New Pathways to Civil Justice

Xandra Kramer • Alexandre Biard •
Jos Hoevenaars • Erlis Themeli
Editors

New Pathways to Civil Justice in Europe

Challenges of Access to Justice

 Springer

Editors
Xandra Kramer
School of Law
Erasmus University Rotterdam
Rotterdam, The Netherlands

Alexandre Biard
School of Law
Erasmus University Rotterdam
Rotterdam, The Netherlands

Jos Hoevenaars
School of Law
Erasmus University Rotterdam
Rotterdam, The Netherlands

Erlis Themeli
School of Law
Erasmus University Rotterdam
Rotterdam, The Netherlands

ISBN 978-3-030-66639-2   ISBN 978-3-030-66637-8   (eBook)
https://doi.org/10.1007/978-3-030-66637-8

This Springer imprint is published by the registered company Springer Nature Switzerland AG.
The registered company address is: Gewerbestrasse 11, 6330 Cham, Switzerland

Preface

Access to civil justice has been a topic of academic debate and a concern of policymakers, legislators and practitioners for a number of decades. In recent years, new trends in civil justice have evolved that reveal current challenges to accessible civil justice as well as opportunities for a civil justice system of the future. These not only develop at the national level but increasingly also at the European level. National, European and global dynamics in civil justice provide a fascinating insight into how justice systems try to adjust to these challenges and make use of new opportunities. Cuts to public spending on legal aid on the one hand and opportunities opened up by technological developments on the other force policymakers, administrators, judges and legal professionals to adapt to a quickly changing legal environment. With all these developments, innovations and experiments in civil justice happening in a very patchy and often divergent fashion, there exists a need for a more systematic approach to a twenty-first century civil justice. This book brings together a collection of perspectives from different corners of the civil justice field and by authors with different (academic, policy or professional) backgrounds, with the aim to gain a more comprehensive understanding of current and new pathways to civil justice.

This book is part of the European Research Council (ERC) consolidator research project 'Building EU Civil Justice: Challenges of Procedural Innovations—Bridging Access to Justice' (2017–2022), carried out at Erasmus School of Law. The project aims to investigate current trends shaping access to justice in Europe and beyond. The focus is on four developments in civil justice: namely, the digitisation of procedures and the use of artificial intelligence (AI); the privatisation of civil justice and in particular the rise of alternative dispute resolution (ADR) mechanisms; the increase in self-representation and the simultaneous disappearance of the legal profession from large parts of the judicial system; and specialisation of courts, in particular the establishment of international business courts in recent years. The contributions to this book result from the conference 'Challenge Accepted! Exploring Pathways to Civil Justice in Europe' that took place at Erasmus University Rotterdam on 19 and 20 November 2018. We had the privilege of welcoming top-notch speakers and over one hundred participants, including academics, judges, lawyers, policymakers and consumer and business representatives from Europe and beyond. One of the goals of this conference was to exchange insights regarding transformations that are taking place in civil justice systems. The great wealth of insights, developments and outlooks that was brought to light during the conference's keynotes (given by Judith Resnik and Ruth de Bock), presentations and lively discussions solidified our conviction that a book bringing together those perspectives would be of great interest to everyone who wants to stay informed about the frontlines of current trends in civil justice.

We are grateful to all conference speakers and contributors to this book, each of whom drew on their experience as an academic, policymaker or practitioner in the field of civil justice to provide, specifically for this book, a unique perspective on the past, current and future pathways to civil justice. We would like to thank the other members of the ERC team who have all contributed to the success of the conference and this book in some capacity. Georgia Antonopoulou, Emma van Gelder, Kyra Hanemaayer and Betül Kas, thank you for your collaboration, insights, creativity and sense of humour. A special thanks to our splendid former student assistant Kyra, whose relentless dedication to our project and hard work in editing this book have been indispensable. We are happy that she will stay in academics to pursue a PhD research. Finally, many thanks to our student assistant, Wouter Hoogeveen, for helping finalise this book, and to Edward Frisken for assisting in the language review.

This book has received funding from the European Research Council (ERC) under the European Union's Horizon 2020 research and innovation programme (grant agreement No 726032). Information on the ERC consolidator project 'Building EU Civil Justice' is available at www.euciviljustice.eu. The editors are principal investigator, postdoc researchers and associated researcher.

While completing the book in COVID-19 times, unfortunately one of the conference speakers and contributors to this book, Roland Eshuis, passed away on 20 April 2020. His empirical work on lead times in civil justice for his PhD research and his passion for empirical data as a researcher for the Research and Documentation Centre (WODC) of the Dutch Ministry of Justice have greatly contributed to evaluating justice reform in the Netherlands. His from time to time confronting but extremely useful comments as a supervisory board member of a study on debt collection carried out for the Ministry of Justice in 2012 was an important and unforgettable pathway to improving the empirical study of civil justice for the PI and first editor of this book.

Rotterdam, The Netherlands   Xandra Kramer
February 2021   Alexandre Biard
                                                                           Jos Hoevenaars
                                                                           Erlis Themeli

Contents

Chapter 1
Introduction: The Future of Access to Justice—Beyond Science Fiction

Alexandre Biard, Jos Hoevenaars, Xandra Kramer, and Erlis Themeli

1.1 New Pathways: A Project for the Future

Access to civil justice has been on the research and policy agenda for a number of decades. Nevertheless, old hurdles—including costs and delays—continue to challenge access to justice, while changes in the justice system and society—the rapid technological advancement at the forefront—create both new challenges and opportunities. At the national, European and international level developments are taking place that merit comprehensive study and discussion. These evolve around four key issues that are central in this book: digitisation and in particular the use of AI in courts; privatisation of civil justice by means of ADR; increased self-representation and its repercussion on the civil justice system and legal professions; and increased specialisation of courts and procedures.

In this introduction, we would like to invite you on a short journey. Close your eyes, relax, and let your imagination run free. Imagine that you have been selected to travel in a time machine to an unknown future, far beyond 2021. Things around you look familiar, albeit somehow different. On the way, you remember that at the turn of the century several observers had written about what was called a 'crisis in civil

This research has received funding from the European Research Council (ERC) under the European Union's Horizon 2020 research and innovation programme (grant agreement No 726032), ERC consolidator project 'Building EU Civil Justice: challenges of procedural innovations – bridging access to justice'; see <www.euciviljustice.eu>.

A. Biard · J. Hoevenaars · E. Themeli
Erasmus University Rotterdam, School of Law, Rotterdam, The Netherlands
e-mail: biard@law.eur.nl; hoevenaars@law.eur.nl; themeli@law.eur.nl

X. Kramer (✉)
Erasmus University Rotterdam, School of Law, Rotterdam, The Netherlands

Utrecht University, Utrecht, The Netherlands
e-mail: kramer@law.eur.nl

X. Kramer et al. (eds.), *New Pathways to Civil Justice in Europe*,
https://doi.org/10.1007/978-3-030-66637-8_1

justice' systems,[1] and for that reason, you decide to have a look at how the situation has evolved. You observe that a vast majority of citizens use their mobile phones and engage with robots and virtual assistants to obtain personalised, tailor-made advice when facing legal issues. Individuals are channelled automatically to specific procedures, depending on the nature of their claims and their needs: for small value cases, they are channelled to one of the out-of-court settlement bodies that will solve their disputes in only a few days and at little or no cost. Where the stakes of the disputes are higher and require judicial intervention, claimants are directed to courts. However, here as well you notice that the profile and functioning of these courts have been transformed in the most surprising manner. Most of them are now operating online. Costly, burdensome, and complex court procedures have disappeared. The use of advanced management systems and artificial intelligence (AI) in courtrooms, which you recall was highly controversial back in 2021, has finally come to facilitate the work of judges considerably. Advanced management systems and AI are now commonly accepted by the legal profession and society at large. You also observe that specialised courts have multiplied to address complex and technical issues and to provide tailor-made justice. Finally, you notice that for a number of disputes many citizens no longer need lawyers. Aided by digital technologies and as a result of simplified procedures, they can represent themselves, and the entire legal system tends to support this practice.

For many of us, this situation will sound like science fiction. Yet, in many aspects, several of these changes are already happening today, albeit at various paces and along very different paths across the globe. Over the past several years, economic and societal needs together with the digital revolution have triggered important innovations for improving access to civil justice. In particular, four trends in justice systems have been fundamental: namely, the digitalisation of procedures and the use of AI; the privatisation of civil justice and the rise of alternative dispute resolution (ADR) mechanisms; an increase in self-representation and the simultaneous disappearance of the legal profession from parts of the judicial system; and a move towards specialisation of courts and procedures.

Many of these changes are currently taking place in a patchy and unsystematic way, without an overarching framework guiding their ongoing developments. Nonetheless, digitalisation, privatisation, self-representation, and specialisation share similar problems: for example, concerning the quality of processes and outcomes, the emergence of new players, the need to rethink and redistribute roles among actors, and the need to enhance visibility and trust among users as well as to foster inclusiveness and accessibility. In a step towards a more comprehensive approach to today's civil justice challenges, this volume brings together insights, developments, and outlooks regarding all four trends. It includes mostly academic contributions, but also a number of policy and practice-oriented contributions to encompass views and experiences from different stakeholders.

---

[1]Zuckerman (1999).

1.2 The Challenge of Artificial Intelligence in Courts

Fast internet connections, massive data collection, technological development, and inexpensive hardware have made digital technologies omnipresent. The technology that stands out as the most futuristic and most promising in the legal realm is AI. Artificial intelligence is an umbrella term that covers many technologies and techniques that try to replicate[2] traits of human intelligence. Using algorithms and data analysis, AI systems perform their tasks much faster than humans and at a much lower cost, and offer considerable benefits with regard to labour-intensive jobs. With technology's ability to simplify, speed up, and, most importantly, lower the cost of court procedures, it is no surprise that government and court officials are looking at it to resolve many of these problems.

The first part of the present book takes on some of the challenges facing the digitalisation of courts and the use of AI in particular. The first three chapters consider different issues of equal importance in the design, implementation, and development of digital innovations in courts. **Dory Reiling** highlights the hypes, hopes, and dreams of digitalising courts. She suggests that court digitalisation should not simply ride the wave of digital optimism but identify the various court procedures and the way information is processed in them. Only after completing this step can court digitalisation proceed to allocate the appropriate technique and technology to the appropriate process. In the end, digitalisation should not be a goal but a means towards better courts. Subsequently, starting from the hype surrounding legal technology and the constant bombardment of news about humans being replaced by robots—even in courts—**Nicolas Vermeys** explores the impact of artificial intelligence on the legal process. For Vermeys, current AI is not sufficiently developed to replace judges in courts. However, AI can be used to support the judges in their decision-making tasks. AI can be used, for example, to prevent conscious and unconscious biases in judges, and in predicting the predisposition of judges to rely on certain arguments. Evidently, there is already a great deal of work AI can do in courts as well as considerable room for further development. Nevertheless, in the third chapter of this section, **Amoroso** and **Tamburrini** argue that technologies that might replace humans with machines also come with ethical challenges. The authors highlight that from a deontological perspective, replacing human judges with machines is questionable, while from a consequentialist perspective such replacement is promising. However, any form of AI in courts should have meaningful human control. To accomplish this, the authors argue, we should divide the tasks of courts into layers, and, for each layer, decide how the human controller should perform his or her task.

AI may be the appropriate tool to overcome the hurdles of access to court in the future, as it can help courts and court users reach their goals with less effort. At present, an obstacle to access to court for many users is the lack of information or the inability to obtain information about their situation. Is it a case that can go to court?

---

[2]Not replicate but mimic, as one of the scientists in Kubrick's 2001: A Space Odyssey would rebut.

What are my rights in this situation? Can I claim damages? These are just some of the unanswered questions that many people grapple with when faced with a legal problem. And without a proper answer, many of these problems never reach the courts. Here too AI might be of assistance. AI-powered systems that can communicate with the parties and help them in assessing the legal connotations of their problem could go a long way in bridging this very first gap in access. Subsequently, such systems can make a list of the documents that are needed to start a court proceeding, can suggest draft documents, or can suggest relevant legislation. Chatbots are one example of such systems, and recent developments show great potential.[3] Law firms have been using chatbots for some years to answer questions from clients or to suggest appropriate documents.[4] Automated systems may also conduct the service of documents or support the collection or presentation of evidence. While this seems futuristic, we should not forget that every day more and more objects are connected to the internet, and many communications and transactions take place online. In the future, we may expect both the service of documents and the provision of evidence to be mostly or entirely digital. For court users, this may translate into better access to information, faster and cheaper court services, and, consequently, fewer obstacles to accessing courts. In addition, AI may be used as a pre-trial mediator with a duty to bring parties together and to try to resolve their dispute before they consider starting court proceedings. This may have enormous benefits not only for small claims, where claimants want to avoid a long and costly trial, but also for many disputants who are interested in a fast and inexpensive settlement.

From the court administrators' point of view, AI can be used to manage court infrastructure, predict the complexity of a case, allocate the appropriate resources, and reduce costs. While these systems do not directly reduce the number of obstructions to access to court, they help the court better manage their resources, which can improve access in multiple ways. Court automatisation may be the first stage in a wholesale deployment of AI in courts.[5]

In addition, AI can assist in the actual administration of justice. Sophisticated and data-fed machines are able to assist judges by reading long documents and summarising them or highlighting important parts. Machines can browse databases to find legislation, case law, and academic or non-academic articles that can be used in deciding a case. Even more advanced machines can draft court decisions based on the documents presented or the input of the judge. It is then the duty of the judge to review and approve the document drafted. This support may reduce the time needed to decide a case or may simply give judges more time to spend on other cases. Courts

---

[3]The Beijing Internet Court in China is specialised in the resolution of online disputes. With an ever-growing number of e-commerce transactions, China has created similar courts also in Hangzhou and Guangzhou. The Beijing Court became the first to use AI in the form of chatbots to resolve cases. See: Liangyu (2019).

[4]Brown (2018) and Goodman (2017).

[5]Wu (2019).

will see an increase in capacity, process times will go down, and, as a result, court users will see their costs diminish.

As noted above, however, a good balance is necessary between what technology can achieve and what is appropriate. AI development and quality depend on the data available. This data should be enough for the system to understand its duty and clean enough to avoid mistakes after deployment. Numerous examples indicate that AI systems have indeed failed due to gaps in the data used in the development phase.[6] The development of AI itself may also be problematic. Who is going to develop court systems: private companies with public supervision? Maybe. But are public institutions able to supervise the development of complex algorithms? Will these algorithms be available for the public to review? Transparency indeed might be the biggest problem for algorithm-based systems. Anyone who wants to review these algorithms will have a difficult job because reviewing algorithms requires very specific skills. Even specialists find it difficult to review an algorithm without data to run it. So how can we make sure that algorithms are transparent for the general public? If people have little confidence in these algorithms, deploying them in courts may be futile.

More specific problems or dilemmas exist, especially when we look at technology from the user's perspective. As humans, is it more appropriate for us to be judged by other humans rather than by a machine? Courts and the court process have been created, shaped, and adjusted to accommodate human-to-human communication. Therefore, the introduction of machines that partially or entirely replace humans may have negative effects on the perception of courts and justice. But not all cases are the same. Some cases are so simple and clear-cut that machines can solve them without much difficulty. If we accept this, we may witness justice delivered both by humans and by machines: namely, some problems will be judged by humans, while others will be judged by machines. Will we have a problem with this idea? Is the machine or the human a premium service, and does this mean that some receive a better service than others? For the common court user, perhaps the most important problem is digital literacy, or the ability to understand how the new system works, and the possibility of accessing and using these systems. If users fail in any of these requirements, electronic systems and AI become ornamental rather than functional. It is the duty of court administration to educate and reach out to court users who lack digital literacy, while system developers are tasked to create systems that are easy to use and understand.

Finally, we should consider the perspective of the judge when deploying AI in courts. As noted above, AI systems are trained by data that represent past experiences, and function by trying to emulate these past experiences in the present context. Some argue that AI systems will not be able to develop new jurisprudence, but will only reinforce past choices and with them also past biases.[7] The same may be true if AI is used to draft or suggest final court decisions, because judges in

---

[6]Fenton and Neil (2018), Zhang et al. (2003).

[7]See Amoroso and Tamburrini in the present book, Chap. 2.

overwhelmed courts may rely on these systems to finish their job quickly, and thus fail to correct past errors or biases. And what if AI is a good judge and resolves many court cases? Will governments deploy them in higher courts? But if we have good AI and we deploy it in the first instance court, will it still make sense to deploy similar AI in a second instance? Replacing human judges with AI judges may signal the twilight of appeals.

Evidently, there is a long and winding road ahead in the development of good AI systems. But more importantly, governments and stakeholders should engage in an open discussion about principles, objectives, and fundamental values that AI can uphold or alter, and can bring or destroy. It is in our hands to decide how smart court artificial intelligence will be.

1.3   Privatisation of Dispute Resolution: The Controversial Rise of Consumer ADR in Europe

Within just a few decades, alternative dispute resolution (ADR) mechanisms have increasingly been described as one of the key components of modern civil justice systems. In 2002, the EU Green Paper on ADR in civil and commercial law highlighted that 'ADRs are an integral part of the policies aimed at improving access to justice'.[8] Similarly, EU Directive 2008/52/EU of 21 May 2008 on certain aspects of mediation in civil and commercial matters stressed that 'the objective of securing better access to justice (. . .) should encompass access to the judicial as well as extrajudicial dispute resolution methods'. The added value of ADR has been discussed extensively. It has been presented as an informal, accessible, fast, and cost-effective way to access justice while preserving court resources.[9] Yet voices have also warned against the development of a second-class and opaque justice, as ADR schemes may not be subject to the same procedural constraints and requirements as those usually applying in courtrooms.[10]

To remedy these issues, to enhance trust and ultimately to ensure that ADR fully delivers its potential, the European Union adopted Directive 2013/11/EU (the 'Consumer ADR Directive'), which has renovated the regulatory framework applying to consumer ADR in Europe.[11] Among others, the Directive ensures that consumers can turn to quality-certified entities.[12] It sets several binding quality

---

[8]EU Commission (2002) Green Paper on Alternative Dispute Resolution in Civil and Commercial Law COM/2002/0196 final, para 9.

[9]EU Commission (2002), para 9.

[10]Eidenmüller and Engel (2014), Haravon (2011), Lindblom (2008).

[11]EU Directive 2013/11/EU of the European Parliament and the Council of 21 May 2013 on alternative dispute resolution for consumer disputes.

[12]Biard (2019a) Impact of Directive 2013/11/EU on Consumer ADR Quality: evidence from France and the UK; Cortés (2015).

requirements applying to ADR schemes and their procedures: namely, the principle of accessibility, expertise, independence, impartiality, effectiveness, transparency, fairness, liberty, and equality. Compliance with these requirements is ensured by a network of national 'competent authorities' monitoring the quality of their national ADR bodies on an ongoing basis.[13] As the Directive was one of minimum harmonisation, Member States were also free to adopt additional quality requirements to ensure a higher degree of consumer protection in their countries. In its report of September 2019 on the implementation of the consumer ADR Directive, the EU Commission noted that the 'Directive has consolidated and complemented consumer ADR in the Member States and upgraded its quality'.[14] The Commission further noted, 'Overall, the transparency of ADR entities and procedures has increased considerably, case handling times have been reduced, ADR entities offer more staff training and users are more satisfied with the services provided by ADR entities. The establishment of high-quality ADR infrastructures has also provided an incentive for traders to review and improve their internal complaint handling processes'.[15] Despite these improvements, the EU Commission highlighted that the perceptions of traders and consumers still remain an issue, as many misconceptions about ADR and ADR entities continue to exist.[16] Some consumers and traders, for example, still hold the view that ADR bodies are not fully impartial or that they propose a form of 'justice behind closed doors'. This situation tends to prevent the diffusion of a climate of trust among all stakeholders.

During the conference, we asked our speakers coming from various parts of Europe to reflect on the development of consumer ADR in their respective countries. In addition, we asked them whether, in their views, ADR was indeed a synonym for 'justice behind closed doors'. Contributions presented in this book come from academics and practitioners from Belgium, France, Germany, and the United Kingdom, and who are actively involved in the daily functioning of ADR schemes.

Christopher Hodges sets the scene and puts ADR in a broader perspective, by placing it into the context of all existing dispute resolution mechanisms. He considers that improving access to justice may first require looking at all existing dispute resolution pathways from a holistic perspective. He stresses that many different pathways have emerged progressively, depending on the type of disputes and the needs at stake. However, these different pathways may compete with each other, and the multiplication of options ultimately makes the situation difficult for users to understand and to navigate. As Hodges points out, 'What users of disputes resolution services need are easily identifiable and effective pathways rather than a multiplicity of different options'. **Lewis Shand Smith** builds on his experience as a former ombudsman in the United Kingdom, and highlights the different functions of an ombuds service, which is one particular type of ADR scheme. As he highlights, trust

---

[13]Biard (2018).

[14]EU Commission (2019b) Report from the Commission, p. 8.

[15]*Idem.*

[16]*Idem.*

is a fundamental component of all ADR bodies and can only emerge 'through transparency and openness, easy access, clarity of procedures, sharing of data and insights in order to drive learning, and regularly reporting to key stakeholders on its own performance'. As Shand Smith concludes, 'To build trust in the service and in the way by which it delivers justice, the doors of an ombuds service must never be closed, but be visible, open and accessible to all comers'. **Stefan Weiser** and **Felix Braun** from the General Consumer Conciliation Body ('*Universalschlichtungsstelle*', the German residual entity) present the state-of-play of ADR in Germany, and provide practical insights into the work carried out by the Universalschlichtungsstelle as well as highlight the various challenges faced by ADR entities in their country. **Frédérique** Feriaud and **Pierre-Laurent Holleville** from the French energy ombudsman (*Médiateur national de l'énergie*) emphasise that several safeguards exist to avoid opacity and to enhance trust. According to the authors, confidentiality, which is different from the notion of 'secrecy', remains an essential aspect of ADR. As they point out, 'by ensuring that discussions remain confidential, the law enables parties to speak freely, which is in their best interest'. However, as Feriaud and Holleville also underline, there can be situations where public interest may supersede the need for confidentiality (in particular where rogue practices may harm a high number of consumers). Finally, **Pieter-Jan de Koning** from the Consumer Mediation Service (*Service de Médiation pour le Consommateur/Consumentenombudsdienst*, the residual consumer ADR entity in Belgium) presents the functioning of the Belgian Consumer Mediation Service, and stresses that consumers' and professionals' perceptions about its work remain a challenging issue. Together, these contributions shed light on a multi-faceted European consumer ADR landscape that is consolidating, albeit at different speeds in different countries. If confidentiality is one of the key elements of ADR procedures, it will continue to attract criticism.

In *Nadja*, the French writer André Breton (iconic figure of the French surrealist movement) wrote:

> I myself shall continue living in my glass house where you can always see who comes to call; where everything hanging from the ceiling and on the wall stays where it is as if by magic, where I sleep at night in a glass bed, under glass sheets, where who I am will sooner or later appear etched by a diamond.[17]

Building an 'ADR glass house' where transparency is ensured for all their activities and decisions is and will continue to remain a daily challenge for all ADR entities. However, this also represents a *sine qua non* condition for their full integration into modern civil justice systems.

---

[17]Breton (1928), p. 18—in French: "Pour moi, je continuerai à habiter ma maison de verre, où l'on peut voir à toute heure qui vient me rendre visite, où tout ce qui est suspendu aux plafonds et aux murs tient comme par enchantement, où je repose la nuit sur un lit de verre aux draps de verre, où qui je suis m'apparaîtra tôt ou tard gravé au diamant").

1.4 Self-Representation in Civil Justice: Taking Lawyers Out of the Equation?

With legal procedures often designed to be adversarial and, as a result, hard to navigate for the uninitiated, attempts at reducing material and immaterial barriers to accessing the legal system have historically relied heavily on a privileged legal profession. For a long time, the general supposition has been that in order for people to exercise their right to access the justice system they need the help of lawyers or other legal professionals to translate their everyday problems and conflicts into legal claims. As such, legal representation has always been at the centre of the quest for accessibility in the administration of justice. At the same time, professional legal assistance tends to constitute a large share of the cost of litigation and may turn out to be a barrier to effective access in and of itself.

Over the past three decades, the seemingly entrenched position of the legal profession has been challenged by several dynamics. Firstly, public legal aid systems established during the post-war *Access to Justice movement* have undergone significant overhauls. These have been partly due to financial crises and a related increase in demand for legal aid, but are predominantly a result of successive economic austerity policies and related cutbacks and reforms. Many jurisdictions have seen a stark reduction in the public expenditure on legal aid.[18] Consequently, especially in common law jurisdictions, lawyers are—directly, through permitting more self-representation, and indirectly—through public legal aid cuts—being removed from the civil justice process.

Secondly, technological developments are significantly changing the landscape of legal advice. As discussed above, automated document assembly, predictive AI, and online diagnostic tools are among the 'disruptive technologies' Richard Susskind identified as altering the face of the legal profession.[19] Similarly, technological innovations in the administration of justice itself—aimed at reducing the time, costs, and complexity of legal procedures—are chipping away at the need for litigants to hire a lawyer altogether. Susskind's *The End of Lawyers?* has underscored the existential need of the legal profession to adapt to an ever-changing landscape of legal services under the influence of the increased use of information technology.

Lawyers are not only subject to change in the way they work; lately, we see that, in attempts at making the administration of justice cheaper, faster, and accessible, lawyers may not be part of the equation at all. With policymakers trying to minimise the cost of litigation but recognising the challenges for citizens to navigate the legal system without professional assistance, attempts at reducing the need for professional help—through simplified procedures, aforementioned technological innovations, and expanding alternative dispute resolution options—aim to find a balance

---

[18]Moore and Newbury (2017).
[19]Susskind (2013).

between the accessibility of court procedures and effective legal protection. Experiments with, among others, full digital procedures, mediation-like courts, and low-threshold local civil courts all try to provide simple, fast, and inexpensive procedures with the aim of reaching a solution to disputes in joint consultation, often without the costly inclusion of legal professionals.

While all jurisdictions deal with their own particular dynamics, we can witness an international trend in constricting public spending on the civil justice system in general and subsidised legal aid specifically, with significant consequences for justice seekers of limited means. In particular, the fairly recent reforms in England and Wales following the Legal Aid Sentencing and Punishment of Offenders Act (LASPO) of 2012 have led to a dramatic increase in the number of litigants appearing in court unrepresented.[20] However, such dynamics are not limited to common law jurisdictions without mandatory representation rules. In the Netherlands, the threshold for cases in which legal representation is not compulsory was raised from 5000 to 25,000 EUR in 2011, drastically increasing the pool of cases that can be litigated without legal assistance. At the EU level, several new procedures—for small claims and debt collection claims—are designed to be predominantly digital in nature and are explicitly geared towards litigation without a lawyer.

As a result of these trends, the number of parties to civil proceedings who do not have legal representation has risen steadily in a number of jurisdictions, creating very specific challenges to the effective administration of justice. In legal systems designed for an adversarial process in which both sides are assumed to be represented by legal professionals, self-representing litigants are often viewed as challenges to the efficient administration of justice. As such, they are treated as a potentially frustrating factor in the day-to-day practices of the institutionalised judicial system. Lawyers, however, are seen progressively as an excessive financial burden on both legal aid budgets and litigating parties themselves.

The issue of (self-)representation effectively encapsulates a host of civil justice challenges for the 21st century. It urges the question of accessibility for those without means, the issue of rising costs of public legal aid, and questions of effective legal protection and the integrity of the legal system. The rise in litigants appearing unrepresented in court reveals the problem of the complexity of the law and legal procedures, while at the same time providing a proving ground for the promising developments of technological innovations.[21] The third section of this book deals with the trend towards increased self-representation in civil courts, and questions the future role of lawyers in the administration of civil justice. It bundles three contributions that approach the issue from, respectively, a policy, an empirical, and a theoretical perspective.

Paulien van der Grinten raises the question 'what is self-representation?' Is it just taking the lawyers out of the equation of justice administration or is it more than that? Van der Grinten notes that within the Dutch Ministry of Justice there is more

---

[20]Grimwood (2016).

[21]Barton and Bibis (2017).

focus on solving the actual problem underlying legal disputes than on ensuring that all matters are effectively dealt with in court. There is a wide call for cheaper and more simplified procedures, and the goal is for civil procedure to reduce conflict between parties. Van der Grinten questions how lawyers fit into this new type of procedure, and uses the recent debates and experiments in the Netherlands to tackle the issue. She concludes that while many procedures are open to innovation—which often results in a diminishing role for the legal profession—in complex cases lawyers will not disappear any time soon. **Roland Eshuis** presents results from empirical research on legal representation in Dutch civil court cases. This research studied the effect of a relatively recent increase in the threshold for small claims in civil commercial cases from 5000 to 25,000 euro, effectively bringing a broad range of cases under the jurisdiction of the sub-district courts before which representation is not obligatory. The data shows that self-representation is more popular among defendants, and, although they rarely win a case, they experience the procedure as fair to the same extent as litigants who have professional help. Eshuis presents some lessons to be learned from these insights. The conclusion that still very few claimants use the opportunity to start a court case without professional help raises the question of whether it is in fact possible to shape the law and its procedures in a manner simple enough for anyone to understand. He posits that the fact that we still need lawyers to handle most of our court cases is a symptom of our failure to design a legal system that is accessible to all. **John Sorabji** subsequently tackles the idea of diminishing the role of legal professionals, and directs our attention to the consequences of the wholesale removal of lawyers from the administration of justice. Analysing the main challenges to the legal profession—funding and technological innovation—Sorabji warns us not to throw the baby out with the bathwater. He points to two important risks associated with this development. Firstly, there is the risk of deskilling lawyers who are then effectively reduced to being process managers in a technological environment. And secondly, taking lawyers out of the courtroom also takes away the essential function of lawyers in keeping judges accountable. Sorabji concludes that while in certain classes of litigation the presence of lawyers advising and representing litigants may not be an essential feature of the administration of justice for some purposes, overall they remain a crucial feature of any civil justice system that is committed to securing effective participation, open justice, and democratic accountability.

The movement in many jurisdictions towards more 'Do-It-Yourself Justice' and a diminishing role for lawyers provide a fertile testing ground for procedural innovations that allow for greater access and simpler, more cost-effective procedures, while maintaining the integrity of the justice system as a whole. With the trends pointing in the direction of more justice without lawyers, the pressing question is how much the role of lawyers in the administration of justice can be scaled back without undermining their integral part in the administration of justice. The focus of considerable debate on the civil justice system has to do with the precarious balance between cost-efficiency and substantive justice in addressing civil disputes. Nonetheless, the goals of an effective civil justice system go beyond the quick and low-cost resolution of disputes.[22] In addition to resolving disputes, an effective civil justice system serves the important social function of demonstrating the effectiveness of the law and allowing judges to perform their function of applying, clarifying, and developing the law.[23] With that in mind, the question remains as to what extent a civil justice system can be designed in a way that it can perform this function in any real sense without the presence of legal professionals to assist litigating parties in effectively claiming their rights. It is clear that the question of representation will remain a pressing topic for years to come.

1.5   Court Specialisation and the Rise of International Commercial Courts

The fourth part of this book focuses on court specialisation. While court specialisation is not a new phenomenon, in recent years this topic has gained a lot of attention because of the rise of international business or commercial courts in Europe and beyond.[24] This trend of establishing business courts is also important in the context of access to justice in the broad sense, because it furthers customised court adjudication of international commercial disputes. The present section will briefly address court specialisation as a perceived need to improve access to justice as well as the rise of international business courts in this context.

Specialisation in the judicial system, either by establishing special courts or having divisions or chambers within the general court, has a long history. In France, for instance, the commercial court, the *Tribunal de commerce*, was already established in 1563, and this makes it the oldest court in the French judiciary.[25] For civil law cases, countries usually have a number of special courts or court divisions for certain cases; these include, for instance, labour law, family law, consumer law, and commercial and maritime cases. Civil procedural codes often include special rules for these types of cases, tailored to the parties involved (e.g. weaker parties) and in line with the substantive law. Having separate courts or court divisions also enables judges to acquire the necessary expertise and experience. In some cases the court composition also differs from the general civil court (e.g. the inclusion of lay persons). In that respect, court specialisation is in alignment with Adam Smith's ideas on the division of labour,[26] and furthers access to justice by

---

[22]Clark (2007), para. 9.

[23]Jolowicz (2000).

[24]See *inter alia* Kramer and Sorabji (2019a).

[25]Royer et al. (2016), no. 717.

[26]Smith (1779).

enhancing the efficiency and quality of the judicial process.[27] Specifically in relation to commercial courts, it is not surprising that the World Bank's Doing Business Reports highlight their importance. In the 2019 Report, for instance, it is commented that the 'top 10 economies in the ease of doing business ranking share common features of regulatory efficiency and quality, including [. . .] specialized commercial courts'.[28]

As **Elisabetta Silvestri** also points out in the present book, specialisation is, however, not the solution for poor access to justice. The risk of tunnel vision or monoculture, compartmentalisation, two-tiered justice, and the pressure on impartiality are some of the disadvantages attributed to court specialisation. Silvestri draws attention to the fact that there is little empirical evidence that specialisation improves procedural efficiency and leads to judgements that reflect higher judicial expertise. She discusses developments in Italy, where in recent years the courts designated in the commercial law area have been advertised as providing justice of the highest quality, but so far in practice they have not been able to demonstrate the advantages of specialisation. As Silvestri argues, pros and cons need to be balanced in making decisions about the desirability of court specialisation and how far this specialisation should go.

The rise of international commercial or business courts in recent years cannot be explained only on the basis of the desire to improve access to justice by securing the appropriate expertise and accompanying procedural rules. The emergence of internationally focused courts has also been triggered by other considerations. Firstly, establishing such courts is often activated by economic motives and the desire to raise the profile of the jurisdiction so that it is seen to be an attractive venue for international business litigants. While virtually all initiatives to set up these courts in Europe date from before the Brexit vote of June 2016, discussions have been fuelled by uncertainty about the international litigation framework, by business relocation, and by the opportunities this may create for boosting local legal markets. Secondly, bigger and more complex commercial disputes are increasingly not confined to one jurisdiction. This requires not only subject-matter expertise but also knowledge of the details regarding international business relations, foreign legal systems, and private international law rules. A common feature of the recently established courts is that they offer parties the possibility of litigating in English, and therefore require appropriate language skills from the judges. These courts could further access to justice by providing tailor-made justice and could strengthen the rule of law. Consistent with this aim is the desire expressed explicitly in some countries, including the Netherlands, to offer business litigants an alternative to commercial arbitration. Over the last couple of decades, commercial arbitration has taken over a substantial part of commercial litigation. In fact, the 2018 White & Case and Queen

---

[27]See, *e.g.* Mak (2008), Silvestri (2014). See in relation to the Unified Patent Court: Schovsbo et al. (2015). Research conducted for the Council for the Judiciary on court specialization in the business context in the Netherlands: Böcker et al. (2010) and Havinga et al. (2012).

[28]World Bank (2019), at 1.

Mary survey concluded that 97% of the respondents prefer international commercial arbitration.[29] To counter what has been called the vanishing trial—a phenomenon that was first evidenced in the United States[30]—some governments justify the creation of international business courts governed by procedural regimes that in part are modelled on arbitration rules (e.g. the Belgian legislative proposal). These courts should provide a high-quality and less costly alternative to international commercial arbitration. That the creation of these courts is not unproblematic is illustrated by the fate of the proposal for the Brussels International Business Court (BIBC). Political parties started to withdraw their support at the end of 2018 and early 2019, arguing that the proposal would lead to a two-tiered justice system, and joining earlier critiques qualifying the court as a 'caviar court'.[31] It seems unlikely that this court will see the light of day in the near future, if ever.

In the present book, **Marta Requejo Isidro** discusses the development of international business courts in Europe and beyond. Starting in the Middle East, with the Dubai International Financial Center (DIFC) being the most prominent, in recent years other countries have created similar courts. In Asia, this includes Singapore and China, and in Europe most notably France, Germany, and the Netherlands, while proposals for the creation of international commercial courts elsewhere are on the table.[32] She highlights the Dubai project "Courts of the Future" which aims at establishing a division with the DIFC Courts to deal with technically complex claims, having no or multiple geographical nexuses or involving parties from different jurisdictions. Finally, the author reminds us not to pay attention only to specialisation but also to the need for international cooperation. In this regard, the adoption of the Hague Judgments Convention in July 2019 is a true highlight that—together with an increased number of ratifications of the 2005 Hague Choice of Court Convention—will hopefully better regulate the enforcement of judgments at the global level.

Ianika Tzankova focuses on what may in part be considered a reversed trend, using the image of the 'Global Village' where cases like the Volkswagen case, Trafigura, Apple v Samsung and Philip Morris are subject of transnational litigation and arbitration. She positions the (anti)specialisation trend in judicial law-making against that background. She argues that modern international commerce and consumerism give rise to disputes on a worldwide scale but that national legal systems are not fit to deal with these disputes and at the same time the 'inhabitants of the Global Village' use the divergences between systems to maximise their interests. She concludes that the future of dispute resolution is being shaped by these big players while their interests may not be aligned with those of national legislators and ordinary consumers.

---

[29]White & Case and Queen Mary University of London (2018), at p. 1.

[30]See, e.g. Galanter (2004). In England and Wales: Dingwall and Cloatre (2006).

[31]Kramer and Sorabji (2019b), pp. 1–2; Van Calster (2019), pp. 107–114.

[32]See also Kramer and Sorabji (2019a).

1.6 Concluding Remarks, Future Pathways, and New Frontiers

In the concluding chapter **Judith Resnik** takes a step back from the discussions on the procedures to pose questions about the 'normative aspirations, the doctrinal mandates, and the pragmatics of contemporary civil justice systems'. She focuses on three highly relevant intertwined aspects: the substantive entitlements civil justice protects; the extent of governmental support for courts, other forms of dispute resolution and for those seeking justice; and the role of the public in dispute resolution systems. As regards the latter, she stresses the importance of the public, referring to Jeremy Bentham who already two centuries ago taught that 'access by the public is requisite to the capacity to scrutinize, let alone to discipline, the decision-making and the norms that undergird it'. She concludes by stating 'We lose the very capacity to debate what our forms and norms of fairness are. Whether called "court," or "ADR," or "ODR," we cannot, without all forms of openness, decide whether the paths, processes, or resolutions are just'.

It is clear that today civil justice finds itself at multiple crossroads. Technological innovations, political turmoil, and economic constraints all contribute to a situation in which civil justice systems are forced to continuously reinvent themselves. The persistent development of technological innovations, and especially the promises of AI, stand to significantly change the face of civil justice and rightfully take up a central spot in the current access to justice and the justice innovation debate. Ostensibly positive moves towards a system of justice in which the regular citizen is able, without the assistance of legal professionals, to access the courts and has his case decided on by a judge, have resulted in an increase in the number of people that enter the courtroom without professional legal assistance. Alternative dispute mechanisms have, over the past couple of decades, proven themselves to be a viable alternative to traditional court procedures while also attracting criticism for creating a two-tiered legal system and 'justice behind closed doors'. Court specialisation is yet another measure to further access to justice, as it leads to increasing both the efficiency and the quality of adjudication. However, a multitude of courts and procedures may also have the opposite effect, and specialisation entails the risk of tunnel vision. In this regard, the rise of international business courts in Europe and beyond that focus on access to justice for international commercial disputes is a fascinating phenomenon. It emerges not only from the desire to increase expertise within courts but also because the establishment of these courts is triggered by economic and competitive motives. In addition, as is explicated in some countries, these courts are also intended to provide an alternative to international commercial arbitration and to counter the vanishing trial. However, the experience in Europe so far seems to indicate that the impact of these new courts on the international litigation market is limited.

The Covid-19 crisis that emerged in 2020 has also served as a catalyst in the move towards digitalisation of court procedures, with courts forced to offer their services almost exclusively online under the influence of widespread lockdowns. Courts in many countries have adapted to the crisis and embraced technology. Online hearings and digital documents suddenly became the norm and, perhaps, will become the new normal. Above all, this situation shows that digital technology is a need rather than a luxury. With this in mind, courts should take advantage of the situation and push themselves to make more use of AI and digital technologies. The health crisis, however, may result in long-term economic instability and legal disputes regarding safety, with many people facing financial difficulties and uncertainty. As a result, the traditional hurdles obstructing access to justice are suddenly very high.

While it is difficult to measure the extent to which each of the four trends— digitalisation, privatisation, self-representation, and specialisation—in civil procedure contribute to improving access to justice, it is clear that they are intertwined and strengthen each other. Digitalisation and the rise of artificial intelligence have evidently not only found their way to courts but have also changed the face of ADR, as indicated by the many providers that have moved online. Several ADR entities, are now using AI-powered tools to assist and guide users during the dispute resolution process. This trend is expected to expand in the foreseeable future.[33] In fact, private online dispute resolution (ODR) often proves more advanced and more flexible in integrating technology than do public courts and bodies. Digitalisation also supports self-represented litigants, as online sources and access to procedures can facilitate the journey to courts and to other dispute resolution mechanisms. Technology and online information play an important role in improving the interface between court and out-of-court dispute resolution. At the pan-European level, the e-justice portal and the ODR platform—despite certain flaws—have played an important role in improving access to information, in connecting some of the dots, and in simplifying access to out-of-court and court procedures.[34] Lastly, ADR mechanisms have made clear that customised and low-threshold justice is essential, and court specialisation enables tailoring procedures to the needs of specific litigants and disputes. International commercial courts as they have been established are better geared to the needs of commercial parties in high-value international disputes, among others, by enabling litigation in English and adopting features of commercial arbitration as the 'alternative'—though in fact often the main method of dispute resolution—and they are better equipped technologically.

Over the past two decades, civil justice at the European level has developed rapidly, and the contours of a genuine European civil justice system are visible. European legislation, for instance in the area of ADR, has influenced law and practice in the Member States, but to a certain extent developments at the national and pan-European level take place in parallel. Plagued in part by the financial crisis, by Brexit, and by various political and economic controversies and challenges, the speed at which the European civil justice system is evolving has slowed down.

---

[33]Biard (2019b) Justice en ligne ou Far Www.est? La difficile régulation des plateformes en ligne de règlement extrajudiciaire des litiges.

[34]Hoevenaars and Kramer (2020). Van Gelder and Biard (2018).

Emphasis is placed on instruments that support economic development as well as on the proper implementation and evaluation of existing instruments, judicial training, and the exchange of best practices.[35] The most noteworthy developments over the past few years have been the EU 'New Deal for Consumers' (in particular the Directive on representative action for the protection of the collective interests of consumers),[36] the further development of the ODR platform as announced by the European Commission in September 2019,[37] and a strong policy emphasis on digitalisation and the modernisation of civil justice cooperation.[38] Improvements regarding the European e-justice portal—which are somewhat helpful for self-represented litigants—increase access to information. However, considering the limits of technological interconnectivity and the decentralisation of e-justice, a more revolutionary digitalisation of justice at the European level is not to be expected. As regards court specialisation, it is important to note that the court organisation and national judicial infrastructure are not within the EU competence. The struggles to found a single European Patent Court signify how complicated it is to establish a specialised court at the pan-European level. Interestingly, in the context of a study on building commercial competence by the European Parliament also at the pan-European level, the idea of setting up a European commercial court has been launched.[39] However, it seems unlikely that this will be followed up in the near future.[40]

An overarching issue in the context of access to justice that has not been addressed specifically so far is that of the financing of the justice system as a whole, and of individual or collective litigation or other forms of dispute resolution in particular. Costs and funding are crucial to access to justice, and increased digitalisation in the justice context, the advancement of ADR schemes, increased self-representation, and the desire of court specialisation are to a great extent triggered by the need to increase efficiency and to reduce costs. Two important developments in this are the shift from public to private funding (in particular third-party funding and crowdfunding) and the reform of cost rules (including fee-shifting, proportionality rules, and cost sanctions). While these developments are promising in terms of bridging the access to justice gap, they also pose challenges,

---

[35]Hess and Kramer (2017).

[36]Directive (EU) 2020/1828 of the European Parliament and of the Council of 25 November 2020 on representative actions for the protection of the collective interests of consumers and repealing Directive 2009/22/EC, OJ L 409/1.

[37]EU Commission (2019a) Implementation Report on the European Framework for Alternative Dispute Resolution (ADR) and Online Dispute Resolution (ODR).

[38]For instance, the modernisation of the EU Service and Evidence Regulations to better reflect digital means of serving documents and taking of evidence.

[39]See Rühl (2018). Evas (2018). Criticised by Themeli et al. (2018).

[40]Response European Commission to European Parliament resolution of 13 December 2018 with recommendations to the Commission on expedited settlement of commercial disputes (2018/2079 (INL)), at https://www.europarl.europa.eu/legislative-train/theme-area-of-justice-and-fundamental-rights/file-expedited-settlement-of-commercial-disputes (last visited 8 July 2020).

are surrounded by legal uncertainty, and measures to reduce or redistribute the collective and individual costs of litigation have so far not always been effective. A new project, financed by the Dutch Research Council under its Vici scheme[41], which commenced in late 2020, will add another layer to the ERC research project from which the present book results. Joint efforts and the cross-fertilisation of research in these areas will enable a comprehensive mapping and analysis of recent developments and new frontiers, and will provide new pathways to civil justice in Europe.

References

Barton B, Bibis S (2017) Rebooting Justice – more technology, fewer lawyers and the future of law. Encounter Books, New York

Biard A (2018) Monitoring consumer ADR in the EU: a critical perspective. Eur J Priv Law 2:171–196

Biard A (2019a) Impact of Directive 2013/11/EU on Consumer ADR quality: evidence from France and the UK. J Consum Policy 42:109–147

Biard A (2019b) Justice en ligne ou Far Www.est? La difficile régulation des plateformes en ligne de règlement extrajudiciaire des litiges. Revue Internationale de Droit Économique 165–191

Böcker A, Havinga T, Jettinghoff A, Klaassen CJM (2010) Specialisatie loont?! Ervaringen van grote ondernemingen met specialistische rechtspraakvoorzieningen. Den Haag, Sdu

Breton A (1928) Nadja, translation by R. Howard, 1960. Grove Press, New York

Brown T (2018) Your Court-Appointed Chatbot – is artificial intelligence threatening the legal profession? IT Chronicles. https://itchronicles.com/artificial-intelligence/your-court-appointed-chatbot-is-artificial-intelligence-threatening-the-legal-profession/

Clark A (2007) The Importance of Civil Justice: Nationally and International. http://webarchive. nationalarchives.gov.uk/20131203081256/http://www.judiciary.gov.uk/Resources/JCO/Docu ments/Speeches/mr_american_bar_assoc_031007.pdf

Cortés P (2015) A new regulatory framework for extra-judicial consumer redress: where we are and how to move forward. Legal Stud 35

Dingwall R, Cloatre E (2006) Vanishing trials?: an English perspective. J Disp Resolut 51

Eidenmüller H, Engel M (2014) Against false settlement: designing efficient consumer rights enforcement systems in Europe. Ohio St J Disp Resol 29:261–297

EU Commission (2002) Green Paper on Alternative Dispute Resolution in Civil and Commercial Law COM/2002/0196 final

EU Commission (2019a) Implementation Report on the European Framework for Alternative Dispute Resolution (ADR) and Online Dispute Resolution (ODR), COM/2019/425 final

EU Commission (2019b) Report from the Commission. 2019. Brussels, 25.9.2019 COM 425 final. https://ec.europa.eu/info/sites/info/files/com_2019_425_f1_report_from_commission_en_v3_ p1_1045545_0.pdf

Evas T (2018) Expedited settlement of commercial disputes in the European Union. http://www. europarl.europa.eu/RegData/etudes/STUD/2018/627120/EPRS_STU(2018)627120_EN.pdf

---

[41]Vici project 'Affordable access to justice: towards sustainable cost and funding mechanisms for civil litigation in Europe', financed by the Dutch Research Council (NWO), Erasmus School of Law (PI Xandra Kramer), 2020–2025.

Fenton N, Neil M (2018) Criminally incompetent academic misinterpretation of criminal data - and how the media pushed the fake news. Available via ResearchGate. https://doi.org/10.13140/RG.2.2.32052.55680

Galanter M (2004) The vanishing trial: an examination of trials and related matters in Federal and State Courts. J Empirical Legal Stud 459(1)

Goodman J (2017) Legal technology: the rise of the chatbots. The Law Society Gazette. https://www.lawgazette.co.uk/features/legal-technology-the-rise-of-the-chatbots/5060310.article

Grimwood GG (2016) Litigants in person: the rise of the self-represented litigant in civil and family cases in England and Wales. House of Commons Library. https://commonslibrary.parliament.uk/research-briefings/sn07113/

Haravon M (2011) La fin de la justice civile? Réflexion sur l'éviction du juge. Recueil Dalloz 2427

Havinga T, Klaassen C, Neelis N (2012) Specialisatie gewenst? De behoefte aan gespecialiseerde rechtspraak binnen het Nederlandse bedrijfsleven. Sdu, Den Haag

Hess B, Kramer XE (2017) From common rules to best practices in European Civil Procedure. Nomos/Hart, Baden-Baden/Oxford

Hoevenaars J, Kramer XE (2020) Improving access to information in European Civil Justice: a mission (im)possible? In: von Hein J, Kruger T (eds) Informed choices in cross-border enforcement. Intersentia, Cambridge, pp 503–525

Jolowicz JA (2000) On civil procedure. Cambridge University Press, Cambridge

Kramer XE, Sorabji J (2019a) International business courts – a European and global perspective. Eleven International Publishing, The Hague

Kramer XE, Sorabji J (2019b) International Business Courts in Europe and beyond   a global competition for justice? Erasmus Law Rev 12:1–9

Liangyu (2019) Beijing Internet court launches AI judge. XinhuaNet. http://www.xinhuanet.com/english/2019-06/27/c_138178826.htm

Lindblom P (2008) ADR – the opiate of the legal system? Perspectives on alternative dispute resolution generally and in Sweden. Eur Rev Priv Law:63–93

Mak E (2008) Balancing territoriality and functionality; specialization as a tool for reforming jurisdiction in the Netherlands, France and Germany. Int J Court Adm 2(1)

Moore S, Newbury A (2017) Legal aid in crisis: assessing the impact of reform. Bristol University Press, Bristol

Royer JP, Jean JP, Durand B (2016) Histoire de la justice en France. Presses Universitaires de France, Paris

Rühl G (2018) Building competence in commercial law in the member states', study European Parliament. http://www.europarl.europa.eu/RegData/etudes/STUD/2018/604980/IPOL_STU(2018)604980_EN.pdf

Schovsbo J, Riis T, Petersen C (2015) The unified Patent Court: Pros and Cons of specialization – is there a light at the end of the tunnel (vision)? IIC 271

Silvestri E (2014) Judicial specialization: in search of the 'Right' Judge for each case? Russian Law J 2:165

Smith A (1779) An inquiry into the nature and causes of the wealth of nations. Oxford University Press, Oxford

Susskind R (2013) Tomorrow's lawyers: an introduction to your future. Oxford University Press, Oxford

Themeli E, Kramer XE, Antonopoulou G (2018) International commercial courts: should the EU be next? – EP study building competence in commercial law. http://conflictoflaws.net/2018/international-commercial-courts-should-the-eu-be-next-ep-study-building-competence-in-commercial-law/

van Calster G (2019) The Brussels International Business Court: a Carrot sunk by Caviar. In: Kramer XE, Sorabji J (eds) International Business Courts – a European and global perspective. Eleven International Publishing, The Hague, pp 107–114 van Gelder EM, Biard A (2018) The online resolution platform after one year of operation: a work in progress with promising potential. Tijdschrift voor Consumentenrecht & Handelspraktijken 2:77–82

White & Case and Queen Mary University of London (2018) International Arbitration Survey: The Evolution of International Arbitration. www.arbitration.qmul.ac.uk/media/arbitration/docs/2018-International-Arbitration-Survey%2D%2D-The-Evolution-of-International-Arbitration.PDF

World Bank (2019) Doing Business Report 2019. https://www.doingbusiness.org/content/dam/doingBusiness/media/Annual-Reports/English/DB2019-report_web-version.pdf

Wu J (2019) AI Goes to Court: The Growing Landscape of AI for Access to Justice. Medium. https://medium.com/legal-design-and-innovation/ai-goes-to-court-the-growing-landscape-of-ai-for-access-to-justice-3f58aca4306f

Zhang S, Zhang C, Yang Q (2003) Data preparation for data mining. Appl Artif Intell 17 (5–6):375–381

Zuckerman A (1999) Civil Justice in crisis: comparative perspectives of civil procedure. Oxford University Press, Oxford

Part I
Digitalisation and AI

Chapter 2
The Human Control Over Autonomous Robotic Systems: What Ethical and Legal Lessons for Judicial Uses of AI?

Daniele Amoroso and Guglielmo Tamburrini

Abstract This contribution provides an overview of normative problems posed by increasingly autonomous robotic systems, with the goal of drawing significant lessons for the use of AI technologies in judicial proceedings, especially focusing on the shared control relationship between the human decision-maker (i.e. the judge) and the software system. The exemplary case studies that we zoom in concern two ethically and legally sensitive application domains for robotics: autonomous weapons systems and increasingly autonomous surgical robots. The first case study is expedient to delve into the normative acceptability issue concerning autonomous decision-making and action by robots. The second case study is used to investigate the human responsibility issue in human-robot shared control regimes. The convergent implications of both case studies for the analysis of ethical and legal issues raised by judicial applications of AI enable one to highlight the need for and core contents of a genuinely *meaningful* human control to be exerted on the operational autonomy, if any, of AI systems in judicial proceedings.

2.1 Introduction

Recent advances in robotics and artificial intelligence (AI) have paved the way to robots autonomously performing a wide variety of tasks[1] that may significantly affect individual and collective interests, which are worthy of protection from both ethical and legal perspectives. Exemplary cases are the application of lethal force by

---

[1]A robotic system may be counted as "autonomous" at given tasks if, once activated, it is able to carry out those tasks without further human intervention.

D. Amoroso (✉)
University of Cagliari, Cagliary, Italy
e-mail: daniele.amoroso@unica.it

G. Tamburrini
University of Naples Federico II, Naples, Italy
e-mail: guglielmo.tamburrini@unina.it

autonomous weapons systems (AWS) and the circulation of autonomous vehicles on public roads. But one may also think of increasingly autonomous surgical and care robots.[2] To this list of robotic systems one may certainly add the judicial use of AI software systems, notwithstanding the lack of their (direct) kinetic interaction with the physical world. Indeed, the use of AI in the Court is aimed at replacing or supporting the human judge in decision-making processes and tasks that, *by their very definition*, are supposed to have an impact on legal rights and duties.[3]

These technological developments have fuelled, together with new machine autonomy issues, longstanding discussions on Ethical, Legal and Socio-Economic implications of robotics and AI (ELSE issues in robotics and AI); the origins of which can be traced back at least to Norbert Wiener's seminal reflections on the ethics of information technologies and robotics.[4] Present debates about machine autonomy in ethically and legally sensitive domains have now reached out well beyond academic and specialist circles, entering the political debate and receiving considerable media coverage.[5] Over and above the specificities of each technological application domain, there are a few overarching issues arising in connection with most artificial systems endowed with autonomy in the execution of tasks that are ethically and legally sensitive. First, there is the *technical question* concerning whether artificial agents are inherently unable to carry out properly certain functions governed by law (e.g. making proportionality assessments in the context of a military attack), insofar as they would (allegedly) require uniquely human capabilities. Second, there is the (strictly) *legal problem* of determining how to allocate responsibility if harmful events caused by the machine occur. Third, it is debated—from the perspective of *deontological ethics*[6]—whether it is morally acceptable to remove human agency from decision-making processes that are likely to impinge on individual rights and duties. Fourth and finally, from a *consequentialist* perspective in normative ethics,[7] there is the question concerning the opportunity, or perhaps even the moral and legal duty, to replace human operators with autonomous machines, whenever the latter's performances ensure better protection of the interests at stake (e.g. by reducing the number of road accidents and fatalities).

Although these issues have been raised in recent times especially with regard to autonomous robots, they appear to be at least equally relevant when one considers the use of AI in the courtroom. To begin with, one may question whether it will ever be *technically possible* to program software that is able to reliably replace human

---

[2]With regard to autonomous vehicles and care robots, which will not be examined in this contribution, see respectively Lin (2015), Decker (2008).

[3]See, on this issue, the recent monograph by Nieva Fenoll (2018).

[4]Wiener (1950, 1964).

[5]See, among many others, The Guardian (2019), Schwarzman (2019), Metz (2019).

[6]Broadly speaking, deontological ethics identifies moral duties as guides for acting and judging the moral worth of choices.

[7]Unlike deontological ethics, consequentialism focuses on criteria to distinguish between morally good and bad consequences of choices, and prescribes to judge the moral worth of choices in the light of consequences only.

judges in performing tasks involving discretionary reasoning and/or equitable evaluations. Also, not differently from what happens in relation to robotic systems, the problem may arise as to who is to be blamed for wrongful AI-based judicial decisions that might trigger disciplinary responsibility or compensatory proceedings. Finally, even in relation to judicial applications of AI, one may detect an ethical tension between consequentialist reasons favouring the use of these applications (e.g. the need to avoid decisions tampered by typically-human biases) and the view, ultimately based on deontological ethics, whereby human agency should always be retained in the judicial decision-making process.

Against this background, the present contribution provides an overview of normative—both ethical and legal—problems posed by increasingly autonomous robotic systems, with the aim of drawing some lessons for the use of AI technologies in judicial proceedings, especially focusing on lessons concerning the shared control relationship between the human decision-maker (i.e. the judge) and the software system. After briefly expanding on the notion of *operational* machine autonomy (Sect. 2.2), we will focus on two case studies: autonomous weapons systems (Sect. 2.3) and increasingly autonomous surgical robots (Sect. 2.4). These case studies enable us to highlight—respectively   the issue of acceptability of autonomous decision-making in ethically and legally sensitive domains, and the issue of human responsibility for harmful events caused by autonomous artificial agents. Finally, we zoom in on the implications of this analysis for addressing ethical and legal issues raised by judicial applications of AI (Sect. 2.5). Section 2.6 concludes.

2.2   A Preliminary Distinction: Personal vs. Operational Autonomy

It is important to allay a possible source of confusion deriving from the prevalent use of the word "autonomy" in both legal and philosophical parlance. Definitions employed therein in relation to so-called "*personal* autonomy" are not helpful to grasp ascriptions of "autonomy" to robotic systems and other artificial agents. Personal autonomy is attributed only to self-aware entities, conscious of the surrounding world, and capable to act on their own genuine intentions.[8] No educated guess can be presently made as to whether a machine will be built meeting the conditions to enjoy personal autonomy. Whether this will ever happen in some undetermined technological future may be the object of stimulating speculations; but this is of no avail for significant ethical and legal questions arising today, in relation to already existing or imminent autonomous systems.

As anticipated in the introductory section, a notion of "autonomy" more suitable for our purposes is that of "*operational* autonomy". In this perspective, the "autonomy" of a robotic system stems from (and is solely relative to) its capacity to carry

---

[8]See, among many others, Buss and Westlund (2018).

out one or more tasks without requiring any intervention by human operators/users.[9] Systems that are endowed with operational autonomy form a broad and heterogeneous class. Indeed, the repertoire of tasks that a machine can autonomously perform includes both complex activities, such as the execution of parts of a surgical intervention, and very simple ones, like a thermostat switching a boiler on or off. Analogously, the autonomous performance of judicial functions by some software system may—at least as a matter of principle—either concern repetitive activities and tasks (e.g. the issuance of injunctive reliefs based on electronic invoices) or very demanding ones, including evidence assessment or the working out of the grounds for a judicial decision.[10]

We are presently interested in novel ethical and legal problems raised by some of these systems. These problems usually arise in connection with the performance of tasks requiring perceptual, cognitive and evaluative capabilities that, until recent times, were in the exclusive purview of human beings. It is clear, therefore, that in the present contribution we will mainly look at the current technological frontier of systems endowed with operational autonomy, the realization of which has been now made possible by the technological advances in the fields of AI and robotics and their synergic confluences. Systems of this kind are the autonomous weapons systems, which we now turn to consider. These systems raise novel ethical and legal issues concerning the conduct of warfare operations and the forms of control that humans ought to exert on their action.

2.3 Autonomous Weapons Systems and the Boundaries of Normatively Acceptable Autonomy

According to a widely held view, which is consistent with the broader notion of operational autonomy set out above, a weapons system is autonomous only if it is able to select and engage targets without any human intervention.[11] On the initiative of civil society, the international community has recently begun debating the legality and ethical acceptability of autonomous weapons systems (AWS), mainly within the institutional framework of the Convention on Conventional Weapons (CCW), first in the context of informal meetings (2014–2016) and then, starting in 2017, within a Group of Government Experts.[12]

---

[9]Vamvoudakis et al. (2015).

[10]Nieva Fenoll (2018), pp. 24–30.

[11]See, in almost identical terms, US Department of Defence, Directive 3000.09, 'Autonomy in Weapons Systems', 21 November 2012, 13–14; International Committee of the Red Cross (2016), p. 1.

[12]Awareness about this topic has been raised by the Campaign 'Stop Killer Robots', which was launched in 2013 by an international coalition of NGOs with the primary goal of banning lethal robot weapons. For a full chronology of Campaign's activities, see https://www.stopkillerrobots. org/action-and-achievements/. The proceedings of the CCW debates are available at https://www.

The reason why this technological development has created so much interest (unlike, for example, a drone that autonomously executes navigation tasks) is that AWS autonomy concerns the critical functions of target selection and engagement in warfare operations. These functions are "critical" because their performance (i) is crucially regulated by international law of armed conflicts (or international humanitarian law, IHL); (ii) is a key factor for the purposes of individual and state responsibility; (iii) implies moral choices that affect, and even profoundly so, ethically relevant and legally protected individual positions (the right to life and physical integrity, the right to housing, and so on).

The ethical and legal acceptability of autonomous weapons systems (AWS) is questioned from both deontological and consequentialist standpoints, while arguments for the ethical and legal acceptability of AWS are mainly framed in consequentialist terms.[13] Let us briefly summarize the AWS acceptability debate cast in deontological and consequentialist terms, starting from three deontological arguments against AWS.

(1) The first deontological argument supports the claim that AWS would be unable to comply with the principles of distinction, proportionality and precaution under IHL.[14] The development of AWS fulfilling distinction and proportionality requirements at least as well as a competent and conscientious human soldier presupposes the solution of many profound research problems in artificial intelligence (AI) and advanced robotics.[15] Furthermore, it is questionable whether the elimination of human judgment and supervision is compatible with the obligation to take all feasible precautions to prevent (disproportionate) damage to the civilian population, insofar as the regular behaviour of AI and robotic systems is perturbed by unpredicted dynamic changes occurring in warfare environments. Notably, systems developed by means of advanced machine learning technologies (e.g. deep learning) have been extensively demonstrated by adversarial testing to be prone to unexpected, counter-intuitive and potentially catastrophic mistakes, which a human operator would easily detect and avoid.[16]

---

unog.ch/80256EE600585943/(httpPages)/8FA3C2562A60FF81C1257CE600393DF6? OpenDocument.

[13]For a first, comprehensive exposition of the ethical and legal problems at stake, see Heyns (2013), paras 63–97.

[14]See, respectively, Protocol Additional to the Geneva Conventions of 12 August 1949, and relating to the Protection of Victims of International Armed Conflicts (Protocol I), 8 June 1977, Articles 48, 51(2) and 52(2) (distinction), 51(5)(b) (proportionality), and 57 (precaution).

[15]This is acknowledged also by roboticists who, in principle, are in favour of autonomy in weapons systems. See Arkin (2009), pp. 211–212 (listing the "daunting problems" to be addressed in order to develop an IHL-compliant AWS).

[16]Szegedy et al. (2014), who showed how a change of a few pixels into a schoolbus input image forced a neural network to change its initially correct "schoolbus" classification into an "ostrich" classification. The small image perturbations causing this surprising switch in the neural network classification go completely unnoticed to the human visual system. Indeed, the latter is not similarly

(2) The upshot of the second deontological argument is that AWS are likely to determine an accountability gap. One cannot exclude that AWS will assume targeting decisions that, were they taken by human agents, would trigger individual criminal responsibility. Who will be held responsible for this conduct? The list of potentially responsible persons in the decision-making chain includes the military commander in charge and those overseeing the AWS operation, in addition to manufacturers, robotics engineers, software programmers, and those who conducted the AWS weapons review. People in this list may cast their defence against responsibility charges and criminal prosecution in terms of their limited decision-making roles, as well as of the complexities of AWS systems and their unpredictable behaviour in the battlefield. Cases may occur where it is impossible to ascertain the existence of the mental element (intent, knowledge or recklessness), which is required under International Criminal Law (ICL) to ascribe criminal responsibilities. Consequently, no one would be held criminally liable, notwithstanding the conduct at stake materially amounts to an international crime. This outcome is hardly reconcilable with the moral duty of military commanders and operators to be accountable for their own actions, as well as with the related principle of individual criminal responsibility under ICL.[17]

(3) The third deontological argument supports the claim that AWS would run counter to the principle of human dignity, which would dictate that decisions affecting the life, physical integrity and property of human beings should be entirely reserved to human operators and cannot be entrusted to an autonomous artificial agent. Otherwise, people subject to AWS' use of force would be placed in a position where any appeal to the shared humanity of persons placed on the other side—and thus their inherent value as human beings—would be a priori and systematically denied.[18]

As regards consequentialist approaches to the AWS debate, a distinction should be drawn between *narrow* and *wide* arguments. Narrow consequentialist arguments focus on AWS battlefield performances and their immediate expected outcomes. Wider approaches bring into the picture expected geopolitical consequences for peace and stability of AWS development and deployment. The main argument for permitting AWS on consequentialist grounds is based on a narrow appraisal of expected consequences:

---

fooled to change its initial "schoolbus" classification. Clearly, mistaken classifications of this sort by an AWS perceptual system may lead to an AI disaster in warfare scenarios, whereby an object normally protected by international humanitarian law (such as a schoolbus) is mistakenly classified as an object which normally is not protected in the same way (such as an ostrich). Additional adversarial testing results that are relevant from an international humanitarian law perspective were reported by Athalye et al. (2018). Specifically, a model of a turtle obtained by a 3D printing process was initially classified correctly as a turtle by a suitably trained AI system. However, by slightly modifying the 3D model - in ways that go unnoticed to the naked human eye - the AI system was induced to classify the newly produced object as a rifle.

[17]See, also for further references, Amoroso and Giordano (2019).

[18]See, also for further references, Amoroso (2020), pp. 161–215.

(4) AWS have the potential to bring about reduced casualties in each single battle-field. This expectation is grounded in the expectation that AWS will perform more accurate targeting than human soldiers, and will take more conservative firing decisions, insofar as they can be programmed to have no self-preservation concerns. When these conditions are obtained, the choice of permitting AWS deployment ought to be preferred on consequentialist grounds.[19]

The force of argument (4) depends on the other-things-being-equal assumption that the deployment of AWS will not have a significant impact outside battlefield scenarios. This *ceteris paribus* assumption is challenged by argument (5), which is based on a broader approach to consequence appraisal:

(5) The spreading of AWS is likely to bring about comprehensive consequences for international security and peace, which outweigh any local and short-term advantage one may envisage on the battlefield. Destabilization risks include AWS proliferation with oppressive regimes and terrorists, a new arms race among state actors, fewer disincentives to start wars on account of reduced numbers of involved soldiers, unpredictable interactions between AWS and their harmful outcomes, cyber-vulnerabilities leading to unintended conflicts, acceleration in the pace of war beyond human reactive abilities.[20]

Diplomatic discussions about the ethical and legal acceptability of granting autonomy to weapons systems are essentially based on arguments (1–5). In this regard, however, it should be noted that, over the years, the debate has been progressively focusing on the so-called "human element", that is to say on the identification of a normatively acceptable human-weapon shared control policy. Notably, a growing consensus developed during the CCW proceedings around the idea that all weapons should be subject to a "meaningful human control" (MHC) and that their use should be regulated accordingly.[21]

But then, what is it that makes human control truly "meaningful"? The ethical and legal principles appealed to in the above arguments—and especially in deontological arguments (1–3)—go a long way towards shaping the content of MHC, by providing criteria that enable one to distinguish perfunctory from truly meaningful human control: human control over weapons systems should ensure compliance with the IHL law of targeting; should avoid responsibility gaps in case of harmful events; should ensure that it is a *moral agent*, and not an artificial one, to take decisions affecting the rights of the human beings involved in an armed conflict.

The application of these broad principles in concrete situations must be facilitated by considering a variety of contextual factors guiding human judgments about the

---

[19] Arkin (2009), pp. 29–36.
[20] Tamburrini (2016), Altmann and Sauer (2017).
[21] The UK-based NGO Article 36 must be credited for putting MHC at the centre of AWS debates by a series of reports and policy papers making the case for MHC over individual attacks as a legal requirement under international law (see the documents available at http://www.article36.org/issue/autonomous-weapons.).

presence of conditions for exercising MHC over weapons systems. These factors include defensive or offensive operational goals, anti-personnel or anti-materiel character of the mission (more generally, the *what* of targeting actions), temporal and spatial frames of the attacks to deliver, dynamical features of the environment and its overall predictability (the *where* of targeting actions), and the perceptual and cognitive capabilities that the weapons system is endowed with (the *how* of targeting actions). By piecing together combinations of these factors, one should be put in a position to evaluate what kind of control would be ethically and legally required on each single use of a weapons system. Following a taxonomy proposed by Noel Sharkey (only slightly modified below),[22] one may sensibly consider five basic types of human-machine interaction, ordered according to decreasing levels of human control and increasing levels of machine control in connection with the critical target selection and engaging tasks:

- (L1) A human engages with and selects targets, and initiates any attack;
- (L2) A program suggests alternative targets and a human chooses which to attack;
- (L3) A program selects targets and a human must approve before the attack;
- (L4) A program selects and engages targets, but is supervised by a human who retains the power to override its choices and abort the attack;
- (L5) A program selects targets and initiates an attack based on the mission goals as defined at the planning/activation stage, without further human involvement.

As we argued elsewhere,[23] the ethical and legal calling for MHC examined above dictates that, as a general default policy, the higher levels of human control (L1 and L2) be exerted on AWS. Under this proviso, lower levels of human control may become acceptable only as internationally agreed on exceptions, provided that the fail-safe, accountability, and moral agency conditions for exercising a genuinely MHC over weapons systems can be actually satisfied at those lower levels of human control. In this way, the residual autonomy of weapons systems, if any, would be purified of its ethically and legally problematic aspects concerning humanly uncontrolled target selection and attacking functions. Defensive systems autonomously targeting incoming missiles and ballistic projectiles are a significant case in which lower levels of human control may be granted without jeopardizing MHC.

2.4 Machines' Autonomy and Human Responsibilities: The Case of Surgical Robots

Ethical and legal motivations for applying MHC over increasing robotic autonomy emerge in medical robotics too. In setting up a hierarchy of autonomy levels for medical robots, Yang and co-authors advanced at the same time the requirement that

---

[22]Sharkey (2016). Deviations concern, notably, levels L4 and L5.

[23]Amoroso and Tamburrini (2019).

treating physicians should be "still in control to a significant extent".[24] The proposed levels of autonomy (which partly overlap Sharkey's taxonomy) are as follows:

- L0: The robot has no autonomy but only responds to and follows the user's commands;
- L1: The robot provides mechanical assistance, by constraining or correcting human action;
- L2: The robot autonomously carries out tasks that humans designate and supervise;
- L3: The robot generates task execution strategies under human supervision;
- L4: The robot performs an entire medical procedure with human supervision;
- L5: The robot performs an entire medical procedure without human supervision.[25]

In the medical domain of Robot-Assisted Surgery, L0 autonomy systems are used as slave devices for scaling motion, attenuating tremor and enhancing the precision of surgical gestures.[26] The MHC requirement is unproblematically satisfied when these settings are in place. More subtle MHC issues arise at L1–L3.[27]

Various surgical robots deployed in operating rooms are already granted L1 autonomy. A significant case in point are robotic systems assisting surgeons to move the manipulator along desired workspace paths or preventing robotic manipulators from entering selected workspace regions. Robotic systems identifying and applying these active constraints (a.k.a. as Virtual Fixtures) are more than slave devices, as they on occasion correct the surgeon's intended motions. To exert MHC at this autonomy level, one must have the option to override robotic corrections, by means of second-level human control privileges enabling the surgeon to prevail on first-level robotic corrections.

At L2, humans select a task for surgical robots to perform. The surgeon's supervising role consists in hands-free monitoring and possible overriding of robotic execution. Thus, the robotic system is under the surgeon's discrete (rather than continuous) control. The ROBODOC system for orthopaedical surgery is a relatively early example of a system deployed in operating rooms and endowed with L2 autonomy, insofar as it carries out bone milling preoperative plans under human supervision.[28] A more recent research prototype endowed with L2 autonomy is the experimental Smart Tissue Autonomous Robot (STAR) platform, which carries out intestinal suturing (anastomosis) on pig tissue. In experimental tests on this animal

---

[24]Yang et al. (2017).

[25]Be it noted that L4 surgical robots are technologically more distant and L5 ones are currently in the realm of science fiction. Yang et al. (2017).

[26]The da Vinci robotic system for laparoscopic surgery is typically configured as a teleoperated system with L0 autonomy, where surgeons exercise direct control over the entire surgical procedure, including data analysis, preoperative and intraoperative planning, decisions and actual execution. Ackerman (2014).

[27]Ficuciello et al. (2019).

[28]Netravali et al. (2016).

model, STAR was found to outperform expert human surgeons in manual laparoscopic surgery conditions on account of various clinically used suturing metrics.[29]

The ROBODOC and STAR surgical systems are presently characterized by
different Technology Readiness Levels. The former system is used for clinical
standard procedures, while the latter is still at the research level. This disparity
crucially depends on the nature of their respective operational environments and
predictability properties. ROBODOC's surgical sites are rigid anatomic structures,
whereas STAR operates on deformable soft tissues. The structured environments
where ROBODOC operates allow for safe autonomous task execution due to the
possibility of making accurate measurements and scene changes predictions. In
contrast with this, the soft and deformable surgical sites where STAR operates
raise more severe challenges for the accurate detection and tracking of both surgical
tools and anatomical parts. These differences in the ROBODOC and STAR operational environments suggest that the human perceptual and cognitive vigilance must
be suitably modulated to achieve MHC of individual surgical robots that one brings
together under the broad category of L2 autonomous robots. Discrete perceptual
sampling and cognitive evaluation of robotic task execution are arguably more
demanding in the case of STAR-like systems, in view of scene changes due to
physiological blood flow and respiration, and the corresponding need to assess the
robot's adaptive response. Accordingly, one size of discontinuous MHC control
does not fit all L2 autonomous surgical robots.

L3 autonomous surgical robots generate task strategies under human supervision,
and conditionally rely on humans to select from various generated strategies or to
approve an autonomously selected strategy. To a limited extent, STAR achieves this
level of conditional autonomy as far as anastomosis strategies generation is
concerned, along with systems dynamically identifying virtual fixtures and generating optimal control parameters or trajectories.

MHC for L3 autonomy distinctively requires surgeons to decide competently
whether to approve one of the robot-generated strategies. This decision presupposes
that surgeons understand the rationale for proposed strategies, are in the position to
compare their respective merits, and to make up their mind in due time about which
strategy to prefer over alternatives. Depending on the complexity of proposed
strategies and surgical sites, MHC may incrementally raise human interpretability
and decision-making challenges about robot-generated strategies. Similar issues may
emerge in connection with strategies that surgical robots may *learn* to propose on the
basis of machine learning methods, in view of interpretability and explainability
problems affecting learning systems.[30] Today, the learning of surgical strategies is
bound to be based on data sets formed by humanly generated strategies. In a more
distant future, interpretability and explanation issues arising in the context of MHC
for L3 robotic autonomy may become increasingly acute if datasets for learning
how to generate intervention strategies progressively shift from data concerning

---

[29]Shademan et al. (2016).

[30]On this problem, as well as on the attempts to address it, see Chakraborty et al. (2017).

human-generated strategies to robot-generated strategies and corresponding clinical outcomes.

Similarly to the AWS case examined in the previous section, to identify proper MHC policies for robot autonomies one has to consider the functionalities that are appealed to define the tasks assigned to increasingly autonomous surgical robots (the *what* of autonomy), the bodily environments in which these robots operate (the *where* of autonomy), and the system capabilities that are deployed, e.g. learning, to undertake given autonomous actions (the *how* of autonomy). From an ethical standpoint, the identification and application of MHC policies on increasingly autonomous surgical robots are motivated by the bioethical principles of beneficence and non-maleficence,[31] and by the prospective deontological responsibilities of surgeons that these principles entail.

A thorough analysis of prospective responsibilities induced by the MHC requirement is needed to shape training programs for surgeons in Robot-Assisted Surgery. In particular, the non-maleficence bioethical principle requires proper training to provide conceptual tools countervailing positive machine biases, which may wrongly induce human surgeons to trust more what the robot does or proposes to do rather than their own contrasting judgment. Consideration of MHC-related duties plays an equally significant role in evaluating what are the surgeon's retrospective responsibilities, if any, when something goes wrong. Indeed, a surgeon might be held responsible for damages caused by an autonomously performing robot if she failed to exert MHC properly and the harm in question might have been averted had she carefully complied with her MHC duties. By the same token, retrospective responsibility allegations against surgeons for damages caused by an autonomously performing robot might be rebutted and possibly diverted towards other human agents by showing that the specified MHC duties were judiciously complied with.

2.5 Lessons for Judicial Applications of AI

The ethical and legal debate on autonomous robotic systems and the need to exert properly modulated MHC on them may contribute to better frame the discussion on judicial applications of AI in several respects, which we elaborate on in this Section.

2.5.1 Assessing the Normative Landscape for Human-Machine Shared Control in Judicial Affairs

As mentioned in the introductory paragraph, and similarly to what happens with regard to AWS, discussions about the ethical and legal desirability of increasing

---

[31]Beauchamp and Childress (2013), Chapters 5 and 6.

reliance on AI technologies and their operational autonomy in the courtroom are characterized by deontological and consequentialist arguments pulling into different directions.

In a *deontological perspective*, replacing human judges by algorithms is viewed as a questionable move, insofar as it runs against the moral/ethical prescription to guarantee the fundamental "right not to be subject to a decision based solely on automated processing", especially when such a decision "significantly" affects individuals, which is enshrined in the EU General Data Protection Regulation[32] as well as in the Protocol amending the Council of Europe (CoE) Convention on the Automatic Processing of Personal Data,[33] and which *a fortiori* may be deemed to apply also to decisions having a judicial character.[34]

In a *consequentialist perspective*, the promise of better performances of AI in terms of impartiality[35] and uniformity of decisions[36]—and thus the societal benefits deriving therefrom—provides an argument in favour of its pervasive application in judicial proceedings. Yet, and we may find here another analogy with the AWS debate, favourable consequentialist arguments capture only a fragment of the overall picture (*narrow* consequentialism), as they fail to consider the negative backlashes, on the judicial system as a whole, of systematic resort to AI (*wide* consequentialism).

From a *wide consequentialist perspective*, a less optimistic view of judicial applications of AI ensues from an assessment of present and foreseeable limits of artificial agents' moral and legal autonomy. Indeed, artificial agents (be them robotic or not) are generally endowed with the capability to learn a moral or legal rule from their experience with relevant cases (possibly from the vast amounts of relevant cases processed by means of big data techniques), and to apply the learned rule uniformly to settle new and previously unseen cases. This form of *performative*

---

[32]European Parliament and Council Regulation (EU) 2016/679 of 27 April 2016 on the protection of natural persons with regard to the processing of personal data and on the free movement of such data, and repealing Directive 95/46/EC (General Data Protection Regulation) [2016] OJ L 119/1, 71st preambular paragraph and Article 22 (providing exceptions to this right, but maintaining "the right to obtain human intervention on the part of the controller, to express his or her point of view and to contest the decision" (para 3).

[33]Protocol amending the Council of Europe Convention on the Automatic Processing of Personal Data, Strasbourg 10 October 2018, not yet into force, CETS 203, Article 11. Interestingly enough, the Explanatory Report to the CoE Protocol establishes a connection, which is again reminiscent of the debate on AWS, between this fundamental right and the principle of human dignity, having particular regard to the need to put in place adequate safeguards "when processing personal data, in order for *individuals not to be treated as mere objects*" (Explanatory Report to the Protocol amending the Convention for the Protection of Individuals with regard to Automatic Processing of Personal Data, Strasbourg 10 October 2018, para. 10, emphasis added).

[34]See, in this sense, European Commission for the Efficiency of Justice (CEPEJ) (2018), Appendix I, fn 58.

[35]See, for instance, the way Public Safety Assessment (an algorithm helping judges in deciding on requests for pre-trial release on bail) is advertised by its own developers. https://www.psapretrial.org/about/what-is-psa.

[36]Van Ettekoven and Prins (2018), p. 435.

autonomy of moral or legal kind enables the machine to apply a uniform policy in its decisions. The latter, in other words, is stable over time, insofar as they are based either on explicitly formalized ethical and legal rules implemented by the programmers or on rules extrapolated by machine learning methods from past decisions processed by the machine. What artificial agents cannot presently do (and will plausibly not be able to do, at least for a long time to come) is to autonomously modify these uniform policies based on their own comprehensive judgments about the dynamic evolution of societal beliefs and moral judgments (one may sensibly call *reflective* this form of moral and legal autonomy). Accordingly, while judicial applications of AI may foster the uniformity of decisions and therefore legal certainty, they will also bring about the risk of an undesirable stagnation of the case law,[37] which would become irresponsive to changes in public opinion, due to the lack of reflective autonomy in present and foreseeable AI systems, so failing to fulfil its crucial function to "bridge the gap" between law and society.[38]

2.5.2   Preserving Meaningful Human Control in the Courtroom

Deontological and consequentialist arguments (of both narrow and wide scope) must be properly amalgamated to identify appropriate forms and levels of MHC over AWS, increasingly autonomous surgical robots, and other sorts of artificial agents, including AI systems for use in the courtroom, and more generally judicial applications of AI. A significant landmark in this discussion is provided by the *European ethical Charter on the use of Artificial Intelligence in judicial systems and their environment*, adopted by the European Commission for the Efficiency of Justice of the Council of Europe on December 2018 (from now on "Ethical Charter"), whose Principle 5—significantly entitled "under user control"—is aimed at ensuring "that users are informed actors and in control of their choices", by precluding a "prescriptive approach", i.e. one that considers AI decisions as binding and final.[39] One should be careful to note that this deontological principle does not rule out that some operational autonomy of AI systems in the courtroom may still be allowed and beneficial. However, a more fine-grained approach is needed to outline which tasks are admissible for autonomous machine execution, and which functions ought to be prescriptively reserved to human control in relation to artificial agents operating in

---

[37]See CEPEJ (2018), p. 23 and Nieva Fenoll (2018), pp. 31–32. On the need to avoid the immutability of case law, see *Greek Catholic parish Lupeni and Others v Romania* App Nos 76943/11 (ECtHR [GC], 29 November 2016), para. 116, where it is contended that "a failure to maintain a dynamic and evolutive approach" to case law "would risk hindering reform or improvement", being ultimately detrimental to the proper administration of justice.

[38]On this function of the judiciary, see Barak (2006), pp. 3–19.

[39]CEPEJ (2018), p. 12.

ethically and legally sensitive domains. In other words, one has to give a more precise content to the idea of MHC over judicial applications of AI.

General properties of truly meaningful human control over intelligent machines can be extrapolated from the previous case studies. However, these must be made more specific for the judicial domain. First, human control must afford a *fail-safe mechanism*, where human responsibilities and corresponding control privileges come into play; to prevent (or remedy) erroneous legal interpretations and/or fact assessments that autonomous systems may bring about, in accordance with the principle of good administration of justice, as well as—to the extent that the parties are allowed to contest the machine's decision and to obtain a human revision thereof—with the fundamental right to a fair trial. Second, it must serve as a *catalyst for accountability*, in that it avoids responsibility gaps, and facilitates the distribution of moral and legal responsibilities in case of harmful decisions; which may prove crucial to ascertain the civil and/or disciplinary liability of judges. Third, it must ensure compliance with an overarching ethical requirement, already set forth in the European legal framework on personal data protection: genuine *moral agents*, rather than artificial systems, must be the recognizable (and ultimate) sources of decisions concerning freedom, welfare, and material properties (not to speak of life and death) of persons.[40] This characteristic feature of MHC in the courtroom context might well be viewed as the expression of a fundamental right to have access to *human* justice.[41]

But how to preserve human agency in connection with these various properties, and in front of increasingly autonomous (and complex) artificial agents? The analysis above shows that two problems have to be addressed and solved: (i) how to ensure a proper *quality* of human involvement; (ii) how to establish the kind of human-machine distribution of control privileges that is normatively demanded on ethical and legal grounds.

2.5.2.1 The Quality of Human Control

It is crucial that the human operator does not blindly trust the machine, but takes advantage of AI technology without forfeiting human judgement and critical sense, and without succumbing to so-called automation biases.[42] This is ensured, on the one hand, by training the final users with a view to making them aware of both

---

[40]See above footnotes 32–34 and the accompanying text. See also Organisation for Economic Co-operation and Development (OECD) (2019), 1.2(b): 'AI actors should implement mechanisms and safeguards, *such as capacity for human determination*, that are appropriate to the context and consistent with the state of art' (emphasis added). More explicitly the French text of the Recommendation states that 'les acteurs de l'IA devraient instituer des garanties et des mécanismes, *tels que l'attribution de la capacité de décision finale à l'homme*, qui soient adaptés au contexte et à l'état de l'art' (emphasis added).

[41]See, in a similar vein, CEPEJ (2018), p. 47.

[42]*Ibid.*, p. 23 ('User autonomy must be increased and not restricted through the use of artificial intelligence tools and services').

ascertained and likely limits in the functioning of the artificial systems; and, on the other hand, by putting them in a position to get a sufficient amount of humanly understandable information about machine data processing (*interpretability* requirement), and to additionally obtain an account of the reasons why the machine has taken (or is suggesting or is going to take) a certain course of action (*explainability* requirement).

Meeting the explainability requirement might prove particularly demanding in relation to systems endowed with machine-learning capabilities. Indeed, currently used learning technologies are often based on sub-symbolic data representations and other information processing methods that are not transparent to human users. Notably, deep neural networks are achieving statistically excellent classification and decision-making results, but are mostly unable to fulfil the interpretability and explainability requirements. Moreover, adversarial testing of these learning systems shows that some advanced AI might able to generate excellent decisions (in the case under analysis, solutions to legal problems) in a wide majority of cases; but may occasionally incur into mistakes that no competent human decision-maker would ever make (so-called AI-disasters).[43] The combination of these factors (lack of interpretability for machine decisions and occasional but serious mistakes) does not put human users in the position to understand what happened when the machine goes (badly) wrong. Significantly enough, the demand for AI systems that are capable of providing humanly understandable explanations for their decisions and actions is addressed by and is the focus of the rapidly expanding XAI (eXplainable AI) research area.[44]

The importance of ensuring interpretability and explainability as legal requirements has been well underscored in a recent judgment by the Italian Council of State,[45] where the acceptability of algorithmic decision-making has been scrutinized in relation to a field where the use of AI has already gone a good deal further than the judicial one: that of public administration.[46] The Italian Court, while acknowledging that the automatization of standard procedures through algorithms may be beneficial to the efficiency of public administration, stressed the need to ensure that the artificial decision-maker justifies its choices in terms that are intelligible by citizens and judges. Such a translation of the "algorithmic technical formula" into a "legal rule", in the Court's view, is indeed instrumental to ensure both the transparency of

---

[43]See, in this regard, the remarkable results by Szegedy et al. (2014) and Athalye et al. (2018), discussed above.

[44]Scientifically challenging issues in XAI are, by no coincidence, central themes of research programs supported by the US Defense Advance Research Project Agency (DARPA). See Dickson (2019).

[45]In the Italian judicial system, the Council of State (*Consiglio di Stato*) is the highest administrative jurisdiction.

[46]Council of State, *Mariateresa Altomare and others v. Ministero dell'Istruzione e della Ricerca and others*, Judgment of 8 April 2019, No. 2270.

the administrative procedures and the effectiveness of judicial review.[47] In a similar vein, but this time with reference to the use of AI by judicial institutions, Principle 4 of the Ethical Charter posits the duty to foster the transparency and understandability of data processing methods.[48]

2.5.2.2 A Normative Approach to Human-Machine Distribution of Control Privileges

The aforementioned training and transparency requirements are crucial to an exercise of human control that is compliant with the MHC requirement. Here we may draw another significant lesson from the analysis of various autonomous robotic systems: one size of human control does not fit all judicial applications of AI. After all, it is intuitively obvious that the issuance of an injunctive relief regarding a small amount of money should not necessarily be subject to the same level of human control required for a decision impinging on personal freedom.

The identification of the level of human control normatively required for each application of AI could be facilitated by the formulation of a set of rules bridging the gap between ethical and legal principles on the one hand, and specific software and their concrete uses on the other hand. These "if-then" bridge rules should be able to express the fail-safe, accountability, and moral agency conditions for exercising *in context* a genuinely MHC in the courtroom.

Analogously to what we already said in relation to both AWS surgical robots, the "if-part" of these rules should include properties concerning *what* task the software is entrusted to, *where* (that is, in which judicial domain) it will be employed and *how* it will perform its tasks. The "what-properties", in particular, must concern the judicial activities that the machine is expected to perform autonomously or support (formal verifications, evidence assessment, elaboration of legal grounds for the decision, and so forth). Unlike robotic systems, the "where-properties" must here be understood as related to the areas of law *where* the machine operates (e.g. small claims, family law, or criminal law) rather than to the physical areas and contexts where the robot operates (battlefields, human body in operating theatres, and so on). The "how-properties", finally, must regard the information processing that the system puts at work to carry out its tasks and that may affect its overall controllability, predictability and explainability. Machine-learning capabilities, which may be increasingly implemented on future legal software, are a significant case in point of one kind of how-property that may raise serious concern from an MHC perspective.

---

[47] *Ibid.*, para 8. See also General Data Protection Regulation (n 32), 71st preambular paragraph ('[data] processing should be subject to suitable safeguards, which should include [...] the right [...] to obtain an explanation of the decision reached after such assessment and to challenge the decision'). On this point, see the stimulating analysis by Sileno et al. (2018).
[48] CEPEJ (2018).

The "then-part" of bridge rules should establish what kind of human control would be ethically and legally required on each single judicial application of AI. To this end, one may imagine four basic types of human-machine shared control interaction, ordered according to decreasing levels of human control privileges:

– L0. The judicial activity is carried out by a human with the support of a program;
– L1. A program suggests a course of action and a human decides whether to approve it or not. Deviations from the solution recommended by the program must be justified;
– L2. A program issues a binding judicial decision and a human verifies its legality/correctness only if requested by the concerned party;
– L3. A program issues a judicial decision, which is both binding and final.

Against this background, suitable bridge rules should be formulated to establish what level is required to grant the fulfilment of a genuinely *meaningful* human control, as well as the values of the what/where/how properties (or combinations thereof) that justify the identification of some specific level in the above list. To this end, one should take into account (at least) the following observations:

– To the extent that the freedom of human deliberation is unaffected by machine biases, the L0 level of human control should be considered as unproblematic, provided that the training and transparency requirements are met;
– The use of capabilities that may reduce the overall predictability of the software system functioning, such as deep learning-based decision-making (*how-property*), should be treated as a compelling factor pushing towards the application of the higher level (L0) of human control;
– Obviously enough, routine activities (e.g. those concerning the admissibility of evidence; *what-property*) are best candidates for being carried out at lower levels of human control (L1 or L2);[49]
– Decisions impinging on fundamental rights (such as those regarding personal freedom or family relationships; *where-property*) must be taken at L0 (or at most L1) level of human control. L2 human control, instead, should not be considered adequate, in that it would let an artificial agent decide—although provisionally—with respect to individual interests worthy of enhanced protection from both an ethical and legal perspective;
– L3 level of human control should be in principle deemed contrary to the MHC requirement. Exceptions may be allowed in relation to so-called "disposable rights" (*where-property*), provided that there is informed consent by all concerned parties.

---

[49]Nieva Fenoll (2018), pp. 33–42.

2.6   Concluding Remarks

Principles for moral judgment and action that normative ethical theories make available do not come with a recipe that one applies mechanically to derive ready-made solutions to moral problems. As we saw above, moral choices based on deontological ethics and consequentialism may occasionally come into conflict with each other. Indeed, the pursuit of collective well-being may well motivate, from a consequentialist perspective, the warrant of greater autonomy to artificial systems in ways that are, at least *prima facie*, at odds with deontological imperatives to preserve human decision-making in the execution of certain critical tasks. Therefore, one must think through each moral problem under scrutiny, with the aim of identifying moral norms that appear to be relevant, interpreting them in context and figuring out their situational implications. Suitable prioritization of moral principles and thoughtful compromise is often needed to advance conflict resolution proposals and defuse moral tensions, in order to lay the ground for identifying consistent ethical policies and adopting proper legal regulations.

This intellectual effort is well epitomized by current attempts to understand how to keep AI-based judicial software under MHC (or, in the words of the Ethical Charter, "under user control") without giving up the benefits of automation of decision-making, or at least of certain aspects thereof. In the present contribution, we have tried to show that the debate on autonomous *robotic* systems, such as AWS and surgical robots, may provide useful insights in this regard and may contribute to shape the content of a possible regulation of judicial uses of AI (be it legally binding or soft law).

In the first place, such analysis brings out a three-fold role (fail-safe actor, accountability attractor, and moral agency enactor) that the human operator ought to perform in relation to *any* artificial system operating in legally and ethically sensitive domains, including AI-based judicial software. Also, it enables us to pinpoint distinctive human obligations in the way of human control over judicial artificial agents, which may be differentiated in primary and ancillary ones. Primary obligations concern control functions, with their attending privileges and duties, that must be carried out by human controllers of artificial system, and that no machine should ever be entrusted with. Ancillary obligations (which include training and design requirements) are aimed at ensuring that human-machine partnership conditions are fulfilled for the informed exercise of primary human obligations. Finally, it has been observed that what human controllers of judicial artificial systems must do to fulfil their primary and ancillary obligations depends in significant ways on what task the system is entrusted with, in what legal context it is employed and how it performs its tasks. The what-where-how dimensions of the judicial uses of AI suggest that the MHC formula (or, equivalently in our perspective, the "under user control" principle) does not admit a one-size-fits-all solution, but requires a differentiated approach that is based on the unifying ethical and legal framework that we tried to sketch out above.

References

Ackerman E (2014) New Da Vinci Xi surgical Robot is optimized for complex procedures. IEEE Spectrum

Altmann J, Sauer F (2017) Autonomous weapon systems and strategic stability. Survival 59 (5):117–142

Amoroso D (2020) Autonomous weapons systems and international law. A study on human-machine interactions in ethically and legally sensitive domains. ESI/Nomos, Napoli/Baden-Baden

Amoroso D, Giordano B (2019) Who is to blame for autonomous weapons systems' misdoings? In: Lazzerini N, Carpanelli E (eds) Use and misuse of new technologies. Contemporary challenges in international and European law. Springer, Cham, pp 211–232

Amoroso D, Tamburrini G (2019) What Makes Human Control Over Weapon Systems "Meaning-ful"? Report submitted by the International Committee for Robot Arms Control (ICRAC) to the GGE on lethal autonomous weapons systems of the CCW, Geneva, 20-21 August 2019 https://www.icrac.net/wp-content/uploads/2019/08/Amoroso-Tamburrini_Human-Control_ICRAC-WP4.pdf

Arkin R (2009) Governing lethal behavior in autonomous robots. CRC Press, Boca Raton

Athalye A et al (2018) Synthetizing robust adversarial examples. In: Proceedings of the 35th International Conference on Machine Learning, Stockholmsmässan, Stockholm Sweden, 10-15 July 2018, pp 284–293

Barak A (2006) The Judge in a democracy. Princeton University Press, Princeton

Beauchamp TL, Childress JF (2013) Principles of biomedical ethics, 7th edn. Oxford University Press, Oxford

Buss S, Westlund A (2018) Personal autonomy. In: Zalta EN (ed) The Stanford Encyclopedia of Philosophy. https://plato.stanford.edu/archives/spr2018/entries/personal-autonomy/.

Chakraborty S et al (2017) Interpretability of deep learning models: a survey of results. In: IEEE, Smart World Congress, San Francisco, 7–8 August 2017. https://orca.cf.ac.uk/101500/1/Interpretability%20of%20Deep%20Learning%20Models%20-%20A%20Survey%20of%20Results.pdf

Decker M (2008) Caregiving robots and ethical reflection: the perspective of interdisciplinary technology assessment. AI Soc 22(3):315–330

Dickson B (2019) Inside DARPA's effort to create explainable artificial intelligence. TechTalks, 10 January 2019

European Commission for the Efficiency of Justice (CEPEJ), European ethical Charter on the use of Artificial Intelligence in judicial systems and their environment, Strasbourg, 3–4 December 2018

Ficuciello F et al (2019) Autonomy in surgical robots and its meaningful human control. Paladyn 10 (1):30–43

Heyns C (2013) Report of the Special Rapporteur on extrajudicial, summary or arbitrary executions. UN Doc. A/HRC/23/47

International Committee of the Red Cross (2016) Views on autonomous weapon system', paper submitted to the Informal meeting of experts on lethal autonomous weapons systems of the Convention on Certain Conventional Weapons (CCW), Geneva, 11 April 2016

Lin P (2015) Why ethics matters for autonomous cars. In: Maurer M et al (eds) Autonomes Fahren: Technische, rechtliche und gesellschaftliche Aspekte. Springer, Heidelberg, pp 69–85

Metz C (2019) Is ethical A.I. even possible? The New York Times. https://www.nytimes.com/2019/03/01/business/ethics-artificial-intelligence.html

Netravali NA et al (2016) The use of ROBODOC in total hip and knee arthroplasty. In: Ritacco LE et al (eds) Computer-assisted musculoskeletal surgery thinking and executing in 3D. Springer, Cham, pp 219–234

Nieva Fenoll J (2018) Inteligencia Artificial y Proceso Judicial. Marcial Pons, Madrid

Organisation for Economic Co-operation and Development (OECD), Recommendation of the Council on Artificial Intelligence, OECD/LEGAL/0449 (22 May 2019)

Schwarzman SA (2019) Can we make artificial intelligence ethical? The Washington Post. https://www.washingtonpost.com/opinions/2019/01/23/can-we-make-artificial-intelligence-ethical/?noredirect=on

Shademan A et al (2016) Supervised autonomous robotic soft tissue surgery. Sci Transl Med 8(337)

Sharkey NE (2016) Staying the Loop: human supervisory control of weapons. In: Bhuta N et al (eds) Autonomous weapons systems: law, ethics, policy. Cambridge University Press, Cambridge, pp 34–37

Sileno G, Boer A, van Engers T (2018) The role of Normware in Trustworthy and Explainable AI. *arxiv.org*

Szegedy C et al (2014) Intriguing properties of neural networks. https://arxiv.org/

Tamburrini G (2016) On banning autonomous weapon systems: from deontological to wide consequentialist reasons. In: Bhuta N et al (eds) Autonomous weapons systems: law, ethics, policy. Cambridge University Press, Cambridge, pp 127–128

The Guardian (2019) The Guardian view on the future of AI: great power, great irresponsibility. The Guardian. https://www.theguardian.com/commentisfree/2019/jan/01/the-guardian-view-on-the-future-of-ai-great-power-great-irresponsibility.

Vamvoudakis K et al (2015) Autonomy and Machine Intelligence in Complex Systems: A Tutorial. In: IEEE (ed) Proceedings of the American Control Conference (1-3 July 2015, Chicago). Curran Associates, New York, pp 5062–5089

van Ettekoven BJ, Prins C (2018) Data analysis, artificial intelligence and the judiciary system. In: Mak V et al (eds) Research handbook in data science and law. Edward Elgar, Cheltenham, p 435

Wiener N (1950) The human use of human beings. Houghton Mifflin, Boston

Wiener N (1964) God & Golem, Inc. – A comment on certain points where cybernetics impinges on religion. MIT Press, Cambridge

Yang GZ et al (2017) Medical robotics – regulatory, ethical, and legal considerations for increasing levels of autonomy. Sci Robot 2(4):2

Case Law

ECtHR [GC], *Greek Catholic parish Lupeni and Others v Romania* App Nos, Judgment of 29 November 2016, 76943/11

Council of State, *Mariateresa Altomare and others v. Ministero dell'Istruzione e della Ricerca and others*, Judgment of 8 April 2019, No. 2270

Chapter 3
Court Information Technology: Hypes, Hopes and Dreams

Dory Reiling

Abstract This chapter aims to provide some insights into digital justice from historical, practical, and future-oriented perspectives. First, it provides an overview of the historical development of information technology (IT), from early tools to present-day digital environments. It shows how IT makes ever larger demands for change on organizations. Then, to understand how information technology can work in courts, the chapter looks at how courts process the information in court cases. How courts process information determines what IT courts need if they want to go digital. Next, an example from practice in the Dutch courts shows how a digital court procedure works, and how it improves court performance. The Dutch courts planned to go completely digital in 3 years, but abandoned their plans in 2018. Courts elsewhere also face difficulties going digital, and the next sections examine some of the reasons behind this. First, a look at how IT increasingly demands complements in order to work, then a model of court information processing, then a description of the workings and the technology of a digital commercial claims procedure developed in the Netherlands and a short summary of the knowledge about IT implementation failures. Fortunately, it closes with a few examples that provide some insights into more successful ways to digitalize courts. They are presented in the final section of this chapter.

There are some people who live in a dream world, and there are some who face reality; and then there are those who turn one into the other.—**Desiderius Erasmus**.

D. Reiling (✉)
Amsterdam District Court, Amsterdam, The Netherlands

© The Author(s), under exclusive license to Springer Nature Switzerland AG 2021
X. Kramer et al. (eds.), *New Pathways to Civil Justice in Europe*,
https://doi.org/10.1007/978-3-030-66637-8_3

3.1 Introduction: Courts and Information Technology

Digital justice has been a buzzword around the judicial reform community for quite a while.[1] We dream about improving access to justice, realizing faster procedures, and increasing justice in general. We are confronted with people trying to sell us artificial intelligence, predictive justice and robot judges, and we wonder how much of it is hype and how much has actual potential. While our lives are increasingly digital, courts hope to improve their performance with information technology: faster, more accessible, better justice. In practice, we see court systems struggle to digitalize their procedures.[2] At the same time, their caseload is shrinking,[3] We also see a rise of online tools for "alternative" dispute resolution.

This chapter aims to provide some insights into digital justice from historical, practical, and future-oriented perspectives. First, the chapter provides an overview of the historical development of information technology (IT), from early tools to present-day digital environments. It shows how IT makes ever larger demands for change on organizations. Then, to understand how information technology can work in courts, the chapter looks at how courts process the information in court cases. How courts process information determines what IT courts need if they want to go digital. Next, an example from practice in the Dutch courts shows how a digital court procedure works, and how it improves court performance. The Dutch courts planned to go completely digital in 3 years, but abandoned their plans in 2018. Courts elsewhere also face difficulties going digital, and the next sections examine some of the reasons behind this. First, a look at how IT increasingly demands complements in order to work, then a model of court information processing, then a description of the workings and the technology of a digital commercial claims procedure developed in the Netherlands and a short summary of the knowledge about IT implementation failures. Fortunately, it closes with some examples that provide some insights into more successful ways to digitalize courts. They are presented in the final section of this chapter.

---

[1]Susskind (1998). In this, his first and very influential book, Richard Susskind outlined his vision for the future of law with information technology.

[2]For more information on court IT development in Europe, see The European Commission on the Efficiency of Justice's bi-annual evaluation reports, at https://www.coe.int/en/web/cepej/cepej-work/evaluation-of-judicial-systems.

[3]As expressed by participants in two round tables on court IT by the European Network of Judicial Councils, Amsterdam, May 2017 and 2018.

3.2 Three Worlds of Information Technology

IT has come a long way since its early beginnings, yet its implementation in a judicial setting has been rather laborious and slow. In order to understand why court IT is so difficult to implement successfully, it is helpful to put the IT development in a broader developmental perspective. Andrew McAfee, professor at the Massachusetts Institute of Technology, distinguishes three worlds in information technology.[4] Each of these worlds enabled activities, but also required complements in order to make the IT work. As IT gradually enabled a larger proportion of human activities, it required more complements for implementation to be feasible. This makes increasingly heavier demands on the governance of the implementing organization.

Function IT Function IT, which supports the execution of a discrete task, for example registering cases, document production or researching case law. This is the world we know from the 1980s. This IT works stand-alone, it works without a network. It is relatively easy to implement because it does not require standardizing work processes or security.

Network IT Network IT, such as the internet, e-mail, more sophisticated case law databases or digital files needs a network to be able to work. This IT enables collaboration but does not enforce a specific working method. Users can share documents, but the system does not require a standardized way of doing it. In this second world, a user takes a tool, uses it, and then puts it back.[5] In the courts of this world, the paper case file is still the main carrier of information. The IT does affect the primary work processes by requiring standardization. This world emerged with the arrival of the Internet for everyone. In its simplest form, this world is a website that provides information to the reader. As web site technology evolves, the user can also perform an activity, for example download a form. The form can be filled in by hand and then sent in by mail or email. In a next phase, the user can also fill in the form and submit it online. Still a step further, and the user also receives the result of the transaction in digital form. But by then, we have already entered the third world of IT.

Enterprise IT McAfee calls this the world of Enterprise IT. Here, organizations interact digitally with external users. In a fully digital primary process, IT is no longer a tool, it has become an environment. Users can only work within this environment. Workflows are managed digitally. This form of IT requires that work processes are predetermined and standardized. The work process only exists within the set rules. As such, the rules, regulations or formal laws, and the process merge; they become one and the same. The rules are no longer a tool that is external to the

---

[4]McAfee (2006).

[5]My favorite analogy is that of a bucket. The user takes it from the kitchen cupboard when needed and puts it back after cleaning the kitchen floor. An enterprise IT system is an environment, it is an entire kitchen.

work process. They are coded into the digital work process. Regulation and code are merged into one. McAfee has studied the process of introducing Enterprise IT at many large companies. The transition from network IT to Enterprise IT, McAfee says, is the most difficult transition there is. Only organizations recognizing this in advance and taking measures for it will successfully manage this transition. Such measures include establishing decision rights about the process and about changes to the system, and they must be established in advance. Hence, for courts, in this third world, procedural law as well as practice rules and internal work processes will be encoded in the digital process. To facilitate development, decision rights about all of them—procedural law, practice rules and internal work processes, need to be established beforehand. Courts are organized to process cases. They are production organizations with very limited resources for innovation. Decision rights about work processes and regulation are geared to paper processes. They tend to respect the independence of individual judges to manage and decide their cases. If there are bodies setting standards, enforcement mechanisms tend to be weak or absent. The changes required by Enterprise IT to make digital processes work, are hard to make. To create some understanding of which IT may be useful for courts, and where to start with digitalizing primary court processes, the next section examines the court processes.

3.3   Courts Process Information

This section takes a step back. After realizing that implementing IT is difficult because it requires changes in the court governance and organization that are hard to make, this section looks at a different set of problems. To understand how information technology can be useful for courts, we need to know how courts process information. Case registration, word processing, search engines for case law are all different kinds of court IT. They all support different court work processes. Judges, lawyers, court staff and IT experts tend to discuss court IT without specifying what they mean by IT.[6] In order to facilitate conversations about court IT among judges, IT experts, and between judges and IT experts I have developed a matrix that visualizes what courts do when processing information in those different work processes.[7] This matrix provides a conceptual framework to help make such conversations easier and more effective.[8] It may also hold some surprises for traditional thinkers.

---

[6]In my discussions with judges, court staff and others over the past 25 years, I discovered how judges talk about IT and mean their search engines, IT experts mean system development, and everyone imagines IT to be a case management system.

[7]Reiling (2009). On pp. 120–122 of the book there is a full description of the methodology used.

[8]The matrix was developed for network IT, but it will work just as well for enterprise IT.

Courts Decide Disputes Their decisions also serve as a guideline for behaviour by others than parties to a case. This is generally referred to as the "shadow function of the law". When courts decide disputes, they process information. How courts process information is relevant for the kind of IT that is useful for courts. Parties, be they the prosecution, someone appealing an administrative decision, a couple requesting a divorce or a party to a civil case, bring information to court. In most cases, another party is involved: the defendant, an administrative body, a party contesting a civil claim. The court processes the information, and at the end of the process produces an outcome. This outcome is new information. Courts transform information and turn it into new information that can be of use for the parties involved, as well as society at large.[9]

Court information processing is largely determined by two factors: (1) How unpredictable is the outcome, is the information provided sufficient to determine the outcome? (2) What is the relation between the parties? Do they exchange information for a win-win result, or do they withhold information to win for a zero-sum result? Below is first a description of how that works out.

A package of information comes into the court (someone files a case), that information can be sufficient to decide the outcome of the case in question. For example, a money claim that remains undefended, or a one-sided request that does not involve a second party. Cases like that belong in **group 1**. All the court does is provide a title for execution, for instance a payment order or a default decision. For this outcome, no information exchange between the parties is necessary.[10]

In **group 2**, parties bring a proposal to court, but the law requires the court to examine the request for legality. Here, parties do exchange and share information, and work together to put together their proposal. Most family cases are in this group, as do certain labour cases. The cases in this group have in common that they largely deal with long-term relationships and regulation is light. In this group, the court has a primarily notarial role, in verifying that all legal requirements have been met.[11]

So far, the outcome of the case was largely predictable. In more unpredictable cases, more activities are needed to transform the information to produce an outcome. Such activities can be requests for further information, another reaction from the other party, a hearing, a witness hearing, or a site visit to examine a location.

Sometimes, while the procedure is in progress, parties still reach an agreement between themselves to settle their dispute. This is **group 3**. In this group, parties work together, that is, they exchange and share information, for a settlement, a win-win outcome.

If parties do not reach an agreement, a judgment is needed to bring the case to a close. This is **group 4**. In this group, whether the parties exchange information between them is not relevant for the outcome.

---

[9]Genn (1999). This research has shown that court decisions do not always solve the underlying problem.

[10]This is the equivalent of the concept of a zero-sum game in game theory.

[11]Here, the configuration is similar to a win-win game.

Fig. 3.1 How courts
process information

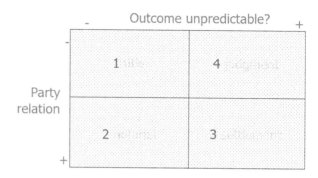

This gives us a first impression of the way courts process information. Figure 3.1 provides a visual representation of these four groups.

Next, it is helpful to find out how the total case load I distributed over the groups. In my research, I have found that for first instance civil cases in the Netherlands, group 1 is about 41% of the total case load.[12] Group 2 is about 36%. Group 3 is about 12%, and group 4 11%.

Group 1 lends itself to automation: with e-filing, court staff no longer need to enter the data into the court system. Because the outcome of the case is largely predictable, automating the process, or at least parts of it, is an obvious use of IT for this group. Most courts already do some of this. There may be some use for artificial intelligence in this group, for instance to sort cases into streams. This kind of technology belongs in the Enterprise IT world. It would require some regulation as well as agreement on decision rights.

For group 2, the IT of choice is the same, and additionally some form of internet support to help parties put together a proposal that will comply with the criteria the court uses to examine it. This support can be static information or a more interactive tool that can react to user input. Potentially, AI may have a role to play here.

For group 3, an added benefit can come from negotiation software.

Group 4 is what we regard as the main activity of courts and judges. It takes most of the judges' time, but in terms of case load, it only is a little over 10%. This may come as a surprise. In group 4 cases, the amount of information in the case file can be considerable, legal research needs to be undertaken to bring the case to a close. This is where digital case files, knowledge systems and search engines come in. Artificial intelligence may be helpful for structuring large case files and for research purposes. Figure 3.2 gives a visual representation of the appropriate IT systems per group.

Meanwhile, some courts in Europe and elsewhere have started to digitalize their procedures. Between 2012 and 2018, the Dutch courts strived to digitalize their

---

[12]Reiling (2009). On pp. 120–122 of the book there is a full description of the methodology I used. The percentages in the book represent the total case load including bankruptcy cases. A later insight made me exclude bankruptcies from the case load for the purpose of this breakdown, since their process is, in the Netherlands, not comparable to case disposition. In this article, I used the new figures.

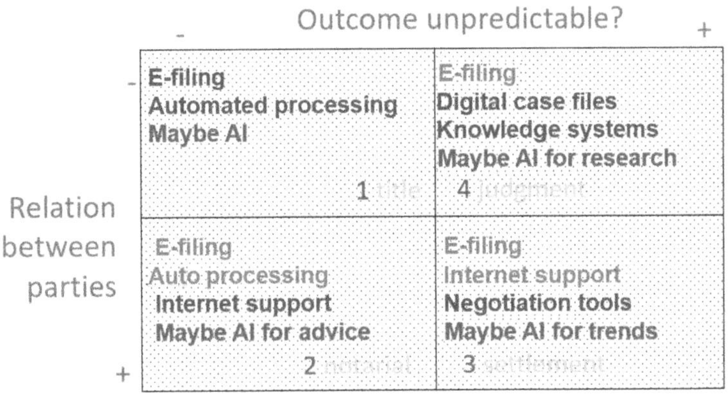

	Outcome unpredictable?	
	−	+
	E-filing Automated processing Maybe AI 1	E-filing Digital case files Knowledge systems Maybe AI for research 4
	E-filing Auto processing Internet support Maybe AI for advice 2	E-filing Internet support Negotiation tools Maybe AI for trends 3

Relation between parties (− top, + bottom)

Fig. 3.2 Information Technology for each Group

procedures. I was responsible, as the "product owner" in agile development terms, for designing and building several procedures, notably a small claims procedure for amicable settlement and the civil commercial procedure.[13] They were both designed to support full group 4 processing. The next section describes the digital court procedure for commercial claims built for the Dutch courts.

3.4 Hope, Dream, or Hype? Digital Procedures

What can a fully digital court procedure look like? The following section presents insights from the digital procedures I built for the courts in the Netherlands. I describe the digital commercial claims procedure I developed for the Dutch courts.

Starting September 2016, two first instance courts have piloted the digital commercial procedure system. Digital filing became compulsory for those two courts in September 2017. In June 2018, The Netherlands Judicial Council decided not to implement the digital commercial claims procedure in the other nine first instance courts.[14] The pilot courts went back to paper filing on October 1st, 2019. At that time, 3792 cases had been filed.[15] Those cases are disposed with full use of the system, that stays in operation for the duration of the cases filed during the pilot phase.[16]

---

[13] A product owner is responsible for ensuring IT is effective for users. More on agile development in the section on options.

[14] Raad voor de Rechtspraak (2018a, b, c).

[15] Information from the NL judiciary's IT organization.

[16] The Dutch administrative courts use a similar system that was built on the same platform for all immigration habeas corpus procedures nationwide. They have processed more than forty thousand cases since the start.

Although the system was never implemented in all courts, it is useful to sketch how the system works. Not many court systems have fully digital procedures. That makes it informative to discuss the system, both as a factual description of a working system, as well as an example of how a digital civil court procedure may look. The procedure described here is supported by enterprise technology, in McAfee's terms. It is a digital environment that supports all four groups of court activity. It first describes the way a digital procedure may run. It then discusses the specific digital functionalities designed for the procedures.

3.4.1 The Procedure

This section describes the court procedure as it works with the digital system, from starting a case to receiving a judgment. The description does not go into the details of procedural law.

Starting a Case A lawyer can start a civil case in different ways.[17] (1) The lawyer of the claiming party first submits the claim with grounds and evidence to the court. (2) The lawyer first serves the claim on the defendant and then submits the claim to the court. E-filing is restricted to lawyers and their authorized support staff because authorization to access the information in the case files requires a secure identification of the person accessing the court system. In the Netherlands, lawyers log in to the court system through the Netherlands Bar portal, with their lawyer's pass, a smart card. Their support staff can log in with their own pass.[18] The system stores which card was used for the login.[19] The system calculates the court fees based on the stated claim. Lawyers can pay the calculated court fee in the filing process via their current account with the court system, their bank account, or they can request an invoice and pay within 28 days from filing.

Immediately upon filing, the court's case management system generates a case number, creates a digital case file, provides the lawyer with the URL to the case file, and assigns the administrator the task to check the filing, and also the court fees. All this usually takes no more than 10 s.

Involving the Other Party Involving the other party is usually the next step in the case. Involving a defending party can be very complex. There are several ways for involving a defending party: notification by the court, or by the claiming party's lawyer, either before or after filing the case in court. In the Dutch case, the claiming

---

[17]New Civil Procedural Law, Wetboek van Burgerlijke Rechtsvordering, in force from September 1, 2016 to October 1, 2019 for pilot courts Midden Nederland and Gelderland.

[18]Article 5, 1 f, REGULATION (EU) 2016/679 (EU General Data Protection Regulation), which replaced Directive 95/46/EC on May 27, 2018.

[19]This secure identification is, for others than lawyers, in place in some countries, but in most countries it is not.

party's lawyer notifies the defending party. For notifications after filing, Dutch civil procedural law allows informal notifications. The lawyer can also opt for formal service by a bailiff, both before and after filing the case with the court. In all cases, the summons notice is generated by the court system in a standard format. The system monitors whether the defending party joins the case. The defending party's lawyer can access the case file using the access code that is included in the summons notice. The defending party's lawyer can decide to join the case on behalf of one or more parties. The lawyers will pay the court fee online, as calculated in the filing process, using their current account with the court system, their bank account, or they can request an invoice.

The system sends a message to the claiming party's lawyer: defending party joined the case and assigns the defending party's lawyer a task to file a defence within 6 weeks from joining the case.

If the defending party did not join the case within the term specified in the summons, the system reports this in a message to the claiming party's lawyer. Generally, the system will then assign a task to check the claim, and have an administrator issue a default judgment, subject to instructions and sign-off by the responsible judge. This makes it a group 1 case.

The Case in Court Now that the case file is complete with a claim, a defence, possibly a counterclaim and a counter-defence, the system generates a task to assign a judge to the case. The court determines who can or may assign a judge to the case. Whoever performs this task will assign a judge or a panel to the case. Assignment of judges to cases is also decided by the court itself.

The system then assigns the case judge the task of deciding whether a hearing should be held in the case or not. In case of a hearing, the judge sets the agenda for the session, the time allotted to the hearing, and any detail relevant for hearing planning. The hearing planner, using this information from the judge, plans the hearing. The hearing planner can request availability dates from the lawyers in an exchange of messages. As there is no standardized procedure to set hearing dates, the system allows courts to either set a hearing date and time directly or use the messaging system to request availability for hearing dates.

The administrator will finalize the hearing invitation. The agenda for the hearing is in the invitation. The system places the invitation in the digital case file and sends the lawyers a message and a notification. The lawyers can use messaging to request a date change for the hearing. The administrator may change or cancel a hearing.

The Hearing The hearing team—the judge and a paralegal or a hearing clerk—can prepare for their hearing in the case file viewer with a form designed for hearing preparation. In the case file viewer, they can: filter or sort documents, annotate, bookmark, and include links in the preparation form. During the hearing, the judge can present a document to the parties and the audience on a large screen using the case file viewer. The court clerk can create session notes in an ordinary word processor and add them, as pdf A, to the internal part of the file.[20] At the end of the hearing, the judge determines the next process step. The system has assigned the judge a task for this purpose. These are the options:

- The case is settled (group 3): the case can be closed. Someone will be assigned a task to close the case.
- More information is needed (group 4): one party will be assigned the task of providing it, after which the other party gets the task of reacting to it.
- More discussion is needed (group 4): a new session can be scheduled immediately in consultation with the parties.
- The information is sufficient for a decision (group 4): The judge can deliver a judgment orally during the hearing, or a hearing team member, assigned with drafting a judgment, will get the task to do this. The judgment must be proclaimed within 6 weeks from the hearing date.

The hearing clerk can make an official report with an ordinary word processor. It will be saved as a pdf-A document and signed by the judge. It is part of the case file.

Judgment The judgment can be drafted either by the judge or by support staff. The courts use templates and standard texts for the judgment, and of course, considerations and decisions pertaining to the individual case. Party names and other information will be retrieved from the case data. Information in the case file and from sources of law and case law can also be inserted by cutting and pasting from those sources and the knowledge systems. The judge finalizes the judgment with a digital signature. The administrator/registrar makes the decision ready to be shared with the parties and uploads it to the case file. The system sends the parties a message and a notification to signal that the judgment has been issued. The administrator registers additional information for accountability purposes and closes the case. Case information remains accessible for the parties at least until the term for appeal has expired.

3.4.2   Key Features of the System

Digital Case Management: Tasks and Activities The backbone of the system is digital case management, balancing strict process control with flexibility in case management. To do this, the system includes tasks and activities. Tasks are required by the process, activities are optional.

Some tasks are required by law or lower regulation. Therefore, they are assigned by the system based on the previous event. So, immediately after the defending party joins the case, the system automatically assigns a task to file a defence to the defending lawyer. The system sends a message to the defending lawyer containing

---

[20]Hearings are not routinely recorded on either audio or video.

the task and the term within which the task needs to be completed. The case management system also monitors the term within which the task needs to be completed. Sometimes the system cannot automatically set a given task for a participant in the system. This is the case when someone sends a letter or makes a request that needs to be decided by a human. The system will then assign a task to determine the next step, first to an administrator. The administrator can refer the task of determining the next step to the case judge. The court can also, when needed, assign tasks to case-related persons. Tasks are actions prescribed by the law, by procedural rules or by a decision of the case judge. Tasks have a due date. Due dates, for example for lawyers, are usually regulated by law. If they are not, then the practice rules set the due date at 2 weeks. In our example, internal tasks for the courts have a due date of five working days.[21] Besides tasks, there are activities. In exceptional situations, a court user can digitally decide to perform an activity, like sending a message to a party. An activity will then generate a task.

Roles The judge, the clerk, the session planner, and the court administrator have different roles in the process. These roles determine which tasks and activities they need to be able to perform. Role assignment is flexible. Not all courts are organized in the same way. The courts determine who has which role, who can perform which tasks and activities and which judge can be assigned to a case. The administrator role, for example, does not have to be a single person; it can be performed by members of the administration team.

E-filing Lawyers file cases either through the web portal or the systems interface. Information can be sent to the court in a structured way in a form or as a document. Filing a case will usually involve a combination of both information in a form that will feed into the court case management system and information about the content of the case. The content information can either be entered in a form with text fields, or in a document that is attached to the filing. In our example, the information filed feeds into the court system directly. The system turns it into a case file automatically upon filing.[22] There is a single case file in each case. In our example, all parties have access to the case file. The court has a dedicated section in the case file that is not accessible to the parties.

Messages and Notifications The lawyers, the judge and other parties involved in the case communicate with each other via messages. Messages are a simple way to exchange information quickly, for instance about procedural and hearing planning issues and part of the case file. With every event in the case, the system sends case-related lawyers a notification on a self-chosen email address. Notifications alert

---

[21]This was the compromise reached after some discussion. Individual courts now work with due days on a standard day of the week. Court staff process incoming documents always on this day. And although this is no longer necessary with 24/7 e-filing, they wanted to still be able to process incoming information on this standard day. With a due date of five working days for processing, court staff can still keep processing on their standard day.

[22]In some countries, the information filed is first examined, and then admitted to the court system.

lawyers to new information in the file. In the system interface, the notification is sent to the law firm's system. As email can be a non-secure way of transmitting information, the information does not contain any personal information, only the case number and the event, just enough to alert the recipient to a change in the case. What the event is, contained in the message that is in the secure case file itself.

Forms and Documents For formal steps (steps with legal consequences) in the process, the system provides smart forms. The form gathers information from the participants by asking questions and providing text fields for more detailed information. Participants can attach documents to the form as well. The system manages steps in the case with structured information from the form. Two examples: After a filing, the system assigns two tasks to the administrator role: checking the filing and the court fee. And if the defending party's lawyer submits the statement of defence with a form, this can include evidence and possibly a counterclaim. In the event of a counterclaim, the system automatically gives the claiming party's lawyer a task to file a defence to the counterclaim within 2 weeks.

The forms also contain information in text fields. The system extracts this information from the form and lays it down in a pdf-A document.[23] All documents are kept in a digital case file in pdf-A format. This format ensures the documents in the case file are unchanged.

3.4.3 Hope or Dream Come True? Improvements

Article 6 of the European Convention on Human Rights (ECHR) sets the standard for court cases in Europe. Court cases are governed by the right to a fair procedure. The digital procedure can bring considerable improvements to the way this procedure complies with article 6 ECHR. Experience with the digital procedure in the two pilot courts has already shown that compliance with the right to a fair procedure in Article 6 of the European Convention on Human Rights may increase in several ways:

- Easier court access through digital case filing that is instantaneous, instead of filing documents through a fax machine. The lawyers included in the pilot schemes were happy with this much more efficient way of filing their cases.
- Equal access to information and increased transparency since parties' lawyers all have access to the single original digital case file, instead of separate paper files that may not be complete and identical for each party and for the court.
- Less delay with instant messaging and automated case management. One full adversarial procedure, including a hearing, was completed in 7 weeks.[24]

---

[23]Pdf-A is an ISO-standardized version of the Portable Document Format (PDF) specialized for use in the archiving and long-term preservation of electronic documents.

[24]Netherlands Judiciary case data, not public.

There are also other improvements. The civil procedure was simplified, which made both the IT and the case management less complex. Digital documents are kept in a persistent format with metadata on their status, which increases information security. Information on the status of court procedures was made publicly accessible.[25]

The most important element of how a fully digital court may work is its digital case management: the combination of procedural rigour of tasks that need to be done and due dates that need to be kept, with flexible case management using message traffic and activities in reaction to events. Unfortunately, the Dutch courts never fully experienced the improvements of the new system, since they decided to not implement the system in all first instance courts. The next sections will try to explore some lessons that can be drawn from this unfortunate development.

3.5 Nightmares: Why Is Reforming Court Procedures with IT So Difficult?

Why is court IT so difficult? More than 10 years ago, my fellow judges plagued me with this question when I was writing my book about Technology for Justice. So, I decided I had no choice but to investigate. The shortest answer to this question is that, in all IT projects, complexity is underestimated.[26] This section examines this insight in more detail, in order to better understand what made the Netherlands judiciary ultimately abandon the digitalization program.

Spray polyurethane (PUR) foam into a space, and it will extrude from all the weak spots. Just like PUR foam, developing and implementing IT will bring up all the weak spots in an organization. IT projects often do not go well. They do not deliver the desired result, they take longer or cost more than expected.[27] More than half of all IT projects—not just those of the government—partly fail, and between 4% and 15% of projects fail altogether.[28] A project that costs more or takes longer has not failed as long as the functionality is used. An IT project can be regarded as a failure if the developed functionality is not implemented. The previous section showed that the digital civil procedure was implemented in two courts, it is in use, but not in all courts.

We now know from countless evaluation reports of failed IT projects what causes IT projects to fail partially or even completely. Usually this is due to an underestimation of complexity. The development, implementation and control of IT are always more complicated than we can oversee in advance. The failure lies in the

---

[25]https://www.rechtspraak.nl/Registers/Zaakverloopregister.

[26]Reiling (2009), pp. 60–80 provides a more detailed description.

[27]At the request of the House of Representatives, the Court of Auditors investigated large government IT projects. The Court of Auditors reported in 2007. See Algemene Rekenkamer (2007), p. 9.

[28]Algemene Rekenkamer (2007), p. 9.

underestimation of the fact that complications may occur, and of the complications that occur during the course of the process. Below are a few examples, with illustrations from the Dutch practice.

Government IT projects are politically complex. The Committee on Fundamental Reconsideration of Civil Procedure, set up in the early 2000s, had advised to omit the distinction between claims and requests procedures in civil justice.[29] Because legal practice resisted this change, the distinction in the procedural legislation stayed. Consequently, that meant different procedures, more software, more work and higher costs.

Another example: The development of the digital procedure had to follow the development of the new civil procedural code in parallel. This meant that adaptations in the proposal for the law caused changes in the design of the digital procedure. In the course of the process, an article that allowed involving the other party before bringing the case to court was introduced, to meet a demand from the bailiffs. The design for digital access in civil cases had to be drastically revised. It led to serious security concerns. All this caused considerable delays and extra cost.[30]

Third example: The Ministry of Justice wanted to implement the digital civil procedure in one operation in all nine non-pilot courts. From the point of view of introducing the new procedural legislation, this was the easiest way. But from the point of view of introducing a completely new digital working environment for the courts, it is risky because all nine courts will be confronted with new procedural legislation, new working methods and new technology at the same time. In early 2018, the Ministry decided it would no longer bear the cost.

Programs and projects are too ambitious. The ambition for the Dutch courts was to digitize all court processes in 3 years. That would result in a savings of 43% in the administrative workload. Those savings would provide financing to complete the projects. When the development took longer than expected (see the previous point) and the procedures were not implemented within the expected time frames, the cost savings were not realized in time.

Programs and projects also underestimate the risks and what is needed to change the organization and the users. At first, the costs of change in the organization were not included in the budget, and later they were still underestimated. In administrative procedural law little changed. But the innovations in civil procedural law and the requirements imposed by legislation on implementation in civil procedure - compulsory digital, implementation in one operation - made implementation extremely complicated.

In the development of the Dutch civil commercial claims procedure, all complexity and risks came together in a toxic conflagration. Important changes were made to civil procedural legislation to speed cases up. These changes mostly had nothing to do with digitalization itself. Translating the new digital procedure into work processes, something that was ongoing with the two pilot courts, was far from

---

[29]Asser et al. (2006), p. 100.
[30]Article 113 New Civil Code.

complete. Implementation in the other nine first instance courts, so much was clear, was going to be very complicated. To make matters worse, funding ran out before the procedure could be implemented in all courts.

3.6 Making the Dream Come True: Options for Court IT

So, after all this, the question to be answered is: how to effectively develop, build and implement court IT? The short answer is: Simplify, simplify, simplify. The longer answer says it depends on several elements.

Agile Development and Experimentation Nowadays, information technology enables fully digital processes. As McAfee has pointed out, this is radically different from introducing tools that can be used as needed.[31] The standard for developing digital processes is agile development. Agile development is a strict methodology to design, develop, build, and test technology in an integrated way.[32] It is a framework for experimentation. Its starting point is not what the technology can do, but what the user needs to be able to do. Consequently, for development to be successful, users need to be involved—one way or the other—in the development and implementation process from the start. Testing will gradually become more like real life, and at some point, the first real case will need to be conducted using the new technology. This means that the line between design, development and implementation becomes blurred. The development process, of both the work processes and the technology, will continue after implementation, it will never stop. Agile development requires experimentation, finding out what works and what does not. Finding out what does not work means things will go wrong a lot of times. This does not match well with legal and court culture. Legal culture tends to be quick to find someone to be blamed if something goes wrong. Blaming in retrospect does not help innovation. More specifically, court culture is also a concern. Courts and judges are the guardians of the existing legal order. Their work is looking back and deciding who should get the blame for what went wrong. This means that looking ahead and envisioning how to innovate does not come naturally to them.

McAfee's findings imply that successful implementation of a digital environment needs decision rights and work processes to be in place before the start of the project. This makes governance an issue: who decides what, and when?

A final aspect is the legal basis for the experiments. For judgments to be enforceable, the procedures need a legal framework once they go live. At this point, the development process is not complete. How to legally frame the development is a serious concern. Concluding, the legal basis for the transition, governance in regarding decision rights and work processes, requirements of agile development

---

[31]McAfee (2006).

[32]https://agilemanifesto.org/.

and pilots, and the capacity for implementation are the main determinants of IT approaches for courts.

Three Approaches From all the above, three approaches for court IT development emerge.

Replace existing processes completely. For relatively short, simple procedures, like the ones in groups 1 and 2, replacing entire processes may work if the aspects discussed in the previous section can largely stay the same:

- The legal basis for this procedure already exists.
- Decision rights can also stay the same when the work processes, although digitalized, basically stay the same as well.
- Agile development is viable if the process can be piloted in a single case, on a voluntary basis.

If these conditions are met, implementation will still not be easy, but it can be successful.

Reform Existing Processes Longer running procedures like group 3 and 4 cases, for instance adversary civil proceedings, turn out to be the most difficult to digitalize. Replacing longer running existing processes in one operation is extremely complex and costly. Existing processes were designed for processing information on paper. They will need a redesign, for processing digital information is quite different from handling paper case files. If they should provide the full advantage of digital processing, they will need a thorough redesign. They will most likely need changes to the legal basis, decision rights and work processes. Starting from the front can be done by designing a process for the cases in my group 1. This would involve e-filing for all cases, and digital case handling for cases in which no defence is filed. There are examples of reforming existing processes, either starting from the front, with e-filing, or from the back, starting with a digital case file.[33] Now that the digital commercial claims procedure will not be implemented any further, the Netherlands judiciary is planning to develop simple e-filing. It is also developing a digital case file.

Design an Entirely New Process This model appears to be successful. Designing and building an entirely new process or even a new institution for processing cases, is not burdened with the constraints of existing legislation, decision rights, and work processes. An early example is the United Kingdom's Money Claim Online.[34] This tool, a "one-trick-pony", was designed for handling relatively small money claims only. It quickly became immensely popular, since e-filing meant that small businesses no longer had to come to a court building with restricted opening hours in person to file a claim. Apart from its user-friendliness, another lesson is in the gradual development of Money claim; first only e-filing for the claiming party,

---

[33]An early example of e-filing is that of the courts in Austria, followed by the courts in Spain. The Austrian courts as well as the Dutch courts are now experimenting with digital case files.

[34]www.moneyclaim.gov.uk.

later also e-filing for the defending party. Another, more recent, example is the Civil Resolution Tribunal in British Columbia, Canada. The Tribunal is a new institutional body set up to handle disputes between owners and tenants of subsidized housing. Its jurisdiction is now gradually expanding into other areas of civil justice.[35] Using agile development, it also increased services to the users, with a solution explorer to help users decide what to do in their individual situation. Since it is fully digital, it has had no difficulty working during the COVID-19 crisis in 2020.

These models may not exist in their pure form, there will be hybrids. However, in each case, factors to be considered are the legal basis for the transition, decision rights and work processes, requirements of agile development and pilots, and implementation. The more change in the existing situation is needed, the more difficult, time-consuming, and costly the transition will be.

3.7 Conclusion

Digital court procedures can improve court performance in terms of access to justice, transparency, and faster case disposition. However, the dream of fully digital court procedures can easily turn into a nightmare. Experience is that introducing information technology to courts is difficult, slow, costly, and not always successful. Courts process information in different ways, depending on the cases in question. Different processes are best served with different kinds of technology. Simple, predictable processes profit most from e-filing and automation, complex processes involving research need search engines and knowledge systems.

The chapter included a—necessarily—general description of the digital commercial claims procedure developed in the Netherlands. Digital case management combining procedural rigour where needed with flexibility when necessary is the backbone of this procedure.

Introducing a fully digital process to replace a paper-based process with supporting IT tools is complex. The chapter discussed, in order to understand the complexity of moving from a paper-based process using IT tools to a fully digital process, some aspects of this transition for courts: governance, legal and court culture, understanding information processing and underestimating complexity. Finally, the chapter identified three approaches for developing and implementing IT for courts, based on the known factors involved. And with implementation as well as with the technology choices, different procedures will need an approach based on the factors involved: the law, decision rights, and work processes. Implementation will be more complex as more change to the existing organization is needed.

---

[35]https://civilresolutionbc.ca/.

References

Algemene Rekenkamer (2007) Lessen uit ICT-projecten bij de overheid. Deel A

Asser WDH et al (2006) Uitgebalanceerd. Eindrapport Fundamentele herbezinning Nederlands burgerlijk procesrecht. Boom Juridische uitgevers, Den Haag

Genn H (1999) Paths to justice: what people do and think about going to law. Hart Publishing, Oxford

McAfee A (2006) Mastering the three worlds of information technology. Harv Bus Rev 11:141–149. https://hbr.org/archive-toc/BR0611

Raad voor de Rechtspraak (2018a) 5 vragen over digitalisering rechtspraak. https://www.rechtspraak.nl/Organisatie-en-contact/Organisatie/Raad-voor-de-rechtspraak/Nieuws/Paginas/5-vragen-over-digitalisering-rechtspraak-.aspx

Raad voor de Rechtspraak (2018b) Letter to the Minister for Legal Protection 'Digitale toegankelijkheid bestuursrecht en civiel recht'. https://www.rechtspraak.nl/SiteCollectionDocuments/11244-brief-digitale-toegankelijkheid-bestuursrecht-en-civiel-recht-6-november-2018.pdf

Raad voor de Rechtspraak (2018c) Nieuwe ontwikkelingen rond digitalisering Rechtspraak. https://www.rechtspraak.nl/Organisatie-en-contact/Organisatie/Raad-voor-de-rechtspraak/Nieuws/Paginas/Nieuwe-ontwikkelingen-rond-digitalisering-Rechtspraak.aspx

Reiling D (2009) Technology for Justice, how information technology can support judicial reform. Leiden University Press, Leiden. www.dory.reiling.com

Susskind R (1998) The future of law. Oxford University Press, Oxford

Chapter 4
The Computer As the Court: How Will Artificial Intelligence Affect Judicial Processes?

Nicolas Vermeys

Abstract Artificial intelligence (or augmented intelligence as we argue it should be referred to) has already permeated into many different areas of society, including the legal process. From algorithmic decision-making or "predictive" tools to robot-judges, numerous AI-powered solutions are being developed to replace the Court in both of the acceptations of the term. Whether it is understood as the alter-ego of the judge and the institution he or she represents, or as a physical place (the courtroom), algorithmic tools are currently being developed to replace or rather reenvision the Court as we know it. However, before looking into using AI tools in this context, we must first understand their possibilities and limitations. This chapter therefore offers an overview of how AI can and should be deployed and exploited within the legal process. It explores why we and others believe that, in most cases, the ideas of replacing judges with algorithms is flawed while examining the ways in which these same algorithmic tools could be better used to help facilitate settlement and guide all legal stakeholders in making more informed choices.

4.1 Introduction

Current fervour around developments in the field of artificial intelligence (AI) has permeated most if not all societal structures and activities. Not a day goes by without the media reporting on how AI will revolutionize the way we play, do business, or otherwise interact with one another.

The legal community has not escaped this new trend. Lawyers, who only a few years ago were told that the probability that they would be replaced by algorithms

The author would like to thank Ms. Sarit K. Mizrahi for her comments and suggestions which helped improve this chapter.

N. Vermeys (✉)
Faculty of Law, Cyberjustice Laboratory, Centre de recherche en droit public (CRDP), Université de Montréal, Montréal, QC, Canada
e-mail: nicolas.vermeys@umontreal.ca

61

was marginally higher than 3%,[1] are now constantly bombarded with headlines that predict their demise.[2] AI algorithms are now passing Bar exams,[3] conducting audits and document reviews,[4] drafting legal opinions,[5] etc. In fact, according to at least one study, algorithms are statistically faster and better at these tasks than even seasoned attorneys.[6] Could we be witnessing the beginning of the end of lawyers, to steal a phrase from Richard Susskind?[7] While we think it highly improbable that this will be the case, there is a need for those within the legal community to ponder on how algorithms will affect their practice.[8]

Of course, lawyers are not the only participants in the legal process whose livelihood is being threatened by algorithms. Tools and technologies that purport to replace court clerks, stenographers,[9] and even judges[10] are currently being developed and implemented. For example, the Estonian Ministry of Justice has asked researchers "to design a "robot judge" that could adjudicate small claims disputes of less than €7,000".[11]

All of these examples beg the question: what place should (and will) AI take within the legal process? To this end, our title, "the computer as the court", is a voluntary *double entendre*. On the one hand, it constitutes a twist on the idea that "[t]he court is the judge or judges who are in charge of the way a legal case happens and sometimes make decisions about it".[12] In other words, "the computer as the court" signifies "the computer as the judge". On the other hand, our title is reminiscent of the first Second Life Courtrooms,[13] and the idea that the legal process can be transported online.[14] Far from being antithetical, both understandings are quite complimentary since, in a world where judges and lawyers are replaced by algorithms, what use is there for courthouses? These two ideas constitute the backdrop of this short contribution on the possible impacts of AI on the legal process.

---

[1]Frey and Osborne (2013).
[2]Cellan-Jones (2017).
[3]Snowdon (2017).
[4]Luminance (2018).
[5]Turner (2016).
[6]Lawgeex (2018).
[7]Susskind (2010).
[8]Kowalski (2017).
[9]Invest Foresight (2018).
[10]Snowdon (2017).
[11]Niiler (2019).
[12]Cambridge Dictionary (2019).
[13]Wente (2009).
[14]Online Dispute Resolution Advisory Group (2015).

4.2   The Computer As the Judge

The idea of replacing judges—beings that have personal views and beliefs which could impact their decision—[15] with cold algorithms that will apply the law indistinctly to every litigant is not a novel one.[16] The concept of robot judges or algorithmic decision-makers has however gained renewed support with recent developments in the field of artificial intelligence. As Max Tegmark phrases it:

> Since the legal process can be abstractly viewed as a computation, imputing information about evidence and laws and outputting a decision, some scholars dream of fully automating it with robojudges: AI systems that tirelessly apply the same high legal standards to every judgement without succumbing to human errors such as bias, fatigue or lack of the latest knowledge.[17]

While this quote offers an excellent overview of the arguments for algorithmic decision-makers, it relies on a series of disputable premises and claims. First, that the legal process is purely a computational exercise and second, that AI systems are free of biases and other flaws attributed to human decisionmakers. In order to properly address these notions (Sect. 4.2.2), we must first understand what artificial intelligence is, and how it works (Sect. 4.2.1).

4.2.1   What Is Artificial Intelligence?

The classic definition of "artificial intelligence" or, rather, the "artificial intelligence problem," was drafted by those credited with branding the term: John McCarthy, Marvin L. Minsky, Nathaniel Rochester, and Claude E. Shannon. In their now famous paper, "A Proposal for the Dartmouth Summer Research Project on Artificial Intelligence",[18] the authors defined artificial intelligence as: *"making a machine behave in ways that would be called intelligent if a human were so behaving".*[19] This description, which circles back to a test devised by Alan Turing in 1950[20] to establish whether machines can think, seems to have molded current dictionary definitions that present artificial intelligence as *"[a] branch of computer science dealing with the simulation of intelligent behavior in computers"*, or *"[t]he capability of a machine to imitate intelligent human behavior".*[21]

---

[15]Tegmark (2018), p. 105.

[16]Ronkainen (2011), pp. 48–53.

[17]Tegmark (2018) p. 105.

[18]Portions of the paper have since been reprinted in McCarthy et al. (2006), pp. 12–14.

[19]McCarthy et al. (1955).

[20]Turing (1950).

[21]Both these definitions have been taken from the Merriam-Webster dictionary (2019).

While helpful, these definitions remain inconclusive. After all, following the proposed logic, a relatively simple tool such as a calculator could be considered to be AI. For this reason, the Oxford dictionary's characterization of artificial intelligence seems more helpful. According to this source, AI can be described as *"[t]he theory and development of computer systems able to perform tasks normally requiring human intelligence, such as visual perception, speech recognition, decision-making, and translation between languages".*[22] By referencing "tasks", the concept becomes clearer, if still somewhat diffused. However, we would suggest that it's how these tasks are completed by the algorithm (through a process that resembles autonomous decision-making rather than following a simple form of binary programming) that helps better explain modern AI. While there are many different types of artificial intelligence algorithms, most recent advances in the field are linked to a form of AI referred to as machine learning.

Machine learning can be summarized as *"[t]he capacity of a computer to learn from experience, i.e. to modify its processing on the basis of newly acquired information".*[23] It *"uses computers to run predictive models that learn from existing data to forecast future behaviors, outcomes, and trends".*[24] Machine learning is therefore dependant on data. The more data it can access, the better it can "learn". This is one of the reasons why machine learning has become so prevalent in the last few years: we now have access to large pools of data, and sufficient computing power to exploit it. Of course, the quality of said data, the way the data is inputted into the system, and how the system is "trained" to analyze the data will have a direct impact on the validity, accuracy and usefulness of the information generated by the algorithm.[25] As we will see, this might be an important impediment to the use of AI to replace judges in certain contexts.

---

[22]Oxford Dictionary (2019a, b, c), artificial intelligence. It should be pointed out that the proposed tasks can be directly linked to the types of technologies encompassed in "Artificial intelligence" according to co-founder of Ross Intelligence Andrew Arruda (see Arruda (2016)). Mr. Arruda presents Artificial Intelligence as a blanket term encompassing four types of technologies: machine learning, speech recognition, natural language processing, and image recognition. Although we would agree that these four concepts fall within the boundaries of artificial intelligence, it could be argued that they do not actually represent distinct technologies as speech recognition and natural language processing could be seen as two sides of the same coin, while both these technologies, as well as image recognition, can, and often do, rely on machine learning algorithms.

[23]Oxford Dictionary (2019a, b, c), machine learning. Machine learning should be envisioned as a spectrum that ranges from relatively simple algorithms to complex self-teaching systems that could eventually mirror the human brain in their complexity (if not their structure). This later subset of machine learning is usually referred to as "deep learning", i.e. "a sub-field of machine learning, where models inspired by how our brain works are expressed mathematically, and the parameters defining the mathematical models, which can be in the order of few thousands to 100+ million, are learned automatically from the data". EDX (2018). Deep learning relies on what are referred to as neural networks, an interconnected group of nodes said to be modelled after the human brain.

[24]EDX (2018).

[25]Domingos (2012).

4.2.2   *Replacing Judges with Algorithms*

Following our admittedly oversimplified explanation of how machine learning works, it's possible to state that an algorithm could be trained using different types of legal texts to answer certain questions and offer conclusions such as court documents, articles from reputable law journals, case law and legislation. For example, Ross, a now defunct AI-based research tool designed to help lawyers find legal authorities[26] was trained using *"complete collections of United States federal and state cases, federal statutes and regulations, selected state statutes and regulations, administrative decisions from the Trademark Trial and Appeal Board, Patent Trial and Appeal Board and National Labor Relations Board, and a selection of decisions from state and federal specialty courts such as military and tribal courts"*.[27]

While this might be the case with certain well-defined high-volume areas such as housing disputes,[28] what happens when there is insufficient data to support a finding? For example, what if a given legal question has yet to be addressed by the courts? As Harry Surden summarizes:

> machine learning algorithms often require a relatively large sample of past examples before robust generalizations can be inferred. To the extent that the number of examples (e.g., past case data) are too few, such an algorithm may not be able to detect patterns that are reliable predictors.[29]

In other words, the quality of an algorithm's decision will depend on the quantity of structured data it can access. For example, Watson—an algorithm developed by IBM to help advise those in the medical profession—can pull from millions of medical records to make a diagnosis.[30] However, while healthcare needs are somewhat universal (basic human biology does not vary according to nationality), laws are territorial. Therefore, one cannot pool data from outside his or her own jurisdiction when training an algorithm, which can become quite problematic in smaller states, like Quebec, where the number of decisions rendered each year represents a fraction of what is needed to properly train an algorithm.[31] Furthermore, since laws are often revised and replaced, legal texts have a limited shelf-life, meaning that past decisions, articles, and other references will need to be regularly taken out of the training pool to ensure accuracy:

> Another challenge that future research in AI and The Law will face is related with the changing nature of the laws. Indeed, in civil law systems, the frequency of legislation changes is higher and higher [...] From the technological point of view, for [...] systems that work in civil law domains (tendentiously rule-based), this means that whenever a legal

---

[26] Ross Intelligence (2019a).

[27] Ross Intelligence (2019b).

[28] Forum (2018).

[29] Surden (2014), p. 105.

[30] IBM projects that there will be over 2310 exabytes of healthcare data by 2020. See IBM (2019).

[31] According to the Canadian Legal Information Institute (CanLII), Quebec courts rendered approximatively 20 000 decisions in 2018. See: CanLII (2019).

norm changes someone will have to search the system for the rules or ontologies that implemented that norm and change them accordingly. Thus, there will be a growing effort to manage such systems and keeping them up to date without creating ambiguities.[32]

The need for machine learning algorithms to have access to important pools of data therefore constitutes the first hurdle to the creation of an algorithmic decision-maker to resolve complex or unusual cases. For example, in 1994, Quebec replaced its then Civil Code of Lower Canada[33] with the Civil Code of Quebec.[34] While the new code was, in certain cases, a mere rewording of older dispositions, other sections were completely reimagined and changed the rights and obligations of Quebec citizens. Had algorithmic decision-makers been used at the time, they would have been incapable of interpreting these new dispositions since they consti-tuted a shift from previous applicable law. In other words, the data was simply insufficient. As Luc Julia, one of the minds behind the creation of Siri, explains:

> [translation] "For a machine to recognize a cat with a 95% success rate, we need access to somewhere in the vicinity of 100 000 pictures of cats. That's a lot. A lot more than it takes a human to recognize a cat. [. . .] If you question psychologists, they will tell you that children only need to see two pictures of cats to recognize them for the rest of their lives, in any circumstance, and in a quasi-infallible manner. Machines are incapable of contextualizing. If, during the learning phase, we didn't produce images of cats taken at night, the chances are slim that the system will recognize a cat at night. . . We can always change the parameters and input more data, but other than the fact that it will be difficult to model all states and all circumstances (can we represent feeling?) memory capacity and computational power problems will emerge."[35]

It goes without saying that, in most cases, legal arguments and interpretations are more complex that recognising whether an animal is or isn't a cat. Therefore, while human judges can look at a new law and interpret how it should be applied based on limited precedents, in view of Julia's analysis, algorithmic decision-makers would fail at the task since they are incapable of contextualizing. Yet, within the legal process, "*[c]ontext is everything [. . .] and every [. . .] case should be dealt with on a case-by-case basis without attempting to define a general approach other than that set out in the relevant legislation*".[36] But this isn't how algorithms "think" (for lack of a better word)—a problem underlined in the American case of State v. Loomis.[37]

The Loomis case revolved around trial courts' use of *Correctional Offender Management Profiling for Alternative Sanctions*, or COMPAS, a decision support tool described as follows:

> COMPAS is a fourth-generation risk and needs assessment instrument. Criminal justice agencies across the nation use COMPAS to inform decisions regarding the placement,

---

[32]Carneiro et al. (2014), p. 230.

[33]29 Vict., ch. 41, (1865).

[34]CQLR c CCQ-1991.

[35]Julia (2019), p. 123.

[36]*Husky Oil Operations Limited* v. *Canada-Newfoundland and Labrador Offshore Petroleum Board*, 2018 FCA 10, par. 58.

[37]2016 WI 68.

supervision and case management of offenders. COMPAS was developed empirically with a focus on predictors known to affect recidivism. It includes dynamic risk factors, and it provides information on a variety of well validated risk and needs factors designed to aid in correctional intervention to decrease the likelihood that offenders will reoffend.[38]

In practice, a series of 137 information points ranging from items such as age and gender, to gang affiliations and community support are collected from the accused and fed into COMPAS.[39] The system then attributes a recidivism score to that individual based on prior compounded data. Mr. Loomis was convicted and sentenced by a circuit judge who relied, among other things, on his recidivism score as produced by COMPAS. According to Mr. Loomis, this violated his right to due process. The Supreme Court of Wisconsin ultimately found that "a circuit court's consideration of a COMPAS risk assessment at sentencing does not violate a defendant's right to due process".[40] Nevertheless, it did feel the need to circumscribe how these types of tools can be used and cautioned circuit courts that:

> because COMPAS risk assessment scores are based on group data, they are able to identify groups of high-risk offenders—not a particular high-risk individual. Accordingly, a circuit court is expected to consider this caution as it weighs all of the factors that are relevant to sentencing an individual defendant [41]

Of course, COMPAS isn't—nor was it ever meant to be—an independent decision-making tool or, to reuse the term proposed by Max Tegmark, a robojudge. But what would happen if a similar tool was to be given the last word in a case? Let us posit that an algorithm can be perfectly trained using a database that includes all current legal texts. Now imagine an individual is convicted of manslaughter by said algorithm, an offense that, under Canadian law, carries a minimum penalty of 4 years in prison,[42] and a maximum penalty of a life sentence.[43] The algorithm would then analyze a series of datasets to establish the ideal penalty for the accused according to his past crimes, affiliations, etc. This decision would then be added to the general pool of data and, before long, algorithmic decisions would simply become self-fulfilling prophecies.[44] Although this would offer greater certainty, it would create a static state of things where legal interpretation would cease to evolve. Yet, as we are reminded by the Canadian Supreme Court, a law is "as a living document" that "grows with society and speaks to the current situations and needs of Canadians".[45]

---

[38]Northpoint (2015).

[39]Angwin et al. (2016).

[40]State v. Loomis, 2016 WI 68, ¶ 120.

[41]State v. Loomis, 2016 WI 68, ¶ 74.

[42]It should be pointed out that said minimum penalty only applies if a firearm is used. See *Criminal Code*, RSC 1985, c C-46, section 236.

[43]*Criminal Code*, RSC 1985, c C-46, section 236.

[44]De Vries and Van Engers (2019).

[45]*Health Services and Support - Facilities Subsector Bargaining Assn.* v. *British Columbia*, [2007] 2 SCR 391, par. 78.

Although there are those who dispute this claim,[46] the fact remains that important legislative changes could not have happened had courts chosen to uphold laws that no longer reflected societal norms and values. An algorithm trained to find its answers in previous decisions would be incapable of such transformative changes.

This approach would also forgo the principle of fundamental justice that is the adversarial nature of the trial process.[47] Since it is questionable whether an algorithm can be agonistic,[48] we must be vigilant in our attempts to incorporate algorithmic computation into the aspects of legal reasoning and decision-making that rely on agonistic tendencies. If too much of this process is outsourced to a machine, this might further contribute to the stagnation of legal interpretation.[49]

Furthermore, the idea that an algorithm can be perfectly trained using a database that includes all current legal texts is, to be polite, difficult to fathom. Therefore, when replacing a human judge with an algorithm, we're simply trading one set of biases for another, or, to be more precise, one set of perceived biases with incomplete data sets. This statement merits explanation.

While studies have shown that a human judge's biases can sometimes affect the outcome of a trial,[50] statistical anomalies in a judge's decision are not necessarily linked to conscious or unconscious prejudice. As explained by the European Commission for the Efficiency of Justice:

> An a posteriori explanation of a judge's behaviour, in particular the revelation of bias, would require all the potentially causative factors to be identified through an interpretative framework and a contextualised analysis. The fact that, statistically, childcare is more often entrusted to mothers than fathers does not demonstrate a bias on the part of judges but reveals the need to mobilise different disciplines from the social sciences to shed light on this phenomenon."[51]

Furthermore, one cannot forget that programmers are human as well. Therefore, even when the data is accurate, structured, and available in a sufficient quantity, the individual "training" the AI could infuse his or her own biases into the system. For example, the COMPAS algorithm used in the previously cited Loomis case was famously claimed to be racially biased by a ProPublica study.[52] According to said study, the algorithm is "*particularly likely to falsely flag black defendants as future criminals, wrongly labelling them this way at almost twice the rate as white defendants*", while "*[w]hite defendants were mislabelled as low risk more often*

---

[46]For example, former US Supreme Court Justice Antonin Scalia was famously quoted as saying that the US Constitution "is not a living document. It's dead, dead, dead."

[47]*R* v *Cook*, [1997] 1 SCR 1113, par. 39.

[48]Crawford (2016).

[49]De Vries and Van Engers (2019).

[50]Chen (2019).

[51]European Commission For The Efficiency Of Justice (2018).

[52]Angwin et al. (2016).

than black defendants".[53] Although subsequent studies have criticized those results,[54] algorithmic bias is far from a theoretical problem:

> The math-powered applications powering the data economy [are] based on choices made by fallible human beings. Some of these choices [are] no doubt made with the best intentions. Nevertheless, many of these models [encode] human prejudice, misunderstanding, and bias into the software systems that increasingly [manage] our lives.[55]

Even when all precautions are taken, what happens when the data used to train an algorithm is biased? For example, let us posit that a "robojudge" was trained using the case law of a given court from the last 10 years, and that an analysis of the algorithm's decisions shows racial bias. If we can surmise that said bias is not linked to the programmer, it implies that the previous case law was racially biased. This puts whoever is training the algorithm in somewhat of a quandary. How does he or she choose which decisions to remove from the database to limit said bias? Not being a judge, that individual does not possess the qualifications or standing to make such a decision.

Finally, what will happen when the algorithm simply does not "know" the solution to a problem because of lack of data? When touting how artificial intelligence is superior to that of humans, AI proponents will often refer to the famous 2011 Jeopardy tournament which pinned Watson against two of the best Jeopardy players of all time. While most remember the algorithm's dominance, few recall that Watson missed some questions. For example, when asked "In May 2010, 5 paintings worth $125 million by Braque, Matisse & 3 others left Paris' Museum of this art period", Watson replied "Picasso". While being fallible should not automatically disqualify an algorithm—after all we don't hold humans anywhere near this type of standard—the fact that the mistake was so egregious shows what happens when a question simply falls outside the scope of an algorithm's training.[56] One must not forget that AI algorithms are based on statistical or probabilistic analyses. Therefore, lack of data—or the presence of contradictory or indeterminate data—will make the predictive model unreliable. This is why the suggestion that "the legal process can be abstractly viewed as a computation, inputting information about evidence and laws and outputting a decision"[57] is flawed. This would be true if all laws were clear, and all evidence valid and trustworthy, but that is unfortunately not the case.[58] In fact, interpretation plays an important role in "outputting a decision":

> The objective of interpretation, the determination of the intent of the legislature, is achieved readily when the enactment is clear, and with difficulty when it is obscure. In the latter case, the detection of intent necessitates a method of eliciting meaning, so as to overcome the problem. This method comprises principles of interpretation which are supposed to point to

---

[53] *Ibid.*

[54] Flores et al. (2016).

[55] O'Neil (2016), p. 3.

[56] Kawamoto (2011).

[57] Tegmark (2018), p. 105.

[58] Côté et al. (2011), p. 3.

the true meaning of the enactment. The quest for meaning is deemed to lead the jurist, in all cases, to determination of the will of the author. The judge cannot shrink from this search for legislative intent: he or she cannot 'refuse to adjudicate under the pretext on the silence, obscurity or insufficiency of the law'.[59]

However, if an algorithm is stunted by lack of data and a proper definition, it will refuse to adjudicate or, possibly worse, will adjudicate based on incomplete data sets. While it could be argued that human judges will do the same, they can pull from other cognitive experiences in a way that computers can't, which explains why we only need to see two pictures of a cat to recognise one while an algorithm needs thousands. In a way, this is somewhat reminiscent of American Supreme Court justice Potter Stewart's famous quote about pornography in Jacobellis v. Ohio:[60] "*I shall not today attempt further to define the kinds of material I understand to be embraced within that shorthand description; and perhaps I could never succeed in intelligibly doing so. But I know it when I see it, and the motion picture involved in this case is not that*". Such a statement, which has come to define a judge's true role, could not be uttered by a computer under the current state of technology.[61]

For many of the above-stated reasons, and in hopes of curtailing the issues surrounding the use of algorithmic decision-making tools, the Canadian Treasury board published a Directive on Automated Decision-Making.[62] As stated in section 4.1 of said Directive, its purpose is to "ensure that Automated Decision Systems are deployed in a manner that reduces risks to Canadians and federal institutions, and leads to more efficient, accurate, consistent, and interpretable decisions made pursuant to Canadian law". To reach this goal, the Directive sets out to impose a series of obligations on those who would develop or use algorithmic decision-making tools. These obligations can be summarized as follows:

- Parties must complete an algorithmic impact assessment prior to launch and make the results public;
- Parties must provide notice of the use of an algorithmic decision-making tool, as well as an explanation as to why and how the algorithm came to a given decision (which can include the release of source code to allow third-party validation);
- Parties must offer quality assurances (testing and monitoring, quality of data, etc.)
- The system must allow for the challenge of the algorithm's decision; and
- Parties must publish information on the effectiveness and efficiency of the system.

It should be noted that these requirements reflect concerns raised by other governments and stakeholders.[63] For example, the possibility to challenge the algorithm's decision is reminiscent of section 22 of Europe's General Data

---

[59]*Ibid.*,p. 8.

[60]378 U.S. 184.

[61]Julia (2019), pp. 153–159.

[62]Government of Canada (2019).

[63]European Commission For The Efficiency Of Justice (2018).

Protection Regulation (GDPR).[64] This provision states that an individual "*shall have the right not to be subject to a decision based solely on automated processing, including profiling, which produces legal effects concerning him or her or similarly significantly affects him or her*".

Does all that precedes imply that artificial intelligence cannot or should not be used in any capacity to help resolve issues? Obviously not. There are arguments to be made for the use of AI to settle low intensity disputes that offer little complexity and revolve around constant and recurrent fact patterns.[65] Expert systems that resolve these types of cases without human involvement have existed for years,[66] and help alleviate clogged systems. Although one could argue that a human decision-maker is still preferable, the choice to be made isn't between a perfect system and an algorithm, but rather between two imperfect systems: one where lack of funding and overburdened dockets cause interminable delays,[67] and the other with expeditious, yet flawed algorithms. In many low intensity cases, this second option, while limited, could remain preferable—especially if an appeal process as that imposed by section 22 of the GDPR or by the Canadian Directive is present.

Furthermore, these same documents open the door for reasoned use of AI to aid in the decision-making process—something we will explore in the next part of this chapter.

4.3   The Computer As the Courtroom

As we posited in our introduction, "the computer as the court" can refer to the idea that the legal process can be transported online. For example, in February 2015, the Online Dispute Resolution Advisory Group—created at the behest of the UK's Civil Justice Council—produced a report that recommended that "Her Majesty's Courts & Tribunals Service (HMCTS) should establish a new, Internet-based court service, known as Her Majesty's Online Court (HMOC)".[68] The idea was simple: the state should stop building courthouses and allow certain cases to be settled online. In order to reach this goal, the report goes on to indicate that:

> The establishment of HMOC will require two major innovations in the justice system of England and Wales. The first is that some judges should be trained and authorized to decide some cases (or aspects of some cases) on an online basis. The second innovation is that the

---

[64]Regulation (EU) 2016/679 of the European Parliament and of the Council of 27 April 2016 on the protection of natural persons with regard to the processing of personal data and on the free movement of such data, and repealing Directive 95/46/EC.

[65]Philipsen and Themeli (2019).

[66]De Vries and Van Engers (2019).

[67]Lafond (2012).

[68]Online Dispute Resolution Advisory Group (2015).

state should formally fund and make available some online facilitation and online evaluation services.[69]

While this report could be seen as simply following a worldwide trend[70] towards what we refer to as virtual courts or tribunals (i.e. online platforms aimed at settling disputes within a state-sanctioned legal process), it highlights the two main components of these platforms: the use of online dispute resolution mechanisms (Sect. 4.3.1), and what we will qualify as "augmented intelligence tools"[71] (Sect. 4.3.2).

4.3.1 Online Dispute Resolution for the Courts

As we just stated, the idea of incorporating online dispute resolution (ODR) mechanisms into the court process has been gathering steam over the last few years.[72] Of course, this begs the question: what is "ODR"?

Envisioned broadly, online dispute resolution can be defined as *"[t]he use of online environments to facilitate communications and dispute resolution"*.[73] However, most analysts will offer a more restrictive view of what ODR is and does. As explained by Ethan Katsh and Janet Rifkin:

> ODR draws its main themes and concepts from alternative dispute resolution (ADR) processes such as negotiation, mediation, and arbitration. ODR uses the opportunities provided by the Internet not only to employ these processes in the online environment but also to enhance these processes when they are used to resolve conflicts in offline environments. [. . .] Like ADR [. . .] at its core is the idea of providing dispute resolution in a more flexible and efficient manner than is typical with courts and litigation.[74]

While this definition seems at odds with the possibility for courts to incorporate ODR tools and practices in their processes, Thomas Schultz explains why this is not the case:

> Cybercourts are simply court proceedings that use exclusively (or almost exclusively) electronic communication means. They should be, and often are, considered to be part of the ODR movement, for two reasons. First, because the ODR movement emerged because of the clash between the ubiquity of the Internet and the territoriality of traditional, offline dispute resolution mechanisms. The term ODR is thus opposed to offline dispute resolution mechanisms, not to courts. Online ADR is only one part of ODR. Second, courts do not only provide litigation. As I said before, there also is court-based mediation and non-binding arbitration.[75]

---

[69]*Ibid.*

[70]Vermeys and Benyekhlef (2012).

[71]This expression is borrowed from Julia (2019), p. 150.

[72]Vermeys and Benyekhlef (2012).

[73]Hörnle (2003), p. 782.

[74]Katsh and Rifkin (2001), p. 2.

[75]Schultz (2003), p. 5.

In fact, the three-stage process associated with ODR, i.e. "negotiation; facilitated settlement; and a third (final) stage",[76] is now being replicated by courts and tribunals around the world.[77] For example, in Canada, the Condominium Authority of Ontario launched its Condominium Authority Tribunal (CAT), an online tribunal aimed at settling disputes between condominium owners and condominium boards, back in 2017.[78] Based on technology developed by the Cyberjustice Laboratory,[79] the CAT process can be described as follows:

1. Filing a case: In this stage, you will tell us who is involved in the case, and what the case is about;
2. Joining a case: In this stage, the other User will join the case. Once they have joined, you will automatically move to the Negotiation Stage;
3. Negotiation: In this stage, Users can try to resolve the case between themselves;
4. Mediation: In this stage, a CAT Mediator will join the case and will help the Users resolve the case;
5. Tribunal Decision: In this stage, a CAT Member will join the case and will make a decision that the users must follow.[80]

While the inner workings of these virtual tribunals are beyond the scope of this chapter, platforms such as that used by the CAT offer incontrovertible proof that the idea of holding online trials is not only feasible, it's a successful way of settling disputes. This is not to say that the online process is flawless or universal; there are undoubtedly drawbacks to moving the courts partially or completely online, but studies show that said drawbacks are outweighed by the benefits associated with easier access to justice.[81] As we and others posited elsewhere:

> ODR practices can and should be adopted by the courts to help settle those cases that are adapted to the online environment. Such measures could go a long way in making the courts more efficient by freeing up judges from hearing cases which could easily have been settled through negotiation or mediation. However, these measures come at a cost. As past and current State-run ODR services have demonstrated, the State needs to invest both financially and politically in these programs for them to work. [. . .] But one should not throw good money after bad in the sense that we should not invest in ODR programs without first establishing what ODR solutions are compatible with the practices, customs, and principles underpinning our court systems. There is a good reason why ODR mainly developed outside of the courts: because it was not hindered by the normative order associated with legal systems. However, this order serves a purpose, and simply discarding it because it is incompatible with new technological advances is a mistake. The key to incorporating ODR practices into the courts is to first identify how the technology will impact our practices beyond the simple statement that ODR will make the legal system more efficient and less

---

[76]United Nations Commission on International Trade (2017).

[77]European Commission For The Efficiency Of Justice (2018).

[78]See Condominium Authority of Ontario (2019a, b) The Condominium Authority Tribunal.

[79]See Labratoire de Cyberjustice (2019).

[80]See Condominium Authority of Ontario (2019a, b) The CAT Process.

[81]Roberge (2019).

costly, because a system that is not in line with our values will never work, no matter how inexpensive and expedient it is.[82]

In the same vein, as some authors suggest, *"[s]ome types of dispute are less likely to be solved by online proceedings than others. E-commerce, for instance, seems better adapted to ODR than family law disputes or criminal cases. Small claims benefit more from the low costs of ODR than large claims"*.[83] While we would agree with the general statement that ODR is better suited to resolve certain types of disputes than others, the way these platforms have evolved in the past few years shows that properly conceived tools can help settle conflicts that one would have never fathomed settling online,[84] an observation that was recently also made by the European Commission for the Efficiency of Justice:

> the scope of these online dispute resolution (ODR) services seems to have gradually extended. They have gone from restricted online services to alternative dispute resolution measures before the complaint is brought before the court, and are now being introduced increasingly into the court process itself, to the point of offering electronic court services'. They do not only concern low-value disputes, but also tax disputes or disputes relating to social security services, or divorce proceedings.[85]

Furthermore, to tie in with the first section of this chapter, we are now seeing the enhancement of these platforms with AI tools—not to replace judges and lawyers—but rather to allow them, as well as the parties themselves, to access better and more complete information to help in the dispute resolution process.

4.3.2 Augmented Intelligence As a Tool Towards Access to Justice

As we just eluded to, virtual courts or tribunals are now contemplating the use of AI (or already using algorithms) to either automate certain steps in the decision-making process, or to offer tools to assist in said process. In this context, legal literature that addresses the use of machine learning to help legal stakeholders gather information will usually talk of predictive justice[86] based on artificial intelligence.[87] While these concepts have permeated our legal lexicon, and while we agree that we face an uphill climb should we try to replace them, the fact remains that—in hindsight—they were poorly chosen. Regarding artificial intelligence, as explained by Luc Julia:

---

[82]Vermeys and Benyekhlef (2012), p. 310.
[83]Schultz et al. (2001).
[84]Susskind (2010), p. 221.
[85]European Commission For The Efficiency Of Justice (2018).
[86]Sève (2018).
[87]Goodman (2016).

[translation] "The very first apparition of the term "artificial intelligence", credited to John McCarthy [...] was then accepted by all. Yet the working group's results fell far short of their ambitions. If they made certain progress in what would later become "expert systems", they in no way determined the steps to simulate intelligence. The use of the word "intelligence" for this discipline is nothing but smoke and mirrors since it is based on wishful thinking that is far from reality. [...] I submit that artificial intelligence does not exist. If we must keep the acronym, AI should no longer signify "artificial intelligence", but rather "augmented intelligence". [...] Whether we call them expert systems, machine learning, or deep learning, they are nothing else than what we humans have decided they are. All of these technologies serve the purpose of assisting us in accomplishing punctual tasks that are often repetitive and highly codified. They offer help to amplify our humanity and augment our physical or intellectual capacities, but can in no way replace them. There is no artificial intelligence that escapes our control and will precipitate our extinction. There is augmented intelligence that must benefit from just regulation in order to support our own intelligence."[88]

As for the expression "predictive justice", it too is highly misleading. The idea of predictive justice refers to tools that "provide a graphic representation of the probability of success for each outcome of a dispute based on criteria entered by the user (specific to each type of dispute). These systems claim to be capable to calculate the likely amount of compensation distributed by the courts",[89] Yet, AI algorithms are not oracles; they are mere tools that can help identify patterns and pertinent information in a sea of structured data. As the European Commission For The Efficiency Of Justice surmises:

A distinction must be made from the outset between what is a "prediction" and what is a "forecast". Prediction is the act of announcing what will happen (prae, before – dictare, say) in advance of future events (by supernatural inspiration, by clairvoyance or premonition). Forecasting, on the other hand, is the result of observing (aiming, seeing) a set of data in order to envisage a future situation. This abuse of language and the spread thereof seems to be explained by a transfer of the term from the "hard" sciences, where it refers to a variety of data science techniques derived from mathematics, statistics and game theory that analyse present and past facts to make hypotheses about the content of future events.[90]

As so-called predictive tools are actually based on probabilities "established through the statistical modelling of previous decisions",[91] they do not predict. Rather, they simply offer insight into past events in the same manner as actuarial tables, which have been used by courts for decades. But "statistical models" do not offer the full picture. As addressed earlier, small shifts in fact patterns might result in very different verdicts. For this reason, we take exception with the use of simple statistical tools and prefer a holistic approach where users are given access to information, not mere indicators. AI shouldn't be used to predict results, but rather to identify useful data that could help legal stakeholders—including judges—better inform themselves on possible outcomes.

---

[88] Julia (2019), pp. 118–151.
[89] European Commission For The Efficiency Of Justice (2018).
[90] European Commission For The Efficiency Of Justice (2018).
[91] *Ibid.*

This issue is central to the Canadian Directive on Automated Decision-Making which, as explained earlier, requires that explanations be given "as to why and how the algorithm came to a given decision", a position shared by members of the *explainable artificial intelligence*, or "XAI," movement.[92] Lack of explanation and, therefore, lack of context, might have unwarranted effects on judicial independence. Studies have demonstrated that judges treasure their independence and that groupthink—"*[t]he practice of thinking or making decisions as a group, resulting typically in unchallenged, poor-quality decision-making*"[93]—does not seem to plague the judiciary.[94] That being said, judges may feel pressured to follow the recommendation of predictive tools since "it is not easy to contradict a system that reviews thousands of cases".[95] This is particularly true "when you have to deal with time constraints".[96] This same conclusion was arrived at by Karim Benyekhlef and Emmanuelle Amar:

> One of these limitations is the risk of performative effect. In the case of predictive tools for case outcome, they can have the effect of an unwilling harmonization of jurisprudence. The fact of advancing a result contributes to its advent. By having access to an average of decisions on a set topic and an average amount, through a machine learning tool, lawyers pleading the case and judges evaluating it, might be tempted to align themselves with those results and exclude human reasoning and factors. On a similar topic, if litigants and lawyers have access to outcome predictive tools, they will use these tools to decide whether to proceed or not. In other words, people might not go to court if the predictive system says they will lose. We believe this could potentially have a negative effect on Justice itself.[97]

This is why explainability is so important when developing so-called "predictive tools", and why we believe it to be the key to the development of augmented intelligence tools that can help legal stakeholders make informed decisions rather than creating predictive tools that give out statistical information that is void of context and could force the inference of erroneous outcomes.

4.4   Conclusion

Algorithms are not intelligent[98] or, if they are, their intelligence is nowhere comparable to that of a human being and closer to that of a small amphibian.[99] It is therefore ludicrous, at this point and time, to talk about robots taking over the judiciary. This is

---

[92]De Vries and Van Engers (2019).

[93]Oxford Dictionary (2019b).

[94]Cotropia (2010).

[95]Philipsen and Themeli (2019).

[96]*Ibid.*

[97]Benyekhlef and Amar (2018), p. 254.

[98]Julia (2019).

[99]Bengio (2018).

not to say that algorithms cannot do some tasks such as triage to help lessen the load for judges, therefore freeing them up to render complex legal decisions. It simply means that, in most cases, AI should be relegated to an informative rather than decision-making role. In other words, while the computer as the judge is still years away, AI-assisted decision-making seems to be the next logical step in the slow but necessary digitisation of certain judicial processes and procedures.

In fact, bringing things one step further, AI's capacity to detect patterns could also help judges better reflect on their own decision-making skills and the biases and prejudices that might hinder their use. For example, more and more legaltech companies claim to offer tools that can predict a given judge's receptiveness to certain legal arguments.[100] While these tools are criticized by many judges, and were even made illegal in France,[101] they could, if programmed properly, offer "a mechanism to detect in real time, and thereby remedy judicial behaviour that undermines the rule of law".[102] This concept was explored years ago by American justice Richard Posner:

> I look forward to a time when computers will create profiles of judges' philosophies from their opinions and their public statements, and will update these profiles continuously as the judges issue additional opinions. The profiles will enable lawyers and judges to predict judicial behaviour more accurately, and will assist judges in maintaining consistency with their previous decisions—when they want to.[103]

As explained by Daniel L. Chen, current algorithms could even go one step further:

> If algorithms can identify the contexts that are likely to give rise to bias, they can also reduce those biases through behavioural nudges and other mechanisms, such as through judicial education.[104]

Of course, as we stated throughout this chapter, what is perceived as a judge's biases could actually be the result of the judiciary applying a biased law as it is written or of statistical anomalies. However, if a tool simply gives judges information on their track records regarding certain key issues, it might—as Justice Posner seems to suggest—give them the insight they need to identify and address involuntary biases and prejudices.

---

[100]See Premoniton (2019).

[101]Artificial Lawyer (2019).

[102]Chen (2019).

[103]Posner (2006), p. 1050.

[104]Chen (2019).

References

Angwin J et al (2016) Machine Bias: There's software used across the country to predict future criminals and it's biased against blacks. Available via PROPUBLICA. https://www.propublica. org/article/machine-bias-risk-assessments-in-criminal-sentencing

Arruda A (2016) Presentation ROSS intelligence. https://www.youtube.com/watch?v=hJk-dQnn4M8

Artificial Lawyer (2019) France Bans judge analytics, 5 years in prison for rule breakers. Available via Artificial Lawyer. https://www.artificiallawyer.com/2019/06/04/france-bans-judge-analyt ics-5-years-in-prison-for-rule-breakers/

Benedikt Frey C, Osborne MA (2013) The future of employment: how susceptible are jobs to computerisation? https://www.oxfordmartin.ox.ac.uk/downloads/academic/The_Future_of_ Employment.pdf

Bengio Y (2018) Countering the monopolization of research. Available via THE UNESCO COURRIER. https://en.unesco.org/courier/2018-3/countering-monopolization-research

Benyekhlef K, Amar E (2018) Some reflections on the future of online dispute resolution. From e-platform to algorithms. In: Barral I (ed) La resolución de conflictos con consumidores: de la mediación a las ODR. Editorial Reus, Madrid, p 229

Cambridge Dictionary (2019) Court. https://dictionary.cambridge.org/dictionary/english/court

CanLII (2019) CanLII. https://www.canlii.org/en/

Carneiro D et al (2014) Online dispute resolution: an artificial intelligence perspective. Artif Intelligence Rev 41:211

Cellan-Jones R (2017) The robot lawyers are here - and they're winning. Available via BBC NEWS. https://www.bbc.com/news/technology-41829534

Chen DL (2019) Machine learning and the rule of law. Available via SSRN. https://papers.ssrn. com/sol3/papers.cfm?abstract_id=3302507

Condominium Authority of Ontario (2019a) The CAT process. https://www.condoauthorityontario. ca/en-US/tribunal/the-cat-process/

Condominium Authority of Ontario (2019b) The Condominium Authority Tribunal. https://www. condoauthorityontario.ca/en-US/tribunal/

Côté P-A et al (2011) The interpretation of law in Canada. Carswell, Toronto

Cotropia CA (2010) Determining uniformity within the federal circuit by measuring dissent and en banc review. Loyola Los Angeles Law Rev 43:801

Crawford K (2016) Can an algorithm be agonistic? Ten scenes from life in calculated publics. Sci Technol Human Values 41(1):77–92

De Vries DM, Van Engers TM (2019) Explainable artificial intelligence within the Dutch Govern-ment. Paper presented at the Autonomy through Cyberjustice Technologies (ACT) Project Annual Meeting, Université de Montréal, Montreal, 12–14 June 2019

Domingos P (2012) A few useful things to know about machine learning. Commun ACM 55(10):78

EDX (2018) Deep learning explained. Available via EDX. https://www.edx.org/course/deep-learning-explained-microsoft-dat236x-1.

European Commission For The Efficiency Of Justice (2018) European ethical charter on the use of artificial intelligence in judicial systems and their environment. Available via COUNCIL OF EUROPE. https://rm.coe.int/ethical-charter-en-for-publication-4-december-2018/16808f699c

Flores AW et al (2016) False positives, false negatives, and false analyses: a rejoinder to Machine Bias: there's software used across the country to predict future criminals. And it's biased against blacks. Federal Probation 80:38

Forum (2018) JusticeBot: giving tenants better access to legal information. Available via UDEMNOUVELLES. https://nouvelles.umontreal.ca/article/2018/11/30/justicebot-giving-ten ants-better-access-to-legal-information/

Goodman J (2016) Robots in law: how artificial intelligence is transforming legal services. Ark Group, London

Government of Canada (2019) Directive on automated decision-making. Available via GOVERN-MENT OF CANADA. https://www.tbs-sct.gc.ca/pol/doc-eng.aspx?id=32592

Hörnle J (2003) Online dispute resolution. In: Bernstein R et al (eds) Bernstein's handbook of arbitration and dispute resolution practice, vol 1, 4th edn. Sweet & Maxwell, London, p 782

IBM (2019) IBM Watson Health. https://www.ibm.com/watson/health/about/

Invest Foresight (2018) Robots to replace stenographers in court. Available via INVEST FORE-SIGHT. https://investforesight.com/robots-to-replace-stenographers-in-court/

Julia L (2019) L'intelligence artificielle n'existe pas, 1st edn. Paris

Katsh E, Rifkin J (2001) Online dispute resolution: resolving conflicts in cyberspace. Jossey-Bass, San Francisco

Kawamoto D (2011) Watson wasn't perfect: IBM explains the 'Jeopardy!' errors. Available via AOL. https://www.aol.com/2011/02/17/the-watson-supercomputer-isnt-always-perfect-you-say-tomato/

Kowalski M (2017) The great legal reformation. iUniverse, Bloomington

Labratoire de Cyberjustice (2019) CAT. https://cyberjustice.openum.ca/en/logiciels-cyberjustice/nos-etudes-de-cas/tasc/

Lafond P-C (2012) L'accès à la justice civile au Québec : Portrait général. Éditions Yvon Blais, Montreal

Lawgeex (2018) Comparing the performance of artificial intelligence to human lawyers in the review of standard business contracts. https://www.lawgeex.com/resources/aivslawyer/?utm_source=google&utm_medium=cpc&utm_campaign=Global_sch_brand&utm_adgroup=42250155000&device=c&placement=&utm_term—lawgeex&gclid=EAIaIQobChMInrKMxrLJ4gIVDJ-fCh3A0Q7qEAAYASABEgKqo_D_BwE

Luminance (2018) Luminance. https://www.luminance.com/index.html

McCarthy J et al (1955) A proposal for the dartmouth summer research project on artificial intelligence

McCarthy J et al (2006) A proposal for the dartmouth summer research project on artificial intelligence. AI Magazine 27(4):12–14

Merriam-Webster dictionary (2019) Artificial intelligence. https://www.merriam-webster.com/dictionary/artificial%20intelligence

Niiler E (2019) Can AI be a Fair Judge in Court? Estonia Thinks So. Available via WIRED. https://www.wired.com/story/can-ai-be-fair-judge-court-estonia-thinks-so/

Northpoint (2015) Practitioner's guide to COMPAS core. https://assets.documentcloud.org/documents/2840784/Practitioner-s-Guide-to-COMPAS-Core.pdf

O'Neil C (2016) Weapons of Math destruction: how big data increases inequality and threatens democracy. Crown, New York

Online Dispute Resolution Advisory Group (2015) Online dispute resolution for low value civil claims. Available via the CIVIL JUSTICE COUNCIL. https://www.judiciary.uk/wp-content/uploads/2015/02/Online-Dispute-Resolution-Final-Web-Version1.pdf

Oxford Dictionary (2019a) Artificial intelligence. https://en.oxforddictionaries.com/definition/artificial_intelligence

Oxford Dictionary (2019b) Group think. https://en.oxforddictionaries.com/definition/groupthink

Oxford Dictionary (2019c) Machine learning. https://en.oxforddictionaries.com/definition/machine_learning

Philipsen S, Themeli E (2019) Artificial intelligence in courts: a (Legal) introduction to the Robot Judge. Available via the Montaigne Center. http://blog.montaignecentre.com/index.php/1940/artificial-intelligence-in-courts-a-legal-introduction-to-the-robot-judge-2/

Posner RA (2006) The role of the judge in the twenty-first century. Boston Univ Law Rev 86:1049

Premoniton (2019). https://premonition.ai/

Roberge JF (2019) Why consider ODR? Conference presented at the Online Dispute Resolution as a Public Service Conference. Toronto

Ronkainen A (2011) From spelling checkers to Robot Judges? Some implications of normativity in language technology and AI & law. In: Branting K, Wyner A (eds) Proceedings of the ICAIL

2011 workshop applying human language technology to law. Masaryk University, Brno, pp 48–53

Ross Intelligence. (2019a) Features. https://rossintelligence.com/features.html

Ross Intelligence. (2019b) Scope of coverage. https://rossintelligence.com/#coverage

Schultz T (2003) An essay on the role of government for ODR: theoretical considerations about the future of ODR. Proceedings of the UNECE Forum on ODR 2003. http://www.odr.info/unece2003

Schultz T et al (2001) Online dispute resolution: the state of the art and the issues. Schultz, Thomas and bc, a and Langer, Dirk and Bonnet, Vincent, Online Dispute Resolution: The State of the Art and the Issues. Available via SSRN. https://ssrn.com/abstract=899079

Sève R (2018) La justice predictive. Dalloz, Paris

Snowdon W (2017) Robot judges? Edmonton research crafting artificial intelligence for courts. Available via CBC NEWS. http://www.cbc.ca/news/canada/edmonton/legal-artificial-intelligence-alberta-japan-1.4296763

Surden H (2014) Machine learning and law. Wash Law Rev 89:87

Susskind R (2010) The End of Lawyers?: Rethinking the nature of legal services. Oxford University Press, Oxford

Tegmark M (2018) Life 3.0: being human in the age of artificial intelligence. Vintage Books, New York

Turing AM (1950) Computing machinery and intelligence. Mind 49:433

Turner K (2016) Meet 'Ross,' the newly hired legal robot. Available via The Washington Post. https://www.washingtonpost.com/news/innovations/wp/2016/05/16/meet-ross-the-newly-hired-legal-robot/?utm_term=.446e385ca1c7

United Nations Commission on International Trade (2017) UNCITRAL technical notes on online dispute resolution. Available via UNCITRAL. http://www.uncitral.org/pdf/english/texts/odr/V1700382_English_Technical_Notes_on_ODR.pdf

Vermeys NW, Benyekhlef K (2012) ODR and the Courts. In: Abdel Wahab MS et al (eds) Online dispute resolution: theory and practice. Eleven, The Hague, pp 295–312

Wente M (2009) For god's sake, get a second life (Or Not). Available via The Globe and Mail. https://www.theglobeandmail.com/opinion/for-gods-sake-get-a-second-life-or-not/article1345119/

Case Law

Health Services and Support - Facilities Subsector Bargaining Assn. v. British Columbia, [2007] 2 SCR 391

Husky Oil Operations Limited v. Canada-Newfoundland and Labrador Offshore Petroleum Board, 2018 FCA 10

Jacobellis v. Ohio, 378 U.S. 184

R v Cook, [1997] 1 SCR 1113

State v. Loomis, 2016 WI 68

Part II
Privatisation and ADR

Chapter 5
Delivering Justice

Christopher Hodges

Abstract The legal system needs to slay some myths. Focusing on access to justice avoids the critical issue of whether justice is actually delivered, in enough individual cases and as a whole. Retaining an adversarial dispute resolution model avoids the reality that it cannot work absent a consistently reliable source of funding, and more investigative models are cheaper and quicker. Focusing on deterrence avoids the fact that the empirical evidence that imposing deterrent sanctions has at best limited effect of the future behaviour of people or organisations, and that those regulators and organisations that have based their approaches on behavioural psychology and ethical cultures are notably effective in affecting change and future behaviour. In short, for all these reasons, our approach to dispute resolution is now out-of-date. There has been diversification in *techniques* (mediation and other ADR techniques in addition to adjudication), in *technologies* (online process, use of artificial intelligence), in *pathways* (Ombudsmen have replaced lawyers and courts in consumer-trader disputes, and are set to do so in the property sector; new regulatory bodies have been created for disputes involving small businesses), and in *functions* (Ombudsmen and regulators use data from inquiries and disputes as tools of market surveillance and behavioural intervention). The reality is that we need a new start to look objectively at considerable diversity and to design a new system that integrates all techniques, technologies, pathways and functions into a single coordinated system. This chapter summarises a recent holistic review of the system in England (and partly Wales) and outlines its conclusions.

C. Hodges (✉)
Swiss Re Programme on Civil Justice Systems, Centre for Socio-Legal Studies, Oxford University, Oxford, UK
e-mail: christopher.hodges@csls.ox.ac.uk

© The Author(s), under exclusive license to Springer Nature Switzerland AG 2021
X. Kramer et al. (eds.), *New Pathways to Civil Justice in Europe*,
https://doi.org/10.1007/978-3-030-66637-8_5

5.1 Multiple and Diverse Dispute Resolution Pathways

The traditional assumption is that laws are made, enforced and hence observed. The associated assumptions are that the mechanism that produces the outcome of observation of law is that individual rights will be enforced, that such enforcement will be through the courts (and usually by private enforcement, in which individuals bring their own claims), that all decisions by courts will be observed, and that such enforcement will deter future wrongdoing. There are problems with all of these assumptions. People may not know that they have relevant rights, or that they can bring a complaint, or that they can afford a lawyer or the court process. Defendants might not observe rights, or judgments, or change their behaviour after a legal ruling. The theory that deterrence has much effect on future behaviour might not be supported by empirical evidence.[1]

A review of all major types of dispute resolution in England (and partly Wales, where some systems are different) reveals uncomfortable failures in the systems for providing information and support to people and small businesses (SMEs), for providing effective and efficient pathways for solving their disputes, and for providing mechanisms that result in appropriate changes in behaviour and couture of people and organisations.[2] This ab summarises the main points of such a review. The review has examined the pathways that exist for resolution of disputes involving consumers, property, families, employment, SMEs, large companies, personal injuries (from road traffic to workplace and healthcare), and claims against the State, including judicial review, administrative appeals, the public Ombudsmen, public inquiries and coroners).

The review project was inspired by evidence that, whilst a great deal of reform has occurred in many types of dispute resolution processes, the outcomes have been effective transformation in some sectors but not in others. This raises questions like: What reforms have been tried and with what success? What reforms do, or do not, work, or are transformative, and under what conditions?

This article first considers the evidence on whether justice is delivered or not. We then examine major developments in the adoption of new techniques (especially mediation) and new technologies (digitisation and artificial intelligence), before noting the failure of the adversarial model for most cases and the fact that in an increasing number of case types, where they are presented with choice of pathways, users have switched to using new pathways and intermediaries. We then examine important reasons for such switches, which are not only related to advantages in resolving disputes (such as identifiability of pathways, ease of access, user-friendliness, speed, and cost) but also the wider functions that some pathways provide, especially if providing assistance to users with solving their problems and in collating aggregated data that is fed back to improve performance, behaviour and culture. The focus then turns to identifying the key issues that need to be addressed in

---

[1]Hodges (2015a).

[2]Hodges (2019).

designing a new system that integrates the various required techniques, technology and functions.

5.2   Is Justice Delivered?

There has been too much reliance on the mantra of 'access to justice'. That slogan can hide the fact that justice is often not *delivered* to individuals and organisations when it is needed. The real question is whether justice is *delivered*. Answering that question needs a great deal of empirical evidence and not much theoretical input. The research evidence provides a salutary view on how people view the legal system and avoid using it. Justice is too often *not* delivered.

Some studies have looked at consumer problems. Consumer Focus reported consumers making a complaint to companies in six important markets (legal services, gas and electricity, mail, telecoms, water and financial services) most wanted a change in how the service was provided (25%) or a refund (23%).[3] A major 2015 study found that UK consumers experienced an average of 2.4 problems a year (123 million incidents), costing £446 per adult, leading to 1.2 billion hours spent dealing with issues, at a total consumer detriment costing UK consumers £22.9 billion a year.[4] The most important source of consumer detriment (45%, amounting to £10.3 billion) was substandard service. It found that in the majority of cases (55%), survey respondents who had suffered some form of detriment indicated that they had not sought, and had no intention to seek, any form of redress. In 35% of cases respondents had sought some form of refund or compensation, with a further 4% planning to seek it, and 6% unsure. Of those respondents who did not seek redress, 22% failed to do so because they believed that the process was too long or complicated. The complexity of the process of redress was proportionately less likely to deter those with a higher level of educational attainment. A 2017 study for Ombudsman Services reported consumers experiencing 173 million issues with products and services, affecting 57% of people in the UK, yet only a quarter (27%) of these were raised with the provider.[5]

Other studies have looked at people with complaints against public bodies. The Parliamentary and Health Service Ombudsman (PHSO) said in 2015: 'People bring their unresolved complaints to us because they want an explanation, an apology and for the service to improve for others.'[6] An associated survey found that although

---

[3]Vaze et al. (2012). The data was from an online survey of 825 people, plus three group sessions and 18 in-depth interviews.

[4]Oxford Economics (2016). The cost per person figure is inflated by high cost problems in areas like construction that affect a relatively small number of people. For EU figures see Civil Consulting (2017).

[5]Ombudsman Services (2018).

[6]Parliamentary and Health Service Ombudsman (2015a).

most people believe you should complain if you are unhappy about a public service (90%), just one third of people (34%) who were unhappy after using a public service in the Ombudsman's remit had actually made a complaint, leaving 64% who did not complain despite being unhappy.[7] The main reasons why people who felt unhappy with a public service did not complain were that 29% thought that complaining does not make a difference, 14% thought it would be more hassle than it was worth, 9% felt it would be too time consuming, 7% did not know where to go to make a complaint, and 6% did not think it would be taken seriously.

A 2016 Citizens Advice survey found that as many as 15 million people who had a poor experience with a public service had not registered the problem as a complaint and that people generally do not make formal complaints after poor public service.[8] It reported a 63% increase in requests for help to complain about public services over the last 4 years; 45% of people having experienced poor public service recently, but only 22% of them went on to make a formal complaint; 52% of people said they didn't complain about a poor experience with a public service because they felt 'it wouldn't change anything'. However, 73% used informal channels to share their frustrations, with one in five younger people turning to social media. Citizens Advice said that feedback and insight of specific groups is being missed.

The Public Accounts Committee said in December 2017 that 'There is a growing body of evidence that when things go wrong many people simply want an apology, or want to know that the issue is being dealt with and it won't happen again.'[9]

The (most recent) survey of legal problems in England and Wales (LPRS), conducted in 2014/2015,[10] found that in the 18 months before interview almost a third of adults (32%) reported that they had experienced one or more of the civil, administrative or family legal problems asked about. The largest problem types related to purchasing goods or services (8%), neighbours' anti-social behaviour (8%) and money problems (excluding personal debt) (7%). Overall almost a quarter (23%) rated their problem as very serious, of which family legal problems and administrative legal problems were more likely to be considered very serious (38% and 31% respectively) than civil legal problems (20%). The study reached the following general conclusion (emphasis added):[11]

> Experiencing a legal problem is a relatively common experience, with a third of adults having experienced at least one problem in the preceding 18 months, although many people who do have such a problem do not classify it as a legal issue themselves and most problems are dealt with without the use of any legal or formal resolution processes or legal advice. Thus the problems that result in formal legal action are *a very small part of a much larger pool of problems that people experience* and, for the most part, deal with alone or without legal or professional help. These findings are in line with those from previous surveys. Understanding the overall picture and *the extent to which individuals are able to deal with*

---

[7]Parliamentary and Health Service Ombudsman (2015b).

[8]Citizens Advice (2016).

[9]House of Commons, Committee of Public Accounts (2017), para. 5.

[10]Franklyn et al. (2017).

[11]Franklyn et al. (2017). See earlier Legal Services Board (2012).

their problems through less formal means is important in considering what access to justice represents for different groups, and *how people can best be supported in resolving issues effectively and quickly.*

The LPRS study reported that almost all adults with a legal problem (90%) had taken some action on their own to try to resolve their legal problem, but used different means, or combinations of means, which different depending on the type of problem. Almost two-fifths of adults (39%) used some form of legal or professional help and almost one fifth (17%) used a formal legal process or resolution service. Those who experienced a problem relating to a relationship breakdown were more likely to use a formal resolution process (35%) than those who experienced a civil (16%) or administrative (18%) problem. Those experiencing civil or administrative problems were more likely (55% and 49%) to try to resolve the problem without using legal or professional help or a formal legal process than those experiencing a problem relating to relationship breakdown (25%).

Overall, 5% of adults with legal problems had used a court or tribunal process, 14% considered using a court or tribunal but ultimately decided not to (43% of whom said that the problem had resolved), and 80% did not consider using a court or tribunal process at all. Overall, 9% of adults with legal problems had used independent conciliation, mediation or arbitration, 11% considered using it but ultimately decided not to (37% of whom said that the problem had resolved), and 79% did not consider using it at all.

Another large survey of legal needs in England and Wales in 2014/2015 similarly found that people tackled their problems in a variety of ways: 35% obtained legal advice; 34% tried to tackle them alone, 15% got help from family or friends, while 13% did nothing.[12] Almost one in 10 were handled alone for 'fear that doing otherwise would cost too much – either the cost of an adviser's service or the cost of court fees'.

The data, therefore, consistently shows, as Hazel Genn suggested,[13] that people have *problems* rather than legal problems, that they have a significant number of problems, and that many go unraised and hence unresolved. But people want not just money but often for things to change. The legal system can sometimes deliver money but is not good at delivering changes in behaviour or culture. Have dispute resolution systems responded to these challenges? Some have, many have not. It is true that several major changes have occurred in dispute resolution during past decades. Let us focus on changes in techniques and technology before looking at pathways and functions.

---

[12]Ipsos MORI Social Research Institute (2016). 54% of all those who responded had experienced at least one legal issue in the previous 3 years.

[13]Genn (1999) and subsequent studies.

5.2.1 New Techniques: ADR and Mediation

Alternative dispute resolution (ADR) is as old as human interactions and has traditionally focused on restoring the social relationships between people.[14] ADR in the form of arbitration has long been adopted as a principal pathway for resolution of large commercial and international disputes, partly competing with courts but with both tracks staffed by the same senior legal or judicial personnel. Arbitration is sometimes found as an alternative in certain other dispute types, such as consumer and online disputes, but has never gained wide trust or usage. Various other techniques are also relevant, including early neutral evaluation.

Mediation—the generic concept of facilitation of resolution through agreement by assistance of a neutral third party—has been hailed as a transformational tool. The Woolf reforms made mediation a mainstream technique and tried to prioritise it as the standard form of dispute resolution technique both before and during a court claim.[15] But mediation has not solved the problem for courts. There are two reasons for this—failure to integrate mediation and mediators *into* the pathway and hence the need for parties to pay for mediation separately. Mediation is still kept separate from the pathway that is taken by a civil claim—they remain separate and need to be arranged and paid for separately. In contrast, consumer Ombudsmen provide an integrated dispute resolution pathway in which mediation is a stage in a seamless process. Further, neither party needs to pay more for this process. The result is outstanding in terms of speed and cost of resolution of cases.

Two examples stand out where these lessons have not been applied. In employment disputes, a claimant has first to notify ACAS,[16] which then contacts both sides to offer its conciliation services. But it is not mandatory to use ACAS, or any other mediation provider. The claimant just needs a piece of paper before being able to start a claim in an Employment Tribunal (ET). Judicial mediation can be offered in an ET and has a 70% success rate. In 2017/2018, 1,300,000 people contacted ACAS. The ACAS conciliation stage resulted in resolution of 25.8% of cases (plus no further action being taken in 29.6%).[17] However, 8.5% of parties could not be contacted, 16.3% declined to participate, and 19.6% continued to an ET—a total of 44.4%. There were only 109,364 formal notifications of claims to ETs, with 38,491 disposals and 9489 ET decisions. If people had to pass through ACAS and be subject to a process in which automatic investigation of their case led to communication between the parties facilitated by ACAS, more cases would settle at that stage and fewer would proceed to an ET.

A further example of lack of integration of mediation is in family disputes. The Children and Families Act 2014 made attendance at a family Mediation Information & Assessment Meeting (MIAM) mandatory before a person can make a relevant

---

[14]Roberts and Palmer (2005).

[15]Civil Procedure Rules 1999, inspired by Woolf (1995, 1996).

[16]See Employment Tribunals Act 1996 ss 18, 18A and 18B.

[17]Secretary of State for Business (2018), p. 36.

family application, save where there is evidence of domestic violence or of a risk of domestic violence.[18] But attending a MIAM is not the same as agreeing to a mediation. Numbers of people attending family mediation (which needs to be paid for) have remained low. Research published in 2015 found that only 19% of a sample of 300 applicants had attended a MIAM before commencement of proceedings and 81% had not done so.[19] Since the withdrawal of legal aid from most family cases in 2014, the number of MIAMs has fallen dramatically.[20]

5.2.2   New Technology

We live in a digital age. It is no longer acceptable for paper files to be used. People expect to be able to use instant forms of online communication and instant responses. The courts and tribunals in UK are undergoing a 'hugely ambitious'[21] £1 billion upgrade with adoption of online technology and the creation of Her Majesty's Online Court.[22] This massive project is being undertaken in discrete steps and is accompanied by experimentation in new ways of working that are being trialled for particular areas. The techniques include digital files, online processes, case management by officials or judges, telephone and now online hearings. All of these changes would reduce cost and time.

Some areas are already a success, such as the upgraded Money Claim Online (MCOL) service,[23] which issued over 25,000 claims between March and September 2018, with the ability for without prejudice offers to be made and accepted, and with 90% of users being satisfied or very satisfied.[24] Another example is the Intellectual Property Enterprise Court (IPEC) where the streamlined procedure has scale recoverable costs for cases up to £250,000, generally capped at £50,000, and robust case management.[25] A small claims track applies where the value of the claim is not more

---

[18]Children and Families Act 2014, ss 1 and 10. See Department for Education and Ministry of Justice (2014).

[19]Hamlyn et al. (2015).

[20]Ministry of Justice (2017), para. 161.

[21]House of Commons Committee of Public Accounts (2018).

[22]See Her Majesty's Treasury (2015), Ministry of Justice and Her Majesty's Courts and Tribunals Service (2016), Her Majesty's Courts and Tribunals Service (2016), Lord Justice Briggs (2016), Comptroller and Auditor General, National Audit Office (2018) and Her Majesty's Courts & Tribunals Service (2018b).

[23]Her Majesty's Courts & Tribunals Service (2020). See Her Majesty's Courts and Tribunals Services (2018).

[24]Her Majesty's HM Courts and Tribunals Service (2018c), p. 12.

[25]CPR, Part 45 rules 45.30–45.32 and see also PD 45 Section IV.

than £10,000.[26] The model is being piloted from January 2019 in some other Business and Property Courts.[27]

But going online does not solve the overall problem—because others already use the same technology, and other mechanisms can be preferable to the court pathway for a number of reasons, as will appear below. Online dispute resolution has been around for over a decade, such as in Online Dispute Resolution (ODR) platforms operated in-house by online traders or by commercial providers. The leading consumer Ombudsmen in UK all adopted online processes some years ago and have continued to develop sophisticated IT and artificial intelligence that can assist consumers, traders and Ombudsmen in analysing and resolving the substance and emotional impact of cases.[28] We will discuss below the considerably increased functions that effective Ombudsmen deliver, beyond dispute resolution.

An indication of the speed with which consumer Ombudsmen can resolve many disputes with traders[29] is that the LPRS study found that almost three-quarters of problems with purchasing goods and services (74%) had concluded by the time of interview, more than all other problem types.[30] Problems relating to a relationship breakup or personal debt were significantly less likely to have concluded (38% and 43% respectively) than most other problem types, except for problems with neighbours' anti-social behaviour or education. For concluded problems where it was possible to calculate the duration, 60% of adults reported that their problem concluded within 3 months of starting, with 12% reporting that their problem had lasted more than a year.

Another example of early adoption of IT was the Injury Portal[31] developed by the insurance industry to be the single entry port for road traffic injury claims over £1000 and with an upper limit of £25,000, roughly from 2010, and from July 2013 extended to Employers' Liability and Public Liability claims valued at under £25,000. The online format provides standard information fields and expert reports, fixed recoverable costs, and has been a success with a significant percentage of cases settled without court involvement. In 2017/2018 701,638 claims entered the system, 171,734 packs were created for approval of settlement by the court, and 73,823 packs were created for continuing in the litigation process, the reminder being dropped or agreed. The Portal has been in effect restricted to use by lawyers, but a

---

[26]CPR, Part 63 rule 72.

[27]Ministry of Justice (2019b), ch 7 para. 3.

[28]Ombudsman Services has undertaken a Transformation Programme in 2018 which has switched 70% of consumer traffic from phone to online. The technology assists in identifying vulnerable consumers. The Financial Ombudsman Service developed a digital analytical tool to assist with processing the large number of Payment Protection Insurance claims that it received: see Thomas (2016).

[29]From 2014 Ombudsman Services resolved some disputes with energy and communications companies within 30 min.

[30]Concluded problems are those which the respondent described as 'now over' or 'most likely now over' and ongoing problems are those which were 'still ongoing' or 'too early to say'.

[31]Claims Portal (2020).

new model is under development for claimants to use in person. It would be interesting to see if trust or settlement were increased if there were an independent intermediary involved, rather than the basic model remaining negotiation between claimant/lawyer and insurer.

5.3 Failure of the Adversarial Model

The number of claims issued in the High Court Queen's Bench Division has fallen steadily from a high of 18,505 in 2007 to 8400 in 2017.[32] Caseload in the Chancery Division has fluctuated in the past decade but stood at 41,697 in 2017. However, users are often foreign rather than domestic: in 2016, over 80% of commercial cases handled by London law firms involved an international party.[33]

In 2017, 2 million cases were started in County Courts (including Small Claims), of which only 161,000 were allocated to a track (showing that they quickly resolved) and led to 41,000 Small Claim hearings and 17,000 Fast or Multi-Track hearings. In the last quarter of 2018, the average time for those cases that went to trial was 34.4 weeks after issue for a small claim and 57.7 weeks for Fast and Multi-Track claims.[34] The County Court Small Claims track was created to be an informal and cost free means of dispute resolution, but it is nowadays used only for debt claims by individuals or (predominantly small) businesses (since 2018 through Money Claim Online), possession cases by (individual or corporate) landlords, plus personal injury claims that fall out of the negotiation process established under the Injury Portal, and other residual types of claims such as serious neighbour disputes.

The cost-versus-procedure balance is a consistent theme of debates about courts—but not about consumer or property Ombudsmen. The story of procedural reform (Woolf, Jackson, Briggs) coupled with funding and costs reform (legal aid, CFAs, BTE, ATE, recoverability, QOCS)[35] and of the unintended consequences that successive reforms have spawned (Case Management Companies, referral fees, whiplash claims, holiday claims, access fees, fixed costs) leads to the conclusions that the problem is actually insoluble within the existing architecture, and that unanticipated and undesirable consequences consistently arise. Procedures aimed at delivering what is thought to be forensically accurate justice (i.e. putting the focus on the view from the judge) through a court system have proved to be too costly for users. In areas where alternatives to courts have emerged (C2B and recently the SME type of B2B, although arbitration is an historical example of large commercial B2B), and users have voted with their feet. The statistics show that the vast majority of

---

[32]See successive quarterly Ministry of Justice (2007–2017).

[33]The Lord Chancellor, the Lord Chief Justice and the Senior President of Tribunals (2016).

[34]Ministry of Justice (2019a).

[35]Conditional Fee Agreements, before-the-event insurance, after-the-event insurance, qualified-one-way-cost-shift.

claims in courts involve low sums; that most cases can be resolved through expert mediation provided by ombudsmen-type intermediaries; that such mechanisms are *free* to users and that enlightened businesses will fund them because they cost less and offer advantages like greater customer retention and the opportunity for obtaining useful data; and that the outputs and values of users differ from 'accurate application of the law' and can involve wider matters; that some systems can be designed to provide the wider suite of desired extensive functions at efficient cost, and some are now doing this highly effectively, and there is considerable innovation. The adversarial model of dispute resolution is no longer fit for purpose in delivering justice for the claims that most people and most businesses have.

The legal system that we have inherited is based on testing facts and arguments through combat. It encourages people to mistrust and fight each other, and it inherently involves intermediaries representing each party in addition to a judge (and perhaps nowadays a mediator) who all have to be paid. The post-War resettlement of the legal system involved a welfare-based approach through which the State would pay for lawyers for then most of the population who could not afford lawyers (legal aid) in the continuation of the previous adversarial system. So whereas justice previously could only be afforded by the rich, justice and new rights of many kinds would now be extended to everyone—but still in an adversarial model. Ever since then, successive governments have been cutting legal aid as it became ever less affordable. However, the adversarial model has remained unchanged.

An adversarial model is inherently expensive. It involves too many people— lawyers for both sides, court administrators, judge. An inquisitorial model was for many years unthinkable as an alternative, as the state could not afford that either and some argued that ADR fails to deliver justice. But in investigation, cross-examination and advocacy, the German civil procedure involves a less important role for parties' lawyers than that of the judge, this being the central reason why it is cheap. But it is still not as cheap as other systems that either reduce overhead costs, especially through use of technology, or fuse various functions even further.

Three responses have occurred *within* the traditional court-led context—diversification of techniques, adoption of new technology, and new funding models. In short, mediation, online and privatisation. But effective answers lie *outside* the litigation model.

Lord Woolf faced the reality that most cases settle during the litigation process and are not decided by a judge, so he encouraged this by placing mediation or other ADR techniques before and during litigation process. However, this introduced a paradox because there is an inherent conflict between fighting and settling; one approach drives people apart, the other seeks to draw them together. One is divisive, the other is healing.

Justice comes at a price, and not only must that price be fair (and hence constrained) but also resources need to be rationed if everyone is to have equal but fair access to the system without unfairly using up resources needed by others. As Sorabji has shown, the central aspect of Lord Woolf's reforms was to accept that a new balance had to apply between, on the one hand, ensuring that accurate and substantive justice is done in each individual case and, on the other hand, ensuring that the state's limited resources for delivering justice remain available to all at reasonable cost and without unreasonable delay, as a result of individual parties consuming disproportionate resource in individual cases.[36] Given the 'intractable triumvirate' of complexity, cost and delay that has throughout the history of English and Welsh court systems. Impeded delivering 'substantive justice' in every case, Woolf was driven inevitably to seek the substantive delivery of 'proportionate justice' in order to maximise the number of people and cases who obtained justice.[37] Absolute forensic justice is simply unattainable in human societies, and it is, therefore, important to maximise the number of situations in which some justice is attained rather than not. It is in this context that a series of new intermediaries has emerged that deliver more justice than lawyer-court systems have managed.

5.3.1   The Switch to New Pathways and Intermediaries

The availability of alternative options leads to consumer choice and more innovation. People have voted with their feet, avoiding courts and choosing alternatives that are perceived to be more user-friendly, free, quick and effective. Examples have occurred in disputes involving consumers, tenants, SMEs and employees.

Although ADR has been promoted in the consumer and other sectors, it has been strongly developed in some sectors either by businesses (who fund it) or by governments (who see that it is a necessary tool to support consumer trust in markets). The developed model is a consumer Ombudsman rather than an arbitration-based ADR scheme. Given the availability of consumer Ombudsmen, there has been a significant switch in usage by consumers and some business sectors. The inherent risk in the privatised model of Ombudsmen was controlled by robust forms of governance of Ombudsmen, such as ensuring their structural and operational independence from funders, transparency and increasing professionalism of the profession of Ombudsmen.[38]

In contrast to the restricted usage of Small Claims quoted above, in 2018 the leading consumer Ombudsmen received over 2 million inquiries and resolved 400,000 claims against the businesses that they cover. Consumers have switched to consumer ADR schemes, especially the consumer Ombudsmen that exist in major sectors such as financial services, pensions, energy, communications, motor, furniture and recently rail. The leading consumer Ombudsmen are now linked to

---

[36]Sorabji (2014).

[37]*Ibid.*, p. 21.

[38]The regulatory model was enshrined in EU legislation under Directive 2013/11/EU on alternative dispute resolution for consumer disputes and amending Regulation (EC) No 2006/2004 and Directive 2009/22/EC (Directive on consumer ADR).

platforms such as those of Citizens Advice and Resolver.[39] Since its start in 2014, Resolver has grown massively, and in 2018 its 15 million site visits and 1,400,000 case files exceed the traffic of Citizens Advice, which in 2017/2018 advised 1.4 million clients. The same switch is expected to happen in the property sector. The Property and Housing Ombudsmen and one major ADR body handled 6000 cases in 2018 but many more issues go unraised and unresolved.

Research showed that SMEs have two major types of legal problems—being paid late by, and suffering from abusive behaviour from, larger customers.[40] Passing a law that late payment is illegal, and providing an efficient Money Claim Online procedure, failed to address the debt problem. This was because SMEs feared commercial retaliation or annihilation from their customers if they complained. The solution was to create new public intermediaries, who could investigate and order resolution of problems—the Groceries Code Adjudicator (GCA),[41] the Pubs Code Adjudicator (PCA),[42] and the Small Business Commissioner (SBC).[43] Importantly, all these bodies could respond to anonymous information from SMEs, whilst protecting their identity. Examples of success of the approach are now emerging. In July 2016, the GCA reported that the top ten supermarkets had all acted on issues raised, and she rated the top three as complying 'consistently well' during the previous 12 months.[44] Surveys of direct suppliers found that the number that experienced issues had fallen.[45] In March 2019 the GCA found the Co-operative Group Limited to have been in breach of the Code in, first, de-listing suppliers with no, or short, fixed notice periods, whilst failing to consider the particular circumstances of products or suppliers and, second, variation of supply agreements unilaterally and without reasonable notice.[46]

In the employment area, a sequence of new regulatory authorities has been created, replacing the private enforcement model to protect abuse of workers. The authorities include the Equality and Human Right Commission to address breaches of human rights exploitation and equality legislation, the Gangmasters and Labour Abuse Authority (GLAA) to deal with labour exploitation across the economy, notably under the Modern Slavery Act,[47] the section in Her Majesty's Revenue and Customs that enforces the National Minimum Wage[48] and National Living

---

[39]Revolver (2020).

[40]Blackburn et al. (2015), Federation of Small Businesses (2016, 2017) and Larkin et al. (2018).

[41]See Groceries Code Adjudicator (2016b).

[42]The Small Business, Enterprise and Employment Act 2015, Part 4. The Pubs Code etc. Regulations 2016, SI 2016 No 790.

[43]Enterprise Act 2016, s1.

[44]Groceries Code Adjudicator (2016a).

[45]Press release, Groceries Code Adjudicator (2016c): 62% in 2016, 70% in 2015, 79% in 2014.

[46]Groceries Code Adjudicator (2019).

[47]Immigration Act 2016.

[48]The National Minimum Wage Act 1998, as amended, including by the Employment Act 2008. See Department for Business, Energy & Industrial Strategy (2018).

Wage laws, and the Employment Agency Standards (EAS) Inspectorate to enforce regulations covering employment agencies, particularly focusing on vulnerable agency workers. The last three of these agencies are coordinated under the Director of Labour Market Enforcement.[49]

5.3.2 Wider Functions Delivered by New Intermediaries

A major reason for the creation and success of these new intermediaries is that they deliver more functions than just dispute resolution. That broader mode of operation is their overwhelming advantage over other forms of dispute resolution—whether courts, arbitration or mediation. The consumer Ombudsmen, for example, have the following roles in relation to the dispute resolution function: providing information, assistance and advice to consumers on their rights and claims; investigating the facts; assisting the parties in resolving their disputes themselves; if necessary, reaching a decision that resolves a dispute. In effect, the Ombudsmen in financial services, energy, communications and other sectors deliver functions of lawyer, mediator and judge in relation to the dispute resolution aspects. Mediation is embedded in the pathway at no extra cost: if it is not relevant in a particular case it can be passed over immediately but otherwise it is more difficult for parties to avoid (as it is an inherent part of the evidence-gathering process) and often proves useful.

But they also deliver additional functions that are quasi-regulatory in nature: collecting, aggregating and feeding back data to businesses, markets and regulators on market behaviour and the behaviour and performance of individual traders, that can drive improvements, perhaps through public enforcement or less formal means, such as discussions between relevant parties.

For example, the Financial Ombudsman Service has published data on the types of complaints made against named banks. It holds regular meetings with the Financial Conduct Authority and with individual banks. In the energy sector, tripartite working occurs between regulator Ofgem, the Energy Ombudsman and Citizens Advice, in which data is shared and an action plan is agreed on who will do what in working with the relevant company, and who will act to reduce consumer detriment. The Ombudsman also uses the economic stress model to analyse if any companies might be at risk of liquidation and which others might fit best to take over the customer base if needed.

The same expansion in functions is envisaged in relation to the property sector. The government has commissioned a working party to make proposals for the design of a single new regulator for property agents. The logic of that change would lead to expansion of the model to include landlords and properties: an attractive idea is for a single property portal. Associated with the regulator would be a new single Ombudsman. There are currently several property ADRs and the landscape is too confused.

---

[49]Director of Labour Market Enforcement (2018).

After a consultation in 2018 based on the premises that the landscape was confusing and had various gaps and inconsistencies,[50] the Government set out in January 2019 a general vision for a new integrated 'service to cover all housing consumers including tenants and leaseholders of social and private rented housing as well as purchasers of new build homes and users of all residential property agents'.[51] The new structure would be constructed in stages, ideally involving voluntary action achieved with the agreement of relevant sectors, but against the threat of mandatory requirements from legislation if necessary. The main pillar of the new approach would be a Housing Complaints Resolution Service that would provide a single point of access for all current and future schemes that offer redress and ADR, and provide advice and triage as a first stage.

It has also been proposed to provide a single Property Portal (information, signposting of disputes), behind which would be relevant coordinated tracks involving the current First-tier Tribunal (Property Chamber) and a new independent Property Ombudsman. That would simplify the current position where landlords tend to start cases in the Tribunal and tenants go (if they can) to an Ombudsman/ADR, which can result in the same issues arising in different uncoordinated venues.

The lesson here is to identify the underlying problems that occur, rather than the disputes that might be symptoms of those problems, and to respond to them by designing a specific system. That thinking was behind the creation of the new intermediaries in the SME and employment sectors noted above—the problems were to protect anonymity and to provide more effective systemic intervention. There should be no surprise that new intermediaries are emerging to address wider social and market problems in place of traditional *ex post* private enforcement mechanisms: the latter simply fail to provide solutions to behavioural and cultural problems. Private enforcement has little effect on the behaviour or culture of individuals or organisations. The emerging model is that of new intermediaries that use private information, public power, and low-key involvement, backed by strong public powers, in an integrated system.

In short, we are taking a fresh look at how to address the problems that people and businesses *actually* face, rather than assuming that we can address issues on the assumption that they will surface as a private dispute. One area that remains to be addressed is that of designing an adequate response to one of the most frequent issues identified by the consumer problems surveys—neighbours' anti-social behaviour. Current environmental health and police powers should here be the last resort and community-based mediation by authorities should be the first line response.

---

[50]Ministry of Housing, Communities & Local Government (2018).

[51]Ministry of Housing, Communities & Local Government (2019).

5.3.3   Justice: Fairness As Well As Law

Another advantage that most Ombudsmen (and mediators) have over courts or arbitrators is that outcomes are usually based on the simple basis if what seems fair. For example, the Financial Ombudsman Service is statutorily empowered—if a dispute is not settled between the parties, as many are—to make a decision on the basis of what seems fair to the ombudsman in the circumstances of the case, taking the law into account.[52] To some critics, that basis of making decisions is an attack on the rule of law, or more about settlement of cases than about legal precision.[53] But to others, it is reaching decisions that reflect and support a fair society and market. It is increasingly the case that the relevant consumer protection[54] and sectoral regulatory law that is being applied requires that traders will treat customers fairly,[55] so a fairness standard has been required under law. The jurisdictions of the GCA, PCA and SBC all extend the requirement of fairness to dealings with SMEs. It has long been one of the requirements of mediators that they must ensure fairness in their activities and procedure.[56]

Many people may not be familiar with legal rules and find them complex and strange. But all human beings possess an innate sense of right and wrong—and hence fairness—unless they are sociopathic or psychopathic.[57] This drives immediate 'gut feel' responses to news about the fairness of any subject without knowing the intricacies of whether it is illegal, ranging from Members of Parliament's expenses, and multinationals paying minimal tax, to sexual abuse. Hence, regulators and Ombudsman are connecting with the population at a deep level—whereas the separate world of courts can appear distant and strange in their processes and decisions. Reconnection would be beneficial.

None of this dispenses with the need for rules, and for some rules to have the force of law, backed by State enforcement. But just as in jurisprudence there was a debate 50 years ago between rules and principles,[58] we now return to older historical echoes of the dichotomy between law and equity.

---

[52]DISP 3.6.1: 'The Ombudsman will determine a complaint by reference to what is, in his opinion, fair and reasonable in all the circumstances of the case.'

[53]Genn (2008); Wagner (2014), p. 165; Eidenmüller and Engel (2014), p. 261.

[54]The Consumer Protection from Unfair Trading Regulations 2008, SI 2008 No. 1277, based on Directive 2005/29/EC, updated in Directive 2011/83/EU.

[55]In financial services, see Financial Conduct Authority (2017); see initially Principle 6 of the Principles for Businesses 'to pay due regard to the interests of customers and treat them fairly', Financial Services Authority (2001). The Invoice Finance and Asset Based Lending Code of the Professional Standards Council requires that 'Members shall act with integrity and deal fairly and responsibly with clients and guarantors'.

[56]See European Code of Conduct for Mediators (2004) at http://europa.eu.int/comm.justice_home/ejn/adr_ec_code_conduct_en.pdf; Directive 2013/11/EU on consumer ADR, art 9.

[57]Wilson (2012) and Haidt (2012).

[58]Hart (1961) and Dworkin (1967).

5.3.4 Looking Outside the Box

The history of reforms to the civil justice system in the past few decades has been that of attempts to reform court procedure, costs and funding. It has often been judge-led. But in focusing on courts only, judges have transgressed the first rule of policy analysis and Better Regulation, which is to consider *all* the options.[59] Woolf, Jackson and the Ministry of Justice made strenuous attempts to try to solve a problem inside the courts 'box' when the solution lay outside in another 'box'. They tried to restrain costs to make them proportionate to the sums involved, and to move towards (a low level of) fixed costs.

The major problem for the courts lay in personal injury claims—for which the solution lies in shifting them out of courts. The vast majority of claims against the National Health Service (NHS) involves small sums: in 2017/2018 63% of successful claims involved under £25,000.[60] The system takes time and effort (and hence cost) to investigate claims where the legal test is based on whether or not negligence has occurred. Disproportionality inevitably arises between costs and possible benefits. The test inevitably means that a significant number of clinical negligence claims will fail (45% in 2017/2019).[61] Once they have been investigated, many can be resolved fairly swiftly, but a significant number reach trial, of which a high percentage fail. In 2017/2018, 69.6% of the 16,338 clinical claims were resolved without formal court proceedings and in the early stages more claims were resolved without payment of damages than with payment of damages.[62] Just under one third of claims end up in litigation with less than 1% going to a full trial (where most end in judgment in favour of the NHS).

Further, people bring legal claims if they perceive it as the only option through which they can reach the truth, or hold someone to account, or ensure that 'the same thing does not happen to others', where they perceive that they are starved of a caring and open response.[63] These points suggest that improving responses to patients and families that are perceived by them as caring, fully open, and provides learning would be more effective approaches than allowing litigation to remain as the only option. But we retain an adversarial system based on proving investigating and proving fault, both of which drive people apart and ferment mistrust rather than understanding and healing. The logic points towards an improved approach to responding to complaints and switching injury claims to being decided by a trusted independent intermediary, such as an Injury Ombudsman akin to an administrative

---

[59]See Strategic Policy Making Team, Cabinet Office (1999), Her Majesty's Treasury (2003), Bochel and Duncan (2007), Department for Business Innovation & Skills (2011), OECD (2012), Department for Business Innovation & Skills (2013) and European Commission (2015).

[60]*Annual Report and Accounts 2017/18* (NHS Resolution, 2018).

[61]*Ibid.*

[62]*Ibid.*

[63]For a recent overview see Birks et al. (2018).

redress scheme, as used with great success in all Nordic states.[64] The continuation of a negligence test and an adversarial compensation system is a major barrier preventing the establishment of an 'open culture' in the NHS, as it wishes to do.[65]

Another example of a solution lying 'outside the box' is in collective redress. A litigation model for delivering mass redress is some form of class or group action. But two other models have proved to be highly effective. First, consumer Ombudsmen can respond to multiple individual cases in a number of ways.[66] They are good at processing multiple similar small claims, as has been shown by the story of payment protection insurance. Second, many UK regulatory authorities have delivered mass redress extremely swiftly, either as a result of exercise of powers to order collective redress, or to accept undertakings to that effect.[67] Use of the regulatory technique as a consequence of an Ombudsman identifying the existence of a problem is now commonplace.

Strenuous attempts to reform procedure in various forms of courts have failed to see that answers can lie *outside* courts and in other areas, such as consumer ombudsmen or different intermediaries. This points to the need to undertake a pretty comprehensive review of different mechanisms, and one that does not assume answers, such as that courts must play a central role.

5.4 The Required Sequence of Functions

The matters reviewed above indicate that in evaluating and redesigning dispute resolution pathways, the following main functions are important to provide. We divide the issues into two groups: first those relating to information, advice, assistance, filtering, and triage and, second, those relating to data, feedback and intervention so as to change behaviour and culture.

5.4.1 Information, Advice, Assistance, Filtering, Triage

How are people to be informed about their rights, and how problems that they have might best be solved? They may need assistance, whether from websites or talking to people. Those who have suffered major healthcare or other traumatic experiences may need ongoing assistance from someone they can trust, who can offer expert but

---

[64]Macleod and Hodges (2017).

[65]Hunt (2016) and House of Commons Public Administration and Constitutional Affairs Committee (2018).

[66]Hodges (2012).

[67]Hodges (2015b), ch 5. Hodges and Voet (2018).

disinterested support. The provider should not have a conflict of interest or bias that favours a particular pathway, such as a lawyer who favours litigation.

The LPRS study[68] found that of those who had used a formal resolution process but not obtained any legal or professional help, most (84%) had sourced their own information or advice, for example from the internet, leaflets, family or friends, or the other side of the dispute. Only 4% of adults with a problem who had used a legal process or resolution service did so without obtaining any information, advice or help at all. There should be no surprise that the websites of Resolver, Citizens Advice and consumer Ombudsmen receive millions of hits annually, and their chatline and phone assistance are so widely used.

The Low Commission raised serious concerns over the number of people who have multiple social problems (clustering), which can involve illness, disability, mental health, debt, housing, social support and entitlement, employment and other issues. It proposed a strategy for provision of advice and legal support on social welfare law, which would include:[69]

– *a public legal education system*, making full use of the internet and embedding information about social welfare law issues in community settings locally;
– *national helpline and website services*, providing information and advice on all aspects of social welfare law, building on and developing current services;
– *local advice networks* of generalist and some specialist advisers for each local authority area, providing face-to-face information, advice and legal support;
– *access to specialist national support* providing information and advice for front-line agencies.

There is a real need to avoid responding to multiple symptoms in social problems and instead to identify and address root causes. The categorisation of a problem as legal or economic or social adopts the viewpoint of the provider of a particular solution and can prevent objective analysis of what the root cause of the problem is and how it might best be solved. The better approach requires strong initial analysis and the swift deployment of relevant expertise. Examples of this sort of approach have emerged in 'problem-solving courts' in the context of administrative justice[70] and in Family Drug and Alcohol Courts (FDAC)[71] where judges, social workers and psychologists support parents to quit addictions so as to prevent removal of their children. This approach needs a reconfiguration of expertise and administrative structures at local authority level, coordinating multiple charity and care services, to deliver expert help (healthcare professionals,[72] mental health nurses, debt advisers, personality counsellors, employment counselling, social entitlement assistance and so on)—all adequately coordinated and with appropriate funding. These

---

[68]Franklyn et al. (2017).
[69]The Low Commission (2015).
[70]Centre for Justice Innovation (2015).
[71]Harwin et al. (2014).
[72]Beardon and Genn (2018).

general assistance and triage services need to be delivered where people go and find assistance easy to seek—pilot studies based in doctors' surgeries have been successful—and offer general advice (not necessarily legal advice centres, which may be too narrow in focus).

All this is a salutary reminder that the important and inevitable shift to use of digital online technology has huge benefits but can leave many people behind. The Online Court may enable users to talk to a case officer once a case has been commenced, but where do people get trusted assistance at the start of analysing what to do about their problem? A largely under-recognised function of solicitors when legal aid was widely available was in providing information, assistance, advice, filtering out poor cases, triage, and assistance with bring a complaint progressing in a claim process. The relevance of these functions can now be seen by their absence since the withdrawal of legal aid in 2014 in employment, family and social entitlement cases and in the rise in Litigants in Person.

A criticism made after the EU ODR cross-border portal was opened was that intelligent users still wanted to talk to someone to confirm even straightforward but unfamiliar instructions on the screen in front of them, and ask about their options, but the facility to talk to the experienced European Consumer Centres Network (ECC-NET) officers and for them to access case files was not available. The ECC-NET offices were therefore unable to interceded as they had previously between consumer and trader to reach solutions. The success rate of cross-border claims was disappointingly low.

5.4.2 Dispute Resolution Process

The issue of process is relatively straightforward. There is a notable similarity between several different processes. The Online Court aims to enter all details into the court file, bringing together facts, allegations and proof. That is how the consumer Ombudsmen have operated for some years. Tribunals such as the Social Entitlement Chamber and Immigration and Asylum Chamber are close to operating likewise. The former starts with a claimant seeing a video of the judge who will handle the case introducing him or herself and explaining the process. Case management is increasingly undertaken in all these systems by case officers, sometimes assisting ultimate decision-makers. The process often includes communication between the case officer and both parties that can form the basis of mutual explanation and mediated negotiation. Despite systems being digitised, elements of humanity are still essential. The Legal Services Board's fundamental review concluded that access to justice is fundamentally about *outcomes and relationships* more than legal processes.[73] It noted:

---

[73]Legal Services Board (2012).

justice is more than the resolution of disputes: it includes just relationships underpinned by law. ... Justice is underpinned by legal knowledge, legislative frameworks, dispute resolution and the infrastructure of the legal services market and the court system as well as by the outcomes that consumers secure. Access to justice is the securing of these just outcomes rather than the process of dispute resolution.[74]

People do not always want money or a court injunction. They may want a number of other outcomes, such as being heard and believed, an explanation, of the desire that what happened to them will not happen to others. They may seek systemic change in the culture and behaviour of a public body towards citizens. For example, there is increasing evidence that patients who are injured, and victims of child abuse, do not typically want money, but seek voice/being heard, an explanation & apology, and a feeling that the system has listened and learned from their experience and the risk that the same thing will happen to others has reduced (i.e. confidence that a regulatory feedback system is in place and will function effectively). It is time to ask how these outcomes are delivered.

5.4.3 Data, Feedback and Intervention to Change Performance, Behaviour and Culture

We now expect systems to identify risks and reduce them. In relation to most disputes, that means that we expect the system to identify recurring and avoidable problems and change behaviour and organisational culture so that the problem is not repeated. Decisions by courts or arbitrators do not change behaviour or culture. More sophisticated intervention systems are needed, which we generally find operating through public regulation and rarely through private enforcement systems.

For many years, the public Ombudsmen and Tribunal Judges have highlighted repeated problems with public services. Reports have been produced calling for change, but little occurs. Some recent examples are as follows. A Report[75] highlighted poor decision-making by the Home Office in immigration and asylum appeals leading to some 50% of decisions not being upheld on appeal in the First-tier Tribunal (Immigration and Asylum Chamber), compared with 25% historically.[76] One in four complaints to the Parliamentary Ombudsman in 2016/2017 related to failure in decision-making.[77] The Local Government and Social Care Ombudsman has set himself the goal 'to move the conversation about our work away from simplistic complaint volumes, to the lessons that can be learned and the wider good we can achieve through our recommendations to improve services for the

---

[74]*Ibid.*, para. 3.6.

[75]Justice (2018).

[76]Ministry of Justice (2018).

[77]*Ibid.*, 7.

many'.[78] Innumerable reports have been issued about the NHS, from within[79] and outside,[80] with seemingly little impact on culture. Academic studies reach similar findings, such as Halliday's study of three local authorities' approaches to homeless decision-making, which showed considerable variation in organisational approaches and ability to internalise any learning from judicial review decisions.[81]

In contrast, markets work well where businesses, Ombudsmen and regulatory authorities work as part of a coherent integrated system to identify data, feed it back, intervene and make changes to reduce future risk. Results are improved where the focus is expressly on an open, ethical culture.[82] The theme is that dispute resolution systems need to operate as part of larger systems that are directed at identifying problems, especially though aggregation of data, and supporting interventions to deliver changes in behaviour and culture. Dispute resolution system need to be integrated with regulatory systems, so as to use data to drive the ability to identify and address performance, behaviour and culture. That is exactly the shift that is occurring in the way that the most advanced regulatory authorities have taken,[83] assisted by consumer Ombudsmen where they exist. Their enforcement policies, and entire regulatory delivery strategies, are not based on enforcement (especially deterrence) when individual infringements are identified, but as a constant holistic approach to looking at behaviour, performance and improvement. They try to identify problems, give advice, collect data and so on so as to look at problems in a longer form and timescale.

5.5 Designing an Integrated System

We should accept that the dispute resolution landscape now comprises many options. The dispute resolution eco-system encompasses not just courts and tribunals, various regulatory bodies, but also various kinds of Ombudsmen, private arbitrators and many mediators, some of whom are organised into structures (like ACAS for employment cases) but many of whom are not (in family and commercial cases).

Courts are not the only option. Courts—or anything else—might not be the best or appropriate option in a particular case. That realisation leads to the proposition that courts—or anything else—might not be the 'ultimate' or 'superior' solution.

---

[78]Local Government & Social Care Ombudsman (2018).

[79]Recent examples: Gosport Independent Panel (2018), Oates (2018) and Hutton (2019).

[80]Mid Staffordshire NHS Foundation Trust Inquiry (2010), National Advisory group on the safety of Patients in England (2013), Evans (2014), Public Administration Select Committee (2015) and Department of Health (2015).

[81]Halliday (2004).

[82]Hodges and Steinholtz (2017).

[83]Hodges (2015a) and Cabinet Office (2017).

That proposition challenges some deeply held constitutional ideas, but it has to be faced in the contemporary world. As Sir Geoffrey Vos said in 2018:

> So far as disputes are concerned, technology must change the way we deal with them. . . . the millennial generation, which expect to be able to obtain everything they want in an instant on their mobile devices, will not make an exception for justice. . . . This online world has allowed the litigant in person to flourish. . . . In my view, online dispute resolution, mediation and ombudsman platforms will absorb much of the small legal work in years to come.[84]

The problem is that the more choices people have, the more they may be confused about which option to use. Should justice be a market in which there is, by definition, not only choice between options (courts, tribunals, arbitration, mediation, ombudsmen, regulators, other hybrids or combinations) based on competition between them? Or should justice be regarded as deliverable by any or all of these pathways—since they are, in reality, all components of the same justice system? The landscape is now complex and needs to be viewed objectively as such. It is now too complex, and not delivering justice often enough, nor contributing to reducing the future incidence of problems. A new vision of the justice system is required.

In this fusion of plurality, the 1970s American idea of a multi-door courthouse[85] does not apply to twenty-first century Western Europe—not least because the courthouse is no longer the unique portal for access to justice or the centre of gravity in delivering justice. Other portals and pathways have replaced courts in some areas and the various components of the system are not coordinated. But we need to provide a small number of easily identifiable portals, from which flow integrated pathways that contain all relevant techniques for solving relevant problems.

In evaluating whether pathways deliver justice for people of businesses, we should ask strenuous empirical questions, like 'What do potential users actually seek?', 'Can people identify this pathway easily?', 'How long does it take?', 'How much does it cost?', 'How many people use it, or might want to use it?', and 'Does it deliver justice to enough users?'. We need robust empirical answers to these questions because 'We're paying for all this'[86] and if the individual pathways and the system as a whole do not deliver value then we should change them.

A simple initial question is: 'Can people easily identify the relevant place to get help for their problem?' Having a choice of pathways is all very well except that users may be ignorant of the possibilities or confused between having too many options. At a certain point of diversification, some rationalisation is necessary, both for ease in selecting the right path and in avoiding wasting money on poor choices. Clarity for consumers is achieved in Belgium by a single national consumer website operated by the Consumer Mediation Service (which is the umbrella body of the leading Ombudsmen). That website provides extensive information to consumers

---

[84]Voss (2018).

[85]Address by Sander at the National Conference on the Causes of Dissatisfaction with the Administration of Justice (April 7–9, 1976), reprinted in Sander (1976).

[86]Access to Justice Taskforce, Attorney-General's Department, Australian Government (2009). The holistic Australian approach was noted in Scotland: Civil Justice Advisory Group (2011).

and enables them to click onto the right Ombudsman or other ADR body (not more than one per sector) who can assist with their problem. It is working well. A fusion between Resolver and Citizens Advice would be highly beneficial in UK.

The current system for complaining against the State is a good example of confusion and complexity. Citizens who are poorly dealt with by the State, whether through adverse decisions or inappropriate behaviour, face a bewildering range of options, many of which cost them too much in terms of time, money, and emotional effort. First, every Government Department has a different complaint mechanism, some involving different levels of review or appeal to different officials, adjudicators or others. Second, one may apply for permission to commence a judicial review in the courts, for which funding for lawyers is in effect needed. Third, one might appeal to a Tribunal, for which funding might not be necessary (save against opponents who instruct lawyers, as many commercial or professional or State defendants would) and the adverse costs risk is almost absent, and the procedures are increasingly adopting online and user-friendly approaches. Fourth, one might complain to the Parliamentary and Health Service Ombudsman (but access is through an MP) or the Local Government and Social Care Ombudsman. Fifth, one might lobby for a Public Inquiry. Sixth, after a death one might try to find evidence and a platform from a Coroner's Inquest. Seventh, one might sue the state under a contract. The Government issued a 'pledge' in 2001 that it would use ADR mechanisms rather than litigation[87] but this seems to have disappeared.

There are too many options here. Each of them differs and each has advantages and disadvantages. Why is there no single and integrated pathway that refers complaints to the right type of investigation, assistance and resolution? It would start with accessible information and assistance, linked to a single portal, through which relevant assistance, support, investigation, mediation and decision-making would be provided by experts with relevant skills. Relevant issues would be passed back and forth between the service providers, so that trained mediators would assist communications and healing between parties, ombudsmen would make decisions on issues of fair practice and judges would continue to make decisions on legal issues.

5.5.1 Funding

The consumer Ombudsman model also highlights an important transformation. Businesses pay for the Ombudsmen systems, claimants do not. The insurance sector pays for the Injury Portal: claimants do not. Not many arbitration consumer ADR systems are free to consumers. Courts impose fees and lawyers are not philanthropically-funded charities. Two drivers have led to businesses funding Ombudsmen and the Portal: some sectors wish to retain good relations with their customers so value speedy and helpful complaint systems and the State is attracted to

---

[87]Justice (2011).

the regulatory dimension of Ombudsmen so imposes funding requirements on traders as an adjunct to the requirement to fund a regulatory authority. Those ideas of paying to maintain good relations and obtaining increased outputs from the system to improve performance are worth paying for, if necessary through taxes.

As at 2017/2018, the Her Majesty's Courts and Tribunals Service was in operational deficit: income collected was £742,000,000 against expenditure of £839,081,000, giving a new deficit of £96,472,000 for a throughput of 2,759,948 claims handled.[88] However, the civil and family courts were in fact in surplus (£80,659,000) and the Tribunals service was in deficit (£177,121,000). The PHSO received 114,278 initial inquiries in 2018, accepting 32,389 complaints and completing 2676 investigations, with a budget of around £32 million. Ombudsman Services 245,000 initial inquiries in 2017, and resolved 94,018 cases, with a budget of around £36 million. The Financial Ombudsman Service received 1.4 million initial inquires and 339,967 formal complaints and resolved 400,658 cases in 2017–2018, with a turnover of around £247 million. These bodies all have different processes so comparisons are dangerous but questions certainly arise about differences in productivity and value for money.

5.5.2   Skills

What skills are needed for this new architecture? Let us look at the three core areas of initial advice, resolving disputes, and affecting behaviour. In relation to initial advice, there is a strong need for expert advice to be delivered by various specialists, including law, mediation, medicine, mental health, debt, housing, employment and so on. Some or all of these would ideally be funded by the State, not least because their early intervention would save public resources in preventing problems from arising or escalating. But the level of demand is high and hence a significant level of supply should be higher than currently.

In the second area of resolving disputes, there is a need for intermediaries trained in investigation, analysis, mediation and decision-making. Hence, demand for legal skills remains high, as now. There may be a different configuration between the structures of judges, ombudsmen, case managers, lawyers, mediators and others, but all those skills remain needed. In the third area, of applying lessons and intervening, there is a clear need for data specialists, ombudsmen, regulators and so on, certainly including lawyers.

A new system along the lines identified here would lead to an increase in the number of people who feel that they can raise problems instead of 'just lumping it' or who feel that something will actually be done to improve things. So the volume in the whole system should rise, at least for some time. If the system is capable of engaging the third function and learning, then problems should fall in time. In this

---

[88]Her Majesty's HM Courts and Tribunals Service (2018a).

system, there will clearly be jobs for lawyers, even if the architecture is different. It was said recently that the Financial Ombudsman Service is the largest employer of law graduates in the country. Family lawyers are currently paid very low rates where legal aid applies but the increase in volume of business means that they are still earning decent money. The future may look different, but people and businesses still have problems that need solving by expert intermediaries. So the horses need not be frightened that this is 'an end of lawyers'.

5.6   Conclusion: A Time for Change

The national dispute resolution system needs fixing. The adversarial model is unaffordable for most types of claims. It is no longer fit for purpose. We do not have a coherent system. We have too many possible dispute resolution pathways. Some of them are not easy for people to identify. Some of them do not work well. Many are too complicated for people to use easily. The system does not deliver our objectives. Justice is too often not delivered. We do not solve the root causes of problems. The system does not support learning or preventing problems from arising. The landscape of advice for citizens, tenants, consumers, families, workers and small businesses is disorganised and confusing. The right assistance is not being delivered in an effective and timely fashion. We're paying for all this so the whole system should be both effective and efficient. It is time for change.

The idea that upholding the law in resolving disputes has much effect on future behaviour and culture is a mirage. Changing behaviour needs interventions by parties other than judges and lawyers. But the dispute resolution system can play an important part in collecting and communicating aggregated data and illuminating issues. Some parts of the current system do this well, and it makes a real difference to the prevention of future problems.

We need a system that delivers three elements for people and organisations: assistance in problem solving, dispute resolution, and learning and improving.

Assistance in Problem Solving   The system should focus on solving people's and organisations' problems. It should have an accessible face, that provides information and support. The network for delivering personal and expert assistance should be coordinated. It should be based on providing online information to people—and collecting anonymised data on their problems. Person-to-person assistance should also be available. Expert assistance should be focused at an early stage to solve root causes of problems. Experiments in problem-solving courts and family and addiction courts have demonstrated their value, but these do not necessarily have to be configured around courts and judges. A wider vision is needed.

Dispute Resolution   The system should provide *integrated* dispute resolution pathways. All the relevant stages should be integrated into a simple, single pathway: assistance and triage, mediation, online, decision, enforcement. This means integrating courts, tribunals, arbitration, mediation, ADR, Ombudsmen, ODR and anything else. Pathways for assistance in solving problems and for dispute resolution should be easy to identify, simple to use, quick, usually no cost to applicants, cheap overall, and effective in delivering outputs that are fair and just. The current adoption of Online Justice should be continued. It provides numerous advantages in simplifying processes and reducing cost. But it should also be designed to provide effective data that can be used to address underlying problems in behaviour and culture.

Learning and Improving The dispute resolution and assistance systems must provide effective input into the prevention of future disputes. Data should be captured and fed back to relevant intervention and regulatory systems to support delivery of improvement in behaviour and culture. The system should aim at identifying new problems and solving the root causes of problems, not just resolving individual disputes. Hence expert assistance and systems should be configured to deliver and achieve this.

References

Access to Justice Taskforce, Attorney-General's Department, Australian Government (2009) A Strategic Framework for Access to Justice in the Federal Civil Justice System. https://www.ag.gov.au

Beardon S, Genn H (2018) The Health Justice Landscape in England & Wales. Social welfare legal services in health settings. UCL Centre for Access to Justice, London

Birks Y et al (2018) Understanding the drivers of litigation in health services. University of York and The King's Fund, York

Blackburn R et al (2015) The legal needs of small businesses: an analysis of small businesses' experience of legal problems, capacity and attitudes. https://www.legalservicesboard.org.uk

Bochel H, Duncan S (eds) (2007) Making policy in theory and practice. Policy Press, Bristol

Briggs M (2016) Civil courts structure review: final report. https://www.judiciary.uk

Cabinet Office (2017) Regulatory futures review. https://www.gov.uk/government/publications/regulatory-futures-review

Centre for Justice Innovation (2015) Problem-solving courts: an evidence review. https://justiceinnovation.org/sites/default/files/media/documents/2019-03/problem-solving-courts-an-evidence-review.pdf

Citizens Advice (2016) Learning from mistakes: how complaints can drive improvements to public services. https://www.citizensadvice.org.uk

Civil Consulting (2017) Study on measuring consumer detriment in the European Union Final report Part 1 – main report. European Commission, Brussels

Civil Justice Advisory Group (2011) Ensuring effective access to appropriate and affordable dispute resolution. The final report of the Civil Justice Advisory Group. https://www.catalystmediation.co.uk/download.php?article_id=MTM=

Claims Portal (2020) Claims portal. http://www.claimsportal.org.uk

Comptroller and Auditor General (2018) Early progress in transforming courts and tribunals. https://www.nao.org.uk

Department for Business, Energy & Industrial Strategy (2018) National minimum wage and national living wage. Calculating the minimum wage. https://www.gov.uk/government/publications/calculating-the-minimum-wage

Department for Business Innovation & Skills (2011) Principles for economic regulation. https://www.gov.uk

Department for Business Innovation & Skills (2013) Guidance: better regulation framework manual. https://www.gov.uk

Department for Education and Ministry of Justice (2014) A brighter future for family justice: a round up of what's happened since the family justice review. https://www.gov.uk

Department of Health (2015) Learning not blaming: the government response to the freedom to speak up consultation, the Public Administration Select Committee report 'Investigating Clinical Incidents in the NHS', and the Morecambe Bay Investigation. https://www.gov.uk/government/publications/learning-not-blaming-response-to-3-reports-on-patient-safety

Director of Labour Market Enforcement (2018) United Kingdom Labour Market Enforcement Strategy 2018/19. https://www.gov.uk

Dworkin R (1967) Is law a system of rules? Univ Chic Law Rev 35(14)

Eidenmüller H, Engel M (2014) Against false settlement: designing efficient consumer rights enforcement systems in Europe. Ohio State J Dispute Resolution 29(3):261–298

European Code of Conduct for Mediators (2004) http://europa.eu.int/comm.justice_home/ejn/adr_ec_code_conduct_en.pdf

European Commission (2015) Better regulation for better results – an EU agenda, COM(2015) 215 final. https://eur-lex.europa.eu

Evans K (2014) "Using the Gift of Complaints": a review of concerns (complaints) handling in NHS Wales. http://www.wales.nhs.uk/usingthegiftofcomplaints

Federation of Small Businesses (2016) Tied up: unravelling the dispute resolution process for small firms. https://www.fsb.org.uk/

Federation of Small Businesses (2017) Treating smaller businesses like consumers – unfair contract terms. https://www.fsb.org.uk/

Financial Conduct Authority (2017) FCA mission: our future approach to consumers. https://www.fca.org.uk/publications/corporate-documents/our-mission

Financial Services Authority (2001) Treating customers fairly after the point of sale, DP7. https://www.fca.org.uk/

Franklyn R et al (2017) Findings from the Legal Problem and Resolution Survey 2014–15. Ministry of Justice. https://www.gov.uk/government/publications/legal-problem-and-resolution-survey-2014-to-2015

Genn H (1999) Paths to justice: what people do and think about going to law. Hart Publishing, Oxford

Genn H (2008) Judging civil justice. Cambridge University Press, Cambridge

Gosport Independent Panel (2018) Gosport War Memorial Hospital: The Report of the Gosport Independent Panel. https://www.gosportpanel.independent.gov.uk

Groceries Code Adjudicator (2016a) Annual Report and Accounts 2015–2016 (Groceries Code Adjudicator, 2016)

Groceries Code Adjudicator (2016b) GCA compliance and monitoring policy. https://www.gov.uk

Groceries Code Adjudicator (2016c) Press release: GCA achieving significant progress for suppliers. https://www.gov.uk/government/news/gca-achieving-significant-progress-for-suppliers

Groceries Code Adjudicator (2019) Investigation into Co-operative Group Limited. https://www.gov.uk/government/publications/gca-investigation-report-into-co-operative-group-limited

Haidt J (2012) The righteous mind. Why good people are divided by politics and religion. Penguin Books, Westminster

Halliday S (2004) Judicial review and compliance with administrative law. Hart Publishing, Oxford

Hamlyn B et al (2015) Mediation Information and Assessment Meetings (MIAMs) and mediation in private family law disputes: quantitative research findings. https://www.gov.uk

Hart HLA (1961) The concept of law. Clarendon Press, Oxford

Harwin J et al (2014) Changing lifestyles, keeping children safe: an evaluation of the first Family Drug and Alcohol Court (FDAC) in care proceedings. Brunel University, London

HM Courts & Tribunals Service (2018a) Annual Reports and Accounts 2017–2018. https://www.gov.uk/government/publications/hm-courts-tribunals-service-annual-report-and-accounts-2017-to-2018

HM Courts & Tribunals Service (2018b) HMCTS response to Public Accounts Committee report on court reform programme. https://www.gov.uk

HM Courts & Tribunals Service (2018c) Reform Update Autumn 2018. https://www.gov.uk

HM Courts & Tribunals Service (2020) Money Claim Online. https://www.moneyclaim.gov.uk

HM Courts & Tribunals Services (2018) Money Claim Online (MCOL) – User guide for claimants. https://www.moneyclaim.gov.uk

HM Courts and Tribunals Service (2016) Modernisation of justice through technology and innovation. https://www.gov.uk

HM Treasury (2003) The Green Book: appraisal and evaluation in Central Government. https://www.gov.uk

HM Treasury (2015) Spending Review and Autumn Statement 2015: key announcements. https://www.gov.uk

Hodges C (2012) Best practice in customer care in UK. In: Hodges C et al (eds) Consumer ADR in Europe. Hart Publishing, Oxford, pp 339–354

Hodges C (2015a) Law and corporate behaviour: integrating theories of regulation, enforcement, culture and ethics. Hart Publishing, Oxford

Hodges C (2015b) Mass collective redress: consumer ADR and regulatory techniques. Eur Rev Private Law 23:829–874

Hodges C (2019) Delivering dispute resolution: a holistic review of models in England & Wales. Hart Publishing, Oxford

Hodges C, Steinholtz R (2017) Ethical business practice and regulation: a behavioural and values-based approach to compliance and enforcement. Hart Publishing, Oxford

Hodges C, Voet S (2018) Delivering collective redress: new technologies. Hart Publishing, Oxford

House of Commons, Committee of Public Accounts (2017) Managing the costs of clinical negligence in hospital trusts: Fifth Report of Session 2017–19, HC 397

House of Commons Committee of Public Accounts (2018) Transforming courts and tribunals: Fifty-Sixth Report of Session 2017–19 – HC 976. https://publications.parliament.uk

House of Commons Public Administration and Constitutional Affairs Committee (2018) Will the NHS never learn? Follow-up to PHSO report 'Learning from Mistakes' on the NHS in England Seventh Report of Session 2016–17 – HC 743. https://publications.parliament.uk

Hunt J (2016) Speech at Global Patient Safety Summit, Lancaster House, 10 March 2016. https://www.gov.uk/government/speeches/from-a-blame-culture-to-a-learning-culture

Hutton M (2019) Spinal services: GIRFT Programme National Specialty Report. https://improvement.nhs.uk/resources/spinal-services-report/

Ipsos MORI Social Research Institute (2016) Online survey of individuals' handling of legal issues in England and Wales 2015. http://www.legalservicesboard.org.uk

Justice (2011) Dispute resolution commitment. http://www.justice.gov.uk/courts/mediation/dispute-resolution-commitment

Justice (2018) Immigration and asylum appeals – a fresh look. https://justice.org.uk/wp-content/uploads/2018/06/JUSTICE-Immigration-and-Asylum-Appeals-Report.pdf

Larkin K et al (2018) The legal needs of small businesses 2013/2017. https://www.legalservicesboard.org.uk

Legal Services Board (2012) Evaluation: how can we measure access to justice for individual consumers? http://www.legalservicesboard.org.uk

Local Government & Social Care Ombudsman (2018) Building for the future. Annual report and accounts 2017–2018. https://www.lgo.org.uk/information-centre/about-us/our-performance/lgo-annual-reports

Macleod S, Hodges C (2017) Redress schemes for personal injuries. Hart Publishing, Oxford

Ministry of Housing, Communities & Local Government (2018) Strengthening consumer redress in the housing market. A Consultation. https://www.gov.uk/government/consultations/strengthening-consumer-redress-in-housing

Ministry of Housing, Communities & Local Government (2019) Strengthening Consumer Redress in the Housing Market. Summary of responses to the consultation and the Government's response. https://www.gov.uk/government/consultations/strengthening-consumer-redress-in-housing

Ministry of Justice (2007–2017) Civil Justice Statistics Quarterly. https://www.gov.uk/government/collections/civil-justice-statistics-quarterly

Ministry of Justice (2017) Legal Aid, Sentencing and Punishment of Offenders Act 2012: Post-Legislative Memorandum – submitted to the Justice Select Committee on 30 October 2017 – Cm 9486. https://www.gov.uk

Ministry of Justice (2018) Tribunals and gender recognition statistics quarterly: October to December 2017, Main Tables (October to December 2017), Table FIA.3. https://www.gov.uk/government/statistics/tribunals-and-gender-recognition-certificate-statistics-quarterly-october-to-december-2017

Ministry of Justice (2019a) Civil Justice Statistics Quarterly: October to December 2018 (provisional). https://www.gov.uk/government/collections/civil-justice-statistics-quarterly

Ministry of Justice (2019b) Extending fixed recoverable costs in civil cases: implementing Sir Rupert Jackson's proposals. https://consult.justice.gov.uk

Ministry of Justice and Her Majesty's HM Courts and Tribunals Service (2016) Response to the proposal on the provision of court and tribunal estate in England and Wales. https://www.gov.uk

National Advisory Group on the safety of Patients in England (2013) A promise to learn—a commitment to act. Improving the Safety of Patients in England. http://www.ihi.org/resources/Pages/Publications/APromiseToLearnACommitmentToAct.aspx

NHS Resolution (2018) Annual Report and Accounts 2017/18. https://resolution.nhs.uk

Oates A (2018) Learning from suicide-related claims. A thematic review of NHS Resolution data. https://resolution.nhs.uk/resources/learning-from-suicide-related-claims/

OECD (2012) Recommendation of the Council on Regulatory and Policy Governance. https://www.oecd.org/governance/regulatory-policy/49990817.pdf

Ombudsman Services (2018) Consumer Action Monitor Report 2018. https://www.ombudsman-services.org

Oxford Economics (2016) Consumer detriment: counting the cost of consumer problems. September 2016. https://www.citizensadvice.org.uk

Parliamentary and Health Service Ombudsman (2015a) RESOLVE News from the Ombudsman Service. https://www.ombudsman.org.uk

Parliamentary and Health Service Ombudsman (2015b) What do people think about complaining? https://www.ombudsman.org.uk

Public Administration Select Committee (2015) Investigating clinical incidents in the NHS: Sixth Report of Session 2014–15. https://publications.parliament.uk/pa/cm201415/cmselect/cmpubadm/886/886.pdf

Revolver (2020) Revolver. www.resolver.co.uk

Roberts S, Palmer M (2005) Dispute processes: ADR and the primary forms of decision-making. Cambridge University Press, Cambridge

Sander FEA (1976) The causes of dissatisfaction with the administration of justice. In: Sander FEA (ed) Varieties of dispute processing, F.R.D. 70(111)

Secretary of State for Business (2018) Energy and industrial strategy by command of her majesty good work plan. https://www.gov.uk

Sorabji J (2014) English Civil Justice after the Woolf and Jackson reforms: a critical analysis. Cambridge University Press, Cambridge

Strategic Policy Making Team, Cabinet Office (1999) Professional policy making for the twenty-first century. https://dera.ioe.ac.uk/6320/1/profpolicymaking.pdf

The Lord Chancellor, the Lord Chief Justice and the Senior President of Tribunals (2016) Transforming our justice system. https://www.gov.uk

The Low Commission (2015) Getting it right in social welfare law. The Low Commission's follow-up report. https://www.lag.org.uk/about-us/policy/the-low-commission-200551

The Mid Staffordshire NHS Foundation Trust Inquiry (2010) Independent inquiry into care provided by Mid Staffordshire NHS Foundation Trust January 2005 – March 2009, Volume

I – HC375-I. https://www.gov.uk/government/publications/independent-inquiry-into-care-pro vided-by-mid-staffordshire-nhs-foundation-trust-january-2001-to-march-2009

Thomas R (2016) The impact of PPI mis-selling on the Financial Ombudsman Service. https:// www.financial-ombudsman.org.uk

Vaze P et al (2012) Dealing with dissatisfaction: complaint handling in energy, water, telecoms, Royal Mail and financial and legal services. Consumer Focus

Voss GC (2018) The law society's inaugural lecture on the future of law. https://www.judiciary.uk/ wp-content/uploads/2018/05/chc-speech-future-of-law-lecture-may-2018-1.pdf

Wagner G (2014) Private law enforcement through ADR: wonder drug or snake oil? Common Mark Law Rev 51:165–194

Wilson EO (2012) The social conquest of earth. Liveright Publishing, New York

Woolf H (1995) Access to justice: interim report to the Lord Chancellor on the Civil Justice System in England and Wales. HMSO

Woolf H (1996) Access to justice: final report to the Lord Chancellor on the Civil Justice System in England and Wales. HMSO

Chapter 6
Trust and Transparency and the Ombuds: Justice Behind Closed Doors?

Lewis Shand Smith

Abstract In this chapter I bring together two presentations given by me at separate conferences. The first was entitled 'Consumer ADR/ODR: Justice Behind Closed Doors?' and the second 'Trust: transparency, information, governance, digitisation, vulnerability'. I explain that ADR cannot be used as a blanket term and while arbitration and mediation, for example, can be seen as examples of ADR where the processes and decisions are private and therefore justice is indeed delivered behind closed doors, ombudsman or ombuds schemes have openness and accessibility as fundamental principles. The consumer ombuds model has four parts: giving advice and support to consumers who have complaints; resolving disputes and publishing outcomes; feeding back to traders and supporting improvement; reporting to stakeholders, including regulators and governments, and influencing policy.

Trust is built through experience and knowledge. Personal experience of an ombuds is limited and so openness about the service, easy and appropriate access, and clarity over governance and accountability are critical pathways to building awareness and trust. In linking the two papers I argue that the ombuds model of ADR is essentially transparent and that this transparency is key to building trust.

6.1 The Perspective of an Ombuds

I am approaching this from the perspective of someone who is a practitioner in the world of Alternative Dispute Resolution and an ombuds.

I first served as an ombuds in the public sector, covering complaints about parliament and its arms-length bodies such as regulators, local government, social housing services, health and mental health services, further and higher education institutions and some aspects of school and nursery education. Then for ten years I was Chief Ombudsman at Ombudsman Services (OS)—the UK Energy and Telecommunications Ombudsman. OS was an ombuds for property professionals:

L. Shand Smith (✉)
Business Banking Resolution Service, London, UK
e-mail: lewis@shandsmith.com

lettings agents, estate agents, managing agents and chartered surveyors and is a "residual body" for the UK under the terms of the 2013 EU Directive on Consumer ADR. In 2017 OS resolved in excess of 90,000 disputes.

The term ombudsman is Scandinavian with its origins in the old Norse word *umboðsmaðr*—basically meaning representative, agent or commissioner. My home is in the Shetland Islands, once part of Norway and the Danish Empire. The place-names are almost entirely old Norse and there are several that derive from umboðs. In his nineteenth century Dictionary of the Norn Language in Shetland, Jakob Jakobsen argues that as a place-name the word may mean crown property or national property, suggesting that the inhabitants were agents of the state with full powers.[1]

The 1241 Law of Jutland or Jutland Code has in its preamble the statement: *með lögum skal land byggja* or 'by law shall the land be built'. The Code separated church and state and introduced the concept of law as a contract between ruler and people, laid the foundation for modern social democracy and is the basis for today's law and democracy in the Scandinavian countries. It is thought that the introduction was written by Bishop Gunnar of Viborg and that the law he has in mind is not just law as passed by monarch and councils and upheld by the judiciary, but law that has as its foundation—and he would have argued God given—human rights and individual self-determination.

The Swedish constitution of 1809 was based on the Code of Jutland—it begins with the words *með lögum skal land byggja* and as an integral part of that constitution the first modern ombudsman was created: a commissioner appointed by the state to investigate claims of maladministration by public bodies.

6.2   Consumer ADR, Justice Behind Closed Doors?

The question "Consumer ADR, justice behind closed doors?" seems to carry with it a negative judgement, an implication that there is something not quite right about justice that takes place in private, out of sight. And, as is the case with the EU Directive, it fails to distinguish between different methods of ADR and suggests a level of secrecy across the entire spectrum.

A report for the Legal Ombudsman in England provided a useful description and analysis of different dispute resolution forms and their characteristics,[2] these include:

> Mediation: Involves the use of a [appropriately qualified] third party who facilitates a negotiation to resolve a dispute. Details of the process to be followed are usually set out in an agreement to mediate which is agreed by the parties beforehand. Mediations can be face to face or on the telephone and tend to involve both separate meetings between the mediator and the parties and joint meetings where all are present.

---

[1]Jakobsen (1985).
[2]Gill et al. (2014).

Arbitration: Involves an independent third party [or parties] (the arbitrator) reaching an independent decision on a dispute. The process of arbitration can vary depending on circumstances, but must be agreed in advance in an arbitration agreement. Some arbitrations may involve hearings similar to those used in a court trial, while others will involve only written submissions. In most cases the arbitrator's decision is legally binding on both sides.

(Inquisitorial) Adjudication: Adjudication involves an independent third party with specialist knowledge (the adjudicator) reaching an independent decision on a dispute. Although similar to arbitration, adjudication processes can be simpler and usually produce decisions that are binding on the company but not on the consumer. They can be more flexible and adjustable to meet specific commercial and other needs.

In a mediation the mediator does not adjudicate but holds the process. The outcome is not binding, and if the parties fail to reach agreement they retain the right to take the dispute to the courts. Both parties agree at the outset that what takes place and the evidence exchanged will be completely confidential. Nothing from the mediation process can be brought to a court in evidence. A recent report on mediation in civil justice in Scotland recommends that basic data in relation to mediation should be collected in order to assess the effectiveness, benefits and limitations of mediation services and that it might include: geographical location, general sector of the dispute, duration of the mediation and the outcome   whether a full or partial.[3]

Formal arbitration is generally much more like a court or tribunal process with both sides leading evidence and where the arbitrator can require or call evidence. It is generally subject to arbitration laws of the host country or "seat". Grounds for appeal are limited. It is confidential, and confidentiality may be enshrined in legislation, for example as in the Arbitration (Scotland) Act 2010. While the Act lists exceptions the general rule is that:

Disclosure by the tribunal, any arbitrator or a party of confidential information relating to the arbitration is to be actionable as a breach of an obligation of confidence...

The tribunal and the parties must take reasonable steps to prevent unauthorised disclosure of confidential information by any third party involved in the conduct of the arbitration.

The tribunal must, at the outset of the arbitration, inform the parties of the obligations which this rule imposes on them.

"Confidential information", in relation to an arbitration, means any information relating to:

(a) the dispute,
(b) the arbitral proceedings,
(c) the award, or
(d) any civil proceedings relating to the arbitration in respect of which an order has been granted under section 15 of this Act, which is not, and has never been, in the public domain.[4]

---

[3]The Expert Group on Mediation in Civil Justice in Scotland (2019).

[4]Arbitration (Scotland) Act 2010: Schedule 1, Part 3, Rule 26.(1).

A study of the law and practice of arbitration across the European Union and Switzerland on the point of privacy and confidentiality observed that:

> The place of confidentiality in arbitration varies significantly between jurisdictions. There is little question regarding the "privacy" of an arbitral proceeding, in that it is uniformly accepted that individuals not parties to the arbitration agreement have no right to be present at an arbitral hearing. This contrasts markedly with what is often seen as the right of the public to attend judicial proceedings...

> The "confidentiality" of arbitration, however, is a broader concern, and relates not to attendance at arbitral proceedings, but to both the public accessibility of information about and arising from the arbitration, and to the right of parties and other individuals involved in an arbitration to release information about or arising from it. The confidentiality of arbitration varies significantly between States, with some adopting a rule that arbitration is inherently confidential, while others treat arbitration as not confidential unless it is covered by a confidentiality agreement between individuals/entities involved.[5]

In what may be a majority of cases a judgement (or "award") is reached by the tribunal "behind closed doors", in lower value cases the arbiters may not even give a reason to the parties for their decision. It is no surprise that the likely confidential nature of an arbitration and the award makes arbitration an attractive alternative to the courts for parties involved, particularly in a commercial mediation.

A report by the APPG on Consumer Protection on its Ombudsman Inquiry found that:

> While ADR is generally seen to cover mediation, conciliation, arbitration and adjudication, for the Ombudsman Association it is essential to take a wholly different approach, something they describe as 'inquisitorial adjudication'. With inquisitorial adjudication, time and effort are more concentrated at the 'front end of the consumer journey', as Donal Galligan, [Director] of the Ombudsman Association put it, which includes 'looking for evidence that might be missing'. The result is invariably a deeper understanding of the causes of the problem.[6]

The use of the ombuds system has developed from public administration to widespread use in consumer ADR. Most often ombuds offices are created by statute with the ombuds, or natural or legal person,[7] appointed by the national parliament or government. Alternatively, they can be formed by a particular sector on a voluntary basis with the ombuds being appointed by the board of directors of a private company. In either circumstance consumer ombuds offices are required to be approved and monitored by the competent authorities of the member state. Consumer ombuds cover a wide range of sectors: finance, energy, telecommunications, travel, property, housebuilding... and each member state is required to have a residual body to provide a service where no specific ADR entity exists.

---

[5]Policy Department C: Citizens' Rights and Constitutional Affairs of Directorate-General for Internal Policies (2014), p. 29.

[6]All-Party Parliamentary Group on Consumer Protection (2019), p. 10.

[7]The description used in Directive 2013/11/EU of the European Parliament and of the Council on alternative dispute resolution for consumer disputes for the persons in charge of ADR.

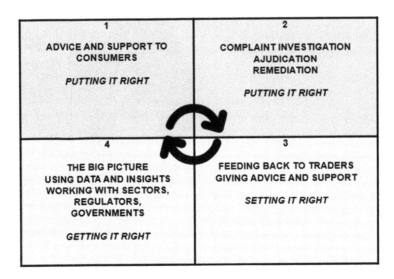

Fig. 6.1 The four parts of the ombuds model

6.3 Characteristics of the Ombuds Model

What then are the characteristics of the ombuds model, which Donal Galligan described as *'a bit of a gold-plated service'*[8]? The model has four distinctive parts as shown in Fig. 6.1.

6.3.1 Giving Advice and Support to Consumers: **Putting It Right**

A consumer has a complaint about a trader, they have approached the trader and had no satisfaction. What next? A trader operating within the EU has an obligation to signpost to an ADR entity whether or not they agree to use it.

Ombuds schemes have an increasingly strong on-line presence, with website pages giving clear information about the role of the purpose and limitations of the service, the processes followed, the range of likely outcomes and ways in which consumers can gain access to the ADR procedure. The website will typically outline governance and funding arrangements, particularly making clear the independence of the service from those under jurisdiction.

Frequently complaints can be made and supporting documents uploaded through a portal on the website and all parties to the dispute can use it to make comments and track progress.

---

[8] All-Party Parliamentary Group on Consumer Protection (2019), p. 10.

Fig. 6.2 Advertising the presence of Ombudsman Services

Accessibility is one of the key principles of all ombuds schemes, but a consumer must first know the service exists and is available. It is often those who are more vulnerable who do not know about or use an ombuds service. To help counter this Ombudsman Services, for example, has run campaigns in conjunction with AGE UK and the National Union of Students to raise awareness and encourage participation. Ombudsman Services has also provided briefing sessions for MPs and Members of the Scottish Parliament, providing briefing packs for their offices and researchers.

Another initiative in 2017 was the Ombudsman Services 'ombudsvan' (Fig. 6.2). Taking the office to areas where take up of the service was low, and where need was considered to be high. Interestingly, while officers were able to take complaints and to give updates on 'live' disputes, the largest benefit was through the information and help given to those who had a problem but did not know how to complain to their supplier or trader.

In ombuds schemes, once an approach or application has been made, the entry point is generally into a unit that will provide information, advice and support. The complaint will be assessed for eligibility. If a complaint has not already been made to the trader the consumer will be redirected, told what to expect and what to do if they are dissatisfied with the outcome. They will be guided as to the kind of evidence and documentation they might be required to submit. If the dispute is one that is not within the jurisdiction of the scheme, they will be signposted to an alternative.

An assessment will also be made to determine whether the consumer has a level of vulnerability or requires special assistance in using the ombuds. Help will be given in framing the complaint and the outcome the consumer regards as necessary to put things right. At all times the officer will manage the expectation of the consumer and be prepared to guide them through the ombuds processes.

If the dispute falls into a category that is frequently seen and dealt with, then the officer may point towards the likely decision and redress and encourage both parties to settle. This negotiated or facilitated resolution, where the officer proposes the

remedy without an investigation, can be either the result of negotiation or conciliation, and is becoming commonplace in the ombuds toolkit. It is often described as
informal resolution or *early resolution.*

6.3.2 Complaint Investigation, Adjudication, Remediation: Putting It Right

The core of an ombuds service is inquisitorial adjudication, the 'gold-plated' service
referred to by Donal Galligan.

When a dispute is accepted for investigation the parties are invited to submit
evidence. The ombuds, or an officer acting on behalf of the ombuds, will examine
the materials asking four basic questions: what does the consumer claim happened?
What is he response of the trader? What should have happened? What did happen?
The ombuds may ask for further information from either party to the dispute and may
provide the facility for a face-to-face discussion with either party and, on rare
occasions, a hearing. In establishing what should have happened the ombuds will
take into account all relevant law and regulation, standards and codes of conduct.
The officer will have a certain level of expertise in the subject matter area, and where
appropriate may ask for technical advice from a qualified and independent
professional.

The officer will make the decision or adjudication based on what is fair and
reasonable in the circumstances of the specific case. While previous decisions will be
taken into account, precedence does not apply, and each case is decided on its merits.
Generally, both parties have the opportunity to appeal and for most consumer ADR
schemes in the UK, when the initial decision or decision following an appeal is
accepted by the consumer, it becomes legally binding on both parties.

If the consumer does not accept, they retain the right to ask that their dispute be
heard in the courts. In cases where a dispute could not be resolved through a given
ADR procedure where the outcome is not binding, the parties should subsequently
not be prevented from initiating judicial proceedings in relation to that dispute.[9]

Importantly, the decision made by the ombuds and the report issued is admissible
in court. It becomes the property of the consumer and can be used by them in
whatever way they decide. A consumer may decide to share it with others similarly
affected or use it to inform the press or media.

Typically, the ombuds will record in the decision whether the complaint has been
upheld or partially upheld in favour of the consumer, or not upheld. Where the case
has been upheld in full or in part, the ombuds may recommend some form of
remediation, an appropriate form of redress that will correct the failure. It may be
a financial award, the restoration or improvement of a service and could include an

---

[9]Directive 2013/11/EU of the European Parliament and of the Council on alternative dispute
resolution for consumer disputes, para 45.

element of compensation of distress and inconvenience caused. If the decision is legally binding, then so is the award. If the trader fails to comply, then the decision and redress are enforceable through the courts.

In summary, a consumer believes that something has gone wrong with the contract or service provided by a trader, they have complained to the trader and remain dissatisfied and then they approach the ombuds. The ombuds provides access to a third-party independent review of the dispute, where appropriate they will investigate and adjudicate, and may require some action to be taken.

While the ombuds process takes place behind 'closed doors', the service is well publicised and accessible, the evidence, decision and report are made available to the parties to the dispute and can be used as evidence in court,[10] and the remedial action can be enforced through the courts. It is important to recognize that the report and adjudication are not confidential.

In the life-cycle of customer service, the consumer journey, the first two elements of the ombuds responsibilities can be described as *'putting it right'*—investigating what has gone wrong. solving problems, resolving disputes.

An ombuds will take a case to investigation where the consumer or trader do not agree a facilitated settlement or conciliation, where the dispute is unusual or complex, where a collection of similar complaints point to some sort of systemic failure or where it is in the public interest to do so. Any or all of the last three reasons could trigger the ombuds service to initiate feedback to traders or alert regulators.

6.3.3   Feeding Back to Traders, Giving Traders Advice and Support: Setting It Right

A distinguishing feature of an ombuds type service is that it exists for more than just resolving complaints. A significant element in what it provides is working with companies and traders.

An ombuds investigation can identify systemic problems, for example a clause in a contract that disadvantages consumers, a failure to deliver specified goods or services—in total or in part, maladministration in the calculation and presentation of bills, geographical or demographic hotspots of complaints, or a lack of consistency between what companies say they offer and what they actually make available. Of prime importance is whether the business has demonstrated adherence to its the ethical and cultural principles.

---

[10]In the UK where a consumer ombudsman has been established by statute, for example the Financial Ombudsman or the Legal Ombudsman, the trader can call for a judicial review. The Energy Ombudsman and Telecommunications Ombudsman and ADR bodies are required by statute but are not themselves creatures of statute; it is likely that they are judiciable but until tested in the courts it is unknown. With voluntary ombudsman schemes such as the Furniture Ombudsman or Motor Ombudsman, it is unlikely that a trader will have access to the judicial review where the outcome of a case has been accepted by the consumer.

In sectors such as Energy and Finance the foundational regulatory requirement is that the supplier of goods and services should treat customers fairly and be able to demonstrate it. It is the ombuds, making decisions on the basis what is fair and reasonable, that can hold the trader to account. In addition, therefore, to requiring redress for an individual, the ombuds may also make recommendations to the business asking for changes to policy and practice.

The ombuds is not a regulator and has no locus in enforcing regulation or law or punishing for a breach. The ombuds will, however, work with a trader, offering guidance and advice, helping to develop good complaint handling, and giving support when a one-off event has caused significant detriment for a large number of customers.

> Across the sector, the percentage of cases that have been "settled" – resolved without the need for us to investigate – increased from 5.95% in Q4 2017 to 21.97% in Q1 2018. The increase was predominantly driven by a significant increase in the number of provider A cases being settled.

> We identified issues with the way in which provider A notified customers of a price rise, which had driven increased complaints numbers to us in January and February 2018. We have discussed the matter with provider A and provider A subsequently decided to accept our recommendations and resolve complaints with affected customers rather than submit case files.[11]

Where there is systemic failure in aspects of the delivery of a contract, or maladministration on the part of a provider or evidence that customers are not being treated fairly then the ombuds, in collaboration with a business, will use the information collected and analysed during the investigation process to drive change and bring about improvement: *'Setting it right'*.

An ombuds within the EU is required to publish such information annually, together with recommendations made:

> Member States shall ensure that ADR entities make publicly available on their websites, on a durable medium upon request, and by any other means they consider appropriate, annual activity reports. These reports shall include the following information relating to both domestic and cross-border disputes:

> (b) any systemic or significant problems that occur frequently and lead to disputes between consumers and traders; such information may be accompanied by recommendations as to how such problems can be avoided or resolved in future, in order to raise traders' standards and to facilitate the exchange of information and best practices.[12]

---

[11]From Ombudsman Services Annual Report (2018).

[12]Directive 2013/11/EU of the European Parliament and of the Council on alternative dispute resolution for consumer disputes, art 7 2. (b).

6.3.4 The Big Picture—Using Data and Insights, Working with Sectors, Regulators and Governments: **Getting It Right**

Consumer ombuds have strong, often statutory, links with regulators and consumer bodies. For example, in the UK the Financial Ombudsman with the Financial Conduct Authority, the Energy Ombudsman with Ofgem, the Telecommunications Ombudsman with Ofcom, and the Legal Ombudsman with the Legal Services Board. In the UK the regulators are also the competent authorities for ADR schemes in their respective sectors.

Ombuds will at the very least have a mechanism for reporting regularly to the regulator about the performance of the sector, and in certain instances it may be a statutory requirement. The UK Energy Ombudsman has a data sharing agreement with the regulator and with the consumer body Citizens Advice. All three bodies provide statistics which are collated and published quarterly by Citizens Advice. The aim is to give consumers an overview of how individual electricity and gas suppliers compare to one another to inform consumer choice.

The Energy Ombudsman will give information on complaints received about specific energy suppliers: overall numbers of complaints made and accepted by the service; updates on signposting—has the supplier informed the consumer of their right to go to the ombuds, at the right time and in the right way; trends, for example the biggest driver of complaints; outcomes, complaint upheld, partially upheld, not upheld and percentage of remedial actions implemented within the obligatory timescales.

Consumer ombuds will also collaborate with sector trade associations, feeding back the information derived from complaints received, outlining trends, highlighting areas of concern, reporting where it seems an association member has breached agreed standards, recommending changes to codes of conduct and standard contracts.

Consumer ombuds that have been created by statute may also have a duty to report directly to parliament and/or government and make themselves available for questioning.

The investigation is indeed 'behind closed doors' providing a level of anonymity for both consumer and trader but the ombuds, in publishing outcomes, names the trader and works with the industry, regulators and governments to bring about change and improvement, constantly asking the question: "in the particular circumstances of the case, has the consumer been treated fairly?". Successive studies have shown that principles or ethics-based regulation are more likely than a system of heavy enforcement and punishment to achieve good outcomes for consumers and citizens.[13] The unique insights an ombuds gains from investigating complaints

---

[13]See, for example, Hodges and Steinholtz (2018).

assists the development of regulation and standards as well as service provision and attitudes towards the customer journey.

The ombuds is a critical element in the dynamic cycle of continuous improvement: putting it right, setting it right, getting it right. *Putting it right* through investigation, adjudication and remediation; *setting it right* by feeding back and working with traders to improve the service they give; and supplying data and offering insights to sectors, regulators and governments to inform a context in which traders are encouraged and empowered to treat customers fairly in ways most appropriate to the circumstances, learn from mistakes and are supported in *getting policy and practice right in the first place*.

Consumer ADR, is it justice behind closed doors? It depends, arbitration is usually bound by confidentiality and by the outcome of the process, and there is limited scope for appeal. Mediation takes place in private, both parties can walk away without agreement and with the option to go to court—none of the information shared during the mediation can be divulged. In consumer ombuds type schemes where inquisitorial adjudication is the core, the service is signposted, there is easy and supported access, the publication of outcomes is the norm, and data and insights are used to drive improvement and inform regulation. Relevant evidence collected and decision reports are admissible as evidence in any subsequent court proceedings. While the beginning to end consideration of an individual dispute is carried out in private, the public availability and the use of the learning, conclusions and recommendations are an integral part of the ombuds model. It is characterised by openness and transparency.

6.4   Trust and Transparency

Trust: transparency, information, governance, digitisation, vulnerability; the given title of a conference session[14] seemed to be no more than a random collection of words. Why these words? And how do they relate? How significant are they to a consumer ombuds?

The colon after *trust* sheds some light, that somehow transparency, information, governance, digitisation and vulnerability are all aspects of trust, or that the ways in which we treat these areas are perhaps ways of building trust.

Tim Hicks writing in *Embodied Conflict* highlights the fundamental importance of trust as the glue of human relationships:

> The primal importance of trust to our fundamental survival concerns runs so deep that we are mostly not aware of it as an omnipresent factor. Trust has to do with the degree to which we can rely upon interfaces we have with external reality, both physical and relational... I need to be able to trust my perceptual experience of the physical world in order to navigate that

---

[14] *Consumer ADR – Delivering Fairness ands Justice for Consumers, Business and Markets.* 18 and 19 March 2019, Wolfston College, Oxford.

world safely and successfully. So it is with my social relationships. We ask to what degree we can rely upon and be safe in the presence of the other. Trust is established on the basis of experience. We learn (encode) how something is, whether a physical object, a person, or relational dynamic, and we expect it to remain consistent. When there is variability, we learn about the pattern from repeated exposure. We can deal with the variability when it includes some constancy. We want the patterns to be predictable.[15]

Hicks is writing in the context of conflict resolution. He reminds us that we are physical organisms, that it is brain function rooted in the experience of the entire body in interaction with its environment that determines our conflict behaviours. Our neural structures are the mechanisms by which we know, think about, create beliefs about, and understand the world in which we live, including the social world.

> Repetition reinforces the neural structures. The longer and more frequent our relationship with a physical and relational phenomenon, the more we have the experience of "knowing" it and the more we trust it to remain as it has been.[16]

If trust depends on knowledge, on experience, on repeated exposure to variability so that we learn and understand patterns, then this presents a challenge to all consumer ombuds. Typically, a consumer will use a particular consumer ombuds only once. A small number may take disputes about different products or services to different sector-specific ombuds, but the large majority of consumers have limited knowledge or experience of ombuds and will almost never have repeated exposure.

The challenge for ombuds then, is building trust where the experience on which it is constructed is generally missing. *Trust: transparency, information, governance, digitisation, vulnerability.* That colon is in the wrong place? The jumble of words takes on new meaning when the colon is moved—*trust (and) transparency: information, governance, digitisation, vulnerability.* The learning and thence the trust that comes from experience has to be replaced by knowledge which the ombuds and their advocates make available in a way that is structured and convincing. Trust is built by the comprehensive dissemination of information—by transparency.

6.4.1   Information and Accessibility

Information: the what? where? when? and who? of the ombuds service. The facts about its core functions, detail about its principles, processes and governance, assurances about its independence and the fairness of its decisions, confidence that the outcomes of decisions and requirements for redress and change are implemented.

What is available, as an alternative to the courts, for a consumer who has a complaint about a trader? An ombuds service of which only a few people are aware is already failing. A Citizens Advice report on consumer experiences of complaint

---

[15]Hicks (2018), p. 72.

[16]*Ibid*, p. 72.

handling[17] found that the majority of people do not escalate their complaints beyond the service provider and that the main reason for this is a general lack of awareness and confusion about which independent organisations are there to represent the interests of the public and how they should be used. When surveyed, only 28% of consumers making a complaint about a regulated sector claimed to be aware of independent organisations that provide mediation[18] in that sector.

Consumer ombuds and the businesses under their jurisdiction clearly need to do more to raise awareness. Consumers need to know that the service exists. They need to know the sectors for which it has responsibility and the criteria for eligibility—for example has a complaint been made to the trader, have they had time to respond, is the dispute about a legitimate commercial decision or the failure to deliver a contract, is the case already subject to court action? In deciding on whether to lodge a case with the ombuds the consumer should have a clear idea of the potential remedies that the scheme is empowered to deliver, for example the limit to any financial award.

The ombuds has a duty to ensure the consumer and trader know what to expect from the service which is handling the dispute. There needs to be clarity on the processes employed, the evidence that might be requested and the timescales for supplying it—in a mandatory scheme the trader should know the consequences of non-compliance. The parties should know at the outset the time the end-to-end procedure is likely to take.[19] *When* are they likely to receive updates, when will they know the outcome, by when should the remedy be implemented?

It should be easy for the consumer to find out *where* to take their complaint and the means by which they can raise it. Belgium's Belmed platform, for example, provides information about how to make a complaint and the agencies responsible. It also provides an online facility through which the complaint can be lodged and settled. Interestingly, while the site is well used, most consumers then go directly to the appropriate ombuds in preference to the online option for making a complaint. The European Consumer Centre Network (ECC-Net) has centres in each member state and also Iceland and Norway. ECC-Net gives advice and support to consumers who have failed to resolve their disputes with traders in these countries, including cross-border disputes.

Ways of making the complaint must be obvious and straightforward and by the means preferred by and the consumer: web-based access through an online portal or by e-mail, by telephone or by letter. Some ombuds will give the opportunity for a face-to-face interview. All ombuds will make known the provision they make for those with particular needs, for example for those suffering sight or hearing loss. The ombuds service will also highlight the support it can make available to those who

---

[17]Slater and Higginson (2016).

[18]The CA report uses *mediation* here to refer to the available ADR/ombuds schemes. See *ibid*, p. 43.

[19]The 2013 EU ADR Directive states that the outcome should be available within 90 calendar days from the date on which the ADR entity has received the complete complaint file. That can be extended for highly complex disputes and the parties informed of the expected length of time until conclusion.

find it difficult to articulate their complaint, or those who may be especially vulnerable.

Just *who* will be handling the dispute needs to be apparent to both consumer and trader. The people, how they were appointed, the training given, steps taken to ensure their independence and neutrality, and to whom they are accountable.

The 2013 EU ADR Directive gives clear guidance on the independence and impartiality of natural persons carrying out ADR activities: type of appointment, length of service, expected expertise, remuneration and conflicts of interest.

The information has to be there and easily accessible, but if the ombuds is to be trusted then the scheme has to be transparent by regularly demonstrating how it has met its commitments and achieved its goals. Key performance indicators have to be agreed and compliance measured and published, customer satisfaction surveys carried out and results made available, some ombuds use focus groups to provide feedback. All ombuds are required to publish an annual activity reports that detail the number of disputes received, the nature of the complaints, the outcomes, the time taken, and systemic problems uncovered and recommendations made. Most important of all, decisions need to be, and be seen to be, consistent and fair.

6.4.2   Digitisation and Vulnerability

It may seem strange to link digitisation and vulnerability other than because both are high on the agenda for consumer ombuds schemes.

Automation is seen to be a means by which accessibility can be improved for those who are technologically literate and willing to 'self-serve' throughout the complaint handling procedures. Algorithms can be developed that can quickly make an assessment on whether a complaint is eligible, judge the emotional state of the consumer, and finally offer a resolution. The algorithms can collect and analyse data, spot trends and systemic failure and produce reports. It is easy to see just how valuable these can be to an ombuds, reducing overall time taken, offering resolution without investigation and creating a rich body of data. Many of tasks once undertaken by trained officers can now be completed by the technology, so reducing costs.

On the other hand, if ombuds are developing this technological capability so are the traders under jurisdiction, especially the very large businesses in regulated sectors. Is it not likely that their own systems will get there first, resolving disputes, spotting trends, finding inherent failings? Will the need for the third-party consumer ombuds become less?

If the consumer ombuds is using artificial intelligence to carry out its related functions, how will it ensure that each case is considered on its merits, in its own context and on the grounds of what is fair and reasonable? Is there a danger that the consumer ombuds will become little more than a machine for resolving disputes? If decisions are automated is there a real risk that transparency will be reduced and the office of the ombuds become even more obscure?[20]

Customer services experts are warning that by removing the personal touch, the ombuds will lose what consumers actually want the service for. By the time a consumer contacts the ombuds they have already been through the complaints process of the trader, they are becoming increasingly disgruntled and what they want more than anything else is to be listened to. They are looking to the ombuds for empathy, understanding and support to journey through the procedures. They are looking for a relationship that is open and honest and for outcomes that are demonstrably fair. The technology has its part to play but it is through transparency in relationships that trust is built and expectations met.

Niall Devlin: *"A relationship that leans on technology"*.
Katrin Herrling: *"Technology frees us from administration to allow concentration on relationships"*.[21]

There are several projects underway to help ADR bodies find ways to identify and better serve those who may be vulnerable or who require special assistance. There are particular demographic cohorts who rarely complain when something has gone wrong and are even less likely to take their dispute to an independent third party. If and when they do, they need to be supported. If the technology is there for those consumers willing and able to use it, then it should allow an ombuds to focus on giving help where it is most needed.

The technology therefore is a valuable tool that will create the space for the ombuds to assist those who need it most, to concentrate on the *advice and support* function referred to at Sect. 6.3.1 above. It is critical that this capacity is well published by the ombuds, by the traders and by the advocacy organisations who work on behalf of specific groups of people. Where the ombuds maintains a continuous dialogue with representative bodies, reporting on progress and open to advice, then this transparency will encourage trust to develop.

6.4.3 Governance and Accountability

The board of an independent company has duties and responsibilities placed on it by legislation and codes of conduct. In most, if not all examples, the governing body or board of an ombuds scheme has, in addition, an obligation to protect the independence and integrity of the ombuds service—of its people and of the scheme itself.

---

[20]Perhaps a greater and more exciting challenge for the ombuds will arise when investigating a dispute about a decision made by artificial intelligence. If there is maladministration in that decision, where does responsibility for that failure lie, and how is it to be uncovered?

[21]From presentations at the UK Finance SME Banking and Commercial Financial Conference, Belfast 2019.

While it has no locus in determining complaints the board has still to demonstrate its own independence and impartiality. For example, while trader organisations may be represented, they must not be in the majority and appointments should be by open competition. For the scheme to operate effectively, the board has to ensure it has sufficient resources and also that those funding the service cannot influence the outcome of disputes. The activities of the board should be published alongside the annual report of the service, especially highlighting income and expenditure and the sources of funding, as well as risks and mitigation.

In some schemes the board may have as part of its duties the appointment of key officers, including the person in charge of the service and should publish its procedure for doing so.[22]

The first line of accountability for the *natural persons in charge of ADR* is generally the board and its chair.

The person in charge and the scheme itself may be answerable to several different stakeholders. As an example, the Energy Ombudsman Service in the UK is accountable to the Energy Regulator, Ofgem, which has responsibility for approving and monitoring the scheme. Ofgem carries out this task on behalf of the Department for Business, Energy and Industrial Strategy and the Secretary of State. The Energy Ombudsman is held accountable to consumers through Citizens Advice, to energy supply companies through Energy UK and network companies through the Energy Networks Association. It maintains dialogue with those directly responsible for service delivery through a liaison panel.

The etymological origins of *ombuds*, or *ombudsman* described at Sect. 6.1., imply a person who carries the authority of the state. All public sector ombuds are appointed by the state and are accountable to the people through their elected representatives. Throughout the EU the same is true of many private sector ombuds. Private or public, all ombuds act in the public interest and if the title ombuds is used then, in the interests of accountability and transparency, the scheme should be created by statute, membership made mandatory on a sector, and the natural person in charge—the ombuds—appointed by parliament. The All-Party Parliamentary Group on Consumer Protection argued for root and branch reform to ensure there is a powerful and accessible statutory ombudsman in all sectors. They made a number of recommendations for simpler changes, that can be introduced quickly, including that:

> All ombudsmen should be required to give evidence to Parliament, via the appropriate select committee.[23]

Transparency of governance and accountability will help users to trust that the organisation and its processes are independent, impartial and fair.

---

[22]"It is generally expected that the initial appointment of the office holder will be through open process without a predetermined outcome and which adheres to appropriate national codes of practice relating to public appointments. Terms of office should be published and be of sufficient certainty and duration to secure independence." See BIOA (2007), p. 17.

[23]All-Party Parliamentary Group on Consumer Protection (2019), p. 10.

6.5 Trust, Transparency and the Ombuds: Justice Behind Closed Doors?

The role of a consumer ombuds is to deliver justice, most often in the sense of what is right and fair, not only about whether a law has been complied with or a contract fulfilled; an alternative to the courts but not a substitute for the courts.

Trust is constructed through repeated exposure to an object, person or procedure. Awareness of ombuds schemes is low, the numbers using them to resolve disputes lower still, and those repeatedly using an ombuds service very few indeed.

How then is an ombuds to build trust? It has to be through transparency and openness, ease of access and of use, clarity of procedures, working with businesses to improve, sharing data and insights to drive learning, and regularly reporting to key stakeholders on its own performance.

A scheme is expected to have a policy on openness and transparency in relation to what is does, how it does it and the results in achieves. This is fundamental to accountability. It enables a scheme to demonstrate fairness of approach, which in turn increases public confidence. It also ensures that a scheme is not perceived as exclusive, secretive or unwilling to be open to public scrutiny.[24]

Trust will be built around better transparency in the process and more explicit governance mechanisms, a wider diffusion of the information, and better acknowledgement of the risks surrounding the different forms of vulnerability.[25]

An ombuds investigation is conducted in private. But everything that surrounds it is public and transparent. An ombuds decision and report becomes the property of the complainant who is at liberty to use it in a court action. Learning is fed back to drive change and improvement.

The doors of an ombuds service are not closed but wide open, offering accessibility and visibility to all comers. It is through transparency that trust in the service, and in the way by which it delivers justice, is built and sustained.

References

All-Party Parliamentary Group on Consumer Protection (2019) Report from the Ombudsman Inquiry, vol 1. https://images6.moneysavingexpert.com/images/documents/Ombudsman%20report.pdf

BIOA (2007) Guide to principles of good complaint handling. https://www.ombudsmanassociation.org/docs/BIOAGoodComplaintHandling.pdf

Cornelis M (2019) At the consumer ADR: delivering fairness and justice for consumers, business and markets conference, University of Oxford, Oxford, 18–19 March 2019

Gill C et al (2014) Models of alternative dispute resolution: a report for the legal Ombudsman. https://www.virtualmediationlab.com/wp-content/uploads/2014/12/ombudsman.pdf

---

[24]BIOA (2007), p. 17.

[25]Cornelis: from a presentation at a Consumer ADR Conference, Oxford University (2019).

Hicks T (2018) Embodied conflict – the neural basis of conflict and communication. Routledge, Abingdon

Hodges C, Steinholtz R (2018) Ethical business practice and regulation: a behavioural and values-based approach to compliance and enforcement. Hart Publishing, Oxford

Jakobsen J (1985) An etymological dictionary of the Norn language in Shetland. The Shetland Folk Society, Shetland

Ombudsman Services (2018) Annual report: January to December 2018. https://www.ombudsman-services.org/about-us/annual-reports

Policy Department C: Citizens' Rights and Constitutional Affairs of Directorate-General for Internal Policies (2014) Legal instruments and practice of arbitration in the EU. https://www.europarl.europa.eu/RegData/etudes/STUD/2015/509988/IPOL_STU(2015)509988_EN.pdf

Slater K, Higginson G (2016) Understanding consumer experiences of complaint handling. https://www.citizensadvice.org.uk/

The Expert Group on Mediation in Civil Justice in Scotland (2019) Bringing mediation into the mainstream in civil justice in Scotland. https://www.scottishmediation.org.uk/wp-content/uploads/2019/06/Bringing-Mediation-into-the-Mainstream-in-Civl-Justice-in-Scotland.pdf

Chapter 7
CDR in Belgium: The Special Place of the Belgian Residual ADR Body

Pieter-Jan De Koning

Abstract This contribution discusses the tasks, procedures, structure and some of the improvement areas of the Belgian Consumer Mediation Service. The Consumers Mediation Service was set up under the impetus of European Directive 2013/11 (the "Consumer ADR Directive") and forms the final piece of the Belgian alternative dispute resolution (ADR) system for consumer disputes. The task of the Consumer Mediation Service is to guide consumers and businesses through the rather heterogeneous Belgian ADR landscape, both by providing information and by correctly referring the parties. If a dispute cannot be referred to a sector-specific entity, the Consumer Mediation Service will try to mediate a solution itself. Fast, free and easily accessible are the key words of the Consumer Mediation Service. The procedures and conditions laid down by law with which the Consumer Mediation Service, as a qualified entity recognized by public authorities, must comply are an expression of this. However, there are also a number of weak points. The contribution elaborates on the fact that a residual service that was previously unknown to the companies can count on little support from these companies. The fact that the recommendations made are unenforceable makes the Consumer Mediation Service sometimes little effective. Finally, the boundary between providing information and giving advice is sometimes also thin. But although still finding its place, there is no denying its relevance.

7.1 Introduction

The Consumer Mediation Service (CMS) is an autonomous public service which has been assigned various tasks, but whose main objective is to inform consumers and businesses about out-of-court dispute settlement. The CMS was established by the

This contribution appeared earlier in Voet (2018).

P.-J. De Koning (✉)
Belgian Consumer Mediation Service (Service de médiation pour le consommateur/
Consumentenombudsdienst), Brussels, Belgium
e-mail: pieterjan.dekoning@consumentenombudsdienst.be

law of 4 April 2014[1] transposing European Directive 2013/11/EU[2] into Belgian law, registered in Book XVI of the Code of Economic Law (CEL). The service was officially launched on 1 June 2015.

The Consumer Mediation Service has a special place in the Belgian Alternative Dispute Resolution (ADR) landscape since it acts as a point of contact for all other qualified entities on the one hand, and as a conciliator in residual consumer disputes on the other hand.

This contribution is intended to give the reader an insight into the operation of the Consumer Mediation Service, as well as the special place that it occupies in the Belgian ADR landscape. In the following, both the tasks (Sect. 7.2) and the procedure (Sect. 7.3) will be discussed. Where possible and relevant, statistics and figures are added.[3] Subsequently, the types of cases that are dealt with (Sect. 7.4) are discussed, as well as the way in which they are handled and the associated perception (Sect. 7.5). The structure and financing are discussed in a sixth chapter. In the seventh chapter a number of concerns are made, in particular with regard to the perception, admissibility, impartiality and recommendations of the CMS. The eighth chapter finally draws some conclusions.

7.2   Tasks of the Consumer Mediation Service

The Consumer Mediation Service has three tasks as laid down by law.[4] In addition to informing consumers and businesses about their rights and obligations, and in particular about the possibilities of out-of-court settlement of consumer disputes, the CMS also takes receipt of any request for the out-of-court settlement of a consumer dispute. If there is a qualified entity competent to deal with the submitted case, the CMS shall immediately forward the case to that entity.[5] If no other qualified entity is competent, the CMS shall process the case itself.

The three tasks of the Consumer Mediation Service are performed by two distinct services. On the one hand, a first-line point of contact[6] answers questions from consumers and businesses, while it also analyses and assesses the incoming cases and forwards them to the competent service. The mediation service, on the other

---

[1]Law of 4 April 2014 on the insertion of Book XVI, 'Out-of-court settlement of consumer disputes', into the Code of Economic Law—Official Gazette, 12 May 2014.

[2]Directive 2013/11/EU of the European Parliament and of the Council of 21 May 2013 on alternative dispute resolution for consumer disputes and amending Regulation (EC) No. 2006/2004 and Directive 2009/22/EC, OJ L 18 June 2013, 165/63.

[3]All figures and statistics in this contribution were taken from the various annual reports of the Consumer Mediation Service, which can all be found on its website, https://consumerombudsman.be/en.

[4]Art. XVI.6 CEL.

[5]Art. XVI.15, §2 CEL.

[6]Art. XVI.13 CEL.

hand, is responsible for handling all residual consumer disputes between a consumer and a business. The CMS is primarily competent for national complaints, but it is also competent for cross-border complaints if the company concerned is established or active in Belgium.

The first task of the CMS consists of informing consumers and companies about their rights and obligations, in particular about the possibilities of out-of-court settlement of consumer disputes. This task is not only very extensive, but also very important. The Consumer Mediation Service aims to be a one-stop shop for all ADR, for both consumers and businesses. In order to foster and optimally support out-of-court dispute settlement in Belgium, it is necessary to have one single point of contact that can provide all the necessary information. After all, the consumer ADR landscape is rather fragmented. There are mediation and ombudsman services in various sectors, while other sectors have reconciliation commissions, and other sectors still rely on dispute commissions. Moreover, the competences of these different services are not always clearly defined. That is why there is definitely a strong need for a single point of contact guiding both consumers and businesses through the ADR landscape and immediately referring both parties to the competent services.

Not only does the CMS provide insight into the out-of-court dispute settlement landscape, it also provides general information about the rights and obligations of consumers and businesses. This obligation overlaps with the services provided to citizens by the government, in particular the contact centre of the Federal Public Service (FPS) Economy. This contact centre informs consumers and businesses on all topics dealt with by the FPS Economy. The contact centre can therefore also provide information about mediation between consumers or between companies, for example by referring to the existence of the Belmed platform. Belmed is an online platform made available to consumers and businesses by the FPS Economy. Through Belmed, commercial disputes can be settled out of court and online, with the intervention of an independent mediator. Belmed is available for Business to Consumer (B2C), Business to Business (B2B) and Consumer to Consumer (C2C) disputes.

The Consumer Mediation Service specialises in consumer disputes, i.e. any dispute between a consumer and a company relating to the performance of a sales or service contract or to the use of a product.[7] The scope of the contact centre and Belmed is therefore broader than that of the Consumer Mediation Service.

The Consumer Mediation Service does not provide information about the legal proceedings that may follow an out-of-court procedure before a qualified entity.

Any request for out-of-court settlement of a consumer dispute is accepted and thoroughly analysed by the CMS, and then forwarded to the appropriate qualified entity competent in the matter. When a case received by the Consumer Mediation Service falls within the competence of a qualified entity, the CMS is obliged to

---

[7] Art. I.19, 2° CEL.

Table 7.1 Cases received by the CMS

Year	Info	Forwarded	Outside competence	Residual competence	Total
2016	174	2374	389	4342	7279
2017	844	3318	358	5043	9563
2018	1115	2660	353	4890	9018
2019	1330	2422	357	4544	8653

Info: These are the written requests for information handled by the CMS. These do not include requests for information by phone. *Forwarded*: These are the cases forwarded by the CMS to another (qualified) entity. *Outside competence*: These are the cases that the CMS was not able to forward or handle itself within the scope of its residual competence (B2B disputes, C2C disputes, …) *Residual competence*: These are the cases that fell under the residual competence of the CMS

Table 7.2 Cases closed by the CMS

Year	Amicable settlement	Recommendation	Termination	Total
2016	1307	956	342	2605
2017	1103	510	706	2319
2018	1308	788	283	2379
2019	1343	1338	173	2854

Amicable settlement: the number of amicable settlements reached after mediation by the CMS. *Recommendation*: The number of recommendations drawn up when an amicable settlement could not be reached. *Termination*: The number of cases abandoned by the complainant

transmit the case to that service. The CMS does not assess the admissibility of the complaint, as this is left to the service receiving the case.

The CMS may only forward the consumer disputes it receives to qualified entities. These qualified entities are either private entities or entities set up by a public authority, engaging in the out-of-court settlement of consumer disputes. These entities are recognised by the competent authority and comply with all the guarantees of accessibility, expertise, independence, transparency, impartiality, fairness and effectiveness provided for by law.

The CMS itself is also recognised as a qualified entity since 14 July 2015.

The third and final task of the CMS is dealing with all received consumer disputes that cannot be forwarded to any other qualified entity; these are the so-called residual disputes. Key CMS figures are presented in Table 7.1. We will discuss these residual disputes and the procedure followed by the CMS in more detail later on.

Remark: the large difference between the number of received residual cases (Table 7.1) and the total number of cases closed (Table 7.2) is striking. It is important to note that after the competence check, the admissibility is also assessed and the completeness of the case is verified. Unfortunately, many cases do not get past this stage, the majority of them remaining incomplete.

7.3 Procedure

This chapter is dedicated solely to the description of the procedure followed by the Consumer Mediation Service when dealing with residual consumer disputes. When the CMS forwards cases to other qualified entities, it only assesses the competence. The further admissibility assessment is left to the qualified entity receiving the case.

7.3.1 Case Assessment

The processing of an application by the Consumer Mediation Service is free of charge. As soon as the application is complete, the Consumer Mediation Service has 3 weeks to communicate to the complainant whether it can and will handle the case. This is done by means of a reasoned letter.

The CMS has both mandatory and optional grounds for declaring a complaint inadmissible. The Consumer Mediation Service refuses to deal with an application (1) if the complaint is fictitious, offensive or defamatory, (2) if the complaint is submitted anonymously or if the other party has not been or cannot be identified, (3) if the complaint has already been dealt with by a qualified entity, even if it was declared inadmissible there, and finally (4) if the complaint is intended to settle a dispute that is or has been the subject of a legal action.

The optional grounds for refusal allow the CMS some leeway to assess the case. The CMS is lenient in this regard, always aiming to help the consumer in the best possible way. The first optional ground for refusal, which is the consumer's failure to submit the complaint in question in advance to the company concerned, is in line with the objective of the Consumer Mediation Service to promote out-of-court dispute settlement. The aim is to provide every opportunity for dialogue between consumers and businesses. The CMS will only start a procedure if the consumer can demonstrate that they have already actively tried to resolve the dispute personally and amicably with the company. Proof of this may be provided by all legal means. Even if the evidence is very difficult to provide, for example if the consumer claims having repeatedly but fruitlessly contacted the company by phone, the case will not be considered inadmissible.

Secondly, if the complaint in question was lodged with the company in question more than a year ago, the CMS may refuse to handle the case. This is another ground for refusal that is not applied that strictly. Say a consumer had a dispute with a company 5 years ago about work done on a kitchen, and despite various attempts to settle everything amicably, the dispute has not been solved and only now are they faced with amicable recovery by a bailiff. In such a case, the CMS will not automatically disqualify their complaint on the sole grounds that it is dated.

Thirdly and finally, complaints can be refused if handling of the dispute would seriously jeopardise the effective operation of the Consumer Mediation Service. The CMS has never had to invoke this ground for refusal.

The number of incomplete cases has proved to be a weakness of the Consumer Mediation Service. In order for a case to be considered complete, the CMS wants to have at least proof that the consumer has attempted to resolve the dispute personally with the company (see above), information on the identity of the company, as well as a detailed but clear description of the complaint. In some cases, other information will also be required, such as proof of purchase in the case of a warranty issue, or a copy of the contract in the case of a simple contractual dispute. Here, too, the assessment is at the discretion of the CMS, which adopts a broad scope. According to the rules of procedure, the consumer is given 10 working days to complete the case. In practice, however, the case will be reopened if the consumer provides additional information to complete the case after this period. Unfortunately, many cases remain incomplete and are therefore closed without any mediation. The reason for this remains unclear. One might suspect that the complaint has been resolved in the meantime and that the parties did not deem it necessary to inform the CMS about this. Another possibility is that the administrative burden imposed on the consumer is perceived as too heavy, and sometimes the mere act of venting one's frustrations by submitting a complaint removes the desire to take any further action.

7.3.2 Case Handling

Once the application is complete, the processing of the case and its contents begins. Case managers have 90 working days to handle and wrap up each case. In the first stage, the case is forwarded to the company and they are asked to respond. This response is then forwarded to the complainant, who discusses it with the case manager. At present, the cases are only handled by e-mail, letter and/or phone. If deemed necessary, the Consumer Mediation Service may also go on-site to consult the company's books, correspondence, reports and any documents and writings directly related to the subject of the request. The CMS may request any and all necessary explanations and information from the directors, agents and appointees of the company, and may carry out all verifications necessary for the investigation.[8] However, this right has never been invoked. The CMS has also never called upon any experts, although this possibility is also provided for by law.[9]

The case manager listens to both parties and tries to reconcile them. He or she does not initially take a position, but searches for possible avenues towards settling the dispute amicably. If it becomes apparent that the law was not observed in a case, the case manager will clearly communicate this to both parties. If, for example, unfair commercial practices or unlawful terms are established, the Consumer Mediation Service will raise them of its own motion. After all, cases are submitted to the CMS before any specific infringements are identified. Consumers want a solution to

---

[8]Art. XVI.19, §1 CEL.
[9]Art. XVI.19, §2 CEL.

their dispute, but do not always name the dispute as such. The case manager analysing the situation can therefore raise infringements of economic regulations with the company and take a position on the basis of these grounds.

The CMS does not invoke precedents and treats every case with a clean slate. Then again, the Consumer Mediation Service is still too young a service to be able to pursue precedent-based case handling. However, what it can do—and has already done—is combine identical cases. For example, several identical complaints were received in a short period of time from consumers who were unable to redeem a recently purchased gift voucher because the issuing company had allegedly ceased its activities. The cases were handled together, with each case retaining its own case number. The economies of scale for the case manager dealing with these cases is significant, while the consumers do not suffer any disadvantage. Each consumer's case is always handled with due care and consideration. In addition, hopes are that the company will settle more readily if more consumers raise the issue, finding strength in numbers.

For the time being, semi-identical cases are not combined, because each case has its own specificities and each consumer has different wishes in terms of the proposed amicable settlement.

The limitation periods of ordinary law are suspended from the date of receipt of the complete application, and the company must also suspend its collection procedure upon reception of the complete complaint.[10] Although this rule is often a thorn in the side of companies, who see this procedure with the CMS as a delaying tactic on the part of the consumer, this is an essential requirement in order to give the procedure every chance of success. After all, it is impossible to reconcile the two parties on an equal footing if one of the parties has a debt collection claim hanging over them like a sword of Damocles. If the case manager notices that the consumer is in bad faith and the procedure has no chance of success, the case will be closed soon enough anyway. On the other hand, a company that constantly keeps sending payment reminders during an ongoing procedure is unlikely to be lauded in a possible recommendation made at a later date by the case manager.

The CMS notifies the parties of the outcome of the dispute settlement within a period of 90 calendar days. The average processing time for a case in 2019 was 64 days. This period starts as soon as the case is declared admissible and ends when the case is closed. There are three ways a procedure with the Consumer Mediation Service can be concluded. The best-case scenario is when an amicable settlement can be reached between the consumer and the company. The case manager informs both parties of this result once more in writing, and closes the case. The CMS cannot verify whether this amicable settlement is actually honoured by the parties. However, since the CMS is only rarely contacted in this respect, it is assumed that the parties fully adhere to the agreed settlement.

If no amicable settlement is reached, the CMS can close the case with a recommendation. Although this is not obligatory, it is standard practice to do so, for

---

[10] Art. XVI.18 CEL.

various reasons. A recommendation reflects the opinion of the CMS with regard to a case in which it has invested significant time and energy. Hopes are that both parties will find this a useful document to refer to later. After all, nothing prevents either party from going to court with the CMS's recommendation in hand. This recommendation can then prove to be a useful instrument in court.

If the company concerned does not follow the recommendation, it is obliged by law to inform the CMS and the complainant of its reasoned position within a period of thirty calendar days. This, too, is a sore spot. All too often, companies fail to provide this response. That is why the legislator decided in 2017[11] to amend Book XV CEL, 'Law Enforcement', so that violations of this rule by the company can be punished with a fine of 26 to 10,000 euros. If the company is in bad faith, this fine can even be increased to 25,000 euros.[12] It should be emphasised, however, that a company can never be obliged to accept the solution proposed by the Consumer Mediation Service.

Finally, the complainant can terminate the procedure at any time. Regrettably, this happens all too frequently, and at an increasing rate. As with the great many complaints that are never completed, this is a big thorn in the side of the Consumer Mediation Service as the service provider it is and wishes to be. Very often, no reason is given for dropping the complaint. Sometimes the complaint is presumed and suspected to have been dropped, i.e. in the absence of any further communication from the complainant.

7.4   Types of Disputes

Tables 7.3 and 7.4 show the ten most common sectors and the ten most common categories of cases received by the CMS in the calendar year 2019.

As indicated above, the Consumer Mediation Service processes residual disputes, i.e. those consumer disputes that do not fall within the competence of another qualified entity. As more sectoral and qualified entities are established and recognised, the types of disputes (frequently) treated by the CMS also change. For example, in 2015 and 2016 there was a peak in disputes relating to the (legal) warranty period. Over the course of 2017, several companies that were at the origin of a very large number of cases in this category set up their own mediation services,[13] resulting in an immediate drop in the number of cases handled by the CMS in the 'warranty complaints' category.

Another striking aspect is that the top ten sectors also include sectors that have their own out-of-court dispute resolution body. This is due to the fact that these

---

[11]Law of 18 April on various provisions relating to the economy, Official Gazette 24 April 2017.

[12]Art. XV.125, §§1 and 2 CEL.

[13]The Ombudsman for retail, see https://www.ombudsmanforretail.be/en.

Table 7.3 Top ten sectors in 2019

Position	Sector[a]	Cases
1	Services relating to home maintenance and repairs	742
2	Furniture and upholstery	406
3	ICT goods (information and communication technology)	283
4	Goods relating to home maintenance and repairs	261
5	Airlines	161
6	Clothing and footwear	153
7	Large household appliances	182
8	Electronics	154
9	Services related to sports and hobbies	166
10	Cosmetics	110

[a]The breakdown by sector and by category used by the CMS follows the system recommended by the European Commission for classifying consumer complaints and enquiries (Commission Recommendation of 12 May 2010 on the use of a harmonised methodology for classifying and reporting consumer complaints and enquiries—2010/304/EU)

Table 7.4 Top ten categories in 2019

Position	Category	Cases
1	Not delivered/not granted	7747
2	Legal warranty not granted	534
3	Defect, damage caused	528
4	Unjustified invoice	320
5	Does not meet order specifications	274
6	Incorrect invoice	263
7	Partly delivered / partly granted	207
8	Dissolution of the contract	174
9	Payments (e.g. Advances and deadlines)	161
10	Right to reject/cooling off period	124

different qualified entities together do not cover their entire sector, as they are only competent for a limited number of complaints in their sector.

For example, the Reconciliation Committee for Construction only deals with technical construction disputes, while legal or contractual construction disputes fall outside its competence. Furthermore, the Reconciliation Committee only intervenes when both parties accept its competence and upon payment of €200.

The Automoto Reconciliation Committee only intervenes when the seller acknowledges the competence of the Reconciliation Committee in its general terms and conditions, after payment of €80 per party, and only with regard to the sale of (new) cars and warranty disputes. Disputes regarding maintenance and repair fall outside its competence.

The Travel Dispute Committee is competent for disputes with a travel agent and/or travel organiser concerning the execution of a trip. However, this only concerns disputes with travel agents/organisers who adhere to the general travel conditions of the Travel Dispute Committee.

So the Automoto Reconciliation Committee cannot automatically be called upon to settle a dispute with just any garage, nor can the Reconciliation Committee for Construction help with a dispute with just any contractor. And finally, travellers cannot always turn to the Travel Dispute Committee.

7.5 Way of Working and Perception

The Consumer Mediation Service handles residual consumer disputes. The idea is that any national or cross-border consumer dispute with a company established or operating in Belgium should be handled by a qualified entity—preferably a sector-specific entity rather than the Consumer Mediation Service. The reasons for this are obvious. A qualified entity competent to deal with consumer disputes from one particular sector will be able to achieve a high degree of specialisation. The designated case manager will have extensive knowledge and will be familiar with all the details of the sector.

Conversely, the company will also be familiar with its sectoral mediation service. Not only will the company be aware of its existence and operation, but it is also likely to have a positive view of and attitude towards this mediation service. Several mediation services even impose mandatory cooperation of the company in the procedure. Since procedures with mediation services are typically based on constructive cooperation and voluntary participation, the importance of the perception of the company should not be underestimated.

Often there is no constructive cooperation with the Consumer Mediation Service, nor can it rely on extensive and technical knowledge in every area.

First of all, the perception that exists among both consumers and businesses is not always the right one. Consumers expect the Consumer Mediation Service to act as their advocate and are surprised when it cannot reach an amicable settlement, when the proposed settlement is not what they had in mind, or when the CMS ends up making a recommendation that is not in their favour. On the other hand, companies also often have a skewed perception of the position of the Consumer Mediation Service, leading them to adopt a less than constructive attitude. Companies tend to assume that the Consumer Mediation Service is acting to protect and defend the consumer at every turn.

Staff members of the Consumer Mediation Service are required by law[14] to have sufficient knowledge with regard to the settlement of consumer disputes. This obligation does not imply that each staff member must be familiar with the subject matter of every case they are assigned. That would be impossible. Nevertheless, case managers must regularly update themselves on the applicable law and on their

---

[14]Art. XVI.23, §1 CEL.

dispute resolution skills.[15] The residual competence of the Consumer Mediation Service means that the subjects to be dealt with are very diverse.

However, when both parties cooperate constructively in the proceedings, thorough knowledge of the subject matter is not always required in order to reach an amicable settlement. It is also inherent to the modus operandi of the Consumer Mediation Service that the parties themselves enter into a dialogue, albeit through a neutral third party. By having the parties listen to each other's points of view, formulate positions and suggest solutions, the CMS fosters conciliation. The search for an amicable settlement is therefore an attempt to find a solution to a problem that will be supported and honoured by both parties. The Consumer Mediation Service aims for a win-win situation.

7.6 Operation

The Consumer Mediation Service holds a unique position in the Belgian ADR landscape. On the one hand, it acts as a true ombudsman's service that tries to resolve individual consumer disputes and makes recommendations to policymakers via its annual report[16] and, on the other hand, it acts as a one-stop shop for consumers who want to settle their disputes out of court.

7.6.1 Management Committee

The Consumer Mediation Service has a special structure, as it is not headed by one ombudsman, but rather by a management committee comprising six sectoral mediation services. This Management Committee[17] is responsible for the management and representation of the CMS and consists of 10 members:

- two members of the Mediation Service for Telecommunications
- two members of the Mediation Service for the Postal Sector
- two members of the Mediation Service for Energy
- two members of the Mediation Service for Rail Passengers
- the ombudsman of the Mediation Service for Financial Services
- the ombudsman of the Mediation Service for Insurances

---

[15] Art. 4, Royal Decree of 16 February 2015 clarifying the conditions to be met by the qualified entity referred to in Book XVI of the Code of Economic Law, Belgian Official Gazette, 25 February 2015.

[16] Art. XVI.7 CEL.

[17] See Art. XVI.8 et seq CEL.

The Minister in charge of the Economy and the Minister in charge of the Budget each appoint a representative to sit on the Management Committee in an advisory capacity for all agenda items not relating to applications for out-of-court settlement of a consumer dispute.[18]

Every 2 years, the Management Committee appoints among its members a chairperson and a vice-chairperson (one Dutch-speaking and one French-speaking). The rules of procedure are submitted to the Minister for approval.[19]

The Management Committee is authorised to carry out all acts of administration and disposal necessary to run the Consumer Mediation Service, thereby fulfilling its tasks as set out in Article XVI.6 of the CEL. The acts of administration include the annual approval of the policy plan, drawing up the budget and monitoring its implementation, drawing up the annual accounts of income and expenditure, and drawing up the personnel plan.

7.6.2 Funding

The Consumer Mediation Service is funded by means of various contributions and subsidies.[20] First, there is a subsidy charged to the general spending budget; second are the contributions of the companies involved in the out-of-court settlement of consumer disputes that are not undeniably unfounded; and third are the mediation contributions levied to finance the mediation services that sit on the Management Committee.

The initially planned federal contribution of €500,000 was reduced to €364,000 in 2016 and €354,000 in 2017. A contribution of €354,000 is also planned for 2018.

The level of contributions was recently determined in the Royal Decree regulating the funding of the Consumer Mediation Service.[21] The companies' contribution is established at:

- 100 euros from the fifth processed request for out-of-court settlement of a consumer dispute;
- 200 euros from the twentieth processed request for out-of-court settlement of a consumer dispute.

The processed requests to be considered are those closed by the CMS in a given calendar year and resulting in an amicable settlement between the parties or a recommendation to the company concerned. The company shall pay the claimed

---

[18]Both ministers did so, and in July 2017 they each appointed a representative to the Management Committee.

[19]This refers to the Minister responsible for the Economy, cf. Art. I.1, 3° CEL.

[20]Art. XVI.11, §1 CEL.

[21]Royal Decree of 1 March 2018 regulating the funding of the Consumer Mediation Service, Official Gazette, 8 March 2018.

amount within a period of 30 days after receipt of the claim. If a company fails to make payment within this period, the Consumer Mediation Service is entitled to levy a surcharge to compensate for the additional costs incurred as a result of the late payment. The Consumer Mediation Service is also entitled to charge late-payment interests.

The contributions of the mediation services referred to in Article XVI.11,3° CEL are laid down in Chapter II of the Royal Decree. These amounts include a share of the operating costs of the Consumer Mediation Service, as well as any recoveries of costs paid or advanced by the Consumer Mediation Service on their behalf. This takes into account the savings and synergy benefits resulting from shared facilities and cooperation. Indeed, both the Consumer Mediation Service and most of the services that are members of its Management Committee have their offices in the North Gate building in Brussels.[22]

The funding is used for the day-to-day operation of the service. The use of the Consumer Mediation Service by consumers is always free of charge.[23]

7.6.3   Annual Report and Recommendations

The Consumer Mediation Service draws up an annual report on the performance of its tasks.[24] The minimum information that this annual report must contain is listed in the Royal Decree of 2015 clarifying the conditions to be met by qualified entities,[25] and it must also be made available to the public.

For instance, the CMS must mention in its annual report any systematic or significant problems that occur frequently and that lead to disputes between consumers and companies. Such information may be accompanied by recommendations on how to avoid or resolve such problems in the future. And this is precisely what the Consumer Mediation Service does. Previous annual reports have included detailed discussions of warranty problems, disputes with regard to unjustified invoices, furniture disputes and problems with airlines. The recommendations are always illustrated with a number of common examples of cases processed and closed throughout the year.

The Consumer Mediation Service is also frequently asked to provide statistics in response to parliamentary questions and maintains close contact with the FPS Economy. The FPS Economy acts as a channel through which cases are funnelled

---

[22] At the time of writing, only the Insurance Mediation Service had its offices elsewhere.

[23] Art. XVI.21 CEL.

[24] Art. XVI.7 CEL.

[25] Art. 8, §1.

to the CMS,[26] but conversely the CMS also reports blatant and/or recurrent breaches of economic regulations to the General Directorate of the Economic Inspection. The CMS intervenes in individual disputes, but also tries to tackle the source of the problems.

When a dispute involves a flagrant violation of consumer law, or when several identical consumer disputes reach the CMS in a short period of time, or whenever it is deemed appropriate, the CMS will transfer the case(s) to the Economic Inspection. The latter will examine the cases submitted to it as it sees fit. There is no further communication about cases or their contents.

In 2017, for example, the Consumer Mediation Service received quite a few complaints in a short space of time about an online appliance vendor who consistently did not deliver the goods consumers had paid for. The website looked impeccable, the payment page was in accordance with the law, and nothing suspicious was found in the Crossroads Bank for Enterprises. However, the company remained deaf to any correspondence from the CMS and from consumers. In light of this, the CMS decided to submit a case to the Economic Inspection. The website was then taken offline. Although the intervention of the Economic Inspection had no direct influence on pending cases at the CMS, the cause of the problem was addressed. The CMS was compelled to close the cases against the appliance vendor with a recommendation.

7.7 Some Observations

7.7.1 Perception of the CMS

ADR in Belgium already has a (fairly) long and positive track record. The major and most important economic sectors[27] in the consumer landscape can rightly boast that they provide a way to resolve disputes out of court, which in many cases also often leads to an amicable settlement that is accepted by both parties. ADR is useful and necessary. However, the parties' perception of this instrument is crucial. As long as the aim of both parties is to resolve a dispute, then they can achieve a lot. But if either party is suspicious, sceptical or indifferent to the procedure and the result to be achieved, nothing will be gained.

The CMS strives to adjust this perception on a daily basis, in contrast to other qualified entities, in particular the other mediation services. Either these sector-specific entities are competent for all companies that are active in the sector, or they bring together companies that are setting up or have set up an out-of-court

---

[26]The Consumer Mediation Service is a partner of the Report (https://meldpunt.belgie.be), through which consumers can indicate that a copy will also be sent to the Consumer Mediation Service when sending their report.

[27]For example: telecommunications, energy, insurances, postal services, the financial sector.

Table 7.5 Comparing residual and sectoral mediation services

Residual Mediation Service	Sectoral Mediation Service
No fixed sector	All companies in the sector are affiliated
Enterprise has not included engagement and is probably not familiar with ADR	The company has a duty or intention to cooperate in the procedure
Companies do not know the residual ombudsman	Companies have a direct contact point for the ombudsman service
General knowledge of almost all regulations	Extensive specialization

dispute resolution entity. It is clear that an economic sector can benefit from supporting and actively cooperating with ADR. In doing so, the sector shows that it cares about customer satisfaction and the level of service offered, and that it is prepared to settle any disputes in an amicable manner. Often, a sector federation will take the initiative to set up an out-of-court dispute resolution entity, but although the initiative comes from the (private) market, every qualified entity must comply with all the guarantees of accessibility, expertise, independence, transparency, impartiality, fairness and effectiveness provided for by law.

In any event, the companies falling within the competence of a qualified entity can be said to have a positive perception of ADR and a positive attitude towards the way of working of 'their' qualified entity. Not only do they fall within its competence, but they also often have employees who are in charge of communicating with the qualified entity. This obviously ensures that the procedures and working methods are known and that things can move quickly.

The chance of a positive outcome to the dispute is therefore much greater from the outset than when a procedure has to be put in motion with a company that has perhaps never heard of alternative dispute resolution and does not see the point of it, let alone allocate time to it.

The CMS is the final element of the out-of-court dispute resolution system in Belgium. Any consumer dispute that cannot be dealt with by another qualified entity falls within its competence. This almost automatically entails that all companies that have not (yet) understood the usefulness and necessity of ADR fall under the competence of the CMS. Starting a procedure with the CMS therefore often involves explaining what it is, what it does and why ADR is useful, which takes up a lot of time. And time, especially in the economy, is a precious commodity. So the whole ADR narrative often falls on deaf ears. Table 7.5 compares residual and sectoral mediation services.

And it is not just the companies' perception that is skewed. Consumers, too, often have misconceptions about the CMS. The Consumer Mediation Service has the task of guiding consumers through the Belgian ADR landscape and informing them of their rights and obligations. All too often, consumers presume that the CMS is there to help them resolve a consumer dispute to their advantage, achieving the result they want. They see the CMS as their first-line advisor and their advocate. They are wrong on both accounts. First of all, the CMS provides information, not advice (see below); and second, the CMS—and by extension any qualified entity—is not the defender of consumer interests, but rather an impartial third party. Once this sinks in, consumers are often disappointed and frustrated. This perception of the CMS being on the consumers' side is also often held by companies. It is therefore very important to provide clear information to both parties from the get-go, so that they know exactly what the CMS is, before any amicable settlement of the dispute can be reached.

Not only what it is, but also what it does, and how, must be made clear before any procedure is put in motion. The CMS is a mediation service that tries to reconcile the parties. If it fails to do so, it may make a non-enforceable recommendation. Participation in the procedure is not compulsory and neither recommendations nor amicable settlements are enforceable by the CMS. This, too, often leads to frustration among consumers, who ultimately can only turn to the courts and tribunals.

7.7.2 Admissibility of the Procedure

The CMS is competent for consumer disputes between a consumer and a company established in Belgium. The CMS is therefore only competent for B2C disputes and only opens consumer cases against a (residual) company. In doing so, in its capacity as a mediation service, the CMS tries to remedy the inequality between the economically weaker (consumer) and the economically stronger party (company). However, the CMS also questions whether this comparison is always valid. After all, not every company is in a strong position and not every consumer is in a weaker position economically. Empowered and skilled consumers often find their way to out-of-court dispute resolution faster than small SMEs. Furthermore, the latter are also in an economically weak position compared to multinationals. Not only will such SMEs not be able to call upon the CMS, they are also not covered by any consumer protection measure.

A B2C dispute must meet a number of conditions in order to be admissible. The grounds for refusal are sometimes absolute, sometimes optional. These do not pose any significant problems in and of themselves. The completeness of a case, however, is another matter. From the day the case is received, the CMS has a legal period of 21 days to declare the case complete. As soon as the case is complete, the 90-day period starts. All too often, cases remain incomplete.

By way of illustration: in 2018, the CMS received 4,890 residual cases, but 2,352 of these remained inadmissible. The main reason for the inadmissibility of the cases was the fact that they were not completed. 1938 cases remained incomplete in 2018.

The high approachability of the Consumer Mediation Service also appears to have its drawbacks.

7.7.3 Impartiality

The Consumer Mediation Service must always be mindful of the way it is perceived by the parties. It is therefore imperative that its impartiality is never compromised. There is only a narrow divide with the CMS's primary task of informing consumers and companies about their mutual rights and obligations and, in particular, about the existing procedures for the out-of-court settlement of consumer disputes.

Consumers' requests for information are often vague, broad and general. More than anything, consumers seek advice and want to know 'what they should do'. They usually do not expect to get bone-dry information about applicable regulations or procedures. They are looking for advice and assistance in the face of a problem that needs solving. Under no circumstances, however, can the CMS offer a subjective assessment of the facts or provide biased legal advice before a case has been opened, both parties have been heard and an amicable settlement has been actively sought. The provision of advice would make further impartial mediation impossible.

7.7.4 Recommendations

The CMS does not give prior advice to either party. During the procedure, and certainly afterwards, it can give an opinion about the facts, also by pointing out the legislation in force that is to be respected. The CMS attaches great importance to the non-binding recommendations it issues. On the one hand, these recommendations could prove useful in a court of law if the parties decide to continue their dispute before the courts, but on the other hand, they can also provide the parties with more insight into consumer law. The recommendations of the Consumer Mediation Service therefore certainly deserve both parties' full attention.

Recommendations to consumers and companies are also given in the CMS's annual report. On the basis of the cases dealt with throughout the year, the CMS compiles a list of the most common issues and the most remarkable problem cases. Using examples, the CMS then issues recommendations to both consumers and companies.

Finally, the CMS also submits reports to the competent supervisory authority, often with the request to further investigate certain practices of a company or to take action against it. The CMS invariably does this on the basis of a number of similar cases against the same company.

7.8 Conclusion

The Consumer Mediation Service was established to bring order in a rather fragmented ADR landscape. Not only does it guide consumers and businesses through the various ADR mechanisms and point them towards the competent service, it also deals with cases that do not fall within the competence of any other qualified entity. As a mediation service for residual consumer disputes, it has also been recognised by the FPS Economy as a qualified entity.

In its relatively short lifespan so far, the Consumer Mediation Service has experienced some growing pains. However, its importance and usefulness cannot be underestimated. In 2019, more than 8,600 cases were received and either answered, forwarded or initiated as a residual consumer dispute. The creation of new qualified entities, rather than detract from the function of the CMS, has actually even confirmed its relevance.

It is clear that the Consumer Mediation Service is the final element of the out-of-court dispute resolution system in Belgium. As a residual mediation service, however, the CMS must strive for a correct and clear perception of its operation and existence. It is important to inform both consumers and companies clearly in advance about the purpose and the way of working of the CMS. Results can only be achieved when both parties want to cooperate constructively in the out-of-court settlement of disputes.

However, the CMS does more than just forward cases and mediate in residual disputes. It also informs consumers and companies about their rights and obligations. Between this legal task of information provision and the act of giving advice there is only a narrow divide. The latter is something that the CMS, as a qualified entity, must never do, certainly not prior to the opening of a case. If an amicable settlement cannot be reached in a case, the CMS can formulate a non-binding recommendation. In this recommendation, the CMS gives an opinion on the case and it can also provide advice in order to reach a solution to the dispute. The Consumer Mediation Service also provides advice, recommendations and counsel in its annual report, as well as in interim reports to the authorities.

Combining a one-stop shop for consumers and companies looking for information, in particular on out-of-court dispute resolution, with a residual mediation service has been a trying endeavour. Although the Consumer Mediation Service is still finding its place, there is no denying its relevance.

Reference

Voet S (2018) CDR in België. Die Keure, Brugge

Chapter 8
How to Avoid a Trial: In Praise of ADR and Ombudsmen

Frédérique Feriaud and Pierre-Laurent Holleville

Abstract Under European rules, it is now mandatory for Member States to provide citizens with easy access to ADR schemes, the aim of which is to make dispute settlement more efficient than the "traditional" legal system.

However, critics have pointed out that the generalization of ADR mechanisms could result in low quality solutions, crafted "behind closed doors", away from public scrutiny. Through careful analysis, this article demonstrates that ADR mechanisms have features that prevent those fears from materializing. However, built-in procedural safeguards are not sufficient; ADR bodies must be closely monitored as well, so as to ensure that their procedural rules and financing allow no bias.

The article also makes the case for setting confidentiality aside, if a dispute cannot be settled properly through ADR, and only if public interest is at stake. It also provides insights taken from the ADR experience in France, as well as from the French Energy Ombudsman's day-by-day handling of cases.

8.1 Introduction

In the past few years, countries across Europe have taken several measures to favour alternative methods for dispute settlement. Among these, a key driving force has been the transposition of the 2013 Directive on alternative dispute resolution (ADR), which has made it mandatory for Member States to provide citizens with easy access to ADR schemes.[1]

Each country has its own preferred scheme, with differences that can sometimes be quite significant. However, these differences should not cloud the fact that they

---

[1]Directive 2013/11/EU of the European Parliament and of the Council of 21 May 2013 on alternative dispute resolution for consumer disputes and amending Regulation (EC) No 2006/2004 and Directive 2009/22/EC (Directive on consumer ADR); for details on the transposition, see Biard and Hodges (2019).

F. Feriaud (✉) · P.-L. Holleville
French Energy Ombudsman (Médiateur national de l'énergie), Paris, France
e-mail: frederique.feriaud@energie-mediateur.fr; pierre-laurent.holleville@energie-mediateur.fr

© The Author(s), under exclusive license to Springer Nature Switzerland AG 2021   149
X. Kramer et al. (eds.), *New Pathways to Civil Justice in Europe*,
https://doi.org/10.1007/978-3-030-66637-8_8

have a common goal: settling disputes better and faster than the "*traditional*" legal system.

Critics have pointed out that these ADR schemes can have flaws. When a case is brought to justice, a trial is held in a courtroom open to the public, and a final, binding decision is issued for the parties; what's more, case law is made available to citizens. There are usually no such things when it comes to ADR schemes. Hence the fear that ADR mechanisms turn out to be schemes where low quality and unfair solutions are crafted, "*behind closed doors*", away from public scrutiny.

Though these fears are understandable, careful analysis reveals that ADR mechanisms have features that prevent those fears from materializing. To illustrate this point, this article will provide insights taken from the ADR experience in France, as well as from the French Energy Ombudsman's day-by-day handling of cases. But to begin, a few words should be said on the Ombudsman and its background.

The French Energy Ombudsman predates European consumer mediation rules: it was created by the law n°2006-1537 of December 7th 2006 relative to the energy sector. As an "*independent public authority*", the Ombudsman is "*protected*" from outside influences.[2] It is also worth knowing that its financing is carried out by the State, which ensures that there is no bias in the Ombudsman's decisions, called "*recommendations*".

The Ombudsman carries out its mediation mission to solve consumer disputes, as well as disputes involving small businesses. However, it should be noted that the Ombudsman has another legal mission: informing consumers about their rights, through the "Energie-Info" scheme.[3]

Some question the benefits of ADR schemes: as they are conducted in private, there are fears that the solutions agreed upon may be detrimental to consumers, who may be "*encouraged*" to accept an unfair solution. This article's aim is to demonstrate that ADR can produce balanced decisions. In order to do so, one must first examine why consumers use ADR in the first place.

8.2 ADR Is an Efficient Option for Consumers

When consumers face a dispute, they often do not wish to go to court. A standard procedure lasts about a year in France (and even longer if the case is appealed), and can be very costly (legal counsel is often mandatory)—especially when compared to the often modest amount at stake in most everyday disputes.

---

[2]It falls within the scope of a 2017 law governing independent administrative authorities and independent public authorities (loi n°2017-55 du 20 janvier 2017 portant statut général des autorités administratives indépendantes et des autorités publiques indépendantes).

[3]Energie-info, the Ombudsman's information service consists of: the energie-info.fr website, which includes a price comparison tool; a call center that can be reached through a toll-free number (+33 0 800 112 212) with agents answering the simpler questions, and a second-level expert center that processes complex phone and written requests.

By comparison, an ADR proceeding is a much simpler and much faster process. A case is often dealt with in a few weeks; by law, the outcome of the procedure is to be made available in a maximum of 90 days, though proceedings can last longer when a case is complicated.

In addition, an ombudsman is not a passive figure, but rather one that tries to build solutions with the parties themselves, proactively. The main goal is to find an amicable solution, which is something the French Energy Ombudsman's services now manage to do in 60% of cases. Part of the reason for this achievement could be that it is a rule to contact consumers by phone at least once, so as to explain matters in a simple way.[4]

As far as the cost is concerned, consumer mediation rules provide that a mediation process must be either free, or accessible for a low fee. By law, the mediation process provided by the French Energy Ombudsman is free: as a result, disputes are settled even where very small amounts are at stake, which would never happen before a court of law.

To make it even simpler for consumers, the Energy Ombudsman has developed an online dispute resolution platform called SOLLEN. It allows consumers to seek assistance from the Ombudsman online, and to communicate with both the institution and the energy companies (suppliers, distribution system operators) within a secure confidential environment. It has now been fully implemented and has made the mediation experience easier for online users.[5] People who do not wish to use this online tool have no obligation to do so.

8.2.1 A Consequence of All This Is That ADR Can Be a Better Option Than the Court System, Especially for Vulnerable Consumers

It is true that Governments also push for ADR because it drives cases away from the justice system. In France, a recent law has tried to increase ADR culture by strongly encouraging parties with small claims to go through an ADR process before they take the case to court.[6] Lawmakers did not make ADR mandatory, because any legislation that would bar citizens from going to court would breach article 6 of the European convention on human rights, which provides that *"everyone is entitled to a*

---

[4]The results of the last edition of the Ombudsman's annual satisfaction survey show the benefits of resorting to the Ombudsman, who was the decisive actor in finding a solution to their problem for 67% of people surveyed. 80% of consumers state they are satisfied with the Ombudsman's intervention and 78% think it was helpful in finding a solution adapted to their dispute or allowed them to better understand it.

[5]77% of respondents think that the tool facilitated the resolution of their dispute, compared to 73% the previous year.

[6]Loi n°2019-222 du 23 mars 2019 de programmation 2018-2022 et de réforme pour la justice.

fair and public hearing within a reasonable time by an independent and impartial tribunal established by law".[7]

One should also keep in mind that, under European and national law, the ADR process comes with built-in procedural safeguards.

8.3 The Procedural Safeguards of ADR

In our view, the most important consumer ADR rules are the ones that state that ADR is not mandatory and that access to the court system remains possible.

Not only is a consumer never forced to go through ADR, but he or she can decide to take the case to court: this can take place when a consumer is not satisfied with the solution, or indeed at any given moment throughout the ADR process. Note that informing consumers that they are free to go to court is a legal obligation under the 2013 Directive.

Under European law, these two main procedural safeguards help ensure that ADR is not *"private justice"*. This is especially true when one considers that the recommendations of an Ombudsman are generally not binding, as is the case with those of the French Energy Ombudsman.

Even though these safeguards exist, there are still fears surrounding the so-called *"secrecy"* of the ADR process. In this regard, close examination reveals that ADR is built upon the principle of confidentiality, rather than secrecy.

8.4 ADR Relies on Confidentiality, Not Secrecy

It is technically correct, but somewhat provocative, to state that ADR proceedings take place *"behind closed doors"*—as opposed to a trial held in an open courtroom. In our view, it is more accurate to say that ADR schemes are confidential. By ensuring that discussions remain confidential, the law enables parties to speak freely, which is in their best interest.

Consequently, confidentiality itself is not a threat to justice for consumers. However, having confidential proceedings does carry some risks, the main one being the risk of a parallel, *"second-rate"*, justice system for people who cannot afford the court system. This risk is enhanced when companies set up their own ADR scheme, with the possibility of biased solutions. This is why ADR bodies must be closely monitored, to ensure that their procedural rules and financing allow no bias.

---

[7]Convention for the Protection of Human Rights and Fundamental Freedoms (European Convention on Human Rights, as amended) (ECHR), art 6.

8.5 ADR Schemes Must Be Monitored

In France, compliance with consumer ADR rules is monitored by a commission called the *"Commission for the Evaluation and Monitoring of Consumption Mediation"*, or CECMC.[8] Including senior magistrates, expert figures, representatives from consumer associations and professional federations, the CECMC issues a certification to the bodies that meet the required standards of quality. The French Energy Ombudsman was one of the first institutions to be certified in January 2016.

In addition to the CECMC, the French Energy Ombudsman is also controlled by other entities: since it is funded by the State budget, it can be audited by the *"Cour des comptes"* (Court of auditors); it is also controlled by Parliament.[9]

All of this helps build consumer trust in ADR. Other mechanisms have a similar effect, such as self-imposed guidelines and procedures; the Ombudsman's ethics charter for instance specifies that collaborators must remain impartial, maintain confidentiality, autonomy and exemplariness.[10]

Nevertheless, accountability and close monitoring are not always sufficient. In some cases, it is the French Energy Ombudsman's view that the confidentiality of the proceedings must be set aside to reveal what is taking place *"behind closed doors"*.

8.6 When Public Interest Supersedes Confidentiality

When a case is settled, a written recommendation is sent to the parties—but it is not published. However, when a case is significant and reveals a problem that is detrimental to a potentially great number of consumers, then the French Energy Ombudsman's decision is published after anonymization. As a result, there is "case law" from the French Energy Ombudsman.

In addition, when the Ombudsman thinks it is necessary to report poor practices, he does so *via* press releases or interviews in the media. If necessary, companies are *"named & shamed"*, as the Ombudsman has done repeatedly in the past few years for companies who use aggressive selling practices (doorstep selling for instance). All this information is available through the website and social media, as well as in newsletters and annual reports.

This sheds light on the problems, and often helps to fix them; to use a famous quote, *"sunlight is the best disinfectant"*.

However, should these actions prove insufficient, the Ombudsman still has the possibility to ask Parliament to legislate on a difficult issue. This has already been

---

[8]The Act of 20th August 2015, which transposed the European Directive of 21 May 2013 relative to the extrajudicial settlement of disputes, stipulates that the activity of certified ombudsmen shall be subject every two years to a review by the CECMC.

[9]The French Energy Ombudsman submits its annual report to Parliament, who votes the budget.

[10]They are available either on the Ombudsman's website or upon request.

done successfully in the past, for the issue of back-billing for instance. Since energy companies could not solve the problem themselves, the Ombudsman asked Parliament to change the rules; by law, back-billing is now limited to 14 months of consumption.

It is generally acknowledged that in-house ADR entities cannot do any of these things: in the energy sector, they have proved consistently reluctant to encourage their parent company to change its ways, and have often had much more lenient compensation rules than those of the Energy Ombudsman.

8.7 Conclusion

As this chapter has tried to make clear, ADR is not exactly "*justice behind closed doors*": under European law, it is a confidential proceeding that comes with several procedural safeguards and is subject to close scrutiny. What's more, the French Energy Ombudsman holds the view that confidentiality must be set aside when public interest is at stake.

However, if there is no reason to fear the disappearing of the "*traditional*" justice system, one must remain cautious, especially with the development of databased predictive software, and the possible rise of algorithm-based dispute settlement. With this caveat in mind, ADR remains the best way to avoid a trial.

Reference

Biard A, Hodges C (2019) Médiation de la consommation: un bilan, des défis, des pistes de réflexion pour l'avenir. Contrats Concurrence Consommation 2

Chapter 9
Analysis–Defiances–Reflections in Germany

Stefan Weiser and Felix Braun

Abstract The German ADR landscape is and has always been diverse and provides ADR entities with a long history as well as new faces. The year 2016 marked a transformation point when the ADR directive was implemented into a functioning yet incomplete ADR system. Then and also along with the recent change in legislation mainly concerning residual ADR entities, the policy maker was faced with the task to convert reports, data and developments of a few years into a new foundation of the country's residual ADR structure. We will take a close look on this landscape, its issues and changes. Along this way, we identify minor and major particularities in Germany and put them into relation to a broader, European context. In our conclusion and outlook, we discuss the rather paradox observation of (residual) ADR as a promising tool of conflict resolution yet not making the quick start the public expected.

9.1 Introduction

The Consumer Dispute Resolution Act (*Verbraucherstreitbeilegungsgesetz—* VSBG[1]) entered into force 1 April 2016 and implemented the Alternative Dispute Resolution (ADR) Directive 2013/11/EU in Germany.[2] The directive's main objective is to contribute towards improving the enforcement of consumer rights by ensuring full sectoral and geographical ADR coverage.[3] Thus, ADR has joined the symphony of consumer law enforcement instruments as a permanent member and

---

[1]Some sections of the VSBG are amended as we draft these lines, hence when citing the VSBG we are using the act's amended version unless stated otherwise; an English translation (of the 2016 version) can be found here http://www.gesetze-im-internet.de/englisch_vsbg/englisch_vsbg.html.

[2]Directive 2013/11/EU of the European Parliament and of the Council of 21 May 2013 on alternative dispute resolution for consumer disputes, henceforth called ADR Directive.

[3]Roder et al. (2017), § 1, margin no. 1.

S. Weiser (✉) · F. Braun
Zentrum für Schlichtung e.V., Kehl am Rhein, Germany
e-mail: braun@verbraucher-schlichter.de

© The Author(s), under exclusive license to Springer Nature Switzerland AG 2021   155
X. Kramer et al. (eds.), *New Pathways to Civil Justice in Europe*,
https://doi.org/10.1007/978-3-030-66637-8_9

for almost all types of consumer contracts—instead of only for certain sector-specific disputes like in the past.[4]

The pre-2016 German ADR landscape provided services for several consumer-to-business (C2B) disputes. By 2011, there were a vast number of (regional and federal) entities, each differing in terms of their characteristics, size and quality.[5] Some of the currently noteworthy larger and sector-specific entities include: *söp_Schlichtungsstelle für den Öffentlichen Personenverkehr e.V.* (founded in 2009) for transport disputes, the *Schlichtungsstelle Energie e.V.* (founded in 2011) for disputes regarding electricity and gas, and the *Versicherungsombudsmann e.V.* (founded in 2001) for disputes arising from insurance contracts. In these and other sectors, the legal framework had pushed or even obliged traders to establish ADR entities at the turn of the millennium or later.[6] However, ADR in Germany has a relatively short history and its landscape is still a rather recent development, especially when compared to countries such as the Netherlands or Sweden.[7]

The gaps between these long years of ADR experience in several sectors were to be filled in 2016 by an *Allgemeine Verbraucherschlichtungsstelle* (General Consumer Concilliation Entity, cf § 43(1) VSBG). This mission was taken up by the *Allgemeine Verbraucherschlichtungsstelle*, hosted by the *Zentrum für Schlichtung e. V.*[8] The Federal Ministry of Justice and for Consumer Protection (*Bundesministerium der Justiz und für Verbraucherschutz*) funded this ADR entity up to the end of 2019 to guarantee full ADR coverage as required by the ADR Directive.[9] In 2020, an amendment to the German ADR Directive transposition act took effect and provides a few modifications for the upcoming years: Inter alia introducing the so-called *Universalschlichtungsstelle des Bundes* which took over a slightly modified residual ADR task starting 2020. This entity is hosted by the *Zentrum für Schlichtung e.V.* as well.[10]

The quality requirements laid down by the legal framework of the ADR Directive and the transposition act are binding only for the notified ADR entities. Other players in the field of ADR who chose not to comply with these rules still can offer dispute resolution. However, they are not permitted to call themselves

---

[4]Cf. the metaphor used by Braun (2019), p. 131.

[5]Cf. the 203 notified entities (Recommendation 98/257/EC): European Parliament (2011), p. 17; Hodges et al. (2012), p. 87 et seq.

[6]Schlichtungsstelle bei der Deutschen Bundesbank (established 1999); Schlichtungsstelle Post der Bundesnetzagentur (established 2001); Schlichtungsstelle Telekommunikation der Bundesnetzagentur (established 1999); Schlichtungsstelle bei der BaFin (established 2011).

[7]Hodges et al. (2012), p. 73; Berlin (2017), p. 28 et seq.

[8]In this chapter, 'Allgemeine Verbraucherschlichtungsstelle (Kehl)' is referring to the residual ADR hosted by the Zentrum für Schlichtung e.V.; when mentioning one of the other German residual ADR entities, this will be indicated.

[9]The list of notified ADR entities published by the Bundesamt für Justiz can be found here: https://www.bundesjustizamt.de/DE/Themen/Buergerdienste/Verbraucherstreitbeilegung/Verbraucherschlichtungsstellen/Uebersicht_node.html.

[10]Bundesministerium der Justiz und für Verbraucherschutz (2019).

'*Verbraucherschlichtungsstelle*', see § 41(1) Nr. 1 VSBG.[11] Thus, in some sectors, there are no notified ADR entities at all. For instance, in the motor vehicle sector, the Arbitration Board for Motor Vehicles (*Kfz-Schiedsstellen*) solves cases within the scope of used car purchases or motor vehicle repairs with one of their guild members.[12] These entities, however, expressly refrain from applying for a notification as an official ADR entity.[13]

In this chapter, we would like to outline the following points: Sect. 9.2 will analyse the status quo of ADR in Germany after the implementation of the transposition act; Sect. 9.3 will highlight the defiances of consumer dispute resolution in Germany: Sect. 9.4 will reflect on our findings and attempt to provide an outlook to conclude.

9.2 Analysing the status quo of ADR in Germany After the Implementation of the Transposition Act

With the German implementation of the ADR Directive[14] in 2016, the existing ADR entities faced a new regulatory system that provided new laws (VSBG, VSBInfoV[15] and FinSV[16]) and adjusted the existing sector-specific laws[17] to the new system.

In this chapter, we use the term conciliation (German: *Schlichtung*) as the term to describe the type of dispute resolution method that is used by most ADR entities in Germany: a neutral person suggests a solution based on the facts presented by both parties, who then are free to accept said recommendation. This person in charge of ADR (Article 6(1) ADR Directive) is called a '*Streitmittler*', which translates to

---

[11]Cf. Greger et al. (2016), VSBG § 1 margin no. 2.

[12]https://www.kfz-schiedsstellen.de.

[13]Cf. Deutsches Kraftfahrzeuggewerbe (2017); more details on non-certified ADR providers, Biard (2018), 171, paragraphs 32 and 33.

[14]Cf. some 'country reports' on the ADR Directive's implementation across the EU: Morais Carvalho and Nemeth (2018), p. 81 (EU); Cortés (2018), p. 82 (ES/UK); Pinto-Ferreira and Campos Carvalho (2018), p. 89 (PT); Fejős (2018), p. 116 (HU); Rott (2018), p. 121 (DE); Loizou (2018), p. 126 (CY); Biard (2019), p. 109 (FR/UK).

[15]Regulation on Information and Reporting Obligations in accordance with the VSBG (Verordnung über Informations- und Berichtspflichten nach dem Verbraucherstreitbeilegungsgesetz) of 28 February 2016; the method of a separate governmental regulation was chosen to make amendments in those rather technical issues easier as it would be for a parliamentary law, cf. Deutscher Bundestag (2015), p. 77.

[16]Regulation on ADR entities in the financial sector in accordance with § 14 UKlaG and their procedure (Verordnung über die Verbraucherschlichtungsstellen im Finanzbereich nach § 14 des Unterlassungsklagengesetzes und ihr Verfahren) of 5 September 2016.

[17]E.g. VVG (insurance); EVO (rail transportation); LuftVG/LuftSchlichtV (air transportation); EU-FahrgRSchG (transportation by ship); EU-FahrgRBusG (transportation by bus); BRAO (solicitors/barristers); UKlaG (banking/finance); EnWG (electricity and gas); PostG (postal services); TKG (telecommunication).

'dispute mediator'.[18] However, this English term is slightly confusing, as a dispute mediator can be either a mediator or a conciliator or both. In Germany in general, most are conciliators. Nonetheless, we will use the term 'dispute mediator'.

If said dispute mediator renders a reasoned recommendation, this has to be based on the law (in general) and, in particular, the compulsory consumer protection laws, § 19(1) sentence 2 VSBG. However, since neither the ADR Directive[19] nor the transposition act define the term conciliation or impose a certain method to be used for dispute resolution, ADR procedures may even implement methodical approaches of mediation[20] or use classic mediation.[21]

Until 2016, ADR was a rather '*pianissimo*' niche instrument for consumers in Germany. Accompanied by the fuss[22] about the information obligation, which was introduced by Article 14 of Regulation (EU) 524/2013 on online dispute resolution for consumer disputes[23] in January 2016, traders, consumers and other stakeholders seemed to mix up the information obligation rolled out by the ODR Regulation and the ones of the ADR Directive. In addition, the combination of voluntary participation and fees only borne by traders proved to be poor incentives. Hence, ADR in Germany had a rather rough start in 2016 and experienced further turbulences in early 2017 when the information obligations of §§ 36 and 37 VSBG (transposing Article 13(1) and (3) ADR Directive) eventually entered into force (1 February 2017). Awareness on this topic in the broader trader public still seems to be limited yet slowly growing within the entire European Union.[24]

9.2.1 ADR in Numbers

Like almost any new idea, ADR (as defined by the ADR Directive) is evaluated—mostly in numbers. However, are the numbers per se an indicator of the success or quality of an instrument like ADR? There are statistics on the number of ADR entities across the European Economic Area,[25] the number of cases filed at the ODR

---

[18]Translation by Rott (2018), p. 121.

[19]The ADR Directive respects the pre-existing procedures in the Member States and their legal traditions, recital 15.

[20]In the sense of Directive 2008/52/EC.

[21]Cf. Außergerichtliche Streitbeilegungsstelle für Verbraucher und Unternehmer e.V. in Leipzig.

[22]Rätze (2016a, b).

[23]Regulation (EU) 524/2013 of the European Parliament and of the Council of 21 May 2013 on online dispute resolution for consumer disputes, henceforth called ODR Regulation.

[24]European Commission (2017a), p. 66.

[25]Bundesamt für Justiz (2018), p. 12.

platform of the European Commission[26] and the recent case development of ADR in Germany.[27]

In the following, we use some of these statistics to compare Germany with two ADR countries with a strong ADR culture—the Netherlands and Sweden. A large consideration as to why EU-wide ADR was implemented using a directive instead of a regulation was that there were already many different pre-existing ADR approaches in the European Union.[28] Different mentalities in conflict resolution and differences in the progression of ADR are only two of the various reasons as to why it is difficult to compare the statistics of the aforementioned countries. However, such an analysis might still be intriguing.

9.2.1.1 Data from Germany

In total, the ADR entities that already existed in Germany before 2016 processed almost 60,000 disputes annually. Hence, in 2015 the draft of the VSBG estimated that the number of annual requests would double to 120,000.[29] It was also expected that 30 additional ADR entities would be created (and notified) initially, followed by 15 new entities each year.[30] These expectations did not materialise, at least they have not yet.

In 2016, ADR entities received a total of 61,694 requests, rising to 68,538 in 2017.[31] Five new ADR entities were notified: three residual ADR entities, one with a regional focus and one with a focus on mediation.[32] As of mid-2019, there were 27 notified ADR entities in total. 21 of these were private ADR entities and six were public ADR entities. The latter are competent in the regulated sectors (finance, telecommunication etc.).[33] The German transposition act does not mention all ADR entities in an exhaustive list.[34] Instead, the legislator estimated that new ADR entities would be established in the years to come and opted for an open-ended approach.

Some entities faced an enormous increase of requests, e.g. *söp_Schlichtungsstelle für den Öffentlichen Personenverkehr e.V.*, where requests doubled in 2018 (32,239 in comparison to 15,601 in 2017[35]). On the other hand, others recorded slightly

---

[26]https://ec.europa.eu/consumers/odr/main/?event=main.statistics.show (live data).

[27]Greger (2019d).

[28]Cf. recital 6 ADR Directive.

[29]Deutscher Bundestag (2015), p. 42.

[30]Ibid., p. 43.

[31]Bundesamt für Justiz (2018), pp. 60 and 61.

[32]Greger (2019a), p. 43; Greger (2018a).

[33]List (Article 20(2) ADR Directive) of the Bundesamt für Justiz as of 23 July 2019.

[34]Cf. for instance the approach of Austria, § 4(1) AStG or—to some extent—of Liechtenstein, § 4 (1) AStG.

[35]Schlichtungsstelle für den öffentlichen Personenverkehr e.V. (2019), p. 9 et seq.

declining figures (financial services in general[36]). Volatility is not surprising, as each year different actual or legal phenomena can occur and create varying demand for ADR. For instance, the aforementioned *söp_Schlichtungsstelle für den Öffentlichen Personenverkehr e.V.* reports that, in addition to 'the increasing recognition of the entity' and 'the general advantages of ADR procedures', the irregularities that have occurred in national and European air transport were responsible for the high volume of requests.[37] In turn, a ruling of the Federal Court of Justice (Bundesgerichtshof) in the area of financial services[38] affected numerous consumer contracts in 2014, which led to a veritable deluge of requests that had eventually been dealt with by 2016. Hence, even these slightly declining figures indicate that ADR is established in the financial sectors.

The *Allgemeine Verbraucherschlichtungsstelle* (*Kehl*), which was set up in April 2016 as a residual ADR entity for the consumer contracts which were not yet covered by sector-specific ADR entities, received 825 requests in 2016. In 2018, the receipt of 2125 requests was almost identical to the previous year's figure (2118).[39] At the regional residual entity *Anwaltliche Verbraucherschlichtungsstelle NRW e.V.*, which has been operating since 15 June 2018 and is competent for traders established in North Rhine-Westphalia, 11 requests have been made by the end of 2018.[40]

At first glance, these statistics may seem disappointing considering the afore-mentioned expectation of the legislator.[41] However, the comparison to the statistics of other countries allows us to draw a different conclusion. As stated at the beginning, ADR in Germany is a relatively new method of dispute resolution, unlike in Sweden or the Netherlands, where it is an established practice.[42]

9.2.1.2 Trilateral Comparison with the Netherlands and Sweden[43]

In both the Netherlands and in Sweden there is a central entity which covers almost all consumer-relevant economic sectors.[44] In Sweden, this entity is called *Allmänna*

---

[36]Greger (2018b).

[37]Schlichtungsstelle für den öffentlichen Personenverkehr e.V. (2019), p. 9.

[38]On 15 May 2014 the Federal Court of Justice (BGH) issued two rulings on the validity of loan fee clauses in banks' general terms and conditions (BGH XI ZR 405/12 and XI ZR 170/13), followed by two other rulings on 28 October 2014 concerning the limitation of reimbursement-claims of said fees (BGH XI ZR 348/13 and XI ZR 17/14).

[39]Allgemeine Verbraucherschlichtungsstelle am Zentrum für Schlichtung e.V. (2017–2019).

[40]Anwaltliche Verbraucherschlichtungsstelle NRW e.V. (2019), p. 1; the in 2018 newly created residual ADR entity Außergerichtliche Streitbeilegungsstelle für Verbraucher und Unternehmer e.V. in Leipzig did not publish an annual report as of this chapter's editorial deadline.

[41]See Greger (2019c); Roder (2018), p. 202, who is exploring potential reasons.

[42]Berlin (2017), p. 23 et seq., margins no. 5 and 11.

[43]Cf. the comparison laid out by Braun (2019), p. 131.

[44]Berlin (2017), pp. 23 and 25, margins no. 8 and 15.

Reklamtionsnämnden (ARN), in the Netherlands the *e De Geschillencommissies* (SGC).

The ARN received 13,537 requests in 2016, 14,363 in 2017 and 17,575 in 2018.[45] However, in 1970—two years after ARN's launch in 1968—the number of requests was just under 6000.[46] Extrapolating these figures proportionally to the number of inhabitants in Germany,[47] there would have been 110,154, 116,875 and 143,012 requests respectively, and 45,750 requests for 1970.[48]

The SGC received 4801 requests in 2016,[49] 4590 in 2017[50] and 4469 in 2018.[51] If these figures were converted to reflect Germany's population, this would result in 23,034, 22,021 and 21,441 requests respectively.

In Sweden, where the ARN has been established for more than 50 years, the figures are almost exactly at the level of the German legislator's estimation. This could indicate that the estimation might prove to be correct—in the medium to long term. It is noteworthy, however, that the ARN procedure is free of charge for both traders and consumers,[52] and ADR fees imposed on traders are often considered to be a significant access barrier.[53]

However, the figures from the Netherlands indicate that a functioning ADR landscape does not mean that all cases end up with ADR entities instead of in court, as is often feared in Germany when mentioning the massive decline in civil actions.[54] To some, Germany's western neighbour has long been a promising role model due to similarities in legal tradition, similar juridical structures and procedural rules as well as its comparable social and economic conditions. However, contrary to Germans, the Dutch seem to avoid lawsuits.[55] The SGC's work started in 1970 and did not take off until the 1990s due to legislative measures.[56] Looking abroad, it seems that ADR and court procedures are complementary and are not necessarily engaged in a predatory competition. This foresight was already stated by *Astrid Stadler* some twenty years ago when (an attempt of) conciliation prior to a court

---

[45]https://arn.se/om-arn/statistik.

[46]According to Braun (2019), p. 131.

[47]End of 2018 the Netherlands had roughly 17,300,000 inhabitants, Sweden 10,200,000, Germany 83,000,000.

[48]Based on the lower population figures of both Sweden and West-Germany in 1970.

[49]Braun (2019), p. 131.

[50]Stichting De Geschillencommissies (2018).

[51]Stichting De Geschillencommissies (2019).

[52]Cf. the information on ARN via https://ec.europa.eu/consumers/odr/main/?event=main.adr. show2.

[53]Deutscher Industrie- und Handelskammertag (2019), p. 5; 'Traders' participation is low in particularly because it is a voluntary procedure which is fee-based for traders.' Creutzfeldt and Steffek (2018), p. 68; cf. l.c. p. 90: interview with ECC Austria.

[54]Wagner (2017), p. 124; Greger (2016).

[55]Stadler (1998), p. 2481 with further explanations and references.

[56]Braun (2019), p. 131.

procedure was mandatory in certain matters in Germany:[57] boosting the voluntary use of ADR as an instrument which is complementary to court procedures might only be possible to some extent—and only by enhancing incentives.[58]

Overall, the comparison over time indicates that ADR in Germany is just getting started. When it comes to residual ADR entities, high figures are not necessarily an indicator of whether they work or not; these entities are not designed for high volumes.[59] Nevertheless, both sector-specific and residual ADR entities need to be prepared for periods of a high volume of cases, as these occur repeatedly.[60] Further-more, the Dutch history suggests that incentives should be carried out carefully and according to each country's specific situation.[61] Nonetheless, the paramount factors seem to be patience and time.[62]

9.2.2 Yea, Nay, Maybe? The Information Obligation

In a way, the information obligation advertises the existence of ADR and makes traders decide transparently on how they position themselves regarding ADR.[63] In this regard, the transposition in § 36(1) no. 1 VSBG of Article 13(1) goes beyond the ADR Directive's requirements (cf. Article 2(3) sentence 2 ADR Directive): German traders also have to indicate if they generally do *not* want to participate in ADR. It was believed that a negative commitment towards ADR would leave a negative impression with consumers.[64] However, it appears that this bold idea did not work out as planned. Traders might be overstrained with the possible nuances[65] of the wording of § 36(1) no. 1 VSBG '*to what extent* they are willing to participate' (or not at all). An explanation might be that there is not enough knowledge about cases in which ADR would be an asset for the trader. Or the idea did not work out, as many

---

[57]Most German states abrogated this feature in the meantime which can be implemented in the cases laid out by § 15a(1) Gesetz, betreffend die Einführung der Zivilprozessordnung; nowadays, § 253 (3) no. 1 Zivilprozessordnung only asks ('shall specify') whether an attempt of ADR has been made prior to the court action.

[58]Stadler (1998), p. 2487 who is emphasizing that implementing conciliation by legal obligation is unlikely to work out when there is no objective reason that this type of dispute resolution would have emerged in the first place.

[59]Schmidt-Kessel (2019), p. 2.

[60]See the phenomena mentioned under Sect. 9.2.1.1 which rapidly lead to increased figures.

[61]A general comparison of incentives per EU Member State is delivered by the European Com-mission (2019b), p. 32.

[62]Deutscher Bundestag (2019), p. 32; Biard (2018), p. 171, paragraph 42.

[63]Deutscher Bundestag (2015), p. 74; Greger et al. (2016), VSBG § 36 margin no. 1.

[64]Greger (2019a), p. 44.

[65]Greger suggests that traders could announce to participate in ADR procedures when the claim at stake exceeds a certain amount or only considering certain types of contracts, Greger et al. (2016), VSBG § 36 margin no. 7.

traders just do not expect the denial of ADR commitment to be a critical issue. Apparently, some are afraid that agreeing to ADR procedures in general could generate a vast number of (chargeable) cases filed at ADR entities.[66] However, the last three years of ADR have shown that the overall numbers of ADR complaints are at a relatively low level.[67] Even the traders who make an affirmative statement regarding their general participation in ADR procedures on their websites[68] have apparently not been engaged in ADR procedures or even been charged by an ADR entity.

It is true that the idea of nudging traders towards participation via the information obligation was intriguing, despite the fact that it did not fully work out—one can assume that if some big players had shown commitment to ADR, others might have followed in large numbers.

On a side note, according to anecdotal feedback, it seems that, after implementing a statement in 2017, traders do not recall which statement they opted for (participation 'yes' or 'no') or why, remembering only that they had to fulfil yet another legal obligation. Hence, their decision at that time may not have had any substantial reasoning behind it—giving the players in ADR one more reason to continue their work of enlightening.

Unlike the general statement whether to take part in ADR procedures or not (Article 13(1) ADR Directive), the information carried out by the trader when a dispute between a consumer and a trader could not be settled ('deadlock letter'), seems to reach the consumer in due time, cf. Article 13(3) ADR Directive. These are the situations in which consumers need further information what options they have, and these are the situations in which the trader can estimate whether a specific dispute is suited for ADR or not.[69]

A broad evaluation of the information obligation and its implementation by traders may provide more insight on this issue.[70]

9.2.3 Residual ADR Entities

The *Allgemeine Verbraucherschlichtungsstelle (Kehl)* was created as a project to fulfil Germany's obligation in the ADR Directive to assure access to ADR for every dispute arising from a consumer contract, Article 5(3) sentence 1 ADR Directive. An

---

[66]Statement of a trader (anonymous) in the intermediary report on the Allgemeine Verbraucherschlichtungsstelle (Kehl), Creutzfeldt and Steffek (2018), p. 90.

[67]Cf. supra Sect. 9.2.1; Braun (2019), p. 132 mentions the example of a large company which announced early on in 2016 to be willing to participate in ADR and did have as many as five cases lodged at the Allgemeine Verbraucherschlichtungsstelle (Kehl) within nearly three years.

[68]Cf. the test arrangement by Braun (2019), p. 132.

[69]To 15% of consumers who addressed the Allgemeine Verbraucherschlichtungsstelle (Kehl), the entity had been mentioned by the trader, Creutzfeldt and Steffek (2018), p. 47.

[70]The German Government is considering such an evaluation cf. Rita Hagl-Kehl (2019), p. 12789.

interesting side effect of the existence of residual ADR entities is the ability to identify relevant sectors that do not (yet) have a functioning ADR system and where ADR is needed in particular. The annual reports show these requirements, and either privately funded or publicly funded ADR entities can be established in these sectors in the long term.[71]

Broadly speaking, the German transposition act defines the relationship between residual and sector-specific ADR entities in such a way that the residual ADR entity is not considered competent if a sector-specific ADR entity is, cf. § 4(2) sentence 1 no. 2 VSBG[72] and the amended § 30(2) no. 1 VSBG. At first glance, this sounds like a clear-cut competence rule.

However, the creation of new ADR entities and even the co-existence with established ADR entities leads to a fundamental legal question that seems to concern ADR entities in other countries as well,[73] namely whether the competence of residual ADR entities ends where a sector-specific ADR entity steps in to cover a certain domain of contracts or not. Both systems coexist in the EU.[74] Sector-specific ADR entities are free[75] to establish their own procedural rules, including their field of competency, according to the sector's peculiarities. These entities will most likely identify the most apt cases which are generally suitable for ADR, as they have sector-specific knowledge and are more familiar with the trader structure in their sector. This explains why there are rarely ADR entities which fully cover a specific sector. Instead they usually opt for a membership-based ADR procedure,[76] are competent only for a certain type of contract,[77] operate in a defined monetary threshold[78] or require a contract that has been concluded within certain time limits.[79]

One could conclude that in case a specific ADR entity makes use of their 'estimation prerogative' and assesses the suitable ADR cases in their sector, that

---

[71]For package holidays, the German government identified such a need in 2017 and funded the söp_Schlichtungsstelle für den Öffentlichen Personenverkehr e.V. to deal with these requests as of 2019: Rott (2018), p. 125; Greger (2019b); Haushaltsgesetz 2019, BMJV, post 684 01-059.

[72]The residual ADR entity is not competent for 'disputes for the resolution of which ADR entities are recognised, commissioned or established by other legal provisions'.

[73]Service de Médiation pour le Consommateur (2019), p. 40; SPF Economie (2018), p. 12 and p. 9.

[74]European Commission (2019c), p. 7 and footnote 38.

[75]Nota bene: the national competent authority has to notify their scope under the ADR Directive, Article 20(1) ADR Directive.

[76]European Commission (2015), p. 10 with an illustrated example.

[77]I.e. competence of the telecommunication ADR entity which does not cover 'purely' civil law disputes.

[78]I.e. rules of procedure of the Ombudsmann Immobilien IVD/VPB (inter alia: construction of new buildings or substantial alterations to existing buildings): § 2(1) 'Rejection of conciliation': 'The Ombudsman shall refuse to carry out dispute settlement procedures if (. . .) 7. the amount in dispute is less than EUR 3,000 (. . .); Contrary to § 2(1) no. 7, the ombudsman rejects conciliation proceedings for disputes within the meaning of § 1(2) sentence 2 if the amount in dispute is less than EUR 600.00 or exceeds EUR 5,000.00.'.

[79]I.e. § 11 no. 3 of the rules of procedure of the Ombudsstelle für Sachwerte und Investmentvermögen e.V. (investment assets).

sector could be considered as covered by ADR. In case a request does not fit the sector-specific ADR entity's competence, the consumer would then not have access to any ADR, not even residual ADR. A reason for this could be found in an economical approach that prevents more than only one (specialized) ADR entity from providing expert knowledge in a certain domain.

Considering that, such an approach would lead to the paradoxical situation that the creation of more ADR entities indeed could narrow access to ADR. Hence, we consider the coherence of Article 5(3) and 5(6), (7) ADR Directive to be a reviving competence of residual ADR entities once the specific case does not enter in the framework of the specialised ADR entity's competence. Thus, residual ADR entities need to be able to deal with every kind of consumer complaint and be well-versed in the specific ADR entities' scope of competence. Some of the 'crumbs' left over from the vast 'cake' of ADR cases can be rather difficult to digest:[80] networking and the exchange of best practices and knowledge with other entities seem to be highly recommended side dishes.

9.2.4 Fundamental Legal Questions: Courts and ADR—A Complementary System?

One reason for the policy maker to establish full coverage of ADR was the lack of easy and low-cost access for every consumer throughout the European Union, cf. recital 4 ADR Directive. However, one might think that this motivation, driven especially by the over-shadowing objective of having a properly functioning internal market, cannot apply to every Member State to the same extent. In Germany, court procedures are relatively easily accessible and function well.[81] Thanks to legal expenses insurances, even court costs do not appear to be a particular threat. However, most consumers will still not engage in court procedures over disputes regarding a few hundred euros.[82]

Both consumers and traders recognize the ADR procedure they experienced at the *Allgemeine Verbraucherschlichtungsstelle* (*Kehl*) as being easier, faster and more cost-effective than a court procedure.[83] Still, this method of dispute resolution is not the one of choice even though conciliation and mediation are estimated as a beneficial dispute resolution method.[84]

---

[80]For instance, cases where consumers invested in the so-called 'grey' capital market (non-regulated yet legal capital market).

[81]European Parliament (2017), p. 64: court costs are at 14.4% of a claim's value; Hodges et al. (2012), p. 74.

[82]Roland Rechtsreport (2014), p. 36.

[83]Creutzfeldt and Steffek (2018), p. 83 (consumers) and p. 62 (traders).

[84]PriceWaterhouseCoopers (2016), p. 39 for the situation in Germany in 2015.

Since the start of the discussions on the German transposition act of the ADR Directive in 2014, the implementation of ADR has met with tremendous scepticism. 'Parallel jurisdiction' and 'more access to less law' are just some of the arguments held against the rather new form of dispute resolution and its implementation.[85] It was even predicted that court procedures in civil cases would decline.[86] However, ADR is not an overlaying instrument designed to render courts superfluous and deprive civil litigation of access to court decisions and supreme court rulings in consumer matters. The reasons for this, in particular, are:

The numbers for newly received court procedures in Germany have shown a declining tendency for over a decade (*Amtsgericht* and *Landgericht* alike[87]).[88] *Monika Nöhre* convincingly argues that the existence of ADR and the declining court numbers are not interrelated. ADR cannot be considered a part of the state's justice system but is instead more of an intermediate step between traders' conflict management and courts.[89] Most requests (87%) made at the *Allgemeine Verbraucherschlichtungsstelle* (*Kehl*) concern a claim value of less than 1000 euros.[90] It seems that a minimum of 1950 euros is the average threshold for German consumers for pursuing their claims in court.[91] The 'rational disinterest'[92] in pursuing claims beneath this amount thus withdraws them from classic court procedures anyway, and so they cannot be taken into account when looking at the decline in court procedure numbers, as these claims would never have been lodged there in the first place. Thus, ADR offers additional (complementary)[93] access for cases in which consumers can complain. The fact that the access consumers are looking for does not create a 'second class' jurisdiction[94] is an important issue the German transposition act by § 6(2) VSBG largely considers: the dispute mediators must prove their legal knowledge, particularly in consumer law, their expertise and their skills that are necessary to resolve the disputes submitted to their ADR entity. On a formal note, the dispute mediator must be qualified to act as a judge or a certified mediator.[95]

---

[85]Rott (2018), p. 121 with reference to Engel (2015), p. 1633.

[86]Wolf (2015), p. 1659 et seq.

[87]The Amtsgericht (county court) has inter alia a competence for civil matters up to 5000 Euros, a barrister is not necessary; in Landgericht (district court) procedures (matters from 5000.01 € upward), representation by barrister is inevitable.

[88]Statistisches Bundesamt (2019), p. 12/13 and p. 42/43; Wolf (2015), p. 1656 et seq.; with a comment on recent developments Rebehn (2019).

[89]Nöhre (2018), p. 99/100; she also wonders at p. 88/89 whether high figures of lawsuits are even an indicator of the state of the rule of law.

[90]Creutzfeldt and Steffek (2018), p. 44.

[91]Roland Rechtsreport (2014), p. 36.

[92]Röthemeyer (2016), p. 16.

[93]Berlin (2016), p. 40 with further references.

[94]Cf. Biard (2018), p. 171, paragraph 7.

[95]This formulation requires the dispute mediator to pass the Zweite juristische Staatsexamen; the certification as mediator was introduced on 1 September 2017 when the Zertifizierte-Mediatoren-Ausbildungsverordnung took effect.

Those consumers who are eager to have a court ruling in their case will always chose the 'traditional' way instead of ADR.[96] Moreover, ADR entities may provide in their procedural rules that a request for ADR is to be rejected if a fundamental legal issue—which is relevant for the assessment of said dispute—has not been clarified (§ 14(2) sentence 1 no. 4 lit. b VSBG). This provision's root according to the German legislator is recital 25 of the ADR Directive and was implemented in a manner that amounts to gold plating.[97] On the one hand, all existing residual ADR entities implemented this ground for refusal to deal with a given dispute.[98] On the other hand, not all sector-specific ADR entities made use of this option. For ADR entities in the financial sector, this ground is mentioned in § 6(2) sentence 1 no. 1 of the FinSV. This procedural regulation also clarifies that the refusal must be justified by the ADR entity. *Matthias Roder* reflects on whether the existence of said ground could have its reason in order to prevent ADR entities from producing precedent cases.[99] However, data in the reports do not give the impression that this refusal ground is used very often.[100]

Being an exception, the refusal ground provided by § 14(2) sentence 1 no. 4 lit. b VSBG has to be applied restrictively.[101] It is very unlikely that the typical reaction of a consumer faced by the ADR procedure ending because of this ground for refusal will be to engage a court procedure.[102] One may expect that said consumer may actually be discouraged from going to court, and that the parties would be satisfied with the ADR entity's recommendation to solve the dispute after it has pointed out that the result of a court decision would be unpredictable.[103]

The two sector-specific ADR entities, *Versicherungsombudsmann e.V.* and *söp_Schlichtungsstelle für den Öffentlichen Personenverkehr e.V.*, implemented a creative solution[104] to prevent the potential scenario of consumers abandoning the pursuit of their claims when their claim is rejected by the ADR entity as it concerns a fundamental legal question, cf. § 14(2) sentence 1 no. 4 lit. b VSBG. This scenario was most likely unintended. The entities thus provide a rule that enables traders—the

---

[96]Geier (2016), p. 1368/1369.

[97]Deutscher Bundestag (2015), p. 61.

[98]§ 2.1 lit. h) no. 2 VerfO Allgemeine Verbraucherschlichtungsstelle (Kehl), § 2.1 lit. h) no. 2 VerfO Anwaltliche Verbraucherschlichtungsstelle NRW and § 2(1) lit. g) no. 2 VerfO Außergerichtliche Streitbeilegungsstelle für Verbraucher und Unternehmer.

[99]Cf. Roder (2018), p. 204.

[100]Bundesamt für Justiz (2018), p. 66 where the diagram indicates a value of ca. 10% for 2017 (ADR entities in the financial sector); Roder (2018), p. 204; Rott (2018), p. 125.

[101]Fichtner (2017), § 14, margin no. 60.

[102]Gössl (2015), p. 85, estimates that in case of a rejection on that ground, 'it is not automatically to be expected that a court will deal with the dispute'.

[103]Gössl (2015), p. 85; ADR entities have to indicate that the recommendation may differ from the result of court proceeding anyway when they render their result, § 19(3) sentence 1 VSBG.

[104]§ 9(3) VerfO Versicherungsombudsmann e.V. and § 7(2) VerfO söp_Schlichtungsstelle für den Öffentlichen Personenverkehr e.V.

ADR procedures of said entities are mandatory[105]—to apply for an end to the procedure (without recommendation) under certain conditions. However, the trader is then obliged to reimburse the consumer if the matter is brought to court (only for a first instance's decision), even if the trader prevails in court.

Such a rule appears to be a way of reducing the uncertainty of whether a fundamental legal question comes to a court's attention. However, the (possible) shortcomings of this rule are openly addressed in the *Versicherungsombudsmann*'s annual report: little use of the rule is made and since the trader pays only one court instance, the consumer might not be motivated to pursue a higher court's decision in case of an appeal.[106] To some extent, ADR entities should bear the idea in mind and observe the impact of this rule in the daily work of the specific ADR entities mentioned.

As a follow-up question one might ask whether a consumer whose request was denied by the refusal ground of § 14(2) sentence 1 no. 4 lit. b VSBG engages in a court procedure to find an answer to the fundamental legal issue?[107] Most consumers (and most likely traders as well) want their disputes to be solved quickly[108] and at low costs.[109] Profound legal reasoning not being of predominant importance, ADR could find itself being lost and abandoned by those consumers and traders who prefer to find a quick solution based on traders' customer service algorithms. However, these take into account factors such as purchase histories, purchasing behaviour, sales strength, complaint rates etc.[110] Today's marketing instruments already take these criteria into account.[111] Extrapolating from these possibilities, customer relationship management (CRM) could rule-base its decisions on this data, setting up an autonomous yet effective mechanism to satisfy consumers' expectation while not necessarily needing to comply with (consumer protection) law.[112] ADR as a law-based solution mechanism could prevent dispute resolution from being a matter solely based on algorithms and has the advantage of also being easily accessible.[113]

Nevertheless, it should not be forgotten that especially consumer law cases which look plain at first glance or involve only a small claim sometimes need 'clarification'

---

[105]§ 214(5) VVG and § 57a(1) LuftVG respectively; additionally, the Versicherungsombudsmann's solution is binding if the claim does not exceed an amount of 10.000 Euros, § 11(1) sentence 1 and § 10(3) sentence 2 VerfO.

[106]Versicherungsombudsmann e.V. (2018), p. 19/20.

[107]Isermann (2018), p. 286 with a pleading on the ADR entities' possibility to provide an accessible and realistic solution for consumers even (and particularly) in cases which concern fundamental legal questions.

[108]Rott (2018), p. 124.

[109]Wernike (2019).

[110]Criteria of other social spheres could also be linked to that data: Sachverständigenrat für Verbraucherfragen (2018), p. 60.

[111]I.e. Nguyen (2011), p. 140; Schafer et al. (1999), p. 158.

[112]Cf. Fries (2016), p. 2865 illustrating the 'PayPal law' example.

[113]The possibility to be represented by a third party, e.g. lawyers, was rarely made use of, cf. Creutzfeldt and Steffek (2018), p. 52.

by the Federal Supreme Court or—where EU law is concerned—the European Court of Justice.[114,115]

Notified ADR entities in Germany find themselves on the open field of dispute resolution schemes and will, hopefully, over time be able to refine their profiles and raise awareness on what their purpose is among traders and consumers alike. Concepts that leverage public pressure created by 'naming and shaming'[116] could endanger the recent attempts and efforts to establish high-quality ADR in Germany by sowing confusion about ADR amongst stakeholders.

Additionally, the findings in the annual reports of ADR entities serve as a general feedback system to consumer protection organisations, cf. especially § 34(3) VSBG and § 4(1) no. 2 VSBInfoV. Consumer protection organisations can localise recurrent problems and investigate further.

9.2.5   Practical Cases to Illustrate the Procedure of the Allgemeine Verbraucherschlichtungsstelle (Kehl)

The following case studies illustrate some ADR cases that are based on actual cases the *Allgemeine Verbraucherschlichtungsstelle (Kehl)* has dealt with. They also demonstrate the range of competence of a German residual ADR entity despite numerous existing sector-specific ADR entities. Whereas some sectors refrain from establishing ADR entities,[117] in others not all disputes are covered by the entities. The ADR entity 'telecommunications', set up by the *Bundesnetzagentur* (national (de-)regulatory authority) deals only with specific disputes from an exhaustive catalogue[118] which does not include any contractual disputes (such as the legal guarantee case hereafter).

9.2.5.1   Case Study 1: 'Fine Tuning'

Mrs and Mr Kupfer ordered a used luxury SUV (purchase price 65,000 euros) from Fancy Car GmbH. A 'Loud & Resonant Sound System with 3D sound' was listed in the order overview as special equipment. It was not until the vehicle was handed

---

[114]Article 267(1) a) TFEU.

[115]For instance, European Court of Justice Case C-681/17 on the right to withdrawal and the 'concept of sealed goods which are not suitable for return due to health protection or hygiene reasons and which have been unsealed by the consumer after delivery'.

[116]E.g. the website www.reklamieren24.de that calls itself 'more than a complaint platform'—however the provider itself ironically declares not to participate in ADR procedures: www.reklamieren24.de/impressum.

[117]See above: end of Sect. 9.1.

[118]Cf. § 47a(1) Telekommunikationsgesetz; and above Sect. 9.2.1.

over that Mrs and Mr Kupfer noticed that a cheaper 'Lohse Sound System with 3D sound' had been installed instead. Nevertheless, the Kupfer family agreed to take the vehicle, and Fancy Car GmbH offered them a compensation payment of 1500 euros after their complaint. Mrs and Mr Kupfer refused the offer and suggested that Fancy Car GmbH could install the missing system in the vehicle. Fancy Car GmbH then stated that retrofitting the system at their own expense was out of the question.

After turning to the *Allgemeine Verbraucherschlichtungsstelle* (*Kehl*), the parties disputed the amount of the depreciation which Fancy Car GmbH would have to pay. The Kupfer family demanded 3000 euros, but Fancy Car GmbH refused to pay this amount and continued to offer the 1500 euros which already had been proposed.

The recommendation examined whether there was a loss in value for the Kupfer family and how this loss had to be estimated. Therefore, the dispute mediator compared the (hypothetical) vehicle models with the respective equipment based on the original prices and a reduction amount of 2200 euros was assessed. Informed about the detailed method of calculation, both parties accepted the recommendation.

9.2.5.2   Case Study 2: 'Ms Communication'

As part of her preparations for a longer stay abroad in Canada, Ms Ucluelet ordered a SIM card from Temagami Communications GmbH for 30 euros for calls using a mobile phone. The SIM card was then sent to her home address. Once activated, the SIM card would be activated for four weeks. Arriving at the airport in Canada, Ms Ucluelet placed the card in her mobile phone and realized that neither telephone calls nor data connections were possible. The instructions sent by Temagami Communications GmbH to remedy the situation were unsuccessful. Thus, she bought a SIM card from another local provider, returned the original SIM card to Temagami Communications GmbH, and informed them that she was demanding a refund of the amount paid. Temagami Communications GmbH stated that, following its own investigation, the SIM card had been in working order and that, contrary to Ms Ucluelet's opinion, the SIM card would in fact have been activated, and so Temagami Communications GmbH refused to reimburse.

In the conciliation procedure, the lack of evidence on the part of the parties meant that the case's facts could not be clarified entirely. In the interests of a quick and uncomplicated procedure, the *Allgemeine Verbraucherschlichtungsstelle* (*Kehl*) thus explained the legal situation in the recommendation and which party would have to bear the burden of proof or the risk of litigation costs in the event of a lawsuit. Having reached the same level of legal knowledge, Ms Ucluelet and the Temagami Communications GmbH were finally able to reach an agreement. Both were not willing to pursue the dispute in court and therefore each accepted to bear a certain percentage of the costs.

9.2.6 Conclusion

The development described above in Sect. 9.2.1 shows that ADR in general—and the volume of requests in particular—may grow slowly over the years. On the one hand, it can be argued that Germany is in a relatively good position when comparing ADR across the European Union. On the other hand, there is still a lot of potential to be unleashed, especially in residual ADR.[119] If this potential is tapped, both the number of requests and trader's participation rates would increase. While traders who are associated with a sector-specific ADR entity already adopt ADR both on the consumer and trader sides,[120] traders in the cross-sectoral residual ADR entities' competence seem to lack a 'change of mind':[121] a more precise knowledge of exactly what ADR stands for and to what extent it also offers traders additional benefit. These and other defiance will be discussed in the following section.

9.3 The Defiance of Consumer Dispute Resolution

The following part contains only relatively short descriptions of some of the challenges that ADR faces in Germany—particularly the residual ADR entities. Likewise, possible answers to these challenges are only briefly outlined. Shortness is key because the transposition of the ADR Directive is still relatively young and it is still difficult to obtain valid findings, as there are many things still in motion.

Nevertheless, it seems clear that:

– some specific challenges are common to cross-border disputes
– the design of costs decisively influences traders' acceptance
– ADR cannot and does not have to be a kind of universal weapon for everything

These points will be addressed below to raise awareness of current key challenges, and new solutions could soon deliver results.

---

[119]Deutscher Bundestag (2019), p. 32.

[120]Concerning traders this realization came along with a more or less strong legislative support, which imposes in some sectors a cost payment obligation for traders if they do not participate in the ADR procedure: e.g. airlines have to pay 290 Euros for the a compulsatory ADR procedure when they are not assigned with a private ADR entity, § 57a LuftVG, § 16a Justizverwaltungskostengesetz and no. 1220 in the act's appendix.

[121]Braun et al. (2019), p. 58.

9.3.1 Cross-Border ADR/ODR and Language Barriers

One of the challenges for legal settlements in general are cross-border cases.[122] They do not only implicate a decision of which country's law has to be applied, but parties who are able to contract in a foreign language are also not necessarily able to resolve a dispute due to language barriers.[123] To prevent high costs and facilitate claim enforcement, the European Union created instruments such as the European Order for Payment Procedure[124] and the European Small Claims Procedure.[125] ADR is another instrument which could increase consumers' and traders' trust in cross-border commerce and thus strengthen the internal market.[126] ADR and the complementary[127] Online Dispute Resolution (ODR) is an appealing method for simplifying the process of addressing complaints when a consumer has an unsatisfactory experience when buying goods or supplies of digital content or services in another country. Statistically speaking, cross-border online shopping in the EU still makes up less than 20% of all trade.[128]

Language barriers are of course also an issue for ADR entities. The creation of the ODR platform in 2017 with its built-in translation tool can be a very helpful instrument for cross-border cases.[129] The common online translation websites[130] currently do not offer the ability to prevent personal data in the input text from being sent to the service provider and are thus not suitable for the translation of requests from consumers or statements from both sides. Even a person who is trained in other languages is unlikely to be able to filter all personal data, e.g. names or addresses, from the input text, especially if this text is written in a language that uses a different alphabet such as Bulgarian (Cyrillic).

Even though such a translation tool can offer some advantages (provided that the text does not contain typos), some obstacles remain to be circumvented.[131] Legal expertise is not easily 'translated' from one country to another. ADR entities have

---

[122]European Commission (2017a), p. 113/114 shows that differences in law/consumer protection rules (38.1% and 37.4% respectively) and potentially higher costs for cross-border disputes (36.2%) represent major obstacles for traders.

[123]Höxter (2016), p. 32.

[124]Regulation (EC) 1896/2006 of 12 December 2006.

[125]Regulation (EC) 861/2007 of 11 July 2007.

[126]Recital 3 ADR Directive; European Commission (2019a).

[127]Recital 16 ODR Regulation.

[128]European Commission (2017a), p. 94: consumers in Germany show a clear preference for domestic retailers, making it the only country with an above-average percentage of online buyers from domestic retailers and a below-average share of consumers buying online from other EU countries.

[129]European Commission (2018a), p. 178.

[130]For instance, deepl.com or translate.google.com.

[131]Consequently, for the more complex translation of recommendations, the resources of the Translation Centre of the Bodies of the European Union are available, yet very little used: Translation Centre of the Bodies of the European Union (2017), p. 11.

already realised this and have created international networks such as FIN-NET[132] and NEON.[133] The European Consumer Centres Network (ECC-Net) combines the translation and the advisory aspects—leaning towards the consumer's role according to its agenda. The possibility for consumers to address their cross-border complaints to this network paves the way for consultation in cases that the ECC personnel identifies as being suited for ADR, cf. Article 7 Vademecum ECC-Net.

The importance of networks is stressed in the ADR Directive itself, in particular in Article 16. Member States shall thus 'ensure that ADR entities cooperate in the resolution of cross-border disputes and conduct regular exchanges of best practices as regards the settlement of both cross-border and domestic disputes'. Furthermore, 'the Commission shall support and facilitate the networking of national ADR entities and the exchange and dissemination of their best practices and experiences'. Several residual ADR entities have been meeting at least once a year since 2016 and have thus created an informal network.[134] In 2017, yet another new network emerged, the TRAVEL-NET.[135] As its name indicates, it brings together ADR entities that deal with travel issues, be it as a residual or a sector-specific ADR entity. Finally, the first ADR Assembly took place in Brussels in 2018 upon invitation of the European Commission, reuniting 350 delegates the biggest group comprising 170 representatives of ADR entities.[136] One of the big achievements was that all workshops were organised in a way that facilitates networking.

These developments show that ADR is in a permanent state of flux and that its challenges and defiance are positively taken up by relevant actors.

9.3.2 Costs

The German legislator opted for traders to bear the costs of voluntary ADR procedures. In practice and in the long run, voluntary ADR procedures are feasible only when adequately funded, be it entirely by traders themselves or via co-funding from the public sector. In sectors where ADR is mandatory, the ADR entities are financed by traders of that sector. *Peter Rott* summarises 'where ADR is not mandatory, as in most areas, the fees are obviously an incentive not to participate'.[137] The fees charged by the *Universalschlichtungsstelle des Bundes* are determined by a separate decree (cf. amended § 31(1) and § 42(2) no. 1 VSBG) and are deliberately not

---

[132]https://ec.europa.eu/info/business-economy-euro/banking-and-finance/consumer-finance-and-payments/consumer-financial-services/financial-dispute-resolution-network-fin-net/fin-net-network/about-fin-net_en.

[133]http://www.neon-ombudsman.org/tag/adr/.

[134]Allgemeine Verbraucherschlichtungsstelle am Zentrum für Schlichtung e.V. (2018).

[135]European Commission (2017c).

[136]European Commission (2018d), p. 1.

[137]Rott (2018), p. 124.

cost-covering.[138] Hence, the idea of publicly funding the entity and charging a moderate fee seems adequate: a structure that provides high-quality ADR cannot survive without funding, especially in its early years.

Again, this could change in the future. Once a sufficiently high number of traders have experienced how beneficial ADR procedures can be for them, they may be more easily convinced to bear the full costs—even those traders for whom ADR is not mandatory.

Neither does a high value of a claim necessarily mean that the legal or factual expertise is complicated,[139] nor are 'low value cases' per se easy to settle. This has to be taken into consideration to anticipate appropriate funding. Finally, the German transposition act envisages that the value of the claim is estimated based on the consumer's claim.[140] With the procedure being free of charge for the consumer, this can lead to the consumer overestimating the value—to the detriment of the trader. This approach, considered only on its own, would lack a corrective measure such as the court fees that have to be paid in advance by the plaintiff. The amendment of the transposition act therefore foresees that the workload of the ADR entity can also be taken into consideration when defining the fees, and that other incentives concerning the fees should be implemented.[141]

9.3.3   Limitations of ADR?

ADR is not the European Union's solution to every consumer's issue with a trader. Both consumers and traders need to learn about the specifics of ADR to assess whether their case is suited for this dispute resolution instrument.

9.3.3.1   Multiple Parties Involved

As soon as a third party joins the dispute (respectively is involved), this added dimension makes the dispute more complex. It is very likely that putting more than two parties together in a procedure that has been designed for bilateral disputes is more difficult. A proper assessment is needed as to whether the ADR entity is competent: does a consumer contract between the parties exist? This is an issue that often arises when an insurance company, the manufacturer,[142] a debt collection agency or the like is involved. Finally, the binary prototype of a dispute is easier to

---

[138]Deutscher Bundestag (2019), p. 38.

[139]Deutscher Bundestag (2019), p. 37.

[140]Liepin (2017), § 31, margin no. 12.

[141]Deutscher Bundestag (2019), p. 40.

[142]Cf. § 443 BGB about the commercial guarantee as defined in Article 2 no. 14 Directive 2011/83/EU.

grasp for the consumer, who often gets lost in naming[143] the correct opponent when filing a formal request to the ADR entity—mostly (and quite intended, cf. Article 8 lit. b ADR Directive) without consulting legal assistance.

9.3.3.2   Unclear Facts Because of Insufficient Evidence

Disputes which primarily concern legal issues can be assessed rather easily from afar by the legal personnel of an ADR entity. Difficulties occur when evidence is unclear or is not produced by the parties, and hence the facts remain disputed. Some invoke that in these cases, ADR entities will prefer to render compromises.[144] To avoid these outcomes from automatically leaning more towards mere haggling than a legally assessed recommendation, one must consider the opportunity that ADR procedures offer. Both for the consumer and the trader, an assessment of whether their statements are not able to clarify the facts and with which party the burden of proof rests can open the way to a compromise. Furthermore, acknowledging the costs of a full examination of the case in court, i.e. fully informing both parties about the possible alternative, could help the parties to reach an agreement compromise. This limitation of ADR could paradoxically turn out to be one of the potential arguments for parties to engage in such a procedure.[145]

9.3.4   Conclusion

ADR in Germany is confronted with various challenges. The ongoing assessment of whether ADR works or not is mostly focused on its statistics. However, the statistics of ADR entities by themselves are a poor indicator of how well the ADR landscape is performing, as a comparison of the Netherlands, Sweden and France indicates.[146] In Germany, the new ADR system and its new players need to deliver high-quality ADR, and the perceptions in other sectors have shown that this leads to an acceptance both by traders and consumers in the long run. Communication campaigns seem to be a good way to promote ADR.[147] However, it seems better to advertise an existing and functioning service, thus providing evidence of best practices. If consumers and traders experience how and in which cases ADR can be an alternative solution, they may use this instrument more deliberately. Providing one free initial

---

[143]Cf. BGH VIII ZR 11/16, margins 18 et seq. concerning the interpretation limits of a designated party in a court procedure.

[144]Rott (2018), p. 124.

[145]Roder (2018), p. 204.

[146]European Commission (2018c), p. 1; Biard and Hodges (2019), p. 16 et seq., describing the French ADR landscape.

[147]European Commission (2018b), p. 95.

participation per trader in residual ADR, for instance, is seen[148] as a tool for breaking the layer of scepticism and would at least allow a more profound decision on the future use of ADR. This participation could lead to more experience in ADR and hence more acceptance of ADR in general.[149] In addition, ADR can be used as feedback for a trader's customer relation management.[150] Finally, the expertise of both residual and sector-specific ADR entities allows the assessment of the current situation on consumer disputes and problems.[151] The latter aspect is even more important due to the potential lack of court rulings in consumer disputes.[152]

A voluntary procedure offers maximum flexibility; yet it can leave one of the parties disappointed when the other party chooses not to pursue ADR any further. In addition, the voluntary participation for both parties combined with an obligatory fee burdened upon the trader seems to be a rather challenging status quo for residual ADR entities for finding motivated traders who are willing to participate in their procedures. Of course, ADR is not a remedy for every broken consumer-trader relationship. However, traders have been given the obligation and opportunity to assess the cases suited for ADR and to inform consumers about their choice, cf. Article 13(3) ADR Directive. Mandatory ADR is only one solution to make traders react to consumers' complaints. At least that is what the early implementation of legally 'nudged' ADR in regulated sectors suggests.[153]

9.4   Reflections and Outlook

As outlined above, ADR in Germany did not start from scratch and is well developed in many ways and areas, both in terms of quality and quantity. However, as also pointed out above, many challenges still linger.

The ADR Directive favours ADR for solving cross-border disputes and high-lights the importance of networking in this sense. Thus, ADR is well-designed for cross-border disputes, and the networking of ADR entities should not limit itself to the national level. Best practices in ADR can be compared across borders as well. The *Allgemeine Verbraucherschlichtungsstelle* (*Kehl*) could identify common issues and discover valuable ideas from residual ADR entities of other Member States.[154]

---

[148]This idea came up in the discussions on the amendment on the VSBG, Deutscher Bundesrat (2019), p. 3.

[149]Berlin (2019), p. 57/57.

[150]Hodges (2019), p. 17.

[151]Schmidt-Kessel (2019), p. 10.

[152]Cf. above Sect. 9.2.4.

[153]Roder (2018), p. 202 evokes the air transport sector as an example showing that ADR cannot 'get off the ground' without pressure from politics and legislators.

[154]Similar to the FIN-Net or NEON, residual ADR entities from Austria, Belgium, Germany and Luxembourg have been meeting on a regular basis for those purposes since 2016.

The sharing cases and exchanging knowledge amongst members of a network can fill the gaps which currently still exist, e.g. in cases which are not covered by the ODR Regulation and where the ODR contact points' framework subsequently does not apply.

Despite the considerable number of commitments towards ADR that can be found on traders' websites (cf. Article 13(1) ADR Directive), the number of traders that frankly refuse any participation is considerably high.[155] However, this may be due to some extent to the misconceptions observed.

We observe traders who agree to participate in an ADR procedure on their website,[156] but in fact they prevent undergoing such a procedure by fulfilling the consumer's claim immediately after being informed by the ADR entity about the request. Although this means a conciliation rate of 16.5%,[157] it is still extremely rare for a complete procedure with an elaborated recommendation to be carried out by the *Allgemeine Verbraucherschlichtungsstelle (Kehl)*.[158] Consequently, most claims are fully complied with by the trader. However, these claims might have proven to be (partially) unfounded if there had been a statement from the trader's side and an examination had been carried out. This issue could have been clarified by the ADR entity's recommendation and could have led to a recommendation 'in favour of' the trader. This would then maybe result in the fees borne by the trader being seen in a more positive light. However, it seems that this realisation has yet to prevail.

The reasoning of the transposition of Article 13(1) ADR Directive had good intentions of promoting ADR in Germany and, at the same time, giving consumers an idea of whether their (potential) contract partner is interested in ADR. Despite the questionable manners[159] in which the information obligation is occasionally carried out by traders, the liberties and nuances § 36 VSBG grants may be too complex for all traders to make use of. Information without any binding content (such as saying that the trader is 'in principle' willing to participate), however, is neither legal nor is it useful.[160] Misleading information is a matter for a consumer protection organisation or a competitor (warning letter[161]). Some traders fear the frequently mentioned 'deluge of (unfounded) ADR requests' and the costs these entail.[162] Hence traders (or their legal advisors) may instead opt for the safest wording: 'We do not participate in ADR'.

---

[155]Braun (2019), p. 132.

[156]The (gold-plating) German transposition of Article 13(1) and (2) ADR Directive was subject of two decisions of the BGH (VIII ZR 263/18 and VIII ZR 265/18).

[157]Creutzfeldt and Steffek (2018), p. 68.

[158]Creutzfeldt and Steffek (2018), p. 68.

[159]Some e-commerce traders do not seem to know that there is no compulsory ADR for distance contracts, nevertheless they inform their consumers 'we are *obliged* to participate in ADR'.

[160]BGH VIII ZR 263/18, margin no. 52; Rott (2018), p. 122.

[161]At least the system of warning letters for traders not complying with the information obligation seems to have worked out in one way: traders in Germany were most likely to put the link to the European Commission's ODR platform on their websites, European Commission (2017b), p. 28.

[162]Braun (2019), p. 134.

During the current amendment procedure of the VSBG, the information obligation will not be amended. For a future amendment, one could debate *Felix Steffek*'s approach of implementing a 'German Conflict Management code' which, on an initially voluntary basis, lets traders decide whether they want to comply or not.[163] Should they decide not to comply, they must then state their reasons for not doing so ('comply or explain'). § 36 VSBG could be omitted, and traders can concentrate on the information obligation in Article 13(3) ADR Directive (§ 37 VSBG). At present, the German legislator intended that at least small companies (ten employees or less) to evaluate their decision annually to generally declare whether they have to declare and thus if they want to participate or not, § 36(3) VSBG. Said code would foster more reflection on ADR for all size of companies (cf. Sect. 9.2.2).

The role of the information obligation and its diverse nuances will be probably even more significant after the *Universalschlichtungsstelle des Bundes* (§§ 29 et seq. VSBG) operates: for instance, a trader who omits implementing a statement concerning a participation will have to answer within three weeks or else will be considered a participant of the *Universalschlichtungsstelle des Bundes*' procedure[164]—including the entity's fee. How this indirect compulsory participation will turn out and how traders across Germany will (re-)react to ADR in general are issues which will certainly be discussed in the months to come.

The study currently carried out by *Naomi Creutzfeldt* and *Felix Steffek* shows that consumers who have turned to the *Allgemeine Verbraucherschlichtungsstelle (Kehl)* are 'clearly predominantly satisfied' (61%). They also gave this residual ADR entity a high rating of expertise: 91% appreciated the neutral position; 90% felt taken seriously; 83% mentioned that their problem had been understood correctly; and consumers considered the entity to be competent (84%) and trusted it (85%).[165] These findings reflect other surveys which concluded that consumers are in general for the most part satisfied with ADR.[166] A high satisfaction level and trust in legal competence, neutrality, easy access and transparency were also attested for three sector-specific ADR entities in Germany by *Naomi Creutzfeldt*'s report in 2016.[167] The results concerning traders are similar, however the survey is not yet representative on their part.[168]

Regarding at least[169] 87,398 requests that consumers lodged at ADR entities in 2018 and coming back to the introduction's metaphor, it appears that ADR in

---

[163]Steffek (2019), p. 5.

[164]Cf. the amended § 30(6) sentence 2 VSBG.

[165]Creutzfeldt and Steffek (2018), p. 63.

[166]European Commission (2017a), p. 59.

[167]Creutzfeldt (2016), passim and in particular the project reports regarding three German ombudsmen.

[168]Creutzfeldt and Steffek (2018), p. 29.

[169]A synopsis provided by Greger (2019c) and based on the annual reports 2018 is not yet complete due to the lack of the figures of one residual ADR entity (Außergerichtliche Streitbeilegungsstelle für Verbraucher und Unternehmer e.V. in Leipzig) and one sector-specific ADR entity (Ombudsstelle Immobilien des IVD/VPB - Grunderwerb und Verwaltung).

Germany is an instrument that takes some space, has its sound volume and sets its own accents. However, it has to be seen as part of an orchestra in which other instruments play their own specific roles that should not be suppressed, and in which all play together harmoniously. This orchestra is open to other instruments, such as the *Musterfeststellungsklage* (§§ 606 to 614 *Zivilprozessordnung*), which was introduced in 2018. The legislator intended for there to be cross-references between this new type of lawsuit and ADR.[170] However, as with all instruments and orchestras, careful coordination and especially fine-tuning is essential for creating an audible, pleasing sound. This includes corrections and improvements by a skilled and considerate conductor (and a careful instrument maker) in the future.

The European Commission's Article 26 Report of 9 July 2019 provides some insights into the EU/EEA-wide development and use of ADR entities and the impact of the ADR Directive on consumers and traders, in particular the impact on the awareness of consumers and the level of adoption by traders.[171] Mayhaps the report will cause further discussions whether amendments of the ADR Directive are necessary. On a more concrete scale, ADR may be considered in the context of bundle contracts on the electricity market, with the explicit mentioning in Article 26 of Directive EU 2019/944.[172] We will see how Member States, residual and sector-specific ADR entities design co-operation on this matter.

As of 1 January 2020, there has been some news in the German ADR landscape.[173] Some basic sketches already provide an inkling of what to expect in the years to come.[174] However, the details and especially the repercussions are not yet all visible. Some topics of the 2020 amendment of the German ADR Directive transposition act concern the *Universalschlichtungsstelle des Bundes* and a broader scope of assistance of the ODR contact point.

The most important issue, however, will be to provide a solution to the paradox of why traders often reject a procedure when a dispute arises, but who more abstractly appreciate the expertise and trustworthiness of ADR—considering it to be simpler, faster and more cost-efficient compared to court proceedings.[175]

References

Allgemeine Verbraucherschlichtungsstelle am Zentrum für Schlichtung e.V. (2017–2019) Tätigkeitsberichte 2016 - 2018. https://www.verbraucher-schlichter.de/ueber-uns/taetigkeitsberichte

---

[170]Deutscher Bundestag (2019), p. 20.

[171]European Commission (2019c), passim.

[172]Cf. National Energy Ombudsmen Network (2019).

[173]Nordhardt (2020).

[174]Universalschlichtungsstelle des Bundes am Zentrum für Schlichtung e.V. (2020).

[175]Creutzfeldt and Steffek (2019), second to last paragraph.

Allgemeine Verbraucherschlichtungsstelle am Zentrum für Schlichtung e.V. (2018) Vom anderen
    lernen: Grenzüberschreitender Austausch bei Schlichter-Treffen in Luxemburg. https://www.
    verbraucher-schlichter.de/presse/pressemitteilungen/pressemitteilung-vom-24072018
Allmänna Reklamtionsnämnden (2016–2019) Statistik: Antal ärenden åren 2016-2018. https://
    www.arn.se/om-arn/statistik
Anwaltliche Verbraucherschlichtungsstelle NRW e.V. (2019) Tätigkeitsbericht 2018. https://www.
    verbraucherschlichtung-nrw.de/taetigkeitsberichte/?file=files/swissy/img/downloads/AVS_
    Taetigkeitsbericht_2018.pdf
Berlin C (2016) Transparenz und Vertraulichkeit im Schlichtungsverfahren – Zur Frage der
    Veröffentlichung von Verfahrensergebnissen. Verbraucher und Recht Sonderheft:36–43
Berlin C (2017) Überblick zur bestehenden Schlichtungspraxis. In: Althammer C, Meller-Hannich
    C (eds) VSBG – Verbraucherstreitbeilegungsgesetz, 1st edn. Wolfgang Metzner Verlag, Frank-
    furt am Main, pp 21–43
Berlin C (2019) Schlichtungspotential am Beispiel Luftverkehr. ReiseRecht aktuell 2:50–57
Biard A (2018) Monitoring consumer ADR quality in the EU: a critical perspective. Eur Rev Priv
    Law 2:171–196
Biard A (2019) Impact of Directive 2013/11/EU on consumer ADR quality: evidence from France
    and the UK. J Consum Policy 42:109–147
Biard A, Hodges C (2019) Médiation de la consommation : un bilan, des défis, des pistes de
    réflexion pour l'avenir. Contrats – Concurrence – Consommation 2:12–21
Braun   F   (2019)   Das   Verbraucherstreitbeilegungsgesetz   im   Konzert   der
    Verbraucherrechtsdurchsetzung. Verbraucher und Recht 4:130–136
Braun F, Klinder A, Weiser S (2019) Verbraucherstreitbeilegung in der Automobilität. Deutsches
    Autorecht 1:54–58
Bundesamt für Justiz (2018) Verbraucherschlichtungsbericht. https://www.bundesjustizamt.de/DE/
    SharedDocs/Publikationen/Verbraucherschutz/Verbraucherschlichtungsbericht_2018.pdf
Bundesministerium   der   Justiz   und   für   Verbraucherschutz   (2019)   Bundesweite
    Universalschlichtungsstelle. https://www.bmjv.de/SharedDocs/Artikel/DE/2019/102919_
    Universalschlichtungsstelle.html
Cortés P (2018) Consumer ADR in Spain and the United Kingdom. J Eur Consum Mark Law
    2:82–88
Creutzfeldt N (2016) Project Report: trusting the middle-man: impact and legitimacy of ombuds-
    men in Europe. https://www.law.ox.ac.uk/trusting-middle-man-impact-and-legitimacy-ombuds
    men-europe/project-reports
Creutzfeldt N, Steffek F (2018) Zwischenbericht zur Funktionsweise der Allgemeinen
    Verbraucherschlichtungsstelle. In: Deutscher Bundestag Drucksache 19/6890
Creutzfeldt N, Steffek F (2019) Empirische Forschung zur Verbraucherschlichtung. https://blog.
    otto-schmidt.de/mediation/2019/05/09/empirische-forschung-zur-verbraucherschlichtung
Deutscher Bundesrat (2019) Entwurf eines Gesetzes zur Änderung von Vorschriften über die
    außergerichtliche Streitbeilegung in Verbrauchersachen und zur Änderung weiterer Gesetze.
    Drucksache 197/19 (Beschluss)
Deutscher Bundestag (2015) Entwurf eines Gesetzes zur Umsetzung der Richtlinie über alternative
    Streitbeilegung in Verbraucherangelegenheiten und zur Durchführung der Verordnung über
    Online-Streitbeilegung in Verbraucherangelegenheiten. Drucksache 18/5089
Deutscher Bundestag (2019) Entwurf eines Gesetzes zur Änderung von Vorschriften über die
    außergerichtliche Streitbeilegung in Verbrauchersachen und zur Änderung weiterer Gesetze.
    Drucksache 19/10348
Deutscher Industrie- und Handelskammertag (2019) Stellungnahme zum Referentenentwurf eines
    Gesetzes zur Änderung von Vorschriften über die außergerichtliche Streitbeilegung in
    Verbrauchersachen. https://www.bmjv.de/SharedDocs/Gesetzgebungsverfahren/
    Stellungnahmen/2019/Downloads/02012019_Stellungnahme_DIHK_au%C3%9Fergerichtl-
    Streitbeilegung-Verbrauchersachen.pdf

Deutsches Kraftfahrzeuggewerbe (2017) Kfz-Schiedsstellen: gut funktionierende Schlichtung. https://www.kfzgewerbe.de/presse/pressemeldungen/kfz-schiedsstellen-gut-funktionierende-schlichtung.html

Engel M (2015) Außergerichtliche Streitbeilegung in Verbraucherangelegenheiten – Mehr Zugang zu weniger Recht. Neue Juristische Wochenschrift 23:1633–1637

European Commission (2015) Directive 2013-11-EU (Directive on consumer ADR) – issues emerging from the meetings of the ADR Expert Group. http://ec.europa.eu/transparency/regexpert/index.cfm?do=groupDetail.groupDetailDoc&id=18896&no=3

European Commission (2017a) Consumer Condition Scoreboard. https://ec.europa.eu/info/sites/info/files/consumer-conditions-scoreboard-2017-edition_en_0.pdf

European Commission (2017b) Online Dispute Resolution: Web-Scraping of EU Traders' Websites. https://publications.europa.eu/en/publication-detail/-/publication/9cafdfce-b4a7-11e8-99ee-01aa75ed71a1

European Commission (2017c) Commission facilitates new network to resolve consumer disputes in the travel sector. https://ec.europa.eu/luxembourg/news/commission-facilitates-new-network-resolve-consumer-disputes-travel-sector_fr

European Commission (2018a) Ex-post evaluation of the Consumer Programme 2007-2013 and mid-term evaluation of the Consumer Programme 2014-2020 – Final report part 1

European Commission (2018b) Ex-post evaluation of the Consumer Programme 2007-2013 and mid-term evaluation of the Consumer Programme 2014-2020 – Final report part 2

European Commission (2018c) Functioning of the European ODR Platform. https://ec.europa.eu/info/sites/info/files/2nd_report_on_the_functioning_of_the_odr_platform_3.pdf

European Commission (2018d) ADR Assembly 2018 - summary report. https://www.risolvionline.com/Documenti_News/ADR_Assembly_2018_-_Summary_report.pdf

European Commission (2019a) Cross-border e-commerce: Commission welcomes agreement on proposal to facilitate sales of goods and supply of digital content and services in the EU. http://europa.eu/rapid/press-release_STATEMENT-19-742_en.htm

European Commission (2019b) The 2019 EU Justice Scoreboard. https://publications.europa.eu/en/publication-detail/-/publication/662909c5-81c0-11e9-9f05-01aa75ed71a1

European Commission (2019c) Report on the application of Directive 2013/11/EU of the European Parliament and of the Council on alternative dispute resolution for consumer disputes and Regulation (EU) No 524/2013 of the European Parliament and of the Council on online dispute resolution for consumer disputes. https://eur-lex.europa.eu/legal-content/EN/TXT/?uri=COM:2019:425:FIN

European Parliament (2011) Cross-border alternative dispute resolution in the European Union. https://publications.europa.eu/en/publication-detail/-/publication/28ad61d2-c58d-11e5-a4b5-01aa75ed71a1

European Parliament (2017) Effective access to justice. https://publications.europa.eu/en/publication-detail/-/publication/2b6745c1-00bc-11e8-b8f5-01aa75ed71a1

Fejős A (2018) Consumer ADR in Hungary. J Eur Consum Mark Law 3:116–120

Fichtner H (2017) § 14 VSBG. In: Althammer C, Meller-Hannich C (eds) VSBG – Verbraucherstreitbeilegungsgesetz, 1st edn. Wolfgang Metzner Verlag, Frankfurt am Main, pp 163–185

Fries M (2016) PayPal Law und Legal Tech – Was macht die Digitalisierung mit dem Privatrecht? Neue Juristische Wochenschrift 39:2860–2865

Geier R (2016) Schlichtung, Schiedsgericht, staatliche Justiz – Drei Akteure in einem System institutioneller Rechtsverwirklichung. Neue Juristische Wochenschrift 19:1367–1371

Gläßer U, Hammes M, Kirchhoff L (2016) In: PriceWaterhouseCoopers AG, Europa-Universität Viadrina Frankfurt/Oder (ed) Konfliktmanagement in der deutschen Wirtschaft – Entwicklungen eines Jahrzehnts, Frankfurt am Main

Gössl S (2015) Ablehnungsgründe für das Verfahren. In: Schmidt-Kessel M (ed) Alternative Streitschlichtung - Die Umsetzung der ADR-Richtlinie in Deutschland. Jenaer Wissenschaftliche Verlagsgesellschaft, Jena, pp 67–86

Greger R (2016) Der Rückgang der Klageeingangszahlen in der Justiz – mögliche Ursachen (Report on the Symposium an der Universität Halle-Wittenberg on 8 Dec 2015). https://www. schlichtungs-forum.de/dateien/2016/07/Kurzbericht-Halle.pdf

Greger R (2018a) Neue Auffangstelle für Verbraucherstreitbeilegung. https://www.schlichtungs-forum.de/neuigkeiten/neue-auffangstelle-fuer-verbraucherstreitbeilegung

Greger R (2018b) Weiterhin kein Durchbruch bei der Verbraucherstreitbeilegung. https://www. schlichtungs-forum.de/neuigkeiten/weiterhin-kein-durchbruch-bei-der-verbraucherstreitbeilegung

Greger R (2019a) Verbraucherstreitbeilegung: Kein Durchbruch, viele Fragen. Verbraucher und Recht 2:43–48

Greger R (2019b) söp meldet steigendes Fallaufkommen und Ausweitung des Tätigkeitsbereichs. https://www.schlichtungs-forum.de/neuigkeiten/soep-meldet-steigendes-fallaufkommen-und-ausweitung-des-taetigkeitsbereichs

Greger R (2019c) Verbraucherschlichtung schwächelt – außer beim Luftverkehr. https://www. schlichtungs-forum.de/neuigkeiten/verbraucherschlichtung-schwaechelt-ausser-beim-luftverkehr

Greger R (2019d) Eingänge und Erledigungen bei den Verbraucherstreitbeilegungsstellen 2018. https://www.schlichtungs-forum.de/dateien/2019/03/Statistische-%C3%9Cbersicht-2018.pdf

Greger R, Unberath H, Steffek F (2016) Recht der alternativen Konfliktlösung, 2nd edn. C.H. Beck, München

Hagl-Kehl R (2019) Rede zur Beratung des Bundestags. In: Deutscher Bundestag Stenografischer Bericht zur 104. Sitzung, 19/104:12788–12789

Hodges C (2019) Consumer ADR - Delivering Fairness and Justice for Consumers, Business and Markets. https://www.law.ox.ac.uk/sites/files/oxlaw/post-conference_report_0.pdf

Hodges C, Benöhr I, Creutzfeldt-Banda N (2012) Consumer ADR in Europe. Hart Publishing, Oxford and Portland

Höxter G (2016) Das Verbraucherstreitbeilegungsgesetz im Kontext grenzüberschreitender Streitigkeiten. In: Verbraucher und Recht Sonderheft:29–33

https://publications.europa.eu/en/publication-detail/-/publication/3aefdcef-22af-11e9-8d04-01aa75ed71a1

https://publications.europa.eu/en/publication-detail/-/publication/5e9ee253-22b0-11e9-8d04-01aa75ed71a1

Institut für Demoskopie Allensbach, ROLAND Rechtsschutz-Versicherungs-AG (2014) Roland Rechtsreport. https://www.roland-rechtsschutz.de/media/rechtsschutz/pdf/unternehmen_1/ROLAND_Rechtsreport_2014.pdf

Isermann E (2018) Rechtsgrundsätzliches und Schlichtung. In: Czerwenka B et al (eds) Festschrift zu Ehren von Marie Luise Graf-Schlicker. RWS Verlag Kommunikationsforum GmbH, Köln, pp 51–62

Liepin M (2017) § 31 VSBG. In: Althammer C, Meller-Hannich C (eds) VSBG – Verbraucherstreitbeilegungsgesetz, 1st edn. Wolfgang Metzner Verlag, Frankfurt am Main, pp 318–329

Loizou S (2018) Consumer ADR in the Republic of Cyprus. J Eur Consum Mark Law 3:126–129

Morais Carvalho J, Nemeth K (2018) Implementation of the Consumer ADR Directive in the EU Member States. J Eur Consum Mark Law 2:81

National Energy Ombudsmen Network (2019) NEON Welcomes Adoption of Strong Consumer-Protection and Out-Of-Court Dispute Settlement Provisions at EU level. http://www. neon-ombudsman.org/2019/03/26/clean-energy-package-neon-welcomes-the-adoption-of-strong-consumer-protection-and-out-of-court-dispute-settlement-provisions

Nguyen B (2011) The dark side of CRM. Market Rev 11(2):137–149

Nöhre M (2018) Wie viel Streitschlichtung verträgt der deutsche Zivilprozess? In: Czerwenka B et al (eds) Festschrift zu Ehren von Marie Luise Graf-Schlicker. RWS Verlag Kommunikationsforum GmbH, Köln, pp 85–100

Nordhardt MM (2020) Universalschlichtungsstelle - Schneller als vor Gericht. https://www.
tagesschau.de/inland/verbraucher-schlichtungsstelle-101.html

Pinto-Ferreira JP, Campos Carvalho J (2018) Consumer ADR in Portugal. J Eur Consum Mark Law
2:89–91

Rätze M (2016a) OS-Plattform zur Streitbelegung ist online. https://shopbetreiber-blog.de/2016/02/
15/os-plattform

Rätze M (2016b) Verbraucherschlichtung: Neue Infopflichten seit Samstag! https://shopbetreiber-
blog.de/2016/01/08/verbraucherschlichtung-neue-infopflichten-ab-9-januar-2016

Rebehn S (2019) Trendwende bei Verfahrenszahlen. Neue Juristische Wochenschrift – aktuell
43:17

Roder M (2018) Zwei Jahre VSBG – eine erste Zwischenbilanz. Zeitschrift für
Konfliktmanagement 6:200–204

Roder M, Röthemeyer P, Braun F (2017) Verbraucherstreitbeilegungsgesetz. C.H.Beck, München

Röthemeyer P (2016) Verfahren nach VSBG und ZPO im Vergleich. Verbraucher und Recht
Sonderheft:9–16

Rott P (2018) Consumer ADR in Germany. J Eur Consum Mark Law 3:121–125

Sachverständigenrat für Verbraucherfragen (2018) Verbrauchergerechtes Scoring. http://www.svr-
verbraucherfragen.de/wp-content/uploads/SVRV_Verbrauchergerechtes_Scoring.pdf

Schafer J, Konstan J, Riedl J (1999) Recommender systems in e-commerce. In: Feldman S,
Wellman M (eds) Proceedings of the First ACM Conference on Electronic Commerce
(EC-99), pp 158 166

Schlichtungsstelle für den öffentlichen Personenverkehr e.V. (2019) Jahresbericht 2018. https://
soep-online.de/assets/files/14.03._soep_Jahresbericht_2018.pdf

Schmidt-Kessel M (2019) Stellungnahme zum Entwurf eines Gesetzes zur Änderung von
Vorschriften über die außergerichtliche Streitbeilegung in Verbrauchersachen und zur
Änderung weiterer Gesetze. https://www.bundestag.de/resource/blob/649428/
d9e23f78d867b530e2204992a2207354/schmidt-kessel-data.pdf

Service de Médiation pour le Consommateur (2019) Rapport Annuel 2018. https://
consumerombudsman.be/sites/default/files/content/download/files/cod-jaarverslag_2018-fr-lr.
pdf

SPF Economie (2018) Rapport sur le REL en Belgique. https://economie.fgov.be/sites/default/files/
Files/Consumer-protection/Rapport-ADR-Belgique-2018.pdf

Stadler A (1998) Außergerichtliche obligatorische Streitschlichtung – Chance oder Illusion? Neue
Juristische Wochenschrift 34:2479–2487

Statistisches Bundesamt (2019) Zivilgerichte - Fachserie 10 Reihe 2.1 2018. https://www.destatis.
de/DE/Themen/Staat/Justiz-Rechtspflege/Publikationen/Downloads-Gerichte/zivilgerichte-
2100210187004.pdf

Steffek F (2019) Der Deutsche Konfliktmanagementkodex (DKMK). Zeitschrift für
Konfliktmanagement 1:4–8

Stichting De Geschillencommissies (2018) Jaarverslagen 2017. https://www.
samenwerkenaankwaliteit.nl/jaarverslag-2017

Stichting De Geschillencommissies (2019) Jaarverslagen 2018. https://www.
samenwerkenaankwaliteit.nl/jaarverslag-2018

Translation Centre of the Bodies of the European Union (2017) Consolidated Activity Report of the
Translation Centre. https://cdt.europa.eu/sites/default/files/documentation/pdf/005_2018_ar_
2017_en_0.pdf

Universalschlichtungsstelle des Bundes am Zentrum für Schlichtung e.V. (2020) Schlichtung kann
helfen – auch und gerade jetzt. https://www.verbraucher-schlichter.de/media/file/77.PM_
Covid-19-Krise_Schlichtung_kann_helfen.pdf

Versicherungsombudsmann e.V. (2018) Jahresbericht 2017. https://www.versicherungsombudsmann.de/wp-content/uploads/Jahresbericht2017.pdf

Wagner G (2017) Rechtsstandort Deutschland im Wettbewerb. C.H. Beck, München

Wernike S (2019) VSBG ist eine vertane Chance. Quote via : https://www.wnews.de/de-DE/Rubriken/Recht-Rat/19-01_Verbraucherstreitbeteiligungsgesetz

Wolf C (2015) Zivilprozess versus außergerichtliche Konfliktlösung – Wandel der Streitkultur in Zahlen. Neue Juristische Wochenschrift 23:1656–1661

Part III
Self-Representation

Chapter 10
Self-Representation and the Courts: Some Policy Observations from the Netherlands

Paulien van der Grinten

Abstract Self-representation in the courts could be seen as a means to improve access to justice. It saves the litigants the cost of a lawyer. These costs have been reported to be the biggest financial obstacle for parties with a dispute. This contribution based on the panel discussion on the topic of self-representation identifies some questions regarding self-representation from a Dutch policy maker's perspective. These questions relate among others to the increasing complexity of society, the role of the courts and the judges in a civil procedure, the financing of the court system, legal aid and the role of oral presentations as a key element of self-representation in relation to IT-based proceedings. The conclusion is that we would need answers to these questions before we decide on a policy on self-representation in our courts.

10.1 Introduction

Self-representation was the topic of one of the panels during the Conference on Pathways to Civil Justice that took place on 19 and 20 November 2018 in Rotterdam. It was one of the last panels of the Conference. By that time, we had heard so many interesting, worrisome, hopeful and inspirational stories about the civil justice systems across the globe that it dazzled me. Whether it was about digitisation of justice, standardisation, artificial intelligence in dispute resolution or alternative dispute resolution schemes, each of the speakers' and panellists' speeches seemed to have at least some link to self-representation. In that respect they underlined the modesty I felt when talking about policy observations from the Netherlands. Before I can make policy observations, I first have to make an inventory of my preliminary

---

This article reflects the author's personal views and is without prejudice to any views of the Dutch Ministry of Justice and Security.

P. van der Grinten (✉)
Ministry of Justice and Security, The Hague, The Netherlands
e-mail: p.van.der.grinten@minjenv.nl

policy questions. So, this is what I can offer now, the Dutch perspective and some preliminary questions from a Dutch policy perspective.

10.2   What Is Self-Representation?

Before we can talk about whether self-representation is a good thing and whether and how it should be promoted, we need to know what we are talking about. What do we mean by self-representation? Is it just taking lawyers out of the equation or is it more than that? In the Netherlands in cases before the Dutch cantonal judge parties can act in person.[1] The cantonal judge deals with claims up to €25,000. Until 2011 the maximum amount was € 5000. It was increased to make the simple, fast and cheap procedure before the cantonal judge available to citizens in a much larger number of cases.[2] In proceedings before the cantonal judge the parties may also seek assistance or representation from any person they want unless such person is not a lawyer or a bailiff and there are serious objections against him or her (art 79–81 Dutch Code of Civil Procedure). This covers the majority of our civil cases. In practice most claimants bring a representative, but not necessarily lawyers.[3]

The landscape is varied as is shown in the Dutch research evaluating the increased competence of the cantonal judge specifically on the point of representation in cases before the cantonal judge.[4] Among the representatives used are bailiffs and legal expense insurance companies as well as lawyers. Especially in money claims (unpaid debts), bailiffs are used as representatives. This is not a coincidence. Most claims other than family law cases start with a writ of summons. A writ of summons means compulsory intervention by a bailiff: to serve the writ. In serving the writ the bailiff acts on behalf of the claimant. This might prevent claimants from acting on their own behalf in the actual court procedure following the writ. A different start of proceedings—self-start—might promote real self-representation in the actual court cases. However, we lack empirical data, and much would depend on other known and unknown—relevant factors. What we do know, is that in cross border cases within the scope of the EU-Regulations on Orders for Payment and Small Claims legal representation and a writ of summons are not required and applications are made with a standard form.[5] However, in the Netherlands this has not led to

---

[1]The cantonal judge falls under the Dutch court of first instance. It deals with cases with a maximum of € 25,000 and with all cases relating to labour law, landlord-tenant case and most consumer cases (article 93 Dutch Code of Civil Procedure). The procedure before the cantonal judge is a single-judge procedure (article 47 of the Law on the Judiciary (Wet op de Rechterlijke Organisatie).

[2]Eshuis and Geurts (2016).

[3]In 2017 in only 1% of the cases (4500) the claimant was self-represented, defendants were self-represented in 10% of the cases (35,600), see Minister for Legal Protection (2018).

[4]Eshuis and Geurts (2016).

[5]Article 24 of Regulation (EC) No 1896/2006 of the European Parliament and of the Council of 12 December 2006 creating a European order for payment procedure, OJ L 399, 30.12.2006,

self-representation by natural persons who are a claimant in these procedures. Natural persons tend to either use a lawyer to file their application (Order for Payment) or not use the procedure at all (Small Claims).[6] Would a simple interactive form which helps the claimant to choose what to claim and to include all the relevant aspects of the claim increase direct access for natural persons? The success of the British Columbia Civil Resolution Tribunal which offers an online dispute resolution mechanism suggests this might indeed be effective.[7]

10.3 Opposing Trends: Increasing Complexity v. Demand for Accessible and Effective Problem Solving

10.3.1 Increasing Complexity of Society and Its Disputes

There seem to be opposing trends relevant for the civil justice system and the role of self-representation therein. A first trend has to do with society becoming ever more complex.[8] As it does, so do its rules and its disputes. In the Netherlands, court files have become thicker over the years.[9] In complex cases between professional parties e.g. about multi-party building or finance contracts or about the liability for climate change hundreds of pages for an admissibility defense alone are not an exception. In these cases, instead of one or two lawyers on a case, a whole team of lawyers may be working on it to look in every corner of the case, thereby increasing the number of pages of each document and the amount of work for the courts with it.

Standardisation of legal work has led to types of work done by others than lawyers or by technology. This standardisation seems to have hit mainly other types of work than litigation like due diligence and more and more the work done in mergers and acquisitions. In this practice area the previously specialised work of drafting a Sales Purchase Agreement has been perfected in Model Contracts.[10] For the moment, complex litigation still seems to be largely unaffected. To me it is rather unlikely that for complex litigation cases this 'lawyers' paradise' will disappear

---

p. 1–32 and article 10 of Regulation (EC) No 861/2007 of the European Parliament and of the Council of 11 July 2007 establishing a European Small Claims Procedure, OJ L 199, 31.7.2007, p. 1–22, as both amended on 7 July, 2017.

[6]The Netherlands country report in the IC2BE project suggests that complexity of the case and language issues may also be a factor here. See EA Ontanu (2020).

[7]Cf. the British Columbia Civil Resolution Tribunal, an online dispute resolution device based on the perspective of the citizen without legal knowledge, https://civilresolutionbc.ca/. The fact that in Canada they have chosen to offer this mechanism out of court rather than within the court does not seem relevant in this respect.

[8]WRR (2017); cf. also Mr. Hans van Mierlo Stichting (2013).

[9]See for example Vranken (2018), about the increased size of the files in procedures before the Dutch Supreme Court.

[10]See also, extensively Susskind (2010).

shortly or that procedures and conflicts are easily simplified. Although this is not a solution to the complexity problem, forcing those same lawyers to present the essence of the dispute in a 'two-pager' instead of those hundreds of pages might—at least, in the short term—be a better way to save time and costs for courts and clients and thereby get better access to justice. In the long run we may need to rethink the way we deal with disputes about complex matters.

But what about the increasing complexity of society in relation to the ordinary and the more vulnerable individual citizens? Could it be that technology and globalisation has made it more complex for citizens to deal with their basic needs like housing, mobile phones, bank accounts and Internet access? For each of those there may be foreign providers involved which only offer their services online. They may use thick and hard-to-read contracts with detailed and complex rules behind it. Could this have created more causes and greater complexity of legal disputes as well? And if so, is representation by a lawyer increasingly important or are there other ways to address this problem of increased complexity of society and its disputes in relation to citizens? This is the point where a second trend, opposed to the first is worth mentioning.

10.3.2 The Need for 'the Actual Problem to be Effectively Solved' in Court for Citizens ('Effective Justice')

A second trend, going in the opposite direction, is that the judiciary, the government and others feel that our civil justice system is failing citizens and SME's. I only have to refer to Ruth de Bock's outstanding keynote speech at the conference from which this book results to illustrate this.[11] Citizens' problems are juridified in court proceedings and court decisions do not always offer long-term solutions to those problems. The role of lawyers and their compulsory partiality may sometimes have the effect of contributing to this juridification of problems.

There is a wide call for cheaper, simplified procedures and de-escalation of conflicts, in family cases, disputes between neighbours and between SME's. In order to reduce the number of persons with problematic debts and to simplify our debt collection court mechanism, there is a call for a total reform of the debt collection system to possibly make it an out of court mechanism, like in Belgium or with a greater focus on the use of realistic payment schemes imposed by the court.

Rather than waiting for new legislation, courts are experimenting with procedures which are 'close to the parties' within the framework of the Dutch Code of Civil Procedure (DCCP). They can use Article 96 DCCP for these experiments as this article provides for jurisdiction of the cantonal judge on a voluntary basis. It can be

---

[11]Ruth de Bock delivered a keynote speech on different pathways to justice and the need for clear signposting, using the example of damage caused by earthquakes in Groningen resulting from gas extraction. This keynote speech was not reworked into a chapter and is not included in this book.

used for all sorts of cases as long as no other court has exclusive jurisdiction in the matter (e.g. family cases must be dealt with by the family judge). The only requirement is that both parties jointly ask the cantonal judge to deal with their case or, if asked by one of the parties, the other party consents to the use of the cantonal judge to solve the dispute. Article 96 DCCP leaves it to the cantonal judge to decide on the rules of procedure for the case. That is why the current experiments are all based on this Article of the DCCP.

At the same time the Dutch Ministry of Justice and Security is working on a project to make our laws of civil procedure more responsive to citizens' legal needs. Based on the perspective of litigants we look for ways to improve the role of our civil justice in dispute resolution. We will also look at the role of our rules of civil procedure to see how they could help reduce the conflict material between the parties rather than induce it. We will yet have to see the role of lawyers in the way disputes are dealt with and how they fit into this new type of procedure.

10.4 An Example: The Consulting Judge

One of the court experiments is the so-called 'Consulting Judge' at the court of Noord-Nederland in the North of the Netherlands. The experiment started on 1 May 2016 and lasted till 1 May 2018. In was evaluated in a study made at the request of the Council for the Judiciary, which was finalized in October 2018.[12] Cases could be brought before the Consulting Judge by mutual consent of the parties and only after referral by either a legal expense insurance company or by the 'Legal Desk', a government organisation which advises citizens with a legal problem on where to go with their problem (ADR, court, mediation). The idea was for the parties to have a 'dialogue with the Consulting Judge and if need be, a court decision' with a lower court fee. In practice the defendant would only consent to use these proceedings rather than the ordinary court procedure after prior direct contact between the Consulting Judge Bureau's support staff with the defendant.

In this experiment no documents were submitted beforehand. The laws on evidence were not strictly applied; the goal was to have a dialogue that would help the parties solve their problem not to do comprehensive fact-finding. Parties could bring a representative to support and advise them. But the parties themselves would have to be the key players in the proceedings and tell their story to the judge. Some parties, especially claimants, did bring a representative, which would usually be someone from the legal expense insurance company that had referred the case to the Consulting Judge in the first place. Such representative would only sometimes be allowed to speak during the court hearing.

More than half of the cases dealt with by the Consulting Judge were disputes between private landowners (neighbours). The other half consisted of building

---

[12]Evaluation report Hertogh et al. (2018).

disputes, consumer purchase agreements, Landlord-tenant disputes, labour disputes and a few family disputes. The number of settlements was high: 58 out 64 cases (91%). Parties were reasonably happy with the procedure before the Consulting Judge.[13]

One would expect that the study's conclusion would be that the experiment was very successful. However, the study concluded that it was only a half success: very successful in some respects, but this success has to be weighed against the costs and time of the experimental procedure. The costs of the support staff to inform the parties about the possibility to bring their case before the Consulting Judge and about the procedure were rather high. A further criticism was that the high number of settlements is highly influenced by the very strict selection of cases admitted as suitable for the Consulting Judge (64 out of 115 original referrals). The study also found that the absence of documents led to lengthy court hearings of three to four hours before the facts were established—and a settlement could be reached. The study does not say much about the impact of not having representatives acting as such. The study's ultimate conclusion is that it would be worthwhile to do a different experiment using some elements of the Consulting Judge. It could be using a kind of triage by a lay judge (like in Germany the *Schiedsamt* or in Norway the *Forlikrad*) or by a having real walk-in hours for the Consulting Judge, not necessarily in a court building. A second experiment has already been taken up by the Rotterdam court, which started the Rotterdam Consulting Judge (*"Rotterdamse Regelrechter"*) experiment in September of 2018.[14] It lasted until December, 2019 and will be scientifically evaluated. The principle of no submission of documents before the hearing is upheld in this experiment. The hearing will be a dialogue between the parties and the judge. If no settlement can be reached in this hearing the court may give its decision or leave room for the exchange of some documents if needed. Legal advisors like lawyers are allowed in the procedure and they may be brought to the hearing but the judge will primarily have the parties speak for themselves. We will have to wait for the evaluation but it seems like lawyers are tolerated in this experiment rather than being a quintessential part of it.

---

[13]Vranken (2018).

[14]See for further information https://www.rechtspraak.nl/Organisatie-en-contact/Organisatie/ Rechtbanken/Rechtbank-Rotterdam/Regels-en-procedures/Paginas/regelrechter.aspx.

10.5   Another Example: Divorce Cases—The Divorce Without Damage Project

Divorce without damage is the rather pretentious name of a project that intends to reduce the damage for children of high-conflict divorces.[15] The project has yet to be further developed and executed so I can only give you a rough impression of the current ideas. The goal is to have sustainable solutions for legal problems in relation to a divorce, especially where children are involved.

Spouses or one of them, are expected to go to a local divorce desk. From there, all help, legal/mental/social, will be organised through a single neutral 'family-representative' for both spouses or through referral to such a neutral person. This neutral family-representative is to act on behalf of the two potentially disagreeing partners and their children if there are any, in a court procedure and to submit documents stating the points of agreement and disagreement. The judge can intervene on the points where the parties disagree, preferably at the early stages, and help them to reach sustainable outcomes on other points, where needed assisted by e.g. a psychologist.

This neutral family-representative, according to the plans, does not necessarily have to be a lawyer. At the same time, many of the criteria we are looking at seem to be taken from the code of conduct of the Dutch specialised Family Lawyers (among which expert legal knowledge). Some judges participating in the discussions on this feel that divorce disputes are escalated rather than de-escalated by lawyers, in particular on the side of lawyers working on a legal aid basis. But do those judges see what conflicts have been solved beforehand between the parties with the help of a lawyer-mediator or a family lawyer? Do we know enough about the role of those lawyers in the majority of divorce cases in which a joint divorce request is submitted to the court?

The need for better access to justice is widely felt in divorce cases, but it is not an easy problem to solve. In a recent example the ex-wife's lawyer helped a divorcing couple to reduce costs, by agreeing to submit their joint divorce request. This request was based on the divorce agreement drafted by the ex-husband and agreed between the two of them. Years later the ex-husband felt his financial interests had not been properly served in the divorce agreement. He sued his ex-wife's lawyer who was ordered by the court to pay a considerable sum of money for neglecting the duty of care to provide legal information about his position to the ex-husband. As she had been the ex-wife's lawyer she was considered—and under the official disciplinary rules for lawyers bound to be—partial on her behalf.

We will have to see how this idea of one neutral family-representative for two disagreeing spouses is going to deal with this type of conflicting interests issue. And what to do if one of the parties simply refuses to have anything to do with this neutral

---

[15]See for information https://www.rijksoverheid.nl/actueel/nieuws/2018/05/09/ministers-dekker-en-de-jonge-starten-samen-met-gemeenten-uitvoeringsprogramma-scheiden-zonder-schade; and the Progress Report of 1 July, 2019, (Parliamentary Documents 2018-2019, 33 835, nr. 44).

family-representative or during the proceedings feels that its interests are not properly represented? How do we respect the adversarial aspects inherent to a case where parties disagree and court intervention is needed? As de-escalating and problem solving the approach of the one neutral family-representative may sound, we still have many fundamental and practical questions to answer.

10.6 Appeals Proceedings from Cases Without Legal Representation

Increasing access to justice by reducing the costs of representation is also on the agenda of the Dutch Parliament. It asked if parties who appeal decisions of the cantonal judge—where no legal representation is required—could act without representation also before the court of appeal.[16] The Ministry of Justice and Security organised an expert meeting in 2018 where the conclusion was that, at least in the short term, this is not a good idea. The experts found that our rules of civil procedure in appeal are too complicated and the quality of the legal debate would suffer in case of self-representation. Parliament was informed that the issue would need to be looked into in relation to a simplification of the rules of procedure in appeal.[17] This raises the question whether simplifying the rules for appeal proceedings would indeed make self-representation easier for litigants. And if so, would self-representation contribute to a better procedure for them? And how are we supposed to measure this?

10.7 Law on Experiments in Civil Justice

Keynote speaker Ruth de Bock mentioned in her speech the plans for a Law on Civil Justice Experiments.[18] Its goal is to improve our civil justice system in order to make sure it de-escalates conflicts and helps solve the actual legal problems that citizens are faced with. The idea is that experiments are needed to see what actually works in this area. A law on experiments is needed to make sure that parties can be forced to use the experimental procedure instead of having to limit the experiment to voluntary use of the experimental procedure.

---

[16]Question asked by Member of Parliament Van Oosten (VVD) in Parliament (Tweede Kamer der Staten-Generaal) (2018).

[17]Minister for Legal Protection (2018).

[18]Keynote not part of this book (see footnote 11 in this chapter). Bill no 35263, Parliamentary year 2018–2019 'Regels inzake invoering van een tijdelijke mogelijkheid voor experimenten in de rechtspleging (Tijdelijke Experimentenwet rechtspleging)' (Rules on the introduction of the temporary possibility for experiments in the judiciary).

At the time of writing, the Bill to introduce this law was pending in Parliament.[19] It is drafted on request of and in cooperation with the Judiciary. It provides for the possibility to deviate from almost all procedural rules, including those on representation by a lawyer, except those that safeguard the essential elements of a civil procedure like impartiality of the judge. It requires that every experiment safeguards the principles of access to justice and fair trial. The Bill provides for a review board, which reviews whether a proposed experiment meets all the requirements of the law, and a compulsory evaluation. The law will only be applicable for 15 years. When an experiment turns out to be successful according to the evaluation, it can be implemented in the procedural rules of the Code of Civil Procedure. The experiments currently discussed are meant to build on the several pilots like the pilot with the Rotterdam Consulting Judge, for example, a "judge-nearby"-experiment with easy access for citizens with their day-to-day legal problems. Self-representation in the sense of actual in person litigation will certainly be an important point to be discussed in these experiments.

10.8   Information for Citizens: A Precondition to Self-Representation?

Without knowledge about the problems and the options for solving them, self-representation seems either almost impossible or a huge burden on the courts. Legal education of citizens and increasing their access to information seems to be increasingly on the agenda. See for example the press release on the UK plans on Public Legal Education from among others the Law Society, the Judicial Office and the Ministry of Justice.[20] In the Netherlands we currently do not have such an education plan. We do have basic information and Q&A's on the government's website on some of the legal events happening to people's lives.[21] The goal is to provide citizens with basic knowledge of their civil and criminal rights. See also the examples in this book about all the Artificial Intelligence systems available. Leaving aside all the doubts we can have about AI as potential replacement for lawyers and judges, there is a lot more legal information 'out there' for citizens. However, to what extent are those systems really accessible for citizens? And more importantly, is providing information to citizens in general and more particularly to the more vulnerable citizens experiencing the greater part of legal problems really helpful in

---

[19]See: Parliament (Tweede Kamer der Staten-Generaal) (2019).

[20]Attorney General's Office and the Rt Hon Robert Buckland QC MP (2018).

[21]E.g. Government (Rijksoverheid) (2020a) Scheiden of uit elkaar: wat moet ik regelen? (Divorce or Separation: what legal steps do I need to take?); Government (Rijksoverheid) (2020b) Wat moet ik doen als ik word ontslagen? (What should I do when I get fired?).

solving their legal problems? Do they have the capacity to process such information? And does it help to increase their capacity to act in person in a court procedure?[22]

10.9 Questions and Conclusions from a Dutch Policy Perspective

We cannot talk about self-representation without discussing what we expect from courts and judges. Is it their task to give a legal decision? Can they realistically be the problem solvers that we may want them to be? Is the judge someone who should have an authoritative dialogue with the parties? Or should the parties in a court case be entitled to a full-fledged procedure with access to all the means of evidence available under the rules of civil procedure? If judges are not instructed by parties 'in the know', should they do their job differently? Do we want them to spend more time on a case to gather the factual and legal information up to the same level? Or do we want them to give different types of decisions without having all the underlying documents and evidence? What would that mean for the principle that the court must base its decision on the material truth? How do we prevent the judge from becoming partial when one party is clearly less suited to represent himself than his opponent?

What would a wider use of self-representation mean for the way we finance our courts? Is it in this respect in the end cost-saving or would it be costlier for the courts to deal with self-represented cases instead? What would it mean for one's right to legal aid? Would that still be guaranteed or would a right to self-representation also mean an obligation to do so? Is self-representation something that is more suitable in specific types of cases like disputes between neighbours? Can we identify disputes that will never be suitable for self-representation?

Oral presentation seems to be important for self-representation. How could we integrate this in a system where IT will become more and more important?

Can Dutch courts do more to make self-representation easier for litigants by providing information e.g. on which steps to follow to start a proceeding and a list of documents to be produced, like we already have in Dutch family cases? By having more uniform standardised procedures and requirements for each type of claim? Or by providing interactive digital forms like the UK courts use now?

If more uniformity in procedures is a precondition for digitised procedures, where does this leave us with our aim for tailor-made procedures as a means to increase access to justice? Can IT-solutions help here and should we in the Netherlands focus more on IT-access for citizens rather than just for lawyers?

And lastly, we have been talking about pathways to civil justice, but isn't one of our problems that our substantive laws in its different layers of supranational, European and national rules are just overly complicated?

---

[22]Cf. WRR (2017).

Within the Dutch Ministry of Justice and Security we do not—yet—have the answers to all these questions. But thanks to the conference on Pathways to Civil Justice I have been able to gain a lot more insight in whether these are the right questions to ask.

References

Attorney General's Office, the Rt Hon Robert Buckland QC MP (2018) Our vision for legal education. https://www.gov.uk/government/news/our-vision-for-legal-education

Eshuis RJJ, Geurts T (2016) Lagere drempels voor rechtzoekenden. Evaluatie van de Verhoging van de Competentiegrens in 2011, Cahiers 2016-14 WODC. https://www.wodc.nl/onderzoeksdatabase/2445-evaluatie-verhoging-van-de-competentiegrens-kantonrechter.aspx

Government (Rijksoverheid) (2020a) Scheiden of uit elkaar: wat moet ik regelen? (Divorce or Separation: what legal steps do I need to take?). https://www.rijksoverheid.nl/onderwerpen/scheiden/vraag-en-antwoord/checklist-bij-scheiden-of-uit-elkaar-gaan

Government (Rijksoverheid) (2020b) Wat moet ik doen als ik word ontslagen? (What should I do when I get fired?). https://www.rijksoverheid.nl/onderwerpen/ontslag/vraag-en-antwoord/

Hertogh M et al (2018) 'Zegt u het eens, wat wilt u van de rechter', evaluatie van de Spreekuurrechter. https://www.rechtspraak.nl/SiteCollectionDocuments/research-memoranda-2018-04.pdf

Minister for Legal Protection (2018) Letter of the Minister for Legal Protection of 19 December 2018, Parliamentary Documents 2018-2019, 29 279, nr. 485. https://zoek.officielebekendmakingen.nl/kst-29279-485.html

Mr. Hans van Mierlo Stichting (2013) De complexe samenleving: idee 34(1)

Ontanu EA (2020) The Netherlands. In von Hein J, Kruger T (eds) Informed choices in cross-border enforcement. Intersentia

Parliament (Tweede Kamer der Staten-Generaal) (2018) Question asked by Member of Parliament Van Oosten (VVD), Parliamentary Documents 2017-2018, 29 279, nr. 438. https://zoek.officielebekendmakingen.nl/kst-29279-438.html

Parliament (Tweede Kamer der Staten-Generaal) (2019) Voorstel van wet - Regels inzake invoering van een tijdelijke mogelijkheid voor experimenten in de rechtspleging (Tijdelijke Experimentenwet rechtspleging), Parliamentary documents 2018-2019, nr. 35 263, nr. 2. https://www.tweedekamer.nl/kamerstukken/wetsvoorstellen/detail?id=2019Z15302&dossier=35263

Susskind RE (2010) The end of lawyers. rethinking the nature of legal services. Oxford University Press, Oxford

Vranken JBM (2018) De omvang van cassatiestukken in civiele zaken. NJB 997:1418. https://www.njb.nl/blogs/de-omvang-van-cassatiestukken-in-civiele-zaken/

WRR (2017) Weten is nog geen doen: een realistisch perspectief op redzaamheid (Knowing is not yet Doing. A realistic perspective on self-reliance). Wetenschappelijke Raad voor het Regeringsbeleid, Den Haag. https://www.wrr.nl/publicaties/rapporten/2017/04/24/weten-is-nog-geen-doen

Chapter 11
With and Without Lawyers: Empirical Research on Legal Representation in Dutch Civil Court Cases

Roland Eshuis

Abstract Empirical research on legal representation in Dutch civil court cases investigated the effect of a relatively recent increase in the threshold for small claims in civil commercial cases from 5000 to 25,000 euro, effectively bringing a broad range of cases under the jurisdiction of the sub-district courts before which representation is not obligatory. The data shows that self-representation is more popular among defendants, and, although they rarely win a case, they experience the procedure as fair to the same extent as litigants who have professional help. This chapter presents us with some lessons to be learned from these insights. The conclusion that still very few claimants use the opportunity to start a court case without professional help raises the question of whether it is in fact possible to shape the law and its procedures in a manner simple enough for anyone to understand.

11.1 Introduction

This chapter addresses the quality of services provided by professional representatives in commercial cases handled at the Dutch Courts. It compares the services provided by professional lawyers,[1] bailiffs and other representatives in civil court cases, and the performance of litigants without representation. The research presented in this chapter is part of a broader study that evaluates the raise of the small claims limit for commercial civil cases (see paragraph 3). This measure ended the 'lawyers monopoly' on the representation of parties in court cases with a financial value between 5000 and 25000 euro, and made self-representation in these cases possible.

At the time of writing Roland Eshuis († 20-04-2020) was senior researcher at the Dutch Ministry of Justice Research and Documentation Centre (WODC).

---

[1]The term 'lawyers', as it is used in this chapter, refers to members of the Dutch Bar Association.

R. Eshuis (✉)
The Hague, The Netherlands
e-mail: kramer@law.eur.nl

199

It provides us with an opportunity to find out what happens if the same group of court cases is handled under different rules for representation. We compare the quality of representation in the (old) condition in which every litigant is represented by a lawyer with the quality of representation under the (new) condition of free choice of representation. In the condition of free choice, the quality of representation by various types of representatives (lawyers, bailiffs, legal expenses insurance, self-representation) will be compared.

The role of lawyers, bailiffs and legal expenses insurance companies has been a recurring subject of debate among legal professionals, and in Dutch politics.[2] That debate is fuelled by incidents, and the role of legal professionals may be 'framed' as indispensable one day, and as a problem the next day. While on the one hand, there is a tendency to impose higher standards and obligations for regulated professional groups such as lawyers and bailiffs, on the other hand there is a tendency to reduce their role, and create room for innovative and less expensive providers of legal services. The latter is in line with Susskind who observed that attempts to make justice cheaper, faster and more accessible could mean "the end of lawyers".[3]

Studying the quality of services provided by professionals as well as self-representing parties should provide answers to various questions in the Dutch debate. Do professional lawyers actually add value to the Court process, are litigants able to handle cases on their own, and how well do the various providers of legal services do their job? How does the quality of services (as seen through the eyes of professionals) relate to the procedural justice experienced by litigants? Do people using a legal expenses insurance company receive the same quality of services as those that hire a lawyer on the basis of an hourly fee?

The first paragraph of this chapter provides a brief introduction to the professionals that provide legal services for litigants in civil court cases. The second paragraph explains the relevant changes due to the raise small claims limit and the design of the study. In the third paragraph, the results of the empirical study are presented. The fourth and final paragraph discusses the results in the relation to the questions in the previous section and the wider debate on (professional) representation of litigants in court cases.

11.2   The Landscape of Legal Services in the Netherlands

Dutch Lawyers and Law Firms The Dutch Bar Association currently has about 18,000 members (2018). Their number has grown by 50% since the start of this century. Members of the Bar Association, addressed as *"Advocaat"*, have a number of special roles and privileges, grounded in Dutch Law.

---

[2]See Eshuis et al. (2012).
[3]See Susskind (2008).

The Bar Association supervises lawyers, handles complaints against them, and can impose various sanctions, including exclusion from the Bar. Lawyers have to provide information on the financial status of their office and spend time on (permanent) education.

Almost 90% of the Dutch law firms are small, employing between 1 and 5 lawyers, while 55% of the total is a one-person office. Big law firms (often part of or associated with global law firms) are the remaining 10%. Common civil cases are mostly handled by the smaller offices.

A common observation in research on access to justice is the problem that one-shotter litigants find it hard to find a capable and affordable lawyer to do their case. Small law firms may offer their services for any type of case, but may lack sufficient expertise in some of the cases they handle.

The common contract between lawyer and client is based on an hourly fee, to be paid after services are provided. Fixed fees are not common, no cure no pay contracts are not allowed.

Bailiffs and Debt Collection Agents Bailiffs are a regulated profession in the Netherlands. In Dutch Law, the name of the profession is '*Gerechtsdeurwaarder*', which translates as 'court bailiff'.[4] Bailiffs have two important functions in civil commercial court cases. First, the writ has to be served by a bailiff, to make sure that the defendant knows that there is a court case again against him/her. Second, bailiffs hold a monopoly on the use of coercive measures in the execution of judicial decisions. In most commercial civil cases—the cases in which no lawyer is required—a bailiff can provide 'one stop shopping' for the court process.[5]

There are unregulated debt collection agents as well. In the smaller claims these agencies can represent their clients in court. A bailiff will be required however to serve the writ, and if coercive measures have to be taken.

Large scale providers of consumer services usually have contracts with one or more bailiffs and/or debt collection agents to collect their unpaid bills. In recent years, there has been a growing custom of selling packages of such claims to debt collection agents (who then become owner of the debt and claimant if they take a case to court).

Legal Expenses Insurance Policies in the Netherlands Legal expenses insurance companies play an important role in the Dutch legal landscape. More than two and a half million households have an insurance policy to cover potential legal costs (36% of all households).

The main providers of legal expenses insurance policies own a foundation that employs lawyers and paralegals that represent clients in court cases. Some smaller

---

[4]However, the bailiffs are not part of the court or the court organization. Bailiffs work in a private organizational setting, like lawyers.

[5]In these cases the bailiff can serve the writ, represent the litigant in court and apply coercive measures in the execution of the judicial decision.

companies share a foundation that provides these services. The companies have contracts with law firms as well, that handle cases for a fixed price.

If a client needs help in a court case, most companies will first suggest a lawyer or paralegal from its foundation or network. The client is allowed to choose a lawyer from outside the companies' network. In practice, many policies limit the amount of help that will be provided if a client chooses a lawyer from outside the company's network.[6]

Insurance policies are limited in the amount of money covered, or the type of cases that are covered. A common exclusion are divorce cases.

11.3   Context and Design of the Study

Civil Commercial Cases at the Dutch Courts   In Dutch Civil Process Law, in court cases with a high financial value, both claimant and defendant are obliged to hire a professional lawyer.[7] In smaller cases, parties are free to choose any kind of representative, or to do without.[8] All Civil commercial cases are handled under a set of general procedural rules. The procedure starts with a writ, which has to be served to the defending party by a bailiff. After the answer from the defending party, a court hearing will be planned (default) or the procedure may continue in writing. Parties are obliged to provide all relevant information in the introducing documents. In the writ, the claimant has to state if the defendant has already denied the claim, and for what reasons. By withholding such information, the claimant risks losing the case. This rule of procedure was introduced in 2002 in order to speed up the court process.[9] It aims to have all relevant information present at the start of the procedure.[10] Recently, this rule has been criticized as limiting access to the court; it adds to the complexity of bringing a case to court, and the necessity to hire professional help.[11]

In commercial cases, the losing party will have to pay a substantial part of the costs the winning party made in the court procedure (including court tax and the representatives' fee).

---

[6]See Steinz (2018).

[7]Critics often frame this as 'the Lawyers Monopoly'.

[8]Wetboek van Burgerlijke Rechtsvordering, Artikel 97.

[9]TK 26855 Herziening procesrecht burgerlijke zaken, in het bijzonder de wijze van procederen in eerste aanleg.

[10]Before the introduction of this procedural rule, parties could hold their cards to their chest and play them one by one. Such strategic behavior could lead to lengthy procedures.

[11]Van der Kraats (2017).

The Raise of the Small Claims Limit In 2011 the small claims limit for civil court cases was raised from 5000 euro to 25,000 euro.[12] So, in cases with a financial value between 5000 and 25,000 the lawyers' monopoly ceased to exist. Bailiffs, debt collection agents, and legal expenses insurances could all represent their clients in court. And litigants were allowed to do without any professional representation in their court case. The quality of legal services had been a main topic in the debate in parliament on this measure, and became a main topic in the evaluation study on this measure.[13]

Design of the Study The design of the evaluation study is quasi experimental, with measurements before (2010) and after (2013 and 2014) the small claims limit was raised. Since the changes took place in cases with a financial value between 5000 and 25,000 euro, those are cases that the research focuses on. We studied the cases before the measure, when all parties were represented by lawyers, and afterwards, when parties were represented by lawyers, other professionals or doing without representation).

Measuring Quality A major challenge was to compare the quality of services provided by the various types of aids, and the performance of litigants who represent themselves in court. Measuring the quality of professional services is not easy, and many attempts to do so are hardly satisfying. In the design of this study, I carefully followed the statement from Henry Mintzberg, that the only ones who can really judge the quality of professional services, are people from within that professional group.[14] Who is competent then, to 'judge' the quality of services of lawyers and other representatives in court cases? We defined that group as all professional workers with a legal education substantively involved in the processing of civil court cases. The quality of representation in this study is lawyers, judges and court employees (judicial assistants).

To be able to compare, one has to focus on the common elements that occur in every procedure. In Dutch civil procedure, the most common elements are the exchange of writ and answer at the beginning of the procedure, and a hearing that takes place after this exchange.[15] We had panels of lawyers, judges and court personnel 'judging' the quality of anonymized documents (writ and answer), and the judges in the court hearings 'judging' the quality of the representation in the courtroom.[16] For both quality measures, respondents filled out a list of 8 to 10 items.

---

[12]Tweede Kamer, vergaderjaar 2008-2009, 32 021, nr. 3 and Tweede Kamer, vergaderjaar 2009-2010, 32 021, nr. 14.

[13]Eshuis and Geurts (2017).

[14]Henry Mintzberg (1983).

[15]Every procedure starts with a writ (100% of the procedures). In about half of the cases, the defendant actually defends himself (answer in 50% of the procedures). A hearing takes place in less than 50% of the procedures.

[16]600 representatives or self-representing parties were rated at court hearings. 415 documents (writ or answer) were rated by panels. 60 documents were rated twice, to check the consistency in the

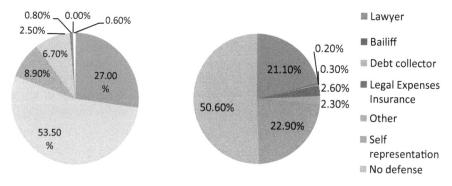

Fig. 11.1 The choice of legal representation, by claimants (left) and defendants (right). Data on representation were established from court files of cases completed in 2014 (a sample of 2250 cases handled at 9 court locations)

This is to make sure that all would consider the same criteria in their ordeal on quality.

In all cases used for quality review, litigants were invited to respond to a survey on client satisfaction and procedural justice. In this way, relations between quality judgements by professionals and the way individual litigants had experienced the court case could be reviewed.

The instruments used for the measurement of quality, client satisfaction and procedural justice are included in the appendix of this chapter.

11.4 Results

The Choice of Representation Before 2011, all parties in commercial court cases with a financial value between 5000 and 25,000 euro had to be represented by a lawyer. After the small claims limit was raised to 25,000 euro, all litigants were free to choose their representative, or to do without. So, what do they choose? Figure 11.1 shows the choice of representation for claimants and defendants, when hiring a lawyer was no longer compulsory. When free to choose, only a quarter of the litigants choses to hire a lawyer. This suggests that the (former) obligation to hire a lawyer forced many to do something they'd rather not *want* to do. The patterns for claimants and defendants are quite different. First of all, claimants hardly use the option of self-representation while many defendants do. Second, most claimants have a bailiff or debt collection agent as a representative. These representatives are deployed almost exclusively by claimants, in cases concerning unpaid bills. The

ratings by different respondents. Three items were omitted from the analysis for lack of consistency. 850 Litigants responded to client satisfaction and procedural justice surveys. For further methodological details, please see Eshuis and Geurts (2017).

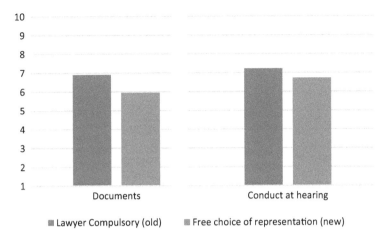

Fig. 11.2 Peer ratings of quality of documents and representation at the court hearing (scale: 1–10), before and after the raise of the small claims limit (higher scores equals higher quality). For documents, the drop in the quality rating is statistically significant. For the 201 conduct at hearings the difference between the old and the new situation is not 202 statistically significant

cases in which lawyers or legal insurance companies are deployed, are quite different in nature (disputes on contracts, torts, intellectual property). The 'other' representatives found in this study include accountancy firms, workers unions, branch associations, and a variety of legal and non-legal advice agencies. The numbers of each of these actors are too small to show separate results for each type. When it comes to defendants, we see that half of this group does not defend itself. Most of these cases, again, involve unpaid bills. If a defendant does provide a defence, in almost half of the cases he chooses the option of self-representation. If a professional is hired, it is most likely to be a lawyer.

Quality by Peer Rating Figure 11.2 shows the quality ratings before and after the raise of the small claims limit. Before, all representatives were professional lawyers. In the new situation, most are not lawyers. The figure includes ratings of self-representation. The rating for the introduction documents dropped one point on the 10-point scale (statistically significant); the rating for the representation on the hearing dropped 0.5 point (not statistically significant). Evidently, the quality ratings dropped, but the change is not that big. In fact, one might say that the surplus quality provided by the highly educated and closely supervised group of professional lawyers is surprisingly small.

Quality in Court Hearings Figure 11.3 provides a closer look at the ratings for representation at the Court hearings. It shows the scores on the list of items that judges filled in at their court hearings. We see that the best ratings on every item are for lawyers. Other representatives, on average, score just a little lower. The ratings for parties representing themselves is substantially lower on all items, with an average below six.

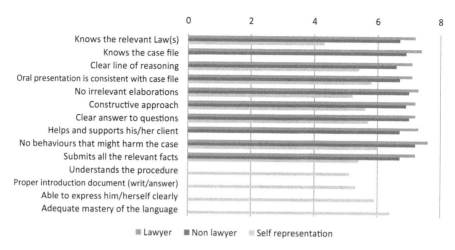

Fig. 11.3 Quality ratings at court hearing (rating by Judges, 10 point scale). On 6 out of 10 items, lawyers' scores are significantly better than non-lawyers scores. Scores of self-representing parties are significantly lower than those of both lawyers and non-lawyers

Fig. 11.4 Percentage of cases with 'insufficient' representation at Court hearing (rated below 6 on 1–10 Scale). The difference in ratings between self-representing parties and others (lawyer or non-lawyer) is statistically significant

Figure 11.4 shows the percentage of overall scores that are below six, categorized by type of representative. This depicts the chance that a certain type of representative will perform insufficiently in the courtroom. This chance is as big for a lawyer as it is for the other types of representatives (taken as a group). Chances that representation is insufficient is much higher for litigants representing themselves, almost 50%. Most problematic are items concerning legal knowledge: relevant law and the court procedure. Least problematic is general language and expression.

Quality in Documents (Writ and Answer) Figure 11.5 provides us with a closer look at some of the ratings for introductory documents: writ and answer. The rating of the documents reveals a similar pattern as seen in the ratings at court hearings. The lowest ratings are for documents issued by self-representing parties. The most problematic elements are knowledge of law and formal requirements, language is the least problematic. The figure shows separate scores for lawyers working under 'normal' conditions (the client hires the lawyer and pays an hourly fee) and lawyers handling cases for legal expenses insurance companies (insurance company hires the

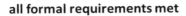

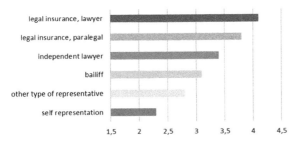

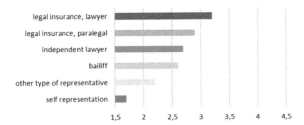

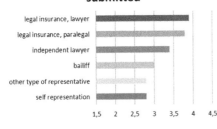

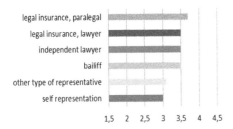

Fig. 11.5 Peer ratings on introduction documents (writ, answer). The overall rating for independent lawyers is different from all other ratings (statistically significant), except for the bailiffs rating

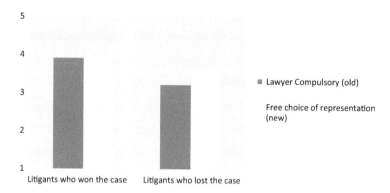

Fig. 11.6 Client satisfaction with services provided by their representative (scale: 1–5), before (lawyer compulsory) and after (free choice of representation). Higher satisfaction by losing parties, under condition of free choice, is statistically significant. Change for winning parties is not statistically significant

lawyer to do a number of cases for a fixed fee).[17] These arrangements are believed to provide different incentives to lawyers, regarding the time they spend on a case and the value they place on reaching a friendly settlement.

A surprise are the consistently high scores for both lawyers and paralegals acting for litigants with a legal expenses insurance. Their average scores are better than those of lawyers in cases without legal expenses insurance. A deeper analysis of the scoring patterns reveals a difference in the distribution of scores; while most independent lawyers perform very well, there are some underachievers. We do not find these 'underachievers' in cases with legal expenses insurance companies.

The chance that a representative will file an 'insufficient' document (rating below 6 on a 10-point scale) is 12% for legal cost insurances, 36% for independent lawyers and 52% for self-representing litigants.

Client Satisfaction How do litigants feel about the services provided by their representatives? Figure 11.6 shows the general satisfaction with the services provided. In the new situation where litigants are free to choose, with various types of representatives, this satisfaction is higher than when all litigants had lawyers as representatives.

For winning parties, the difference is not statistically significant, but for losing parties it is. The reason seems obvious; for those who spent a significant amount of money on the services of a lawyer, a negative result will be harder to bear.

---

[17]The panel rating method made it possible to form samples large enough to compare these groups. In the quality rating of conduct in court we did not have that opportunity; judges would just rate any case that would be presented to them during a period of three months. The number of observations on several types of representatives is too low to allow for comparison between groups.

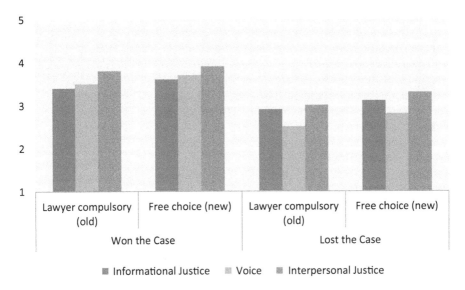

Fig. 11.7 Perceived procedural justice (3 dimensions) in defended cases (likert scale). For losing parties, changes on all three dimensions of procedural justice are statistically significant. For winning parties, only the change in informational justice is statistically significant

Procedural Justice In this research, three dimensions of procedural justice were measured: informational justice, interpersonal justice and voice. The results, in Fig. 11.7, are clear-cut; on every dimension, for both winners and losers, the condition of free choice of representation is experienced as fairer than the former condition, in which hiring a lawyer was compulsory. So, despite the lower peer ratings for the quality of representation, litigants experience the new condition (free choice of representation) more positively than the old one. It is likely that the free choice of representation actually leads to a better fit between the litigants' needs and what they get. The research also suggests that if litigants have the freedom to choose, they feel to some extent 'committed' to their choice and are less likely to attribute unfavourable outcomes to their representative.[18]

How Representation Affects the Court Process Does the participation of professional representatives affect the court process? The brief answer is yes, it does. Various patterns were found in the way court cases develop, in relation to the type of representatives involved.

First, comparing the conditions of compulsory representation by a lawyer and the condition of free choice, the latter leads to higher participation: not only the number

---

[18]This pattern occurs as well among litigants with legal expenses insurance. Litigants who were appointed a lawyer by their insurance company tended to be more critical than those who chose a lawyer by themselves.

of incoming cases rises, the percentage of defended cases goes up as well.[19] Second, the percentage of (defended) cases in which a Court hearing took place, dropped from 66 to 42%. More cases were judged solely on exchanged documents. Bailiffs and debt collection agencies (representatives of over 60% of the claimants under the condition of free of representation, (see Fig. 11.1) commonly state in the writ that they prefer a procedure without a hearing. If not challenged by the defending party, this request will generally be honoured. Third, the percentage of cases in which a friendly settlement was reached, dropped from 46 to 28%. The best chance for a friendly settlement is when both parties are represented by a lawyer. Hardly any friendly settlements are found in cases with a party that does without professional representation. It is clear that professional representatives play an important role in developing friendly settlements.[20] Fourth, procedures with self-representing parties tend to stay very simple, while procedures with professional aids are more complex (and take more time). This could have to do with insufficient knowledge of law and procedure, but might just as well be due to self-selection; defendants that see little chance of winning are less likely to spend money on a professional representative.

11.5   Conclusions and Discussion

Do Dutch litigants (still) need lawyers in court cases or can they do without them? The research shows that after the introduction of free choice in representation in commercial civil cases with a financial value between 5000 and 25,000 euro, most claimants still choose for professional help. It is a risk to bring a case to court without professional help. The need for lawyers, or at least some form of professional help in common court cases, seems to reflect our inability to create laws and procedures that anyone can understand and use. To frame a problem in the right way to have it processed as a court case, one needs to be aware of rules and their exceptions, to be able to handle mutually contradictory principles and to decipher words and phrasings that are hardly used in common language. In theory, the use of self-representation in court cases would be an option to consider for repeat players

---

[19]This cannot be attributed solely to the free choice of representative. There are various other differences in the way small cases and bigger cases are handled that may account for this result. For instance, in the bigger cases the defendant has pay a court fee (not in small cases); small cases are handled at more court locations, which limits travelling distances for defendants. The research attributes an increase of 20% in the incoming to the free choice of representation. The percentage of undefended cases dropped from 61 to 47%. The research cannot separate the effects of free choice of representation, court fees and travel distance.

[20]The highest percentages of friendly settlements are found in cases with lawyers and legal expense insurances as representative. They may negotiate a settlement for their client, and also advice their clients on whether to agree to a settlement.

with in-house legal services. In practice however, a growing number of these repeat players outsource their legal work.[21]

In the choice of representation by claimants there are two main patterns. First, a large volume of cases involves the collection of unpaid bills by repeat players, operating nationwide. The court process will—if they win the case—provide them with a title for execution. The judicial decision entitles the use of coercive actions (for instance, to take possession over income, savings or goods owned by the losing party). Repeat players generally contract bailiffs and debt-collection agencies to handle these cases. Taking the case to court may be a step in that process of collection, without any active involvement—or even awareness—of the claimant. Most of these cases remain undefended.

In court cases that are not simply or exclusively about unpaid bills, the pattern in representation is different. In those cases, claimants will usually hire a lawyer or call on their legal expense insurance for representation. In most of these cases the defendant will be active. About half of the defendants in these cases opt for self-representation. If they choose for a professional representative, it is most likely to be a lawyer.

Choices in representation do affect the way the cases evolve during the court process. Free choice of representation leads to more incoming cases and a higher percentage of defended cases.[22] If both parties have a professional representative, the court process will be more complex and take more time. Friendly settlements are more common if both litigants have professional representation.

In this study, professionals—mainly judges and lawyers—rated the quality of services of professional representatives and self-representing parties. In half of the cases of self-representation, representation was considered insufficient. However, hiring a professional is no guarantee against insufficient representation; representation by professional lawyers was rated insufficient in 10% of the cases.

While the quality of representation—as rated by professionals—became lower after the introduction of free choice of representation, experiences of litigants were more positive under the condition of free choice. It is plausible that being able choose leads to better matches between what the litigant needs, and what he actually gets. Just think of the repeat player that already has a bailiff working on the case, and had to hire a lawyer as well in order to bring the case to court; or the defendant that is not allowed to defend himself, unless he hires a lawyer. It is hardly surprising that these litigants experience the condition of free choice as the fairer than the old condition, in which hiring a lawyer was compulsory.

The difference in patterns of peer ratings and the experience of litigants do raise a new question: what should we value more? The 'fairness' perceived by the people seeking justice, or the 'quality' as judged by legal professionals?

---

[21] A current trend among repeat players is to sell their claims in bundles to debt collection agencies.

[22] Phrasing it in the other perspective: if parties are obliged to hire a lawyer, they are less likely to take a case to court or defend themselves if a case is brought against them.

The analyses of changes in the court process adds an extra layer to the quality discussion. It is clear that free choice of representation leads to the improved access to justice for both claimants and defendants. This is something to be valued positively. The lower numbers of court hearings and friendly settlements on the other hand, are not considered a positive development. Both these developments are associated with the absence of professional representatives, especially lawyers. Professional representatives may negotiate a friendly settlement for their clients or advise them to accept a friendly settlement.

The main development in representation can be labelled as 'displacement': other parties are providing the services previously provided by lawyers. These parties deliver a narrower range of services, with more specialization. This is true for bailiffs and debt collection agents, but also for legal expenses insurers. The high-quality ratings for the representatives operating for legal expenses insurers were a surprise in this study. In the past, several consumer shows on Dutch TV have shown critical topics on legal expenses insurance policies, suggesting that the actual help they provide to their clients is below standard.[23] What is the secret of the legal expenses insurance? Their caseload makes it possible for these firms to develop a high level of specialization for the more common types of civil disputes, including training programs for employees and standardized documents (see Fig. 11.5). For traditional law firms, such specialization does not pay off.[24] Also, the insurance companies have well developed knowledge of the market supply; if special knowledge on fewer common subjects is required, they know which lawyers to hire. Finding the right lawyer for the case remains difficult for inexperienced parties.

The findings are relevant in relation to the principle of equality of arms. The old rule that obliged both claimant and defendant to hire a lawyer is directly related to this principle. The line of reasoning was that if claimants were obliged to hire a lawyer, then defendants would have to be obliged as well; if not, there would be imbalance.

That imbalance does occur in the new situation: only very few claimants go to court without professional help, while most defendants do without. Still, as noticed, these defendants experience the current situation as 'fairer' than the old one. In practice, we find that the percentage of defendants that actually does go to court is increased in under the condition of free choice on representation. It seems that the cost of 'equal' arms (in the old situation) lead to defendants not defending themselves at all.

---

[23]Some of the topics in the research presented here relate indirectly to these shows. For instance, a broadcast from the TV show "Radar" (see: Avrotros.nl) on May, 24th, 2010 lead to discussion in parliament, and placed the comparison of services by lawyers and legal expense insurance companies on our research agenda. Some recent broadcasts include the "Radar" broadcasts of December, 16, 2016 and March 4, 2019 and "Kassa" of March 2, 2019.

[24]The big Law firm have little business in common court cases with limited amounts of money. The small firms that operate in this niche have limited ability to specialize.

Appendix: Research Instruments

In this project, a variety of instruments was developed for the collection of data regarding the quality of representatives in court cases. This appendix includes translated versions of these instruments, and a short introduction text on the way they were used. The appendix includes four parts:

A1. Introduction to the instruments
A2. Survey among litigants
A3. Quality rating of documents
A4. Quality rating of conduct at court hearings

A1 The Use of the Research Instruments

Rating the Quality of Introducing Documents

For the research on the quality of documents exchanged when a court is introduced, two instruments were developed, each in various versions. The first instrument is a survey for litigants (see A2), the second a list of items to rate the quality of documents (see A3).

First, a survey was sent to litigants, in 2700 court cases (in 2011, and again in 2014). From the cases replied to in 2011, court documents were sampled and made ready for the quality rating by professionals. From the information collected in the survey, we knew in which cases litigants had legal costs insurance, and whether they had been free to choose a lawyer. For the quality rating, documents representing these various conditions were collected. In 2014, a comparable strategy was used. This time, the main concern was to have documents with the various types of representation (including bailiffs and self-representation).

The quality rating took place in four sessions, each in a different city. The participants were invited through the local Bar, lawyers' associations, and the court organization. In each session, 15 to 20 participants (mostly lawyers, at least one judge per session) would rate the introduction documents of (at least) 10 court cases. Cases from 2011 and 2014 were mixed and rated at all 4 sessions. A total of 415 documents has been rated. Some of them were rated twice (at different sessions) to check whether the ratings were consistent among the various people that did the rating.[25]

---

[25]Two items were removed from the analysis because the consistency of the ratings on these items was below standard.

Rating the Quality of Conduct at Court Hearings

Two instruments were developed to establish the quality of conduct at court hearings. There is list of items for judges to fill in after the hearing (see A4). These items concern various indicator for the quality of conduct at court cases. Second, there is a survey to be filled by the litigants in the case. This is comparable to survey A2, bus less elaborate.

For the quality ratings on conduct at court hearings, the parties would be handed the survey at the hearing (by a court employee). Most courts offered the possibility to parties to fill the questionnaire after the hearing, and put it in a locked reply box. The alternative was to send it by post to the researchers, for which a free reply envelope was provided. After the hearing, the judge would rate the conduct of the representatives. Judges would do this procedure for every hearing, during two months. Under this data collection strategy, there was no way to make sure that all types of representatives would be included in the study; if certain types of representatives did not (or hardly) show up in court during the two months, they would not be in the study.[26] For the 2011 study, the challenge was to have enough cases representing the various conditions under which lawyers can work for legal insurance companies (varying from free choice by the litigant, and paid on hourly fee, to contracted by the insurance company to handle a bundle of cases for a fixed fee, without free choice for the litigant).[27] The conduct of a total of 565 representatives and self-representing parties was rated.

A2 The Survey Among Litigants

This survey came in six separate versions. There are different versions for claimants and defendants, and for undefended cases, defended cases concluded by a judgment, and defended cases concluded by a friendly settlement. The version shown here is for was used for claimants in defended cases with a final judgment.[28] Question 7 was used as measurement of client satisfaction. Satisfaction can be understood as (positive or negative) discrepancies between expectations, and actual experience. Those are addressed in question 21. Procedural justice items are addressed in questions 8, 20, 22 and 28. Question 30 addresses distributive justice. Please note that the

---

[26]There were enough ratings for lawyers, bailiffs, legal cost insurance and self-representing parties to separate results for these group in the analysis. Less common types of representatives were put in one group 'other'.

[27]The number of observations regarding each type of these contractual relations were too low to handle them separately in the analysis. Regarding the conduct at court hearing, the analysis only separates results for cases with and without a legal cost insurance.

[28]It is the version used in 2014. The version used in 2011 had the same items, but was simpler since all litigants were represented by a lawyer.

questions as presented here are translated from Dutch. Some precision is lost in this translation, while unintended connotations may be added.

7 How satisfied are you with the services provided by your representative?

		Very satisfied	Satisfied	Neutral	Dissatisfied	Very dissatisfied	Does not apply
1.	Listening to my problem	□1	□2	□3	□4	□5	□6
2.	Explaining my chances	□1	□2	□3	□4	□5	□6
3.	Explaining the steps in the court process	□1	□2	□3	□4	□5	□6
4.	Describing the problem in the court documents	□1	□2	□3	□4	□5	□6
5.	The time spent on my case	□1	□2	□3	□4	□5	□6
6.	Speed of action	□1	□2	□3	□4	□5	□6
7.	Accessibility	□1	□2	□3	□4	□5	□6
8.	The fulfilment of agreements	□1	□2	□3	□4	□5	□6
9.	Overall satisfaction with the service	□1	□2	□3	□4	□5	□6

8 To what extend do you agree with the following statements on your representative?

		Strongly agree	Agree	Neutral	Disagree	Strongly disagree	Does not apply
1.	My representative has listened to my story well	□1	□2	□3	□4	□5	□6
2.	My representative handled in court case in the right way	□1	□2	□3	□4	□5	□6
3.	My representative spent too little effort on my case	□1	□2	□3	□4	□5	□6
4.	My representative informed me how a court procedure works	□1	□2	□3	□4	□5	□6
5.	My representative kept me posted on developments during the court procedure	□1	□2	□3	□4	□5	□6
6.	It was easy to find a representative for my case	□1	□2	□3	□4	□5	□6

20 To what extend do you agree with the following statements on the information during your court case?

		Strongly agree	Agree	Neutral	Disagree	Strongly disagree	Does not apply
1.	The court (or judge) has informed me how the court procedure works	□1	□2	□3	□4	□5	□6
2.	Others (than the court or judge) have informed me how the court procedure works	□1	□2	□3	□4	□5	□6
3.	I received accurate information on how the court procedure works	□1	□2	□3	□4	□5	□6
4.	I found the information I received on developments in my court case comprehensible	□1	□2	□3	□4	□5	□6
5.	I was surprised to see how the court case developed	□1	□2	□3	□4	□5	□6
6.	During the procedure the court kept me well informed on the developments in the case.	□1	□2	□3	□4	□5	□6

These items, together with item 8-5, make up the scale used for informational justice. For items 20-1 and 20-2, only one of the scores (the best one) was used. Same goes for the related items 8-5 and 20-6. In both cases, from the concept of informational justice, it is of importance that the litigant receives good information (regardless of who provides that information)

21 To what extend do you agree with the following statements on access to the court and the way your case was handled?

		Strongly agree	Agree	Neutral	Disagree	Strongly disagree	Does not apply
1.	I did not expect the court procedure to be expensive	□1	□2	□3	□4	□5	□6
2.	In the end, taking my case to court was less expensive than I expected	□1	□2	□3	□4	□5	□6
3.	I did not find the procedure complicated	□1	□2	□3	□4	□5	□6
4.	I did not expect to have to invest a lot of time in the procedure	□1	□2	□3	□4	□5	□6
5.	In the end, I invested more time in the procedure than I'd expected to.	□1	□2	□3	□4	□5	□6
6.	I found the procedure to be very formal	□1	□2	□3	□4	□5	□6
7.	I thought a court case would be handled quickly	□1	□2	□3	□4	□5	□6
8.	The court case took longer than I expected	□1	□2	□3	□4	□5	□6

22 To what extend do you agree with the following statements on the way your case was handled?

		Strongly agree	Agree	Neutral	Disagree	Strongly disagree	Does not apply
1.	All angles of the case that I considered important, were reviewed in court	☐1	☐2	☐3	☐4	☐5	☐6
2.	In my opinion, the judge had thoroughly considered the substance of the case.	☐1	☐2	☐3	☐4	☐5	☐6
3.	I think that in his decision, the judge has taken my arguments into account.	☐1	☐2	☐3	☐4	☐5	☐6
4.	I this court case I have been able to present my view on the case	☐1	☐2	☐3	☐4	☐5	☐6
5.	I found the matter was handled superficially	☐1	☐2	☐3	☐4	☐5	☐6
6.	The judge put pressure on me to agree to a friendly settlement	☐1	☐2	☐3	☐4	☐5	☐6

28 To what extend do you agree with the following statements on the handling of your case?

		Strongly agree	Agree	Neutral	Disagree	Strongly disagree	Does not apply
1.	The judge asked me whether I felt properly informed on how the court case would proceed.	☐1	☐2	☐3	☐4	☐5	☐6
2.	I found the language spoken in the court room hard to understand.	☐1	☐2	☐3	☐4	☐5	☐6
3.	The judge acted impartial.	☐1	☐2	☐3	☐4	☐5	☐6
4.	Me and the other party were treated in the same way.	☐1	☐2	☐3	☐4	☐5	☐6
5.	I felt the judge to be more sympathetic to the other party than to me	☐1	☐2	☐3	☐4	☐5	☐6
6.	During this procedure, the judge threated me with respect	☐1	☐2	☐3	☐4	☐5	☐6
7.	I found the judge to be flexible	☐1	☐2	☐3	☐4	☐5	☐6
8.	I was surprised by the decision of the judge	☐1	☐2	☐3	☐4	☐5	☐6

Items 28-3 to 28-6 make up the scale for interpersonal justice

30 To what extend do you agree with the following statements on the judges' dicision?

	Strongly agree	Agree	Neutral	Disagree	Strongly disagree	Does not apply
1. I think the judges' decision is just	□1	□2	□3	□4	□5	□6
2. The judges' decision is advantageous for me.	□1	□2	□3	□4	□5	□6
3. I think the judges' decision is fair.	□1	□2	□3	□4	□5	□6

A3 Peer Ratings of Documents (Writ, Answer)

Legal professionals were asked to rate the quality of court documents. The documents were taken from actual court files, and anonymized. All indications that might provide a clue on whether it was written by a lawyer, a bailiff or any other type of representative were removed from the document.

Statements used for rating the quality of writs and conclusions

	Strongly agree	Agree	Neutral	Disagree	Strongly disagree	Does not apply
1. The document contains all relevant information	□	□	□	□	□	□
2. The reasoning is logically consistent	□	□	□	□	□	□
3. There are no irrelevant dwellings/elaborations	□	□	□	□	□	□
4. The phrasing is clear and comprehensible	□	□	□	□	□	□
5. Relevant law and litigation are mentioned	□	□	□	□	□	□
6. The claim is not or only loosely attached to its legal basis	□	□	□	□	□	□
7. I did not see any language errors	□	□	□	□	□	□
8. The documents comply with all formal requirements	□	□	□	□	□	□

Report mark: …. (1-10)

A4 Quality Rating of Conduct at Court Hearings

The quality of the conduct of representatives at court hearing was established through a rating on 10 items, and an overall rating. A special version was used for self-representing litigants (see Fig. 12.3, the green bars).

Statements used to rate the conduct of representatives at court hearings

The representative...	Report mark								
1 ... knows the relevant law(s)									
2 ... has good knowledge of the case file									
3 ... argues clearly									
4 ... is consistent with the case file									
5 ... does not present irrelevant pleas or elaborations									
6 ... acts in a constructive manner									
7 ... gives clear answers to questions									
8 ... helps or supports his client when necessary									
9 ... abstains from behaviour that could be harmful to the litigants' interests									
10 ... passes all relevant facts									
Overall rating									

The judges were instructed not to adjust their standards to the type of representative, but to rate all representatives (including self-representing parties) to the same standard: the quality that should be expected from a professional lawyer (member of the Bar association).

References

Eerste Kamer, vergaderjaar 2001-2002, 26855 nr 16c Herziening procesrecht burgerlijke zaken, in het bijzonder de wijze van procederen in eerste aanleg

Eshuis RJJ, Geurts T (2017) Lagere drempels voor rechtzoekenden. Evaluatie van de verhoging van de competentiegrens in 2011. Cahier 2016-14. WODC, Den Haag

Eshuis RJJ, Geurts T, Beenakkers EMTh. (2012) Hulp bij juridische problemen: Een verkennend onderzoek naar de kwaliteit van de dienstverlening van advocaten en rechtsbijstandsverzekeraars. Literatuurstudie en secundaire analyses. Cahier 2012-3. WODC, Den Haag

Mintzberg H (1983) Structures in fives: designing effective organizations. Prentice Hall, Englewood Cliffs

Steinz A (2018) Gaat het wel goed met onze rechtsbijstandverzekeringen? NJB 23:1649–1655

Susskind R (2008) The end of lawyers. Rethinking the nature of legal services. Oxford University Press, Oxford

Tweede Kamer, vergaderjaar 2008-2009, 32 021, nr. 3 (Memorie van Toelichting)

Tweede Kamer, vergaderjaar 2009-2010, 32 021, nr. 14 (wetswijziging)

van der Kraats K (2017) De eigen(aardig)heid van de kantonrechter. Over de verschillen tussen het proces(verloop) bij de kantonrechter en de civiele rechter en de betekenis daarvan. Montaigne reeks, deel 5. Boom Juridisch, Den Haag

Chapter 12
Justice Without Lawyers

John Sorabji

Abstract This chapter considers the extent to which lawyers are an essential feature of an effective civil justice system. It does so, first, by examining two contemporary challenges to the presence of an independent legal profession. Those challenges are: first, one that arises from the withdrawal of civil legal aid funding; and secondly, one that arises from technological innovation e.g., digitisation of process, of legal work, and the growth of online courts designed to provide a means of access that does not depend on legal advice or representation. Having outlined these two challenges, it goes on to examine whether and to what extent lawyers are needed to secure effective access to justice. It considers whether, and to what, extent they may simply add to the complexity, cost and delay of litigation, with no attendant positive effect on the achievement of substantively correct decisions in individual cases. Finally, it looks at why it can, and should, properly be understood that lawyers are an essential feature of civil justice systems through the public interest role they play in ensuring effective participation in proceedings, through maintaining open justice and, in that way, through securing the democratic accountability of the courts. A future where lawyers are designed-out of the system is one that would design-out the very features that render a civil justice system one that is committed to securing, and forms part of a constitutional system committed to, the rule of law.

12.1 Introduction

"The first thing we do, let's kill all the lawyers." Those were the famous, or rather infamous words given to Dick the Butcher by Shakespeare in Henry VI, Part II. They were uttered during Jack Cade's Kent Rebellion against Henry. On one level Dick's words portray a not atypical trope in society: that lawyers are at best a necessary evil. At another level they give expression to the hopes of authoritarians throughout history: an end to lawyers would mean an end to law. As John Locke noted,

J. Sorabji (✉)
University College London, London, UK
e-mail: j.sorabji@ucl.ac.uk

© The Author(s), under exclusive license to Springer Nature Switzerland AG 2021   221
X. Kramer et al. (eds.), *New Pathways to Civil Justice in Europe*,
https://doi.org/10.1007/978-3-030-66637-8_12

'*Whereever law ends, tyranny begins*'.[1] Dick's words were those of the proto-tyrant, of one who was not committed to the rule of law. That Shakespeare had Cade's revolutionaries express this idea was, however, something of poetic licence.

The real-life Cade, for all his rebellious tendencies, did not want to see the elimination of lawyers or the law. On the contrary, the basis of his revolt was to bring the King back to acting within the law. His aim, just as it was previously in English history when King John was required to seal Magna Carta, was to ensure that he did not act as if he were above the law. This was made clear in the proclamation Cade and his fellow revolutionaries issued on 4 June 1450. Article 1 of the *Complaint of the Poor Commons of Kent* or the *Proclamation of Grievances* made that clear. It stated, diplomatically for revolutionaries, that the King had been ill-advised and as a consequence, he had taken to act as if he was '. . . *above his laws . . ., and [that] he may make it and break it as he pleases, without any distinction.*'[2] They stressed that the opposite was true: Kings were subject to the law just as everyone else in society was subject to it. For Cade, bringing an end to lawyers as Shakespeare has Dick suggest, would have done little to bring about sovereign compliance with the law. On the contrary, it would have removed a fundamental means by which the King, just as anybody else, could be held to account. An absence of lawyers, as Dick the Butcher would no doubt have wanted, would have meant an absence of law. As Zuckerman has it, there is no justice without lawyers.[3]

In the not-to-distant future latter-day Dick the Butchers might not have to emit blood-thirsty cries for the end of lawyers. They may be more likely to ask 'where are the lawyers'? In many jurisdictions around the world, particularly those where legal representation in litigation is not a mandatory requirement such as the various common law jurisdictions, lawyers are being taken out of the equation. They are being removed from the administration of justice.[4] That they are is the product of two challenges to their continuing relevance: the funding challenge; and the technological challenge. The latter need not necessarily challenge the role that lawyers play in the administration of justice. However, when taken together with the funding challenge, it does so.

In this chapter, first, the nature of the two challenges is outlined. Secondly, the extent to which lawyers are a necessary feature of the administration of justice is discussed. Finally, it is argued that while in some classes of litigation the presence of lawyers advising and representing litigants may not be an essential feature of the administration of justice for some purposes, overall they are an essential feature of any civil justice system that is committed to secure effective participation, open justice, and democratic accountability. Contrary to the arguments advanced, for instance, by Susskind, there ought to be no end for lawyers.[5] Rather than simply

---

[1]Locke (1988), chap. xvii (sect. 202).

[2]Arkenberg (1999).

[3]Zuckerman (2014).

[4]For a discussion of the growth of lawyerless litigants, see Assy (2015).

[5]Susskind (2010).

develop court procedures and processes, as is happening in numerous jurisdictions around the world (England and Wales (England),[6] the United States,[7] Canada,[8] Australia,[9] China[10] etc.), for lawyerless technology-based courts, a number of steps can and should be taken to overcome the funding and technology challenges to reinvigorate the role lawyers play in the administration of justice.

12.2 Challenges to the Place of Lawyers in the Administration of Justice

Adversarial civil justice systems have three fundamental features in common. As Assy has pointed out they are: first, that there are self-interested opponents; secondly, that they present evidence and make reasoned submissions on the application of law to fact according to rules of procedure and of evidence; and, finally, that a neutral third party, the judge, determines the result of the parties' reasoned, evidentiary, debate.[11] Any system is only ever as effective as its parts and their operation; again as Assy notes correctly, a deficiency in any of these three parts of civil justice systems, '*is likely to undermine the functioning of the system.*'[12]

From the 1940s, and what has been characterised as the Access to Justice Movement,[13] there was a recognition, and political acceptance, of the view that to secure the effective functioning of civil justice systems states should promote access to litigation funding for citizens who did not otherwise have the financial means to afford access to the courts. The 'post-war consensus'[14] that this was to be achieved by the provision of civil legal aid in many jurisdictions was predicated upon the idea that such funding was necessary in order to enable impecunious individuals to access the courts and lawyers, the latter of whom would then identify requisite evidence, navigate the pre-trial process, and secure the reasoned argument at trial that was essential for it to be carried out effectively. Funding was thus an essential prerequisite of the first and second features of adversarial civil justice. Removal of such funding, and as a consequence the removal of the ability of impecunious individual litigants to access lawyers has, in the words of a former Chief Justice in England,

---

[6]For England and Wales' online civil process, see Sorabji (2017) pp. 51–69; Etherton (2019).

[7]For Utah's online claims process, see Himonas (2018), p. 875.

[8]For British Columbia's Civil Resolution Tribunals, see Salter and Thompson (2016), p. 113.

[9]See for instance, Evers and Ryan (2016), p. 65.

[10]Hangzhou Internet Court (2020).

[11]Assy (2015), p. 11, Assy drew up Landsman's analysis in making these three points; Landsman (1983), pp. 713–714.

[12]Assy (2015), p. 12.

[13]Cappelletti (1993) p. 282.

[14]As Byrom puts it, Byrom (2017), p. 229.

undermined the ability of England's civil justice system to function adequately. As he put it, without funding for lawyers, the adversarial system cannot work.[15]

Since the 1980s there has, however, been a significant reduction in state provision of civil legal aid across the world. In Australia, for instance, civil legal aid provided to various Legal Aid Commissions has since the late 1990s been reduced significantly. From 1997, when 55% of their budgets amounted to civil legal aid, there has been a steady reduction to around 33%.[16] In England, where at one time approximately 80% of the population were eligible for some form of civil legal aid,[17] by 2007 this stood at 29%. A significant period of financial retrenchment by the state following the 2007 financial crisis left it subject to further swingeing reductions. As from 2013,[18] the civil legal aid budget was subject to a 40% reduction; a £300–£350 million reduction. Some 62% of those previously entitled to receive legal aid prior to the reduction became ineligible i.e., approximately 11% of the population are now within the scope of civil legal aid.[19] As Roger Smith, former chief executive of *Justice* (an independent advisory body) described it, this meant that the United Kingdom was doing no more than providing the *'lowest level of service that [would] comply with [its] minimum obligations under the European Convention on Human Rights at the least possible cost'*.[20]

While the retreat from a welfare state-based approach to the provision of civil legal aid has in a number of jurisdictions been matched by the promotion by legislatures and courts of alternative forms of private litigation funding, they have not filled the gap left by legal aid's withdrawal adequately. The promotion of contingency fee funding agreements through legislative reform, in various forms such as England's conditional fee agreements or damages-based fee agreements, has been of limited scope.[21] The former have focused on discrete areas of litigation funding, such as personal injury. The latter, due to being drafted inadequately, have not been utilised by the legal profession.[22] Equally, courts have sought to develop third-party litigation funding, in the absence of legislative authorisation.[23] Again, however, such developments albeit explicitly driven by the aim of increasing access to justice have had limited impact in respect of those individuals and claims that

---

[15]House of Lords (2014), p. 15.

[16]Noted by Flynn and Hodgson (2017), p. 3. A similar pattern can be seen in, for instance, Canada, see McKillop and McCamus (2014).

[17]Paterson and Goriely (1997) cited in Byrom (2017), p. 228.

[18]As a consequence of legislative reform effected by the Legal Aid, Sentencing and Punishment of Offenders Act 2012.

[19]Flynn and Hodgson (2017), p. 3; and see Sorabji (2015), p. 159.

[20]Smith (2012).

[21]For a discussion, see Peysner (2014).

[22]Civil Justice Council (2015a).

[23]Arkin v Borchard Lines Ltd. [2005] 1 WLR 3055.

would otherwise and previously have been funded via civil legal aid.[24] The focus of third party litigation funding, predicated as it is on the prospect of the third party funder realising significant financial benefits through the provision of such funding, has been on high value litigation. Its utility for lower value claims, debt claims, housing claims, family disputes, immigration and employment claims is thus questionable at best.

The effective evisceration of civil legal aid and a less than adequate response via the promotion of private alternatives has had one significant consequence. It has resulted in the significant growth of individuals who have been left with the choice of not bringing proceedings to vindicate their rights or of bringing such claims without the benefit of legal advice or representation. It is not clear to what extent individuals have taken the former course of action, although the Civil Justice Council anticipated that significant numbers would do so.[25] The increase in litigants-in-person (LiPs), lawyerless litigants, has however been marked.[26] While precise figures are not available, evidence given to Parliament by the English senior judiciary in 2015 was clear: there had been a significant increase in LiPs in civil disputes. Figures in family disputes show a marked reduction in claims, bearing out the Civil Justice Council's fears that parties would 'lump it' and simply take no steps to vindicate their rights. They further show in the remainder of family claims a sharp increase in LiPs. What evidence is available is thus unequivocal: the reduction in legal aid has had a sharp impact on claims being brought, and on the availability of legal advice and representation in those that are issued. Lawyers are thus being priced out of the system. The inevitable consequence of this is that both of the first two fundamentals of the civil justice system have been negatively affected by the withdrawal of legal aid.

The second challenge facing lawyers' involvement in civil justice is a technological one. This has a number of strands. The first, and most longstanding, is that the development of information technology is disrupting, and will be expected to do so

---

[24]As Lord Phillips put it, explaining the justification for the court's endorsement of third party funding, in Gulf Azov Shipping Co Ltd. v Idisi [2004] EWCA Civ 92 at [54], *'Public policy now recognises that it is desirable, in order to facilitate access to justice, that third parties should provide assistance designed to ensure those who are involved in litigation have the benefit of legal representation'.*

[25]Civil Justice Council (2011), p. 8: *'Every informed prediction is that, by reason of the forthcoming reductions and changes in legal aid, the number of self-represented litigants will increase, and on a considerable scale. Such litigants will be the rule rather than the exception. Where there is not an increase the reason will be that the individual was resigned to accepting that the civil justice system was not open to them even if they had a problem it could solve or it could give access to the rights they were entitled to.'*

[26]House of Commons' Justice Select Committee (2015), pp. 90–95; Comptroller and Auditor General of the National Audit Office (2014), p 15; Civil Justice Council (2014); Judiciary of England and Wales (2014), p. 12; Q v Q [2014] EWFC 31 at [11]; Grimwood (2016).

further in the future, legal practice.[27] There are several elements to this. The most significant for present purposes focuses on the effect information technology will, or at least is expected to, have on the role lawyers play in the litigation process. That is the replacement of lawyers by 'robot lawyers', by automated legal processes and processing.[28] By way of example, the disclosure process in English civil procedure can now be carried out via the use of so-called predictive analytics rather than, as previously, by trainee and junior lawyers. That it can be, and can be carried out more cost-effectively, more speedily and more accurately than human lawyers, goes some significant way to explain why its use has been approved by the courts, but equally why it is likely to become the norm over time.[29] Equally, there is a clear expectation that pleadings (statements of case) will in time be fully digitised, and carried out by what might be called robo-pleaders, by technology such as that developed by I-CAN! and used in a number of jurisdictions within the United States.[30] Such 'smart forms', while they may in some cases call for a degree of review by a lawyer, need have no such human involvement in the drafting process.[31] Furthermore, evidence from pilot schemes in England show that they are easier to use than traditional paper-based forms, that they promote efficiency and cost-effectiveness in proceedings and, as also confirmed by evidence drawn from other jurisdictions,[32] promote greater litigant-user satisfaction with the litigation process.[33] A further element, which is being piloted by a number of law firms, such as Berrymans Lace Mawer (BLM), in England, is, again, the use of so-called predictive analytics as a means to predict the likely outcome of legal disputes.[34] Using the application of artificial intelligence to past case data, law firms seek to give initial advice on the merits of claims to guide litigation and settlement strategies. Considered advice by lawyers is thus, to a degree, starting to be replaced, or at this stage augmented, by the application of AI technology.[35]

---

[27]It is the idea that information technology is a disruptive technology, which will engender significant change in the nature and practice of law; see Christensen et al. (2015), p. 44; Susskind (2010); Susskind (2013).

[28]Markovic (2019).

[29]Pyrrho Investments v MWB Property [2016] EWHC 256 (Ch). Also see Moore v Publicis Groupe 11 Civ 1279 (ALC)(AJP), (S.D.N.Y. Feb. 24, 2012); Irish Bank Resolution Corporation Ltd. v Quinn (2015) IEHC 175, (2015) 3 J.I.C. 0306, Irish High Court (Comm.). And see Grossman and Cormack (2011); McGinnis and Pearce (2014).

[30]Ribadeneyra (2012), pp. 251–252.

[31]For a discussion of the various online legal forms available, such as those provided by *LegalZoom*, see Barton (2016).

[32]Barton and Bibas (2017), pp. 120–123.

[33]See, for instance, the summary of the improvements effected by the introduction of a number of online forms as part of the development of online procedures in England in, Burnett (2018a), pp. 21–24.

[34]A predictive programme that can identify liability in personal injury claims has been developed, see Slingo (2019).

[35]See, for instance, Ruger et al. (2004); Aletras et al. (2016); Katz et al. (2017).

There are several consequences that are likely to follow on from these technological developments. It is likely that there will be fewer lawyers in future. Just as in other industries where technology has altered the size of the workforce, IT developments ought to do the same for the legal profession. Automated pleadings, automated disclosure, AI-assisted predictions of litigation outcomes, are all likely to reduce the number of lawyers needed to carry out and manage litigation. Such developments are not just likely to have an impact on the legal profession directly. Taken together with the reduction in litigation funding, developments in IT are also having an impact upon lawyers' place within the civil litigation process itself. The issue here is the role that the development of online dispute resolution is having on the conscious redesign of civil justice systems. One fundamental element of that redesign is the removal of lawyers from the civil court process. In addition, therefore to the scope for a reduction in lawyers from the legal supply-side, demand from the courts is likely to reduce in future too due to IT developments.

Structural and procedural redesign of civil justice systems is, as noted above,[36] a well-established feature across the world. The impetus for this redesign has explicitly been the development, and success, of a variety of online dispute resolutions, such as that developed by eBay.[37] A feature of these ODR mechanisms is the absence of any input from lawyers. The nature of the design, which is focused on the speedy, economical, consensual resolution of broadly consumer disputes is one where it is neither necessary nor cost-effective to resort to legal advice.[38] Two examples illustrate this trend. First, the Civil Resolution Tribunal in Canada. This online tribunal is explicitly designed to be operated by LiPs, without either legal advice or representation. The CRT's online platform, initially, through its '*Solution Explorer*' system, which helps the parties understand the nature of their problem, and then via assistance, for instance, from the CRT's case management, guides litigants through the stages of the dispute resolution process, assisting them to formulate their claim and response.[39] While it does not prohibit parties from seeking advice from legal professionals, the nature of the assistance the CRT provides is intended to remove them from the process; to render them redundant. Legal representation during the resolution process is, however, presumptively prohibited, albeit with a discretion on the part of the CRT to set that presumption aside.[40]

Secondly, and explicitly building on the approach adopted in the CRT, both the Civil Justice Council (a statutory advisory body, the purpose of which is to ensure that the civil justice system remains, amongst other things, fair and accessible[41]) in England and the English senior judiciary both recommended the development of an online court, which would be explicitly designed for individuals to operate without

---

[36]See *supra* n 6–10.

[37]See Katsh and Rabinovich-Einy (2017); Civil Justice Council (2015a).

[38]Civil Justice Council (2015a).

[39]Salter and Thompson (2016), 129ff.

[40]Salter and Thompson (2016), n 53.

[41]Civil Procedure Act 1997, s.6(3).

legal assistance.[42] While the main recommendation, to build a discrete online court to achieve this end was rejected by the UK government, its recommendations concerning the development of digital processes that were designed for the use of LiPs without legal assistance is being taken forward.[43] While the English judiciary have been at pains to reject suggestions that their active support for the development of these online processes has been the reduction in state funding of civil litigation, and particularly of the civil justice system, it is beyond doubt that the growth in LiPs has been a significant stimulus for such developments. As Sir Ernest Ryder explained it, the consequences of the 2007–2008 financial crisis was not the reason to adopt a developmental approach that sought to eradicate lawyers from the justice system. It was the spur, however, to bring about a fundamental reappraisal of how the state delivered justice.[44] On the contrary, however, austerity does appear to have been the spur to action as it contributed, if not caused, a significant increase in the numbers of LiPs as a result of reductions in legal aid provision. Thus austerity resulted in increasing numbers of individuals expected to navigate the civil courts and their procedure, as well as the substantive law, without legal assistance to guide them.[45] As Sir Michael Briggs (the Briggs Review), the main architect of the proposal to develop an online court put it, "*I consider that there is a clear and pressing need to use the opportunity presented by the digitising of the civil courts to create for the first time a court . . . for litigants to be enabled to have effective access to justice without lawyers.*"[46]

The clear and pressing need was the increase in LiPs due to the removal of civil legal aid.[47] Developments in ODR generally and particularly those exemplified by the CRT in Canada provided not only the opportunity to modernise the civil justice system, but to do so in a way that met the needs to the increasing numbers of LiPs. Technological developments, which on their own were putting pressure on the legal profession, or as the Civil Justice Council has it where disrupting it,[48] combined with the consequences of reductions to legal aid, are now seeing the development of

---

[42]For a discussion see Sorabji (2015).

[43]See the various online court pilot schemes set out in: CPR PD 51R (Online Civil Money Claims Pilot); CPR PD51S (The County Court Online Pilot); and CPR PD51V (The video hearings pilot scheme) http://www.justice.gov.uk/courts/procedure-rules/civil/rules#part51.

[44]As he put it in Ryder (2016) at 5, '*Austerity, the product of the 2007–2008 financial crisis, provides a basis upon which we have had to scrutinise the ways in which we secure the rule of law and the citizen's access to justice as part of that. It provides the spur to rethink our approach from first principles. As such we should not see austerity as the driver of reform. It is not a question of cutting our cloth. It is a question of austerity forcing us to do what it took fifty years of failure in the 1800s to do: look at our systems, our procedures, our courts and tribunals, and ask whether they are the best they can be, and if not how they can be improved.*'.

[45]See the design aimed at ameliorating these problems outlined by the Civil Justice Council (2015b), p. 6, and by Briggs (2015), p. 75ff; Briggs (2016).

[46]Briggs (2015), p. 122.

[47]Briggs (2015), ibid. at 7–8.

[48]Civil Justice Council (2015b), p. 5.

courts and court processes explicitly designed to be used without lawyers. As those designs are, as they are in England, intended to result in significant numbers of civil claims coming within the scope of the online, lawyerless process,[49] the future path that is being developed is one where it is intended lawyers will have no, or at best a marginal, role to play. The question then becomes what effect that might have on access to justice.

12.3 The Contingency of Lawyers

Is the absence of lawyers from the civil justice system necessarily a negative development? The language of those involved in reform in England would suggest the answer to such a question is no; removing lawyers from litigation is not necessarily to be regretted. While the Briggs Review, for instance, did not go so far as to suggest that lawyer involvement in the reformed online processes it proposed should be prohibited, it was clear in the direction of travel: the new online court and procedure was to be designed for the use of non-lawyers i.e., the aim was to reduce the need for and presence of lawyers in the reformed system.[50] This was to be done in order to enable claims that would not otherwise be pursued on grounds of costs i.e., legal costs, would now be capable of being pursued effectively by lawyerless litigants.[51] In this respect, it noted that such a development would mean for the first time a civil justice system would not be designed by and for the use of lawyers nor would it thus adopt a '*lawyerish*' approach to litigation,[52] as it would provide the means to guide lawyerless litigants easily through its procedures, would help them diagnose their disputes in legal terms, and guide them in a quasi-inquisitorial way through the evidence-gathering process.[53] Given this, it regretted not being able to call the new online court, a 'Peoples Court', due to the historic

---

[49]The proposed online process is intended, at least initially, to encompass the majority of types of civil claim up to a value of £25,000; see Etherton (2019), p. 3.

[50]Briggs (2016), p. 46, noting it was not a 'design objective' to exclude lawyers. On the contrary their exclusion would simply be a consequence of the design. It could be suggested that is a distinction without a difference.

[51]Briggs (2015), p. 76.

[52]Briggs (2015), p. 79, '*I would summarise the advantages of the OC as a separate court with separate rules as follows. First, this would best achieve the fundamental objective behind the design of the OC, namely to create a court for litigants without lawyers, because it would insulate the OC from all the lawyerish and purely adversarial aspects of the culture of the civil courts generally, including the County Court. The OC is intended from the outset to be a less adversarial environment, in which investigation by the court will form an important and distinctive part.*'

[53]Briggs (2015), p. 75, '*In fact the true distinguishing feature of the OC is that it would be the first court ever to be designed in this country, from start to finish, for use by litigants without lawyers.*'

connotations of such a term.[54] The same points also underpinned the reports by the Civil Justice Council and *Justice* which pre-dated the Briggs Review, and were readily accepted by members of the senior judiciary.[55]

The initial scope of such a development, and it is to be noted that despite the rejection of the central idea of creating a new online court to deliver such reforms its aims are being pursued through the development of online civil procedural reforms noted above, was to be confined to low value and straightforward cases. As such the reforms would see a limited class of claims come within the scope of the lawyerless process. Complex and high value claims would remain outside its scope. This limitation was, however, noted to be a technical one; it was based on the idea that at the start of such a development complex cases would not be capable of being dealt with effectively by the technology underpinning the new online system.[56] The value and complexity restriction, which as the Briggs Review noted could lead to the criticism that a two-tier system of justice was being developed, was merely contingent.[57] Come the technology, come the basis for a wider exclusion of lawyers. The exclusion of lawyers was, in principle at least then, not looked at as necessarily being limited by value and complexity of disputes.

There is some support for the idea that removing lawyers from the litigation process would not be a negative development, and would on the contrary increase access to and effective participation in disputes and not, as suggested, create a two-tier justice system. Thus there is some evidence to support, indirectly and as unpalatable as it may be, the movement away from the proper provision of civil legal aid. The evidence comes from empirical studies of the impact of lawyers and their absence from employment disputes, unemployment insurance appeals, tax appeals, and disability appeals. Studies, as noted by Barton & Bibas, show that in civil cases lawyers add value i.e., are beneficial, where the civil process is adversarial and formal. Where proceedings become increasing informal and less adversarial, the presence of lawyers makes no significant difference to the outcome of the dispute. There are, however, two exceptions to this: the presence of lawyers in such cases has two negative effects: it increases delay and, inevitably as they need to be remunerated, the cost of litigation.[58] As they put it, commenting on the effect of lawyers on employment disputes, *"The only statistically significant effect found by (a) study of unemployment appeals was that lawyers made cases take about 40% longer. In*

---

[54]Briggs (2015), p. 75, '*It would be tempting to capture this essential distinguishing feature by calling it a people's court, were it not for the unfortunate historical connotations which would inevitably attach to that phrase.*'

[55]For a discussion, see Sorabji (2017).

[56]Briggs (2015), p. 76, '*Simplicity is a requirement . . . because it is unlikely that first generation software will prove to be up to the task of accommodating complex issues. . . .*'.

[57]Briggs (2016), p. 37.

[58]Barton and Bibas (2017), pp. 104–109.

other words, adding lawyers had perverse effects – it did not increase clients' chance of success but hurt clients by delaying their eventual recoveries."[59]

The delay arising from lawyer involvement was, they suggested, a consequence of the complexity they brought to litigation i.e., by taking procedural points and making procedural applications that would not otherwise be made. They echo therefore the criticism inherent in the Briggs Review: lawyers create a lawyerish culture. That culture is neither necessary, nor is it beneficial. On the contrary, it simply renders procedure more technical, as Barton & Bibas note, which in turn adds to its complexity, its cost and its delay.[60] As they conclude there is no benefit in such cases to be derived for litigants to counter-balance those costs, as lawyers do not make a significant contribution to the court or tribunal reaching a correct decision. Where, however, there is some evidence that lawyers play a positive role in assisting litigants to achieve a correct decision it is in cases where, *". . . the governing laws were complex, the proceedings were aggressively adversarial with little judicial involvement and the other side was almost always represented by counsel.".*[61]

In other words, as the Briggs Review proposed, and developments in Canada's CRT suggest, a civil procedural system that is designed to reduce complexity in its procedure, to provide a means for the complexity of substantive law to be simplified by online diagnostic tools, to be quasi-inquisitorial or investigative rather than adversarial, and to have no lawyer involvement,[62] is a more efficient and effective system.

The evidence Barton & Bibas examine goes further. One of the underpinnings of the developments of online civil processes, which is evident in the CRT and being taken forward in England post-Briggs, is the management of claims by the court itself. This management, whether it is advice or assistance to litigants in managing the pre-trial process or the facilitation of consensual settlement by negotiation or mediation, is not necessarily to be carried out by trained lawyers. On the contrary, such work could be done by experienced and/or trained court staff.[63] Barton & Bibas's draw on work done by Kritzer,[64] which demonstrated that in a number of selected judicial forums (unemployment insurance, tax, disability appeals and labour arbitration), the assistance provided by non-lawyers to litigants was as effective as

---

[59]Barton and Bibas (2017), p. 108.

[60]Barton and Bibas (2017), pp. 108–109.

[61]Barton and Bibas (2017), p. 106.

[62]Civil Resolution Tribunal Rules, r.1.13 https://civilresolutionbc.ca/wp-content/uploads/2019/03/CRT-Rules-Effective-April-1-2019.pdf. The presumption in the CRT, except for road traffic accident personal injury cases, is that there will be no lawyers involved. That presumption can only be overturned if the litigant obtains the CRT's permission to be represented by a lawyer; see, '*In some cases, you can have a representative speak for you when you use the CRT. For motor vehicle injury disputes, you can automatically be represented by a lawyer. In most other cases, you'll have to ask the CRT for permission if you want to be represented by a lawyer.*' A representative is not a lawyer. https://civilresolutionbc.ca/tribunal-process/starting-a-dispute/helpers-representation/.

[63]Briggs (2015), p. 88.

[64]Kritzer (1998), at 201, cited in Barton and Bibas (2017), p. 106.

that provided by lawyers. The key issue in such cases that was determinative of the value of the assistance was the individual's experience i.e., a non-lawyer with experience of the court or tribunal was as effective as a lawyer. This evidence would seem to suggest that in such forums, where there is a simpler form of process for instance, than is applicable in civil procedure before ordinary civil courts, there is scope for the provision of assistance via court officers. Equally, and again this points towards the superfluity of lawyers, they point out that the same evidence supports the expansion of the availability of technical assistance from non-lawyers to lawyerless litigants through the licensing of non-lawyers who have experience in particular discrete areas of the law. Such 'limited-license legal technicians', and here the parallel with the future developments discussed by Susskind in *Tomorrow's Lawyers* concerning the development of new ways of delivering legal services other than via today's lawyers is patent, could thus provide a cost-effective alternative to lawyers as well as to trained court staff providing advice and assistance to litigants.

The evidence marshalled thus points to the following. First, the more procedure and substantive law can be simplified and the less formal and less adversarial a process is, the less valuable legal representation is to litigants and to the outcome of disputes. Lawyers are not necessary in such circumstances. That civil justice systems have historically been none of these things embedded the necessity of lawyers. That digitisation is enabling civil justice systems to be recast with simpler, more accessible procedures, with a less formality and technicality, and with a less adversarial and more investigative or problem-solving culture, is thus removing those features that support the necessity of lawyer involvement. Reform is rendering lawyers an unnecessary expense. It is, perhaps for the first time, leading to the position advocated by Bentham, that each individual can be their own lawyer due to the simplicity, accessibility and lack of adversariality of the process.[65]

Secondly, their evidence points towards a continuing, for now, need for lawyers in cases where the law, procedural and/or substantive is complex. That necessity is however undercut somewhat by both the assumption underpinning developments in England, which suggest that technological advances could in time expand the scope of its evolving online procedure from simple cases to more complex ones. The necessity of lawyers in those areas where the current evidence shows the added value they provide to litigants via advice and representation may well be no more than contingent. Developments in AI, such as those already being used by BLM (noted above) or through the development of predictive analytics in disclosure suggest a future where legal technicians, either provided by the state via their online courts or private enterprise, rather than skilled and experience lawyers provide and run digital services that replace work currently being done by lawyers generally, and specifically in complex cases. Future technological developments could thus lead to a position where litigants in both simple and complex claims can do as well in terms of

---

[65]Bentham (1843), p. 177; and see Barton and Bibas (2017), p. 203 on the importance for this as a means to secure equality before the law.

outcome without a lawyer as they would do with a lawyer. The necessity of lawyers for resolving individual disputes may thus increasingly decrease over time.

12.4 The Necessity of Lawyers

The digital, online reforms that are currently being developed are quite properly focused on improving access to the courts for individuals, particularly for those who are priced out of the system either due to the withdrawal of civil legal aid or because the cost and time of litigating their dispute is greater than the value of their claim. Their focus is on individual claims, a point which was made evident by Lord Burnett in his explanation of the focus of England's digital reform programme. As he put it: *"We should perhaps remember that the overwhelming majority of civil claims are for small sums, important though they are to the litigants, and that litigants want and expect a swift and inexpensive answer."*[66]

Barton & Bibas's evidence would then support the view that for those litigants the absence of a lawyer provided, as is intended through the digital reforms, the process is simple, non-adversarial and informal such litigants will also receive correct decisions. The reforms have in this way focused on one facet of the civil justice system's constitutional function: the peaceful resolution of disputes via rights-vindication. In so far as the reforms facilitate, and moreover expand the state's ability to secure that aim they cannot properly be criticised, assuming they do achieve that aim. A civil justice system does not, however, simply exist to resolve individual disputes. It has a wider public purpose, which does not feature in either discussions such as those that animate consideration of the future evolution of the legal profession or discussions of reform proposals, such as the Briggs Review. It is in the wider public interest that the necessity of lawyers becomes apparent, and as a consequence ought properly to be taken account of in developing the digital future of civil justice.

The nature and importance of the wider public interest in the provision of civil justice, and effective access to the courts, was recently reiterated in England by the United Kingdom Supreme Court in *R (Unison) v Lord Chancellor*.[67] As Lord Reed explained, courts exist to give effect to laws properly promulgated by Parliament and, in common law jurisdictions, the courts via the common law. They thus ensure accountability of state officials, by enabling them to be held accountable according to law. As such access to the courts constitutes, as Kessler has it, a state-checking function in that it acts as a means to deter arbitrary state action.[68] Equally, and focused on private individuals, it plays the same role in determining non-compliance

---

[66]Burnett (2018b), p. 6.

[67][2017] UKSC 51; [2017] 3 WLR 409 at [68]-[74].

[68]Kessler (2005).

with private law rights.[69] Accessibility secures these ends more generally through the fact of access being genuinely available, than necessarily through individuals having to bring disputes before the courts. The prophylactic role of what is generally known as the 'shadow of the law' is here as important as the court's dispute resolution function in securing compliance with the law.[70] As Lord Reed put it: *"But the value to society of the right of access to the courts is not confined to cases in which the courts decide questions of general importance. People and businesses need to know, on the one hand, that they will be able to enforce their rights if they have to do so, and, on the other hand, that if they fail to meet their obligations, there is likely to be a remedy against them. It is that knowledge which underpins everyday economic and social relations. That is so, notwithstanding that judicial enforcement of the law is not usually necessary, and notwithstanding that the resolution of disputes by other methods is often desirable."*[71]

The public interest in effective access to the courts goes wider than this. The civil courts, through adjudication, as has been powerfully argued by Fiss, Luban, Genn and Resnik for instance, provide a means by which the state can restate and develop public values and norms, focus and lead public debate, or bring about structural reform of our governance structures, and secure constitutional stability.[72] This public role, is as Fiss had rightly argued, adjudication's i.e., the civil justice system's, central function.[73] It is in these various public functions that the necessity of lawyers can be found; it is the necessity that Dick the Butcher would have liked to avoid through their elimination. Absent lawyers it is difficult to see how a civil justice system can properly achieve its public functions. This can be seen in three ways: first, open justice and effective public participation in the civil process; secondly, the constitutional right to legal advice; and, finally, the potential to de-skill the legal profession posed by digitisation.

Open justice is a well-established constitutional principle inherent in civil justice systems. It is, for instance, the means by which the judicial process can be held publicly accountable. It is the means by which the system can be subject to scrutiny to ward against arbitrary conduct by the judiciary. And it is the means by which, through the provision of public and reasoned judgments, individual litigants and members of the public can understand why disputes have been resolved as they are. Ultimately it is the means by which the rule of law is secured. As Toulson LJ put in *R (Guardian News and Media Ltd) v City of Westminster Magistrates' Court (Article 19 intervening)*: *"Open justice. The words express a principle at the heart of our system of justice and vital to the rule of law. The rule of law is a fine concept but fine words butter no parsnips. How is the rule of law itself to be policed? It is an age old*

---

[69]See Genn (2010, 2012). Also see the arguments developed by Resnik on the importance of access to the courts as a means of giving effect to legislation in, for instance, Resnik (2008, 2015).

[70]Mnookin and Kornhauser (1978).

[71][2017] UKSC 51; [2017] 3 WLR 409 at [71].

[72]Fiss (1984); Luban (1995); Genn (2010), ibid.; Resnik (2015), ibid.; Mittal and Weingast (2010).

[73]Fiss (1984), p. 1089.

question. Quis custodiet ipsos custodes - who will guard the guards themselves? In a democracy, where power depends on the consent of the people governed, the answer must lie in the transparency of the legal process. Open justice lets in the light and allows the public to scrutinise the workings of the law, for better or for worse."[74]

Generally, the way in which open justice is secured has been considered to involve effective access to court hearings, court documents, and reasoned judgments by the parties, the public and particularly the media.[75] One class of participant in the open justice process has not generally been identified: the lawyer. The ability of parties through participation in court proceedings, through examining trial documents and scrutinising judgments to ascertain whether the judgment reached is justified by an assessment of the law and evidence before the court is one that is mediated through the prism of independent legal advice. In many cases neither the public nor the media are present in court. In many cases, except those that are high profile and are delivered by higher first instance courts, judgments are not in practice made publicly available. As such in many cases, they are the only effective mechanism to ensure that the civil justice system, the law and in this the conduct of a judge as the means by which the delivery of justice and the application of the law is achieved, is as Harlan Fiske Stone CJ suggested, *'on trial in every case.'*[76]

To give one recent example, it could be asked in the absence of the media, the public, a published reasoned judgment and transcript of the proceedings, and the absence of lawyers representing the parties how might a lawyerless litigant have been in a position to assess their treatment by a judge as going beyond bias to abuse, as was the case in *Serafin v Malkiewicz*.[77] Digital processes may be able to provide the means by which parties could diagnose their dispute, or could even, depending on the nature of the digital system, diagnose whether there were grounds to appeal from a first instance decision, but where that depends on the state providing the 'Solution Explorer' as in Canada or as is intended to England, the question that must be asked is on what basis does this provide an effective state-checking mechanism against arbitrary conduct by the judiciary, or against a lapse in standards in conducting the pre-trial and trial process. It assumes that individual members of the public, whether claimant or defendant in private law disputes, must trust the state to check itself, to police itself. The assumption is that the replacement of independent legal advice, with legal advice or perhaps more realistically legal assistance, dependent on the state is a sufficient means of guaranteeing the necessary scrutiny that only lawyers provide in every case in which they are present.

Reforming the civil justice system so that lawyers are presumptively absent is one way to, inadvertently, remove the sole means by which independent and informed

---

[74][2012] EWCA Civ 420; [2013] QB 618 at (1) as endorsed by the UKSC in Cape Intermediate Holdings Ltd. v Dring (Asbestos Victims Support Groups Forum UK) [2019] UKSC 38; [2019] 3 WLR 429 at [2].

[75]See Jaconelli (2002), p. 3.

[76]Harlan Fiske Stone, cited in Sample et al. (2008), p. 4.

[77][2019] EWCA Civ 852 and [2020] UKSC 23; [2020] WLR 2455.

scrutiny of the judicial process is maintained. Providing lawyerless litigants with means to replace lawyers, where such means are provided by the state, is a way to make them dependent on the state to ascertain whether the state has not upheld the standards required of it in delivering justice. In the short term, and where lawyers are available in many cases if not all of them, this may not have a negative impact on the accuracy of outcomes of disputes, as Barton & Bibas's evidence shows, or of the fairness of process. Overtime though, the removal of the effective scrutiny of the judicial process by lawyers, and dependence on the state as a means to ascertain whether court officers have managed cases properly, impartially and in an unbiased manner, and judges have adjudicated according to law, may through closing justice off from an informed view, lead to a slip in standards and the growth of arbitrary process.[78] In this way the potential arises for the civil justice system to develop regressively so that it is no longer able to properly carry out its public interest functions, as for instance, it ceases to itself uphold and apply public values and norms through the development of poor practices, which then lead to a reduction in the quality of judgments and a general decline in confidence in the courts and judiciary with a weakening of the shadow of the law. Open justice may not be essential in every case to secure the effective administration of justice, but a system predicated on an absence of lawyers in proceedings of a general class or value is one which is moving towards one that is providing the basis for an absence of open justice generally and the negative consequences that follow on from that i.e., a reduction in adherence to the public interest in securing the rule of law.

Secondly, an absence of lawyers from the civil process runs contrary to the effective provision of what is generally recognised to be a fundamental, constitutional and human right: the right to receive independent legal advice.[79] The removal of lawyers as a means to provide advice and assistance by both accepting that the state has no duty to provide effective civil legal aid or by reforming the civil justice system to remove a need for independent legal advice would appear to run contrary to a state fulfilling its responsibility to secure this longstanding fundamental constitutional right. It is no real answer to suggest that that right can be properly secured by the provision of online legal diagnostic tools as part of a digital court process. As with the point concerning open justice, that relies on placing trust and confidence in the state to provide such advice. What basis there is for that in public law disputes, where the state is the respondent, is difficult to see. There may be a greater basis for doing so where private law rights are at stake, as it could be said the state has no reason to favour one party over the other in such cases and thus has no incentive to do anything other than provide advice of a similar quality to that provided by an independent lawyer. That may be true, however it fails to take account of the fact that states often have interests that are not entirely compatible with facilitating access to

---

[78]On this see Zuckerman (2014).

[79]R v Derby Magistrates' Court, ex p B [1996] 1 AC 487; R (Morgan Grenfell & Co Ltd) v Special Commissioner of Income Tax [2002] UKHL 21, [2003] 1 AC 563 at [7]–[9]; and in respect of Canada, Lavallee, Rackel & Heintz v Canada, (2002) 3 S.C.R. 209.

the courts. Such interests may influence the nature of any advice given via their online diagnostic tools. For instance, a state may wish to reduce the number of claims being made through the courts either generally, or in specific areas. Advice via the diagnostic tool could be tailored to point potential claimants and defendants away from the civil process to other resolution forums. Such advice, of a type that might not be forthcoming from a lawyer uninfluenced by such extraneous public interests the aim of which is to reduce litigation. Such advice may thus provide a basis to reduce effective participation of the public in the justice system by reducing their ability to obtain effective legal advice concerning their substantive public and private law rights and obligations.

It might be said in answer to the second point that it assumes that the provision of online diagnosis will only be provided by the state. It could, quite properly, be said that law firms could provide their own, independent, versions of online diagnosis; that legal technicians could provide such advice. Here the final difficulty of removing lawyers from the civil justice system arises, the risk that over-time it will de-skill the legal profession. This is referred to in other areas as the 'auto-pilot' problem. One of the problems that became apparent following the introduction of plane 'auto-pilots' was that over time pilots became increasingly dependent on it, with a consequent reduction in their own skills. As a consequence flying became more risky due to the problem that arose where autopilot either failed or could not deal with novel situations. Due to their reliance on it, pilots no longer had the necessary skills themselves to deal with such situations.[80] The development of online legal diagnostic tools could lead to a similar problem for lawyers, as could the development of predictive analytics replacing disclosure work done by junior lawyers, as could the development of robo-pleaders, again replacing work done by junior and more senior lawyers.

Each of these innovations could retard skills development by lawyers, which would reduce their ability to devise and develop such systems in the future, as well reducing their ability to scrutinise the nature of any work done digitally for error or to consider the application of law creatively in novel situations. Where judges are drawn from the legal profession, as in England, the possibility then arises that future judges will not have the same or equivalent legal skills and experience as previous generations of judges. Setting aside for present purposes the problem that such developments may pose by rendering future lawyers and judges ever more dependent on technology, which itself will call into question how society is able to ensure that the technology used is subject to effective scrutiny and accountability, this raises a fundamental problem for the civil justice system's public functions. As Fiss argued, as noted above, one of the public functions of courts which goes beyond applying those norms embedded in law, is to develop new norms and thereby to reshape society through the creative development of the law. Where lawyers and judges no longer have the legal skills and experience of those of past generations the ability of courts to develop the law creatively may well be reduced in the future.

---

[80]Fry (2019), p. 131.

While it may be the case that artificial intelligence may develop so as to provide creative solutions to novel situations, it is perhaps to be doubted whether it could or should be acceptable for the development of values to be delegated in that way. If one of the civil justice system's public functions is to maintain the '*governance of law*' as a shared enterprise,[81] it might well be expected that it be a shared *human* enterprise. For that, it will require skilled and experienced lawyers advising litigants, making reasoned arguments to judges, who themselves are skilled and experienced lawyers. Such a presence in litigation may well not be called for in any assessment of how individual disputes can be resolved, but it would appear to be a necessity where the public function of developing law, or stating, developing and applying new social norms and values is concerned.

12.5   Conclusion

Where might this leave the position of the legal profession in the future? It cannot but be the case that in future civil justice systems are likely to become increasingly digitised, with a greater role for technology to play in guiding litigants through the system, as is already the case in Canada's CRT and is being developed in England and other jurisdictions. In many cases this will inevitably reduce the necessity of having a lawyer guide a party through the litigation process, and will do so as Barton & Bibas suggest with no adverse effect on the outcome of individual cases. Such technology may also lead to properly effective simplified rules of court, with—due to the application of technology guiding parties through the rules—less scope for procedural error, and hence less need for lawyers to advise parties on the consequences of error, and also to assist them to apply for procedural relief from such consequences. It may also be the case that the work of court staff, managing cases, assisting parties to identify evidence, as well as promoting the use of mediation and other forms of ADR or ODR, will equally reduce the need for lawyers to carry out a further degree of advisory work during the course of litigation. In all these, and undoubtedly other ways not yet appreciated, the potential exists for technology to provide a basis for lawyers to play less of a role in litigation. And for many litigants who are willing to accept a pared-back court process in exchange for a speedy resolution of their dispute, that will be perfectly acceptable a future. Equally, as a policy choice for society that may be perfectly acceptable, in terms of balancing the cost of resolution to individuals and society in general against the benefit of securing an accurate decision.

Such developments should, however, take account of the need to ensure the involvement in lawyers in the litigation process for a number of principled reasons that are focused on the broader public interest rather than the immediate interests of individual litigants. First, lawyers are an essential means through which open justice

---

[81]Fuller (1964).

is achieved. The presence of independent legal scrutiny of the litigation process while it is taking place is a strong prophylactic against the prospect of the arbitrary application of procedural law and substantive law by court administrators and the judiciary. It is the means by which an informed and critical participant can ensure that justice is done, as well as is seen to be done. A court system that is only scrutinised by lay participants, is not one that is capable of being subject to effective scrutiny. As we move to a system that is primarily conducted online, or provides for greater decision-making on the papers rather than at oral hearings, as is suggested in England, the greater the need would seem to exist for independent, informed scrutiny of the system by lawyers.

Secondly, the presence of lawyers is an essential element of effective participation by parties in the civil trial process. It may be acceptable, on grounds of cost and efficiency, to provide through digital processes a means by which an online court process could help lawyerless litigants to determine the nature of their claim, and either with our without the assistance of court administrators, the nature of evidence to submit in support of the claim. The question arises, however, to what extent it is acceptable to establish a system that is predicated upon an online system and court administrators being solely responsible for determining these questions. In terms of questioning and testing the veracity of the guidance given, to what extent is a lawyerless litigant in a good position to do so without expert advice. Are lawyerless litigants to be expected to simply trust the state to provide effective and neutral advice? Equally to what extent can a lawyerless litigant be properly expected to trust or to effectively challenge decisions taken by an online procedure or by a court administrator. Absent legal advice a litigant is unlikely to have, nor should they be expected to have, the means to do so. Establishing a lawyerless system places a significant degree of power and responsibility in the hands of the state and its processes, with doubtful means by which individuals can test or otherwise challenge it.

Thirdly, the absence of lawyers from large parts of the civil justice system, combined with reductions in opportunities for lawyers to gain legal skills, experience and the judgment that stems from that, poses a problem concerning the ability to hold the justice system to account as well as operate it effectively in the future. Any systemic reduction in the ability of junior lawyers to develop the skills commonplace to today's senior lawyers, will inevitably reduce the prospect that the next generations senior lawyers will have the necessary skills and judgment to hold the civil justice system to account. It will equally reduce the prospect that tomorrow's judges, particularly in common law systems, will have the same skill level as today's judges. It poses the problem of a general de-skilling of the legal profession. Such a future profession is one less likely to be capable, to have the ability, to hold Dick the Butcher to account, as well as to hold the state to account.

This is not to suggest that civil justice systems should not embrace technology, that lawyers involvement in litigation cannot properly be minimised in some areas of procedure. It will clearly bring benefits, both in terms of efficiency and economy; thus it will open up access to justice. And in many cases this will be done with no reduction in the quality of decision-making in individual cases. It is to suggest, however, that the redesign of civil justice systems needs to take place with an explicit commitment to there being a defined and essential role for the legal profession, in the wider public interest. It is a suggestion that, at the present time, is not perhaps featuring to the extent it ought to in discussions concerning digital reforms to civil justice. With reform's focus on individual cases, the necessity of lawyers in the wider public interest to ensure the civil courts are able to continue to fulfil their public functions is being neglected. As a consequence, we may, with the best of intentions, be embedding a reformed approach which will undermine our ability to ensure, as Justinian specified, we are able *"to render everyone [their] due."*[82]

References

Aletras N et al (2016) Predicting judicial decisions of the European court of human rights: a natural language processing perspective. Peer J Comput Sci. https://doi.org/10.7717/peerj-cs.93

Arkenberg J (1999) Jack Cade: Proclamation of Grievances 1450. In: Internet medieval source book. Fordham University. http://www.fordham.edu/halsall/source/1450jackcade.html

Assy R (2015) Injustice in person. Oxford University Press, Oxford

Barton B (2016) Technology can solve much of America's access to justice problem, if we let it. In: Estreicher S, Radice J (eds) Beyond elite law. Cambridge University Press, New York

Barton B, Bibas S (2017) Rebooting justice. Encounter Books, New York

Bentham J (1843) Principles of Judicial Procedure, with the outlines of a procedure code. In: Bowring J (ed) The works of Jeremy Bentham, Vol. 2. William Tait, Edinburgh

Briggs M (2015) Civil Courts Structure Review: Interim Report. https://www.judiciary.uk/wp-content/uploads/2016/01/ccsr-interim-report-dec-15-final1.pdf

Briggs M (2016) Civil Courts Structure Review: final report. https://www.judiciary.uk/wp-content/uploads/2016/07/civil-courts-structure-review-final-report-jul-16-final-1.pdf

Burnett ID (2018a) The Age of Reform. https://www.judiciary.uk/wp-content/uploads/2018/06/speech-lcj-the-age-of-reform2.pdf

Burnett ID (2018b) The Cutting Edge of Digital Reform. https://www.judiciary.uk/wp-content/uploads/2018/12/speech-lcj-online-court.pdf

Byrom N (2017) Cuts to civil legal aid and the identity crisis in lawyering: lessons from the experience of England and Wales. In: Flynn A, Hodgson J (eds) Access to justice and legal aid. Bloomsbury, London, pp 221–238

Cappelletti M (1993) Alternative dispute resolution processes within the framework of the world-wide access-to-justice movement. Mod Law Rev 56:282–296

Christensen C, Raynor M, McDonald R (2015) What is disruptive innovation. Harv Bus Rev 93:44–53

Civil Justice Council (2011) Access to justice for litigants in person (or self-represented litigants). https://www.judiciary.uk/wp-content/uploads/2014/05/report-on-access-to-justice-for-litigants-in-person-nov2011.pdf

Civil Justice Council (2014) Civil Justice Council response to Justice Committee Inquiry: impact of changes to civil legal aid under the Legal Aid, Sentencing & Punishment of Offenders (LASPO)Act 2012. https://www.judiciary.uk/wp-content/uploads/2014/05/CJC-response-to-Justice-Committee-inquiry.pdf

Civil Justice Council (2015a) Online dispute resolution for low value claims. https://www.judiciary.uk/wp-content/uploads/2015/02/Online-Dispute-Resolution-Final-Web-Version1.pdf

---

[82]Thomas (1987).

Civil Justice Council (2015b) The damages-based agreements reform project: drafting and policy issues. https://www.judiciary.uk/wp-content/uploads/2015/09/dba-reform-project-cjc-aug-2015.pdf

Comptroller and Auditor General of the National Audit Office (2014) Implementing reforms to civil legal aid. https://www.nao.org.uk/wp-content/uploads/2014/11/Implementing-reforms-to-civil-legal-aid1.pdf

Etherton T (2019) Rule-making for a Digital Court Process. https://www.judiciary.uk/wp-content/uploads/2019/06/mr-oxford-cpr-conference-june-19.pdf

Evers M, Ryan P (2016) Exploring ecourt innovations in New South Wales civil courts. J Civil Litigat Pract 5:65–76

Fiss O (1984) Against Settlement. Yale Law J 93:1073–1091

Flynn A, Hodgson J (2017) Access to justice and legal aid cuts: a mismatch of concepts in the contemporary Australian and British legal landscapes. Bloomsbury, London

Fry H (2019) Hello world: how to be human in the age of the machine. Penguin Random House, New York

Fuller L (1964) The morality of law. Yale University Press, New Haven

Genn H (2010) Judging civil justice. Cambridge University Press, Cambridge

Genn H (2012) What is civil justice for? Reform, ADR, and access to justice. Yale J Law Human 24:397–418

Grimwood G (2016) Litigants in person: the rise of the self-represented litigant in civil and family cases. https://commonslibrary.parliament.uk/research-briefings/sn07113/

Grossman M, Cormack G (2011) Technology-assisted review in e-discovery can be more effective and more efficient than exhaustive manual review. Rich J Law Technol 17:1–48

Hangzhou Internet Court (2020). https://www.netcourt.gov.cn/portal/main/en/index.htm

Himonas D (2018) Utah's online dispute resolution program. Dickinson Law Rev 122:875–898

House of Commons' Justice Select Committee (2015) Impact of changes to civil legal aid under part 1 of the Legal Aid, Sentencing and Punishment of Offenders Act 2012. https://publications.parliament.uk/pa/cm201415/cmselect/cmjust/311/311.pdf

House of Lords (2014) Unrevised transcript of evidence taken before The Select Committee on Extradition Law. https://www.parliament.uk/documents/lords-committees/constitution/Scrutiny/ucCC270416lcj.pdf

Jaconelli J (2002) Open justice. Oxford University Press, Oxford

Katsh E, Rabinovich-Einy O (2017) Digital justice. Oxford University Press, Oxford

Katz D et al (2017) A general approach for predicting the behavior of the supreme court of the United States. PLoS One. https://doi.org/10.1371/journal.pone.0174698

Kessler A (2005) Our Inquisitorial Inheritance. Cornell Law Rev 90:1181–1275

Kritzer H (1998) Legal advocacy: lawyers and nonlawyers at work. University of Michigan Press, Michigan

Landsman S (1983) A brief survey of the development of the adversarial system. Ohio State Law J 44:713–739

Locke J (1988) Two treatises of government. Cambridge University Press, Cambridge

Luban S (1995) Settlements and the erosion of the public realm. Georgetown Law J 83:2619–2662

Markovic M (2019) Rise of the robot lawyers? Ariz Law Rev 61:325–350

McGinnis J, Pearce R (2014) The great disruption: how machine intelligence will transform the role of lawyers in the delivery of legal services. Fordham Law Rev 82:3041–3066

McKillop D, McCamus J (2014) National Report – Canada. In: The Crisis of Legal Aid and Alternative Solutions. International Association of Procedural Law Seoul Conference 2014. https://www.ufrgs.br/caar/wp-content/uploads/2014/10/Session-3.2.pdf

Mittal S, Weingast B (2010) Constitutional stability and the deferential court. U Pa J Const Law 13:337–352

Mnookin R, Kornhauser L (1978) Bargaining in the shadow of the law. Yale Law J 88:950–997

Paterson A, Goriely T (1997) A reader on resourcing civil justice. Oxford University Press, Oxford

Peysner J (2014) Access to justice. Palgrave Macmillan, Basingstoke

Resnik J (2008) Courts: in and out of sight, site, and cite. Vill Law Rev 53:771–810

Resnik J (2015) Diffusing disputes, the public in the private of arbitration, the private in courts and the erasure of rights. Yale Law J 124:2804–2939

Ribadeneyra J (2012) Web-based legal services delivery capabilities. Harv J Law Technol 26:246–256

Ruger TW et al (2004) The supreme court forecasting project: legal and political science approaches to predicting supreme court decision-making. Colom Law Rev 104:1150–1210

Ryder EN (2016) The Modernisation of Access to Justice in Times of Austerity. https://www.judiciary.uk/wp-content/uploads/2016/03/20160303-ryder-lecture2.pdf

Salter S, Thompson D (2016) Public-centred civil justice redesign: a case study of the British Columbia civil resolution tribunal. McGill J Disp Resol 3:113–136

Sample J, Ponzen D, Young M (2008) Fair courts: setting recusal standards. https://www.brennancenter.org/sites/default/files/2019-08/Report_Fair-Courts-Setting-Recusal-Standards.pdf

Slingo J (2019) Robot claims handler 'takes away bias' from PI process. https://www.lawgazette.co.uk/news/robot-claims-handler-takes-away-bias-from-pi-process/5070832.article

Smith R (2012) After the Act: what future for legal aid? https://justice.org.uk/wp-content/uploads/2015/02/After-the-Act-what-future-for-legal-aid-Roger-Smith.pdf

Sorabji J (2015) Austerity's effect on English civil justice. Erasmus Law Rev. https://doi.org/10.5553/elr.000043

Sorabji J (2017) The online solutions court - a multi-door courthouse for the 21st century. CJQ 36:51–69

Susskind R (2010) The end of lawyers? Oxford University Press, Oxford

Susskind R (2013) Tomorrow's lawyers. Oxford University Press, Oxford

Thomas J A C (ed) (1987) Justinian's Institutes. American Elsevier Publishing Co, New York

Zuckerman A (2014) No justice without lawyers—the myth of an inquisitorial solution. CJQ 33:355–374

Case Law

Arkin v Borchard Lines Ltd [2005] 1 WLR 3055

Cape Intermediate Holdings Ltd v Dring (Asbestos Victims Support Groups Forum UK) [2019] UKSC 38; [2019] 3 WLR 429

Gulf Azov Shipping Co Ltd v Idisi [2004] EWCA Civ 92

Irish Bank Resolution Corporation Ltd v Quinn (2015) IEHC 175, (2015) 3 J.I.C. 0306, Irish High Court (Comm)

Lavallee, Rackel & Heintz v Canada, (2002) 3 S.C.R. 209

Moore v Publicis Groupe 11 Civ 1279 (ALC)(AJP), (S.D.N.Y. Feb. 24, 2012)

Pyrrho Investments v MWB Property [2016] EWHC 256 (Ch)

Q v Q [2014] EWFC 31

R (Guardian News and Media Ltd) v City of Westminster Magistrates' Court (Article 19 intervening) [2012] EWCA Civ 420, [2013] QB 618

R (Morgan Grenfell & Co Ltd) v Special Commissioner of Income Tax [2002] UKHL 21, [2003] 1 AC 563

R (Unison) v Lord Chancellor [2017] UKSC 51, [2017] 3 WLR 409

R v Derby Magistrates' Court, ex p B [1996] 1 AC 487

Serafin v Malkiewicz [2019] EWCA Civ 852, [2020] UKSC 23; [2020] WLR 2455

Part IV
Court Specialisation

Chapter 13
The Pros and Cons of Judicial Specialization

Elisabetta Silvestri

Abstract At a time when the search for efficiency is the constant trend of judicial reforms, the establishment of specialized courts could be a viable strategy. Specialized courts means courts equipped with judges who can boast special knowledge and expertise in a specific area of law; and sometimes it also means procedural patterns other than the ones according to which ordinary cases are decided. These features seem particularly appropriate to handle a variety of new cases arising out of novel statutes regulating topics of unprecedented complexity. In fact, judicial specialization is seen as something that can both increase efficiency in the disposition of cases and, at the same time, guarantee high-quality decision-making and uniformity of case law; yet, even specialized courts have their 'dark side'. In particular, one drawback must be emphasized: the establishment of specialized courts can foster the idea of an elitist access to justice that benefits solely selected cases and therefore selected litigants only. This chapter attempts to offer a bird's-eye view of the pros and cons of judicial specialization, avoiding any ultimate conclusions, since conclusions may vary according to the legal system under investigation.

Keywords Specialized judiciary · Generalist courts · Efficiency of justice

13.1 Introduction

The issue of how much specialization is required of a modern judiciary is debated in many legal systems, some of which have a long tradition of generalist judges. How can one define a generalist judge? An Opinion issued by the Consultative Council of European Judges, an advisory body of the Council of Europe on issues related to the independence, impartiality and competence of judges, seems on point. The Opinion reads as follows: 'All judges... must be experts in the art of judging. Judges have the

E. Silvestri (✉)
Department of Law, University of Pavia, Pavia, Italy
e-mail: elisabetta.silvestri@unipv.it

X. Kramer et al. (eds.), *New Pathways to Civil Justice in Europe*,
https://doi.org/10.1007/978-3-030-66637-8_13

know-how to analyse and appraise the facts and the law and to take decisions in a wide range of fields. To do this they must have a broad knowledge of legal institutions and principles.[1] This Opinion depicts in a positive way the generalist judge, a judge who, in principle, is capable of resolving all the cases that are brought to the court in which he sits, independently of the subject matter of the cases themselves. But, in light of the increasing complexity of contemporary society and the emergence of new legal fields, fields in which references to technical concepts abound, can one maintain that an efficient justice system is satisfied by judges who are generically versed in the 'art of judging'? Instinctively, the answer is straight-forward, and it is negative: specialization is needed in law, as it is in many aspects of our everyday lives. Therefore, it is natural to think that a new array of complex cases, raising sophisticated issues of fact and law, deserves to be adjudicated by judges who are highly skilled in the subject matters at stake. After all, the legal profession learned the advantages of specialization a long time ago, and there seems to be no reason to deny that a specialized Bar deserves an equally specialized Bench, most of all these days, when society is challenged daily by the constant changes occurring in the present 'era of hyper-specialization'.[2]

In reality, any discourse regarding judicial specialization should start from a definition that clarifies what the expression means. The distinction between criminal, administrative and civil courts (which is common in many legal systems) can be regarded as a form of judicial specialization, and so is the geographical marking of a court's jurisdiction. It is reasonable to say, though, that the most popular meaning assigned to the expression refers to the so-called functional specialization,[3] in other words to a subject-matter specialization. Therefore, the dichotomy between gener-alist judges and specialized judges can be simplified as a straightforward distinction between judges who hear an extensive variety of cases and judges who hear only a specific type of cases.

It has also been argued that often debates concerning judicial specialization are not immune from generating a good measure of confusion, since there is a tendency to assume that judicial specialization is not different from specialization at the administrative level. The two forms of specialization—it is maintained—are in fact radically different, and to mix them up can bring about serious misunderstandings. While specialization in the field of administration benefits from the consistent pattern and repetitiveness of administrative action, 'the very essence of the judicial function . . . is a detachment from, a dispassionateness about the activity under scrutiny'.[4] In other words, if specialization means very close 'proximity' to a subject matter,

---

[1]Consultative Council of European Judges (CCJE), Opinion (2012) No. 15 of the Consultative Council of European Judges on the Specialization of Judges adopted at the 13th plenary meeting of the CCJE (Paris, 5–6 November 2012), available at https://www.csm.it/documents/46647/0/Opinion+No.+15+%282012%29.pdf/ea52f43d-a8e7-41d2-b59c-02cad9ded476, para 24.

[2]Oldfather (2012), p. 847.

[3]Baum (2009).

[4]Rifkind (1951), p. 426.

judges could lose their ability to distance themselves from the cases requiring their expert knowledge in that very subject matter, and this could affect the impartiality of the decisions they render.

The meaning of judicial specialization can vary according to the status of judges. In legal systems in which the judicial power is entrusted to a career judiciary, specialization is often neither required nor considered an 'added value' to the general knowledge of the law in force that any judge is supposed to possess. Specialization can be gained 'on the field', but that does not rule out the possibility that occurrences such as relocations or promotions force judges to deal with cases having nothing to do with their expertise in a specific area of law.

Another element to be taken into account when analysing the various facets of judicial specialization is whether it affects autonomous courts, meaning special courts with a specialized jurisdiction determined *ratione materiae*, or only subunits or divisions of ordinary courts. Furthermore, one should consider whether specialization is an exclusive prerogative of judicial bodies (whether specialized courts or specialized divisions within generalist courts) acting as first instance decision-makers or can be found at the level of appellate courts as well. Along the same lines, one should consider the fact that in a number of legal systems the element of specialization is satisfied by complementing the adjudicating panels within generalist courts with experts who are lay judges. Another elaboration on the theme of specialization asks whether it is more correct to talk about specialized judges than specialized courts, since it is possible that individual judges are called upon to deal regularly with cases in the subject matter falling within their expertise. The purpose is precisely to avoid the establishment of specialized courts or specialized divisions, a choice made for a variety of reasons, from a lack of financial resources to specific rules of law entrusting the judicial power only with the ordinary courts. These organizational features should not be overlooked, since they can have a bearing on the significance that different legal systems ascribe to judicial specialization and on the effects judicial specialization projects on the administration of justice and its quality.

13.2   Pros and Cons of Specialized Courts

Before scrutinizing the pros and cons of judicial specialization, one might wonder whether it makes any sense to engage in such a survey at a purely theoretical level, disregarding what happens in practice and with no reference to one or more specific legal system. American scholars have emphasized the lack of empirical data on the subject,[5] and the problem is the same on the other side of the Atlantic, too, at least to this author's knowledge. Empirical data are important, but they do not seem enough to dispel doubts about the criteria in light of which the data collected can be

---

[5]Baum (2009), p. 1681; Connors (2019).

evaluated. In other words, and taking efficiency as a possible criterion, how can one say that specialized courts are more efficient than generalist courts in dealing with certain types of cases? By the number of the decisions issued per year? By the speed at which the court's docket is cleared? By the number of judgments subject to appeal and reversed on appeal? Clearly, efficiency is a relative concept, since its meaning varies according to the elements that come into play, elements that depend on the subjective beliefs of the person who is supposed to say what is efficient and what is not. In short, as Professor Lawrence Baum has stated, it is difficult to compare generalist and specialized courts, since 'a good point of reference for comparison does not exist'.[6]

Let us now consider the elements that are conventionally seen as the advantages of having specialized courts. A good starting point is the list compiled by Marcus Zimmer.[7] He identifies the elements in favour of specialized courts as follows: judicial system efficiency and legal system efficiency; uniformity; expertise, improved case management; and elimination of conflicts and forum shopping.[8]

Judicial system efficiency and legal system efficiency are easy to understand. Specialized courts can contribute to the solution of a problem affecting a number of legal systems, that is, the huge caseloads distressing ordinary courts. Surely, the possibility to divert part of the dockets of ordinary courts to specialized courts or specialized divisions could inject efficiency into the justice system and benefit the legal system as a whole. As a matter of fact, legal scholars have emphasized the connection between the difficulties caused by the growing caseload pressure that courts are experiencing in many legal systems and the trend towards the establishment of specialized courts or divisions, since—as Professor Richard Posner has written—'Specialization enables an indefinite increase in caseload to be more or less effortlessly accommodated'.[9] At the same time, one may wonder whether redundant caseloads burdening the ordinary and generalist courts justify, by themselves, the policy choice to establish specialized courts. In fact, other strategies could be adopted to tackle the problem, such as a different arrangement of the judicial geography or the recruitment of law clerks and judicial assistants, just to mention some measures that seem within easy reach. Better yet, a more sensible solution would be to identify once and for all what causes people to believe that all disputes, even the most insignificant ones, deserve to end up in front of a judge. ADR methods, most of all when they are forced upon the parties, as occurs in a few legal systems, can reduce the courts' caseloads, but they leave unresolved the fundamental issue, that is, the issue of discovering the reasons why a certain society is extremely litigious.

---

[6]Baum (2009), p. 1681.

[7]Zimmer (2009), p. 46.

[8]Zimmer lists other elements, too, but they concern specialized courts that are 'outgrowths of administrative agencies of the government', which seems to make reference to bodies that outside the United States would not be deemed courts in the proper sense.

[9]Posner (2006), p. 1050.

According to Zimmer, the judicial system and the legal system as a whole can also benefit (again, in terms of efficiency) from the fact that lawyers appearing before specialized courts have no need to 'educate' the judges on the subject matter of the disputes through the production of numerous briefs and motions or requests for the testimony of one or more expert witnesses.[10] This can help expedite the development of proceedings and curtail their costs, both for the parties and for the public purse.

Expertise and improved case management refer to another highly touted, positive aspect of judicial specialization connected to the fact that an in-depth knowledge of the legal matters at stake is likely to improve the quality of the decisions issued by specialized judges, who can develop a true expertise, by virtue of the fact of dealing constantly with cases revolving around the same subject matter.[11] A specialized judge, thanks to his extensive knowledge of the subject matter at stake, is in the best position to resort to the managerial techniques that are most suitable to the case he is handling. Furthermore, since cases assigned to a specialized court tend to revolve around the same issues, case management can be refined and perfected, so as to guarantee a more effective governance of proceedings and expedite the resolution of disputes.

Another widespread belief is that judges skilled in a specific legal field will produce better decisions than the ones their generalist peers will issue, or at least decisions that the parties will perceive as 'better', and therefore be more inclined to accept. That, in its turn, will contribute to enhancing the authority of specialized judges and reduce the number of appeals.

Continuing with the purported advantages of judicial specialization, one can mention the following: from a general point of view, specialization is conducive to more uniformity and consistency in judicial decisions, which brings about a higher degree of legal certainty. In fact, it has been argued that, 'A specialized court [...] may promote uniformity and predictability across jurisdictions in the interpretation of the law and the development of new legal doctrine'.[12] In their turn, uniformity and predictability reduce the chances of conflicting interpretations of the law governing the subject matter falling within the jurisdiction of specialized courts and, as a consequence, contribute to decreasing the risk of forum shopping.

Finally, an observation related to the performance of specialized judges deserves mention. Specialized judges, faced with similar factual or legal issues arising out of the subject matter that defines their jurisdiction, can gain a deep understanding of the general background underlying the cases that they are called upon to decide, and therefore can come up with solutions better suited to accommodate that background. In other words, specialized judges are more alert to perceiving and understanding the developments of technical, economic and social aspects peculiar to the field of their expertise.

---

[10]Zimmer (2009).

[11]See, for instance, Baum (2010), p. 1531; Rai (2002), p. 878, with reference to cases in the field of patent law.

[12]Kesan and Ball (2011), p. 402.

The elements listed are just some of the purported advantages of judicial special-ization. If one took them for granted, at face value, one could not reasonably deny that the establishment of specialized courts could be a positive step every legal system should take. It would inject into the administration of justice efficiency, high-quality decision-making, consistency of judgments and, last but not least, better 'customer satisfaction'; the parties and the public at large would be inclined to uphold the authority of the judgments issued by highly skilled judges who have mastered the subtleties of the subject matters at stake.

For the sake of argument, though, the 'devil's advocate' must take into account the potential disadvantages of judicial specialization. The Opinion of the Consulta-tive Council of European Judges mentioned above[13] elaborates extensively on the potential disadvantages of judicial specialization.[14] First in the list is the 'separation of specialist judges from the general body of judges'.[15] According to the Opinion, the negative consequences of this are many and of different magnitudes. Probably the most serious one is the risk of tarnishing the image of the judiciary as a united body whose members enjoy the same powers and prestige. The establishment of specialized courts may persuade the public that specialized courts consist of 'an elite group of judges who are different than the others',[16] different in the sense of being superior and more capable, thanks to their expertise. This is a deeply worrisome belief which would likely lower the public confidence in the ability of generalist judges simply because they cannot claim to be specialized in a certain area of law.

The Opinion continues listing other potential disadvantages inherent in special-ization. Specialization, most of all when it concerns a narrow field, may bring about the risk of insularity, a risk emphasized by a number of authors,[17] who stress the fact that compartmentalization of knowledge (even of legal knowledge) often detracts from the ability to see 'the big picture', making it difficult for a specialized professional (and therefore, for a specialized judge as well) to incorporate his expertise into the larger framework that must be considered in order to arrive at the optimal solutions of problems.

Furthermore, the repetitiveness of the issues decided by specialized judges day in, day out can be detrimental to judicial creativity and, in the long run, hamper the development of the law, since the specialized judges 'might tend to reproduce . . . previous decision[s]'.[18] Clearly, this risk is enhanced when a small, selected group of judges are the only ones called upon to decide the same type of issues falling within a limited area of law.

Previously, this author reported the opinion of an American scholar criticizing the lack of empirical data that would allow an educated and well-founded evaluation of

---

[13]Opinion (2012) No. 15, n. 1 above.

[14]For an insightful commentary, see Uzelac (2014), p. 154.

[15]Opinion (2012) No. 15, n. 1 above, at para 14.

[16]Ibid., at para 18.

[17]On this point, see in particular Dreyfuss (1990), p. 412.

[18]Opinion (2012) No. 15, n. 1 above, at para 15.

the performance of specialized courts. Other authors claim the exact opposite, offering charts full of statistical data whose purpose is to prove that specialized judges decide cases neither more swiftly nor more accurately than their generalist counterparts. Furthermore (according to the same school of thought), judicial specialization is not necessarily conducive to consistency and predictability of judgments; to the contrary, the likelihood is high that specialized judges develop a sort of obsession with the subtleties of the legal field that is the realm of their expertise so as to 'focus on minutiae or issues that are not relevant to applicants'.[19]

Another potential disadvantage associated with the establishment of specialized courts is that they can become centres of power, most of all if they handle cases having a strong impact on the national economy; for the same reason, meaning because of the high-profile cases submitted to their judgments, they can be exposed to the pressure of interest groups. One way or another—it is contended—specialized courts are more vulnerable to politicization than generalist courts.[20]

Finally, and returning to the Opinion of the Consultative Council of European Judges (CCJE), specialized judges may give cause for concern regarding their ability to remain independent and impartial much more than generalist judges. According to the CCJE, generalist courts and their virtues must not be underestimated; nevertheless, in light of the ever-growing complexity of the law in a variety of fields, the establishment of specialized courts appears to be a kind of necessary evil. Since it cannot be avoided, it must at least be 'strictly regulated',[21] making sure that there is no difference between generalist courts and specialized courts as far as the guarantees of access to court, due process, right to a fair trial and right to be heard in a reasonable time are concerned.

The list of the pros and cons of judicial specialization could go on and on, but the attempt at drawing the most comprehensive list possible cannot dispel the feeling that judicial specialization is, all in all, simply 'something of a mixed bag'.[22] Perhaps that is the reason why this author has ambivalent feelings towards specialization, since its strengths as well as its weaknesses are equally distinguishable.

13.3   Judicial Specialization in Italy

The starting point for a sketch of the Italian approach to judicial specialization is the constitutional rule forbidding the establishment of special courts, but allowing the legislators to institute specialized divisions within the ordinary courts, and to assign to these divisions lay judges who have an expertise suitable for the cases handled by

---

[19]Morley (2008), p. 386.
[20]On this issue, see Dreyfuss (1990), p. 379.
[21]Opinion (2012) No. 15, n. 1 above, at para 30.
[22]Dreyfuss (1990), p. 407.

the specialized divisions themselves.[23] For quite a long time, the only specialized divisions established within ordinary civil courts have been the ones in charge of cases dealing with matters concerning agricultural land (*Sezioni specializzate agrarie*) and the ones having jurisdiction over juvenile matters (*Tribunale per i minorenni*), the latter being important within the structure of the Italian judiciary because of their broad jurisdiction encompassing all cases, whether civil, criminal or administrative, concerning underage persons. The early twenty-first century has seen a revival of the interest in judicial specialization, and the idea of establishing new specialized divisions within ordinary courts has gained ground, becoming the basis of several reforms. It is hard to say whether these reforms have had a positive effect on the performance of Italian civil justice. One has to keep in mind that the availability of statistics is limited, since in Italy the collection of empirical data is made difficult by a variety of bureaucratic hurdles. And, leaving aside the conventional reference to the growing complexity of the law in force, the pros and cons of judicial specialization have not been the object of in-depth studies, with a view to at least weighing the different choices capable of altering the judicial organization in a beneficially significant way. A disenchanted observer might say that the establishment of new specialized divisions has been essentially a 'cosmetic' reform, presented to the general public as the best strategy to improve the quality of judgments and reduce the length of proceedings most of all in areas of the law that are important for the national economy.

In any event, in the early years of this century the establishment of specialized divisions in charge of commercial cases was one of the prongs of a comprehensive reform of commercial law and company law under consideration by the Italian Parliament. In 2003 the reform was enacted, but the project of setting up specialized divisions was dropped. One of the reasons for this decision was the strong argument that public opinion would likely be against institutions of specialized divisions, perceiving them as a privilege granted to the lobby of businessmen. Interestingly, though, a completely new procedure designed for commercial cases came into force in the same year. Shortly thereafter it became clear that this procedure was a fiasco, and in 2009 it was repealed with no regrets.

Unexpectedly, around the same time, the supporters of judicial specialization were able to claim victory when the legislators resolved to establish special divisions for disputes in the field of intellectual property (IP) law (meaning, for instance, cases concerning patents, trademarks and other trade names and distinctive signs; design and utility models; and domain names and copyright).[24] A feature of the new IP divisions set up within a restricted number of ordinary courts was that they

---

[23] According to Article 102(2) of the Italian Constitution, 'Extraordinary or special judges may not be established. Only specialised sections for specific matters within the ordinary judicial bodies may be established, and these sections may include the participation of qualified citizens who are not members of the Judiciary.' See Dal Canto (2018), p. 273.

[24] Legislative decree no. 168 of 27 June 2003 on the establishment of specialized IP divisions within first instance courts and appellate courts; for a concise commentary, see Casaburi (2003, p. 405).

comprised professional judges only, while the specialized divisions already existing (and mentioned above) all include lay experts.

In 2012, the divisions in charge of intellectual property cases were 'recycled' as 'business courts', the *Tribunali delle imprese* or *sezioni specializzate in materia di impresa*, since the statute establishing them uses both names, underestimating the importance of precision in legal denominations:[25] for the latter is a specialized unit established within an ordinary court, while the former is a 'tribunal', insomuch as the Italian word *tribunale* could bring about misunderstandings regarding the way the judiciary is structured, in light of the constitutional rule preventing the establishment of new specialized courts.

Legal scholars have emphasized that to talk about *Tribunali delle imprese* is a form of 'advertising' which is supposed to both persuade the domestic business community and, most of all, attract foreign investors with the promise of new decision-making bodies capable of granting an efficient disposition of commercial cases.[26] After all, the statute establishing the new business courts had been enacted by one of the many Italian 'technical governments' with a view to strengthening competition and fostering the development of infrastructure, in an attempt to increase the appeal of Italy as a hospitable place for international trade.

The functioning of *Tribunali delle imprese* has highlighted quite a number of issues.[27] First of all, the issue of specialization is not seriously addressed. Even though the explanatory report on the statute establishing the new commercial courts states that they will be comprised of highly qualified judges with a significant expertise in business matters, nothing is said about how and by whom such expertise should be verified, since no procedures for the recruitment of new, allegedly expert judges is contemplated. Consequently, in some courts of first instance it is common to find judges who handle both ordinary cases and cases assigned to a specialized division—needless to say, this is not the best way to help judges acquire specialized knowledge in specific legal matters.

Other issues have to do with the subject-matter jurisdiction of *Tribunali delle imprese*. They retain jurisdiction over disputes in the field of intellectual property law, but now they can also adjudicate other important cases; such as those arising out of antitrust law (domestic and European), as well as an extensive list of disputes concerning company law, a list that is deemed to offer just a few examples of cases that can be handled by commercial courts.

The number of *Tribunali delle imprese* in operation is only 22 (first instance courts plus the appellate level). Since their establishment, their venue has been the subject of several reforms that need not be gone into here. One worth mentioning

---

[25] Statute no. 27 of 24 March 2012, with urgent measures for competition and the development of infrastructure.

[26] Along these lines, see, for instance, Casaburi (2012), p. 517; Celentano (2012), p. 812; Riva Crugnola (2013), p. 520.

[27] An extensive literature exists on the subject; however, it is written in Italian only. Those who are familiar with Italian can get the gist of the matter beginning with Iuorio (2013); Tavassi (2012), p. 1115; Panzani (2012), p. 1786; Santagada (2012).

though identifies by name the commercial courts that are the only ones entrusted with the power of handling disputes involving foreign companies as parties to a case.[28]

There are two recent additions to the jurisdiction of the *Tribunali delle imprese*. The first concerns class actions based upon the new statute governing 'collective proceedings'. The second covers miscellaneous proceedings provided by the reformed rules on bankruptcy and other insolvency procedures. Both statutes were passed in 2019 and will enter into force in 2020.[29]

Will the *Tribunali delle imprese* survive under the pressure of the new cases that are likely to crowd their dockets? And what about their professed specialization, keeping in mind that the disputes falling within their jurisdiction are so diverse that one may wonder whether the legislators understand the difference between specialization and omniscience.

According to one Italian author (Romano 2018), the *Tribunali delle imprese*, grounded on the pillars of specialization and the assignment of cases to a few selected courts, have become a model for the organization of the Italian judiciary. Only time will tell whether or not this model will contribute to improving the performance of Italian civil justice. Meanwhile, the umpteenth reform of civil procedure is under consideration by the Government, in yet another attempt to persuade the public that this time all the problems will be solved once and for all.

13.4 Conclusions

It does not seem possible to come to any firm conclusions on the subject of whether the specialization of the judiciary should be promoted or looked upon with suspicion. Like many issues regarding the administration of justice, judicial specialization has positive and negative aspects. These have to be weighed in order to strike a balance that combines the aim of providing an efficient and competent disposition of cases with the need to avoid that the rush towards specialization causes an unreasonable proliferation of specialized courts, making the role of generalist judges inconsequential. In deciding whether or not to establish specialized courts, the legislators should make the choice that appears to be more suitable to their legal system. But they should never overlook the perspective of the court users. After all, citizens who have faith in their judges probably do not care much whether they are specialized or generalist.

---

[28]On this reform, see Farina (2014) and Casaburi (2014).

[29]On collective proceedings, see statute no. 19 of 12 April 2019; on the reform of insolvency procedures, see legislative decree no. 14 of 12 January 2019.

References

Baum L (2009) Probing the effects of judicial specialization. Duke Law J 58:1667, 1671, 1681

Baum L (2010) Judicial specialization and the adjudication of immigration cases. Duke Law J 59 (1501):1531

Casaburi G (2003) L'istituzione delle sezioni specializzate per la proprietà industrial e intellettuale: (prime) istruzioni per l'uso. Il diritto industriale:405

Casaburi G (2012) La tutela della proprietà industriale e il tribunale delle imprese. Il diritto industriale 516:517

Casaburi G (2014) La riforma del 'tribunale delle imprese' – Storia felice, poi dolentissima e funesta, delle sezioni specializzate. Il diritto industriale:171

Celentano P (2012) Le sezioni specializzate in materia d'impresa. Le società:812

Connors E (2019) Specializing district courts for patent litigation. Case Western Reserve Law Rev 69(771):792

Dal Canto F (2018) Lezioni di ordinamento giudiziario. Giappichelli Editore, Torino, p 273

Dreyfuss RC (1990) Specialized adjudication. BYU Law Rev 377:412

Farina M (2014) Brevi note sul Tribunale delle società con sede all'estero (art 10 D.l. 145/2013). http://www.judicium.it/brevi-note-sul-tribunale-delle-societa-con-sede-allestero-art-10-d-l-1452013/

Iuorio MA (2013) Il Tribunale delle imprese. http://www.judicium.it/il-tribunale-delle-imprese/

Kesan JP, Ball GG (2011) Judicial experience and the efficiency and accuracy of patent adjudication: an empirical analysis of the case for a specialized patent trial court. Harv J Law Tech 24 (393):402

Morley M (2008) The case against a specialized court for federal benefits appeals. Fed Cir Bar J 17 (379):386

Oldfather CM (2012) Judging, expertise, and the rule of law. Wash Univ Law Rev 89:847

Panzani L (2012) Le sezioni specializzate in materia di impresa. Giurisprudenza di merito:1786

Posner RA (2006) The role of the judge in the twenty-first century. Boston Univ Law Rev 86 (1049):1050

Rai AK (2002) Specialized trial courts: concentrating expertise on fact. Berk Tech Law J 17 (877):878

Rifkind S (1951) A special court for patent litigation? The danger of a specialized judiciary. ABA J 37(425):426

Riva Crugnola E (2013) Il tribunale delle imprese. In: Libro dell'anno del Diritto. Istituto della Enciclopedia Italiana, Roma, p 520

Romano G (2018) Il Tribunale delle imprese e le sue competenze. In: Il Libro dell'anno del Diritto 2018. Istituto della Enciclopedia Italiana, Roma, para 1.1.2

Santagada F (2012) Sezioni specializzate per la impresa, accelerazione dei processi e competitività delle imprese. http://www.judicium.it/sezioni-specializzate-per-la-impresa-accelerazione-dei-processi-e-competitivita-delle-imprese/

Tavassi M (2012) Dalle sezioni specializzate della proprietà industriale e intellettuale alle sezioni specializzate dell'impresa. Il Corriere Giuridico, Milano, p 1115

Uzelac A (2014) Mixed blessing of judicial specialization: the devil is in the details. Russian Law J 2(146):154

Zimmer M (2009) Overview of specialized courts. Int J Court Admin 2:46

Chapter 14
International Commercial Courts: Specialised Courts?

Marta Requejo Isidro

Abstract Legal fragmentation creates uncertainty and increases costs. The greater part of the rules in national legal systems focus on domestic transactions; national courts are used to dealing with domestic disputes, as opposed to cross-border ones. Contemporary studies and publications on international commercial law deplore the absence of solutions adapted to the demands of the international business community and litigation. It is claimed that the solution may come from specialized international commercial courts (or chambers). In the last two decades, a number of courts bearing the "international commercial" or equivalent label have been set up. Do they really feature as specialised courts? Whereas the intuitive answer is "yes", a second glance reveals that the new commercial courts do not follow one single model; an "it depends" reply is thus more accurate.

14.1 Introduction

Contemporary studies and publications on international commerce law typically stress the costs caused by legal fragmentation and the associated uncertainty; they also complain about the (alleged) mismatch between the domestic legal systems, conceived for purely domestic cases, and the demands of the international business community. Hence the multiple attempts aimed at the unification of substantive law, best represented by the United Nations Convention on Contracts for the International

---

Opinions expressed are the author's only. At the time of writing the author was affiliated to the Max Planck Institute Luxembourg. The chapter was written in May 2019; developments after this date have not been taken into account.

M. Requejo Isidro (✉)
Court of Justice of the European Union, Luxembourg City, Luxembourg
e-mail: marta.requejo_isidro@curia.europa.eu

© The Author(s), under exclusive license to Springer Nature Switzerland AG 2021
X. Kramer et al. (eds.), *New Pathways to Civil Justice in Europe*,
https://doi.org/10.1007/978-3-030-66637-8_14

257

Sale of Goods and the UNIDROIT Principles of International Commercial Contracts.

Academic writings in the context of dispute resolution, echoing the concerns, accuse the increased costs of facing—at least potentially—a multiplicity of legal disputes before hardly suitable courts. It is claimed that the solution may come from bespoke commercial courts: the "international commercial courts" (or, as the case may be, chambers or divisions within existing courts).

A more in-depth analysis than the one we are allowed to make here may lead to relativize the contentions just mentioned, at least at present.[1] Indeed, not all domestic laws are unsuitable for international commerce: the choice of English law in many international commercial contracts points to the contrary.[2] Regarding the necessity for specialised court services, a proper scrutiny per jurisdiction would most probably show that the pertinent questions to be asked (Does the volume of cases justify special courts?; Is it a matter characterized by the presence of technical or scientific issues that might require special expertise?; Is the demand likely to be satisfied with what already exists, or with minor modifications or additions? and so on) end up with different answers depending on the legal system at stake. The assessment depends on the forum at stake, but also on the availability of other dispute resolution mechanisms.

This notwithstanding, whereas the factual basis of the need for courts devoted to international commercial litigation may be disputed, their opportunity cannot be seriously denied. Suffice it to look at what has been going on in Asia, the Middle East and Europe in the last 15 years: in the Middle East, the Dubai International Financial Centre Courts operate since 2006; the Qatar Civil and Commercial Court are operational since 2010 in a First Instance Circuit and an Appellate Division, in connection to the Qatar Financial Centre; the Abu Dhabi Global Market (ADGM) and the Abu Dhabi Global Market Courts were established at the same time in 2013. The Singapore International Commercial Court ("SICC") exists since January 2015. In Kazakhstan, the Astana International Financial Centre Court has just been set up.[3] The Chamber for International Commercial Disputes of the District Court of Frankfurt am Main started working on January 2018; the International Chamber of the Paris Court of Appeal in 7 February 2018; and the Netherlands Commercial Court ("NCC") barely 1 year later, in January 2019. A Brussels International Business Court ("BIBC") should be active by 2020.

International commercial courts are thus already "out there". But, do they really feature as specialised courts? Intuitively, the answer is "yes": they appear as part of

---

[1]It is expected that the Belt and Road Initiative leads to a non-negligible increase in the number of international commercial cases being litigated over a period of time. At the same time, it must be acknowledged that nowadays all courts seem to struggle with similar issues -cost and resource constrains, maintaining standards, complex litigation, technological change- especially in disputes with cross-border elements.

[2]See in the field of arbitration the findings of Cuniberti (2013–2014) and Cuniberti (2015).

[3]For an introduction to this brand new court, certainly less known than the other, see Jackson Sir (2018).

the current widespread movement towards creating courts or bodies to deal specifically with particular subject matters, just like in IP rights or environmental cases, but also in family disputes.[4] At a second glance the answer is not that straightforward: there is no unique notion of "specialised courts". In addition, and more importantly, the commercial courts we have just listed do not follow one single model. Therefore, an "it depends" reply is likely to be more accurate. To prove it, in what follows we will apply several indicators typically associated to specialised courts - the court is (or not) part of the jurisdiction's general court system; the court has (or not) jurisdiction limited to international commercial matters; the procedure before the court follows (or not) tailor-made rules; specific qualification and experience is required (or not) from the judges and the judicial staff—to some of the bodies previously mentioned.

14.2 Asia and the Middle East

14.2.1 General Remarks

Since the beginning of the twenty-first century several dispute resolution centres in the Middle East and Asia have been equipped with courts specially designed to resolve international commercial cases: in the United Arab Emirates, the *Dubai International Financial Centre Courts* (DIFC Courts) and the *Abu Dhabi Global Market Courts* (ADGMG Courts);[5] in Qatar, the *Civil and Commercial Court of the Qatar Financial Centre* (QFC Courts);[6] in Singapore, the *Singapore International Commercial Court* (SICC).[7] On 29 June 2018, China launched two International Commercial Courts—one in Shenzhen the other in Xi'an, to handle disputes concerning the Belt and Road Initiative;[8] an international commercial tribunal will be established in Beijing to coordinate between the two ICCs.

Broadly speaking, international commercial courts share a number of elements,[9] the most relevant being the use of English as the language of the process and the fact that they all seek inspiration in the common law tradition: substantive English law is directly integrated in the legal system in Abu Dhabi through the Application English

---

[4]See Gramckow and Walsh (2013).

[5]https://www.adgm.com/doing-business/adgm-courts/home/.

[6]https://www.qicdrc.com.qa/.

[7]https://www.sicc.gov.sg/.

[8]The Xi'an ICC will handle disputes concerning the "Land Silk Road", and the Shenzhen ICC will handle disputes concerning the "Maritime Silk Road".

[9]The Chinese model presents nevertheless traits that do not squarely correspond to the text. In particular, the proceedings must be conducted in Chinese and parties must be represented by Chinese lawyers. The judges who will sit in the ICCs are all existing judges in the Supreme People's Court; foreign judges might be included in so called "expert committees" to assist the judges to apply foreign laws, but they will not be invited to sit as judges in the ICCs.

Law Regulation 2015; common law rules have been "transplanted" and codified in Dubai; local law inspired by Sharia and the civil law tradition is put aside. In addition, the composition of the courts is not limited to local judges but open to international figures following the practice of common law countries of appointing members of sister jurisdictions. Further common features comprise the allocation of generous management powers to the court, and representation and legal advice not being necessarily confined to national lawyers. Procedural rules are clear, brief, and compiled in easily accessible documents.

Beyond the common aspects each of the international commercial court presents indeed individual characteristics. In what follows we will address the DIFC Courts and the SICC.

14.2.2 The Dubai International Financial Centre Courts (DIFC Courts)

The Constitution of the United Arab Emirates of 1971,[10] permanently adopted in July 1996, provides that the United Arab Emirates is a federal, independent and sovereign state consisting of the emirates of Abu Dhabi, Dubai, Sharjah, Ajman, Umm Al Quwain, Fujairah and Ras Al Khaimah (Article 1). According to Article 121 the Federation shall solely be in charge of enacting laws on an array of matters, among them the enactment a Financial Free Zone Law. On 27 March 2004 Federal Law No. 8 of 2004 on the Financial Free Zones in the United Arab Emirates (the Financial Free Zone Law), was adopted. Financial Free Zones are exempted from all federal civil and commercial laws within the UAE, although UAE criminal law still applies.

A Financial Free Zone was established in Dubai by Federal Decree (Federal Decree No. 35 of 2004). Dubai Law No. 9 of 2004, 'The Law Establishing the Dubai International Financial Centre', establishes as well the various bodies necessary for the DIFC's day-to-day operations. Dubai Law No. 12 of 2004 "The Law establishing the Judicial Authority at the Dubai International Financial Centre' sets up the DIFC Courts of First Instance and Appeal and the jurisdiction of the DIFC Courts. The act provides for the appointment of the DIFC Courts Justice, including the Chief Justice of the DIFC Courts; it delimitates the jurisdiction of the courts (an amendment was introduced in this respect in 2011, see below). It provides as well for the enforcement of judgments, orders and awards made by the DIFC Courts.

The official establishment of the international commercial courts in the Dubai International Financial Centre (DIFC) was 2004;[11] however, they were not fully operational until 2006. The DIFC Courts consist of a Court of First Instance and a

---

[10] After the retrocession of the British extraterritorial jurisdiction in 1971.

[11] See the DIFC LAW No. 10 of 2004, providing for the independent administration of Justice in the DIFC: https://www.difc.ae/files/1914/5448/9176/Court_Law_DIFC_Law_No.10_of_2004.pdf.

Court of Appeal to hear and determine claims in civil or commercial matters and which involve bodies of the DIFC or any DIFC registered establishments; disputes arising from or relating to contracts involving the DIFC; or disputes in which the parties have consented to DIFC Courts' jurisdiction (parties being able to opt-in to the DIFC Courts' Jurisdiction since 2011, see below). In 2007, a Small Claims Tribunal was established as a Tribunal of the DIFC Courts with power to hear and determine claims within the jurisdiction of the DIFC Courts not exceeding 500,000 EAD (just over 100,000 EUR); claims related to employment contracts, provided all parties elect in writing that it be heard by the SCT; or claims which do not fall within the former provisions, but in respect of which: (a) the amount of the claim or the value of the subject matter of the claim does not exceed EAD 1,000,000; and (b) all parties to the claim elect in writing that it be heard by the SCT, and such election is made in the underlying contract (if any) or subsequent to execution of that contract. In addition, the Chief Justice may order any claim to be heard by the SCT from time to time.

The DIFC Courts were not created to focus primarily on the resolution of international commercial cases, but were rather conceived to support the economic activities of the Dubai International Financial Centre: an onshore financial centre located in Dubai City, independently regulated with its own civil and financial administration, legal system and judiciary. As a consequence, until 2011 the DFIC Courts' jurisdiction was confined to disputes with physical links with the Centre; from 2011 it was extended to disputes lacking physical connection with the Centre, if so agreed by the parties pre- or post-dispute.[12]

In line with the foregoing, from the start the DIFC Courts were not so much intended to become a successful model of international commercial litigation; rather, the idea was to keep them separated from the local legal system of the Emirates, based on Sharia and the tradition of civil law and with Arabic as the official language.[13] Conversely, the DIFC Courts found inspiration in the common law world—they declare themselves "to operate as a common law court which applies legal procedures of the highest international standards"-[14] and made of English a preferred choice: today, the authoritative text of the procedural rules is the English one; the whole of proceedings are conducted in English; orders and decisions to be served in the Emirates must indeed be translated, but if there is divergence between several versions, the English one prevails (Court Rules Part 2 -Authentic Texts and Language of Proceedings).[15] The independence of the DIFC judicial system is

---

[12]See Law No. 16 of 2011 Amending Certain Provisions of Law No. (12) of 2004 Concerning Dubai International Financial Centre Courts; Law No.12 of 2004 in respect of The Judicial Authority at Dubai International Financial Centre as amended: https://www.difccourts.ae/wp-content/uploads/2017/10/Dubai12of2004_amended2011.pdf.

[13]See Carballo (2007), pp. 91–10, on the relation and influence of the Sharia.

[14]See for instance Guide between DIFC Courts and Nishith Desai Associates on Mutual Recognition and Enforcement of Civil and Commercial Judgments in DIFC Courts and Courts in India, September 19, 2018, para. 4.2. See as well DIFC Courts' Chief Justice Hwang (2008).

[15]The rules are accessible here: https://www.difccourts.ae/court-rules/.

stressed by the fact that no right of appeal to the Dubai Court of Cassation exists. In turn, the link with the common law world is further endorsed by the possibility to appoint foreign judges, provided some qualifications are met: the candidate needs to be or have been the holder of high judicial office in any jurisdiction recognised by the Government of the United Arab Emirates, and have significant experience as a qualified lawyer or Judge in the common law system.

The DIFC Courts offer a judicial service characterized by courts with broad management powers "to deal with cases justly", where "justly" means: (1) ensuring that the parties are on an equal footing; (2) saving expense; (3) dealing with cases in ways which are proportionate (a) to the amount of money involved, (b) to the importance of the case, (c) to the complexity of the issues;, and (d) to the financial position of each party; (4) ensuring that cases are dealt with expeditiously and fairly; and (5) allotting to particular cases an appropriate share of the Courts' resources, while taking into account the need to allot resources to other cases (Courts Rules, Part 1, 1.6). Other relevant traits are the openness to appoint foreign judges, "without fear of local protectionism or dependence";[16] possibility of being represented by foreign lawyers—registered with the Dispute Resolution Authority Academy of Law;[17] caveats to the general rule of publicity and transparency (Part 35- Court Rules, regarding the hearing; Part 28, for the documents); the invitation to the parties to participate in the schedule of the process (Part 26 Court Rules); the possibility to choose the law applicable to the merits (Article 6 Law No. 12 of 2004 in respect of The Judicial Authority at Dubai International Financial Centre as amended), with a special treatment given to foreign law (the court has the discretion to apply the rules on evidence in the way it considers most appropriate according to the circumstances of the matter: Part 29 Court Rules). Besides, in determining a matter or proceeding the DIFC Court may consider decisions made in other jurisdictions for the purpose of making its own resolution (Chapter I, Part 6, s. 30 (2), DIFC Law No.10 of 2004.)[18]

Are the DIFC Courts specialised courts? The difficulty to consider them as such lies with the fact that they cannot be considered separate, exceptional courts, within a court system; they are a court system of their own. As already explained, the DIFC is under an independent, common law-based, parallel legal system (outside the Dubai and the UAE federal legal systems), backed by an independent judicial system.[19] The most salient feature of the courts is not specialization, but the independence from a legal environment incapable to attract investors: "An independent and impartial enforcement framework is currently functioning. This system is designed

---

[16]Article 9.3 DIFC Law No.10 of 2004. Carballo (2007), p. 97.

[17]See DRA Order No. 1 of 2016 in Respect of Rights of Audience and Registration in Part II of the Academy of Law's Register of Practitioners (https://www.difccourts.ae/2016/09/20/dra-order-no-1-2016-respect-rights-audience-registration-part-ii-academy-laws-register-practitioners/).

[18]https://www.difc.ae/files/1914/5448/9176/Court_Law_DIFC_Law_No.10_of_2004.pdf.

[19]Carballo (2007), p. 92.

to attract foreign investors, who might otherwise worry about local protectionism, slow local courts, proceedings conducted in Arabic, or application of the Shari'a."[20]

14.2.3 The Singapore International Commercial Court (SICC)

The Singapore International Commercial Court (SICC) was established in 2015 as a division of the Singapore High Court and thus a part of the Singapore Supreme Court.[21] It was specifically created to solve international commerce disputes in view of the exponential growth of transnational commerce in Asia; for this reason, although embedded in the local judicial structure the SICC presents distinctive characteristics with respect to the local courts.[22]

The SICC is part of a strategy to make Singapore, already a main hub for arbitration beyond the region,[23] a focal point for cross-border dispute resolution. In addition, it intends to address some of the weaknesses of arbitration: not only from the point of view of the service offered to the users, but also from the perspective of legislative development and harmonization of international commercial law.[24]

Judging from the cases already solved or pending before the SICC, it is legitimate to conclude the SICC is a successful endeavour. Its strength is based on a combination of features: internationality (regarding the type of disputes, but also the composition of the Bench and of the Bar); procedural flexibility; efficiency in the management of the cases.

The SICC international jurisdiction is very broad: parties can opt-in to the SICC, but the court deals as well (and so far, mainly) with disputes without a choice of court clause transferred from another court after consulting the parties (Rules of the Supreme Court, O. 110, r. 7, r. 12). According to r. 1 of the Rules of the Supreme Court, O. 110, the commercial character of a controversy may result from objective

---

[20]Carballo (2007), p. 98. Bookman (2009), p. 21 ff, refers to them as "investment-minded courts".

[21]*Vid. Supreme Court of Judicature Act (Cap 322)*, s. 18A to 18M: https://sso.agc.gov.sg/ACT/SCJA1969.

[22]For instance regarding service abroad *(Rules of the Court* O. 110 r. 6(2), or the non-application of the *forum non conveniens* doctrine *(Rules of the Court* 110 r 8 (2), at least in the case of an exclusive choice of court clause). The *Rules* implement the *Supreme Court of Judicature Act (Cap 322);* they can be accessed at https://sso.agc.gov.sg/SL/SCJA1969-R5. They are in turn complemented by the *Singapore International Commercial Court Practice Directions*, "a set of procedural guidelines regulating all proceedings in the Singapore International Commercial Court ("SICC"). All users of the SICC are expected to comply with the SICC Practice Directions".

[23]The *Singapore International Arbitration Centre* exists since 1991. According to the Queen Mary/White & Case Survey 2018 Singapore is one of the preferred seats for international arbitration, together with Paris, London and Geneva.

[24]Report of the Singapore International Commercial Court Committee (2013), para. 11, 13, 16, Chief Justice Sundaresh Menon (2015), para. 14, 15.

factors, but also from the agreement between the parties. A claim is international in nature for jurisdictional purposes if (alternatively) the parties to the claim have their places of business in different States; none of the parties to the claim have their places of business in Singapore; at least one of the parties to the claim has its place of business in a different State from (a) the State in which a substantial part of the obligations of the commercial relationship between the parties is to be performed, or (b) the State with which the subject matter of the dispute is most closely connected. In addition, a claim is international in nature if the parties expressly agree that the subject-matter of the claim relates to more than one State.

The SICC offers the services of experienced professionals, adding to its ranks judges and experts from different countries and legal traditions: Australia, the United Kingdom, Hong Kong, but also France and Japan (and Austria, in the past). Legal representation by a foreign lawyer is allowed, although only when lawsuits lack any connection with the forum, or when foreign law applies.[25]

The procedures before SICC operate according to a set of written rules, which are those commonly applicable in the legal order. They provide for a clear frame, thus preserving predictability, but can be modified to a certain extent by the court with the assistance of the parties. Indeed, party autonomy plays an important role in the proceedings: parties can choose the law applicable to the merits; foreign law is considered to be proper law—and not a fact; the SICC may order that any question of foreign law be determined on the basis of submissions, without requiring formal proof by experts or cross-examination.[26] The parties are allowed to participate in the design of the procedural rules relevant to their case: a bulk of procedural rules shaped for litigation with a foreign element applies by default, but the parties are entitled to discard and replace some provisions regarding evidence.[27] For instance, parties may agree on the application of rules of evidence found in foreign law, but also the International Bar Association's Rules on the Taking of Evidence in International Arbitration.

In addition, the parties' may decide *ex ante* to waive their rights to object to the SICC's jurisdiction on several basis (e.g., natural forum or multiplicity of proceedings), as well as any recourse against the judgments[28] and orders and/or the recognition or enforcement of such judgments and orders.[29]

The rule of open court hearings and publication of the judgments applies by default. However, rule no. 30 of Order 110 of the Rules of the Court authorizes the SICC to grant a confidentiality request upon application of one of the parties; in

---

[25] *Supreme Court of Judicature Act (Cap 322)*, s 18M, and *Rules of the Court*, O. 110 r. 25.

[26] S. 18K, 18L, *Supreme Court of Judicature Act (Cap 322)*, *Rules of the Court* O. 110, r. 25, r. 28.

[27] *Rules of the Court*, O. 110, r. 23.

[28] Such possibility, unheard of in Europe, exists in international arbitration upon conditions regarding the right to contest the validity of the award: Scherer and Silbermann (2016), pp. 441–492.

[29] See the document on recommended model clauses *Singapore International Commercial Court Model Clauses*, versions as at 7 June 2018, on the website of the SICC. See as well para. 139 of the Singapore International Commercial Court Practice Directions, November 2018.

doing so the Court may have regard to whether the case is an offshore case and to any agreement on the issue between the parties. A confidentiality order will typically indicate that no person must reveal or publish any information or document relating to the case; an order that the case be heard in camera; or an order that the Court file be sealed. Only under very exceptional circumstances will the actual existence of a dispute, the fact that the party was involved in the proceedings or the judgment remain confidential.

On the duration of the proceedings, available data as of April 20, 2019, indicate that since its creation in 2015 the Court has heard 36 cases, all of them involving high sums. The decisions have been mostly delivered quickly, the average period being of 3 months from the hearing.[30] It is worth mentioning that to the extent that the SICC is integrated in the Supreme Court, it benefits from an electronic filing system established in 2000 which allows for judicial documents to be prepared and filed electronically. In order to keep the system flexible to meet new demands the Supreme Court has worked on expanding the capabilities of the electronic filing facility with the implementation of an integrated electronic litigation system (eLitigation).

Registration fees are specific before the SICC—S$8,000 (approx. 5,200 EUR). The expenses associated with the hearing are detailed in the Rules of Court O. 110, r. 47 and 48. The amount varies depending on the number of judges involved: a claim before a single judge costs slightly more than S$ 3,000 dollars; it increases to S$ 4,950 if there are three judges. An appeal before a formation of two judges attracts a fee of S$ 7,000, and before five judges, the fee is S$ 17,500.

To date, as already said the SICC has dealt with a little bit more than thirty cases; its case law has already served the development of the law of the country with regard to contractual liability.[31] From this perspective the SICC meets the demands allegedly felt by the international business community.[32] All in all, and except for the fact that the Singapore ICC is embedded in the general judicial structure, it can be said that the model corresponds well with that of a specialised court. At this point it is worth recalling that the reason why the ICC was created within the existing architecture is not related to its nature, but rather to a very pragmatic need explained in the Report of the Singapore International Commercial Court Committee: "The SICC must be a superior court of law in order to maximise the international enforceability of its decisions under existing arrangements. This means that the SICC needs to be part of the Supreme Court of Singapore, as any other court would be considered a subordinate court by virtue of Article 93 of the Constitution".[33]

---

[30]https://www.sicc.gov.sg/hearings-judgments/judgments.

[31]See https://www.sicc.gov.sg/hearings-judgments/judgments.

[32]See Introduction, above.

[33]SICC (2013), pp. 11–12.

14.3 The European Landscape

14.3.1 General Remarks

Europe has not remained untouched by the ongoing trend to set up bodies equipped to deal with international commercial disputes. In addition to the already existing chamber in London (the London Commercial Court, created as early as 1895) initiatives were taken which have already come to fruition in France (where a Chamber for International and European Law, now renamed "*Chambre International*", has existed within the Paris Tribunal de Commerce for some time already;[34] on February 2018, an International Chamber was inaugurated at the *Cour d'Appel* in Paris); Germany (in Frankfurt Main, but also in other cities - Hamburg, Düsseldorf, Munich); or the Netherlands (the proposal to create an international commercial court got the final approval in December 2018;[35] the court is already holding hearings.)[36] Other proposals are on the table regarding Belgium, but also other countries such as Kosovo.[37]

The existing European ICCs have some commonalities but present as well heavy differences. To the extent the characterization as specialised courts is conditional upon the presence of specific elements the label cannot be equally attributed to all the courts. A common feature is for instance the fact that all European ICCs are part of the ordinary judiciary—they are rather "chambers" or "divisions", not proper courts. Conversely, the composition of the bench differs: the NCC is exclusively composed of professional judges; cases brought before the Frankfurt ICC will be heard by a mixed panel, consisting of one professional judge and two lay judges experienced about business affairs and business law. Costs are not specific before the French and German ICCs, while they are before the NCC District Court and the NCC Court of Appeal. English may be the language of the whole procedure before the NCC, but not before the Frankfurt ICC. The European ICCs follow the national procedural law to a variable extent.

In what follows we will explain the German model and present the most salient features of the Belgium proposal.

---

[34]A *Chambre de droit international* was created in 1995; a *Chambre de droit de l'Union Européenne*, in 1997. They merged in 2015.

[35]For an introduction to the chamber and its history see The Judiciary/NCC (2020). The procedural rules in English—as of December 2018 "Rules of Procedure for the International Commercial Chambers of the Amsterdam District Court (NCC District Court) and the Amsterdam Court of Appeal (NCC Court of Appeal)", can be accessed from the same website.

[36]*Elavon Financial Services DAC v. IPS Holding B.V. and others*. See de Rechtspraak/NCC (2019).

[37]As stated in the paper Republika e Kosovës, Ministria e Drejtësisë – Ministarstvo Pravde (2019) Justice for Development- Policy Note on Commercial Justice. On file with author.

14.3.2   The Commercial Chamber in Frankfurt am Main

The Frankfurt international chamber of commerce exists within the national judicial order. We can state from the outset that its characterization as "specialised court" does not fit; that of "specialised service" works better, but still, only to some degree. Unlike in other countries where international commercial courts or chambers have been set up, no legislative reforms have been required for the Frankfurt ICC; this alone gives a hint as to the limited degree of specialization of the chamber.

The "Justice Initiative Frankfurt" arose in 2016 in an academic context with good connections to the judiciary and to the Ministry of Justice in the Land of Hesse; representatives of the legal profession and the Chambers of Industry and Commerce took part in the project expressing the needs, expectations and preferences of the main stakeholders.[38] The choice of Frankfurt is due both to its relevance as a commercial and financial hub—which explains why it is also the head office of many renowned law firms—and the commercial experience of its courts and judges—especially in the banking and finance sectors. In 2017, the initiative was endorsed by the Ministry; the chamber has been officially operational within the Frankfurt District Court since January 1, 2018, although the rules governing its functioning have not yet been enacted.[39]

The Frankfurt international commercial chamber is in no sense an independent judicial body. On the contrary, it is embedded in the existing judicial structure and accommodates to the in-force legal framework. The commercial character of a dispute must therefore be identified in light of section 95 *Gerichtsverfassungsgeset* (GVG), which delineates it broadly but not to the point of admitting the simple agreement of the parties in this regard. No definition of "international" appears in the German 2018 Bill on the *Kammer für Internationale Handelssachen*, although the requirement exists and some examples are provided in the commentary to section 114b of the draft of April 2018.[40] It is to be noted that in the Bill the direct agreement of the parties declaring a dispute international is not included.[41]

Access to the Frankfurt ICC requires that the claim not fall under the special jurisdiction of another chamber of the District Court Frankfurt/Main; that it is international; and that the parties have agreed on the jurisdiction of the Chamber and have declared in a timely manner (i.e. before the deadline for the statement of defence has expired) their willingness to plead in English and to waive their right to

---

[38]For the history and an in-depth explanation of the functioning of the chamber see Hess and Boerner (2018).

[39]Entwurf eines Gesetzes zur Einführung von Kammern für internationale Handelssachen (KfiHG), Bundestagdrucksache 19/1717, April 18, 2018: http://dipbt.bundestag.de/doc/btd/19/017/1901717.pdf.

[40]Above, note 39.

[41]The examples are: the contract or contractual documents are written in English; one of the parties is domiciled abroad, or the parties agree that foreign law applies. A claim related to the internal affairs of a company may be considered as well as "international" if the company's internal agreements and its correspondence are written in English, or the company's seat is abroad.

an interpreter.[42] The main differences compared to other chambers in German courts is that the commercial one is staffed with clerks fluent in English; so are the professional judges, who will always chair; finally, the chamber also comprises lay judges from the business sector. It is worth noting that the use of English is allowed only to a limited extent; by virtue of a limitation established by s. 184 of the *Gerichtsverfassungsgesetz* (GVG),[43] only the hearing could be held in English; the orders and judgments of the chamber must be drafted in German, with an English translation being optional but not alternative. Amendments to the current situation have been proposed to Parliament in 2012, 2016 and 2018; should the latest one succeed, the conduct of the entire process in English at the first and second instances (not in the third instance, where such possibility would be left to the discretion of the Court) would be permitted, provided the parties agree thereto.[44]

The procedure follows the ZPO, "bringing out the best" of it by way of interpretation: in as much as possible it follows best practices of specialised courts, in particular that of patent litigation in Düsseldorf. As an example: the faculties of direction of the process attributed to the judge by s. 139 ZPO may be used to establish a "road map" with the parties at the beginning of the proceedings, structuring the course of the litigation in an optimal and efficient way; the first hearing may work as a "case management conference" with the parties. No specific fees are imposed.

The Frankfurt initiative is indeed not comparable with German precedents in highly specialised areas such as patents, where Düsseldorf, Mannheim and Munich stand out at the European level. It was born and remains modest. It was feasible without legislative amendments, neither at the level of the judicial structure nor of the procedural rules. It has not triggered specific investment—although the lack of adjusted IT services is deplored; but the issue seems to be a general one of the German justice systems.[45]

14.3.3 The (Unborn) Brussels International Business Court

Although according to latest news (dating 21 March 2019) the BIBC will not be created for the time being,[46] we would still like to devote some comments to the model and its very unique features in the European legal landscape. The initial bill

---

[42]https://ordentliche-gerichtsbarkeit.hessen.de/sites/ordentliche-gerichtsbarkeit.hessen.de/files/LG %20FFM%20Gesch%C3%A4ftsverteilung%202018%20Stand%2001.01.2018.pdf, at 35. Schedule of Responsibilities of the Chambers of the District Court Frankfurt/Main 2018.

[43]For an English translation: http://www.gesetze-im-internet.de/englisch_gvg/englisch_gvg. html#p0490.

[44]Above, note 39.

[45]Hess (2017).

[46]Van Calster (2019).

was heavily criticized on the grounds of a potential lack of independence of the future judges and the expected economic consequences of the new court on the budget of the Ministry of Justice.[47] A new bill dated May 15, 2018, met severe opposition as well.[48] The latest draft prepared by the House of Representatives was published on December 10, 2018,[49] but as already hinted it is unlikely to see the light.

The projected BIBC would considerably differ from the rest of the European ICCs. To start with, it would not be integrated into the national judicial system: it would be composed of career judges and international trade professionals, not necessarily Belgians, acting *ad hoc*. Procedurally, the common rules are largely replaced by others inspired by the world of arbitration, especially by the UNCITRAL Model Law; conversely, substantive law would be determined by the conflict of law rules (European, conventional, or of national source) generally binding on the judiciary. The BIBC would have jurisdiction over international disputes between companies as a unique instance; no appeal would be possible—only cassation. Parties may decide to submit to the BIBC all disputes, or some of the disputes that have arisen or may arise between them in relation to a legal relationship, whether contractual or non-contractual, but cases may also be referred from another Belgian, foreign or international judicial body, including an arbitral tribunal, provided the parties agree to the transfer. The language of the process would be English although exceptions may apply, such as in the case of an intervention by third parties. The internationality of disputes under the jurisdictional scope of the BIBC accounts for the derogation to the common rule on the language of the process. However, the question of when a case is international has been one of the most debated ones.[50]

14.4   Beyond Specialization: The Need for Cooperation and Interrelated Structures

An admittedly different, but certainly related issue is whether international commercial courts (chambers or divisions), individually taken, can adequately tackle the difficulties experienced by the business community in transnational contexts: uncertainty, plurality of fora, juridical fragmentation and related cost. To the extent that the court—or chambers—remain isolated one from another the answer is likely to be "no". The absence of a common instrument ensuring the cooperation among the specialised judicial services perpetuates the risk of multiple inconsistent interpretations of commercial law,[51] of diverging solutions to similar cases -sometimes

---

[47]*Avis d'Office* du Conseil Supérieur de la Justice (2018).

[48]http://www.lachambre.be/flwb/pdf/54/3072/54K3072003.pdf.

[49]http://www.dekamer.be/FLWB/PDF/54/3072/54K3072011.pdf.

[50]See Requejo Isidro (2019).

[51]Albeit certainly lessened thanks to the openness to appoint foreign judges to the bench.

involving the same actors-, and of applications for enforcement abroad of a judgment delivered by an international commercial court being refused, rendering moot all the effort and investment at the declaratory stage.[52]

To surmount the difficulty some jurisdictions have engaged in undeniably creative efforts. For example, since 2015 parties to a dispute before the DIFC Courts are given a unique possibility, namely that of "converting" a DIFC Court's decision into an arbitral award, on the terms indicated by the DIFC Courts, Amended Practice Direction No 2 of 2015: 'If parties who have submitted (or have agreed to submit) to (or are bound by) the jurisdiction of the DIFC Courts wish further to agree that any dispute arising out of or in connection with the non-payment of any money judgment given by the DIFC Courts may, at the option of the judgment creditor . . . be referred to arbitration under the Arbitration Rules of the DIFC LCIA Arbitration Centre, they may to that end adopt an arbitration clause in the terms of the recommended arbitration agreement'. "Convert" appears between quotation marks to underline that there is no real transformation of the judgment, but rather a submission to arbitration of any dispute in relation to its enforcement arising once the judgment has been given (including of course lack of voluntary compliance of the debtor even if it is due to lack of liquidity and not to a disagreement on the merits).[53] The possibility of referring to arbitration, which is indeed not free from conceptual doubts,[54] entails that the judicial decision will finally adopt the form of an arbitral award, and as a consequence the New York Convention 1958 will most probably apply to its recognition and enforcement abroad.

Of course, recognition and enforcement of decisions abroad can be ensured by way of bilateral or multilateral (or, as it is the case within the EU, regional) instruments.[55] The Emirates are part of the *Gulf Cooperation Council Convention for the Execution of Judgments, Delegations and Judicial Notifications 1996*[56] and of the *Riyadh Arab Agreement for Judicial Cooperation 1983*;[57] international

---

[52]Recognition and enforcement of decisions has been described as "the elephant in the room" by Ramesh (2018), para. 27. It was as well the main topic of the speech of the DFIC Courts Chief Justice given last October 2018 at the Standing International Forum of Commercial Courts. See DIFC Courts Chief Justice (2018).

[53]https://www.difccourts.ae/2015/05/27/amended-difc-courts-practice-direction-no-2-of-2015-referral-of-judgment-payment-disputes-to-arbitration/. The wording "convert" was used for the first time by Chief Justice Hwang (2015).

[54]Demeter and Smith (2016), under 4.

[55]From a broader perspective it is worth mentioning here as well the recent establishment of the International Commercial Dispute Prevention and Settlement Organization (ICDPASO) by The China Council for the Promotion of International Trade, China Chamber of International Commerce, together with the industrial and commercial organizations and legal service agencies from over 30 countries and regions including the European Union, Italy, Singapore, Russia, Belgium, Mexico, Malaysia, Poland, Bulgaria and Myanmar (source: The Second Belt and Road Forum for International Cooperation (2019)).

[56]Bahrain, Saud Arabia, Oman, Qatar, Kuwait, AUE.

[57]Jordan, Bahrain, Tunisia, Algeria, Djibouti, Saudi Arabia, Sudan, Syria, Somalia, Iraq, Oman, Palestine, Qatar, Kuwait, Lebanon, Libya, Morocco, Mauritania, Yemen.

commercial court decisions benefit from those regimes after registration with a local court once translated into Arabic. Singapore has concluded multiple bilateral agreements for the mutual recognition of decisions.[58] Since June 2016, Singapore is also a party to the Hague Convention of 2005 on choice of forum clauses. Other ongoing schemes are multilateral or even nourish a global pretension; it is precisely because of their too high ambition that they may fail. Two projects worth mentioning are the "Judgments Project" of the Hague Convention, the adoption of which is scheduled for the next diplomatic conference (June 2019), but which of course may still be unsuccessful;[59] and the Project on enforcement law harmonization carried out by the Asian Business Law Institute.[60]

The adoption of conventional instruments is a challenging endeavour; it requires a high dose of patience and time—something the international business community usually lacks.[61] Not surprisingly judges have reacted and taken the lead. Memoranda of understanding (MoU) or of guidance (MoG) have been signed between courts as well as with law firms operating abroad to facilitate the reciprocal enforcement of judgments. MoU provide for cooperation—judicial, or broader: see for instance the Memorandum of Understanding between Abu Dhabi Judicial Department and The Dubai International Financial Centre Courts Concerning Judicial Cooperation, of April 2017. MoG provide a detailed explanation on the requirements and procedures for enforcing foreign judgments in the signing jurisdiction; they offer businesses additional certainty should a contractual dispute arise: see for example the Memorandum of Guidance on Understanding the Enforcement of Money Judgements between the Federal Court of Malaysia and the DIFC Courts.

In what can be seen as an attempt to go a step further, on May 2017 judges from 25 jurisdictions met in London at the Inaugural Standing International Forum of Commercial Courts (SIFoCC).[62] A second meeting took place in 2018.[63] Participating jurisdictions range from New York, Delaware, Australia, Singapore, Ireland,

---

[58]As of October 2018, with Australia, Brunei Darussalam, Hong Kong, India, Malaysia, New Zealand, Pakistan, Papua New Guinea, Sri Lanka, United Kingdom, the Windward Islands.

[59]And even if it was adopted, it may be long before it enters into force. For an analysis from the EU perspective see Asensio et al. (2018).

[60]Chong (2017). The project sets the stage for the next step in a larger project, where consideration will be given to convergence or harmonization in the field.

[61]The first (failed) attempt to get to a global treaty on the recognition and enforcement of judgments in civil and commercial matters goes back to 1992; see a summary under Asensio et al. (2018), above note 59.

[62]The Forum has its own understanding of what falls under the scope of "commercial law" (Financial, Business, Corporate, Competition, Consumer Protection, Contract, Construction, Environmental, Intellectual Property, Insolvency, Property, International Trade, Commodities, Energy, Maritime, Aviation, Technology, Investment, and oversight of Arbitration), and it is not limited to international courts: see SIFoCC (2019).

[63]The report is available at SIFoCC (2018).

London (England & Wales), Dubai, Qatar, Abu Dhabi, or Bahrain, to Sierra Leone and Nigeria.[64] The Forum has convened in working on issues such a structure for judges of the commercial court of a number of developing countries to be able to spend short periods of time together as observers in the commercial court of another SIFoCC country. More importantly for our purposes, the SIFoCC is working on a draft multilateral memorandum on current best means of enforcement of commercial judgments between members. The Memorandum will be unique in that it is compiled by judges, provides a comprehensive overview of the rules in common and civil law jurisdictions, and intends to offer the ultimate version of the various bilateral Memoranda agreed between jurisdictions. Albeit not binding, it could serve an important purpose in the absence of a treaty in this area.

Finally, the possibilities opened to judicial cooperation by new technologies shall not be underestimated. According to the news published on July 30, 2018, the DIFC Courts have partnered with Smart Dubai in a project entitled "Court of the Blockchain".[65] The partnership presents itself as "the first step in creating a blockchain-powered future for the judiciary", aimed at streamlining the judicial process, removing document duplications, and driving greater efficiencies across the entire legal ecosystem. The alliance will initially explore how to aid verification of court judgments for cross-border enforcement. With the support of the European Commission a similar research into technologies at the service of justice in order to set up an E-justice environment is being carried out in the EU- the *e-CODEX* project on the cross-border exchange of documents, and its follow-ups (Me-CODEX I/ II).

14.5   Conclusions

Specialised judges and courts are a growing tendency across the globe. International commercial courts, chambers or divisions within existing courts, devoted to dispute resolution in the field of international commerce, are said to "address a market failure" and to be "particularly attuned to the needs and realities of international commerce".[66] They appear thus to be an expression of the mentioned trend. But, are they?

The question cannot be answered in terms of "yes" or "no": it actually depends on the court or chamber at stake. The differences among them are sometimes in the detail; sometimes they go to the very foundational policy which, not surprisingly, materializes in unique distinctive features. The DIFC Courts, sitting within a special economic zone and part of a wider strategy to attract foreign investment, act as sole

---

[64]As of April 30, 2019, the Frankfurt Landgericht is not a member.

[65]Smart Dubai is the government office charged with facilitating Dubai's citywide transformation through technology innovation, in order "to make Dubai the happiest city on Earth": https://www.smartdubai.ae/. On the partnership, see DIFC Courts (2018).

[66]Ramesh (2018), para. 3.

and independent judicial system of the zone; the presence of foreign judges on the bench is due more (or at least, just as much) to the concern for independence than to the wish for subject-matter expertise. The SICC was set up "to grow the legal services sector and to expand the scope for the internationalisation and export of Singapore law";[67] the court processes and their aims differ from those of the local common courts; its integration into the Singapore judicial structure is explained by the need to ensure recognition and enforcement of judgements under the bilateral or multilateral regimes to which Singapore is currently a contracting part.[68] The Frankfurt ICC is deeply rooted into the German judicial and legal system. The projected Belgium Court for International Business would be a class of its own. The correspondence of the courts and chambers we listed at the beginning of this chapter (in China, Kazakhstan, the Netherlands…) to one of the four cases analysed would require an individualized research.

It looks appropriate to end a chapter on international commercial courts as specializes courts recalling the so called "Courts of the Future", a project aimed at setting up a specialist division within the DIFC Courts to deal with claims raising questions of technical complexity, or which have no or no single physical geographical nexus, or where the proceedings are likely to involve multiple parties from different jurisdictions. Examples of the types of claim which may be appropriate to bring as COF Claims would be claims involving international commercial chain transactions; claims relating to liability for the acts or omissions of artificial intelligence, software or any devices or components of devices whether integrated or not that are dependent on or controlled by such software (such as autonomous or semi-autonomous vehicles); claims involving issues of cyber security in respect of data and/or assets stored online; claims relating to competition and/or anti-trust issues in respect of online assets or currency; claims involving online intermediaries and/or online platforms or marketplaces.[69] How the Courts of the Future should look like in terms of knowledge, procedures and efficiency and technology integration, is a core, still open question.[70]

---

[67] SICC (2019).

[68] In the words of Sir R. Jackson (above, note 3): "These new courts seem to have been set up with two objectives: first, to provide a judicial system in the background, which will inspire confidence in overseas investors coming to that jurisdiction; secondly, to catch as much international dispute resolution work as possible. In relation to the first (but not the second) objective the size of the caseload is unimportant". The DIFC Courts try to meet the former objective; the SICC, the latter one.

[69] A complete—but not exhaustive list- is available at: http://www.courtsofthefuture.org/part-40000-principles/ (last visited 27.04.2019).

[70] See http://rethinkingjustice.eu/home/the-challenges/courts-of-the-future/ (last visited 01.05.2019).

References

Asensio P et al (2018) The Hague Conference on private international law judgments convention, in-depth study, European Parliament. PE 604.954, April 2018. https://www.europarl.europa.eu/thinktank/en/document.html?reference=IPOL_STU(2018)604954

Avis d'Office du Conseil Supérieur de la Justice (2018) Avant-projet de loi instaurant la Brussels International Business Court. http://www.hrj.be/sites/default/files/press_publications/avis-bibc-fr.pdf

Bookman P (2009) The adjudication business. https://papers.ssrn.com/sol3/papers.cfm?abstract_id=3338152

Calster V (2019) The Brussels International Business Court – Council of State continues to resist. https://gavclaw.com/2018/11/14/the-brussels-international-business-court-council-of-state-continues-to-resist/

Carballo A (2007) The law of the Dubai International Financial Centre: common law oasis or mirage within the UAE. Arab Law Q 21:91–10

Chong A (2017) Recognition and enforcement of foreign judgments in Asia. Research Collection School of Law (Singapore Management University), Singapore. https://ink.library.smu.edu.sg/sol_research/2496/

Cuniberti G (2013–2014) Three Theories of Lex Mercatoria. Colum J Transnatl Law 52:369

Cuniberti G (2015) The Laws of Asian international business transaction. Wash Int Law J 25:35

De Rechtspraak/NCC (2019) Inaugural hearing of the Netherlands Commercial Court is a fact. https://www.rechtspraak.nl/English/NCC/news/Pages/Inaugural-hearing-of-the-Netherlands-Commercial-Court-is-a-fact.aspx

Demeter D, Smith KM (2016) The implications of international commercial courts on arbitration. J Int Arbitr 33:441

DIFC Courts (2018) DIFC Courts and Smart Dubai launch joint taskforce for world's first Court of the Blockchain. https://www.difccourts.ae/2018/07/30/difc-courts-and-smart-dubai-launch-joint-taskforce-for-worlds-first-court-of-the-blockchain/

DIFC Courts Chief Justice (2018) DIFC Courts Chief Justice delivers speech at standing forum of International Commercial Courts. https://www.difccourts.ae/2018/10/14/difc-courts-chief-justice-delivers-speech-at-standing-forum-of-international-commercial-courts/

Gramckow H, Walsh B (2013) Developing specialized court services : international experiences and lessons learned, Working Paper 24. World Bank, Washington DC. http://documents.worldbank.org/curated/en/688441468335989050/Developing-specialized-court-services-international-experiences-and-lessons-learned

Hess B (2017) The justice initiative Frankfurt am Main 2017. https://conflictoflaws.net/2017/the-justice-initiative-frankfurt-am-main-2017-law-made-in-frankfurt/

Hess B, Boerner T (2018) Chambers for international commercial disputes in Germany - the state of affairs. Erasmus Law Rev 1:33–41

Hwang M (2008) The Courts of the Dubai International Finance Centre — A Common Law island in a Civil Law ocean. DIFC Courts. https://www.difccourts.ae/2008/11/01/the-courts-of-the-dubai-international-finance-centre-a-common-law-island-in-a-civil-law-ocean/

Hwang M (2015) Commercial courts and international arbitration – competitors or partners? Arb Int 31:193

Jackson Sir R (2018) A comparative perspective to hybrid dispute resolution fora: jurisdiction, applicable law and enforcement of judgments. Lecture for the Qatar Conference on 'The Promise of Hybrid Dispute Resolution Fora' 18th November 2018. https://www.4newsquare.com/wp-content/uploads/2018/11/A-Comparitive-Perspective-to-Hybrid-Dispute-Resolution-Fora-by-Sir-Rupert-Jackson-of-4-New-Square.pdf

Menon S (2015) International commercial courts: towards a transnational system of dispute resolution', Dubai International Financial Centre ('DIFC') Courts Lecture Series 2015 (Opening Lecture), Dubai, January 19, 2015. https://www.supremecourt.gov.sg/docs/default-source/default-document-library/media-room/opening-lecture%2D%2D-difc-lecture-series-2015.pdf

Ramesh K (2018) International commercial courts: unicorns on a journey of a thousand miles', Conference, Doha, Qatar, 13 May 2018. https://www.sicc.gov.sg/docs/default-source/modules-document/news-and-article/international-commercial-courts-unicorns_23108490-e290-422f-9da8-1e0d1e59ace5.pdf. Accesed 06 May 2019

Republika e Kosovës, Ministria e Drejtësisë – Ministarstvo Pravde (April 2019) Justice for development- policy note on commercial justice. On file with author

Requejo Isidro M (2019) International commercial courts in the litigation market'. Int J Procedural Law 1:4–49

Scherer M, Silbermann L (2016) Limits to party autonomy in international commercial arbitration. In: Ferrari F (ed) Limits to party autonomy in international commercial arbitration. New York University, New York, pp 441–492

SICC (2013) Report of the Singapore International Commercial Court Committee. https://www.sicc.gov.sg/docs/default-source/about-sicc/annex-a-sicc-committee-report.pdf

SICC (2019) Establishment of the SICC. https://www.sicc.gov.sg/about-the-sicc/establishment-of-the-sicc

SIFoCC (2018) Report of the Second Meeting New York 27–28 September 2018. https://www.sifocc.org/wp-content/uploads/2019/02/Report-of-the-Second-SIFoCC-Meeting-New-York-2018.pdf

SIFoCC (2019) About us. https://www.sifocc.org/about-us/#history

The Judiciary/NCC (2020) Netherlands Commercial Court (NCC). https://www.rechtspraak.nl/English/NCC/Pages/default.aspx

The Second Belt and Road Forum for International Cooperation (2019) List of Deliverables of the Second Belt and Road Forum for International Cooperation. http://www.beltandroadforum.org/english/n100/2019/0427/c36-1312.html

Chapter 15
Anti-specialisation Trends in Dispute Resolution or a Shift Towards a New Paradigm? An Initial Exploratory Analysis of Dispute Resolution in the Global Village

Ianika Tzankova

Abstract This chapter introduces a novel concept of 'The Global Village' in dispute resolution. It sketches the image of this Global Village and describes its inhabitants. It identifies the type of disputes that can arise in this context and the major dispute resolution mechanisms to deal with these: (transnational) litigation and arbitration. It then positions the (anti)specialisation trend in judicial law-making against that background. The true state of modern international commerce and consumerism is that they give rise to disputes on a worldwide scale and yet, notwithstanding this stark reality, the legal systems of individual jurisdictions are not fit to cope with civil disagreements on a global scale. At the same time an increasing number of the inhabitants of the Global Village use the differences in national legal systems to maximise their own economic or institutional interests, whilst the general public is largely unaware of the scope, nature and implications of this development. The future of dispute resolution is being shaped by the big players with (increasing) power and their interests may not be aligned with the wishes of individual governments, judicial systems or ordinary consumers. The essential theme of the chapter is that although it is early days in terms of predicting any trends in judicial law-making in the Global Village, an essential first step in that process is to recognize and acknowledge its existence.

The author is grateful to Dennis van Gulik, Marijne Mevius, and Huguette Knolsfor for their research assistance and Deborah Hensler for the inspiring discussions on the topic over the past ten years.

I. Tzankova (✉)
Tilburg University, Tilburg, The Netherlands
e-mail: I.N.Tzankova@tilburguniversity.edu

15.1 The Global Village

15.1.1 A Few Examples

In 2015 German-owned multinational giant VW admitted that it had included a "defeat device" in the software for its diesel cars[1] such that they could, by fraud, pass US environmental tests and VW was sued collectively by thousands of consumers in state and federal courts in the US. The claims were ultimately settled,[2] as were similar consumer cases in Canada[3] and Australia.[4] Subsequently, in the US a nationwide VW securities class action was also commenced and settled.[5] Meanwhile, a special purpose foundation was established in the Netherlands to seek a settlement with VW on behalf of European shareholders and consumers under the Dutch Collective Settlement Act,[6] and a securities lawsuit on behalf of investors (whose share values had dropped dramatically) was filed in Germany, using that country's special group litigation procedure.[7] In Germany, in addition, a consumer-based collective action for declaratory relief was filed and settled[8] by German, so-called designated entities—well-recognised consumer associations, while Dutch consumer foundations were (and still are) coordinating their actions with US partners and have filed actions for declaratory relief and for damages in the Netherlands.[9] In parallel, the shareholders in Germany are represented by the local partners of a leading US-based litigation boutique, and the shareholder suit is funded by a UK-based international litigation financing firm.

In 2006 citizens of the Ivory Coast sought to recover damages in the English courts from a UK-Dutch multinational Trafigura stemming from environmental contamination.[10] After that action was settled, subsequent damages actions were filed by ad hoc foundations in the Netherlands.[11]

In 2011 Apple sued Samsung for patent infringement in the Northern District of California and Samsung counter-sued in Korea, Japan and Germany.[12] Subsequently the companies agree to focus their litigation battles before the Californian judge.

---

[1]Cremer (2015).

[2]Cronin Fisk et al. (2016).

[3]Shepardson (2018).

[4]Duran (2019).

[5]Matussek (2020).

[6]Sterling (2017).

[7]Reuters Staff (2016).

[8]Reuters Staff (2020).

[9]Haas and Kleywegt (2019).

[10]The Times staff (2008).

[11]Business and Human Rights Resource Centre.

[12]Menn (2011) and Kim (2011).

In 2012 a securities class action against a French-Swiss company was resolved in the New Jersey federal court for US investors and in the Amsterdam Court of Appeals for all other investors world-wide, without formal judicial cooperation.[13]

In 2012 Philip Morris' Hong Kong subsidiary filed a claim in an international arbitration tribunal alleging that Australia's public health protection statute regarding tobacco marketing violated Australia's bi-lateral investment treaty with Hong Kong.[14] The arbitration claim was filed after the parent company unsuccessfully challenged Australia's statute before the High Court of Australia. In December 2015 the arbitration tribunal ruled that it did not have jurisdiction over Philip Morris' claim, effectively dismissing it.[15] Philip Morris then filed (and lost) similar arbitration claims against other countries, such as Uruguay.[16]

All of the above are just a few examples of disputes that used to be contained within national borders, but which became part of a trend for increasingly transnational or global resolution.

15.1.2 Factors

Industrialisation, globalisation and the explosive evolution of mass and social media have changed the world into a 'Global Village'[17] with almost infinite business opportunities arising in modern commerce. However, with global business comes the risk of global harm and global dispute resolution. Economic activity increases the possibility of personal injury, environmental damage, financial loss, data breaches and even human rights abuse. In a global economy, the scale of the world economy is such that virtually anything that goes wrong in the manufacture or delivery of products or services will likely affect a huge number of economic players, including consumers, when compared to previous centuries. Even what might appear at first glance to be an isolated transaction or event is likely to involve a web of complex economic circumstances and a variety of international players, each of whom may have a claim or be subject to a law suit if anything goes wrong. Globalisation also lengthens the causal chain of harm, making the latter more ambiguous and making it more difficult to apportion and contribute blame to the various affected parties. The number of players that potentially contribute to the harm is larger and they are increasingly located in different jurisdictions. As a result, when something goes wrong, its impact is felt on a massive scale and is often more controversial than ever

---

[13]Bosters (2015), p. 71.

[14]Fenner and Schneider (2011).

[15]See Tobacco plain packaging—investor-state arbitration.

[16]Mander (2016).

[17]W.F. McDonald is among the first to use this term, in relation to crime and law enforcement: McDonald (1997).

before, and with the rise of the Internet and social media, people across the Globe know about it, within minutes.[18]

Another consequence of globalisation is that when a conflict arises between private parties, lawyers and domestic judges need to operate in a virtual global court. They are addressing 'global problems', problems that are affecting all of us notwithstanding our nationality or domicile,[19] even while they are operating in their own home jurisdiction. Their rulings impact individuals and corporations far beyond their own national boundaries. In private legal relationships[20] there are no true 'Global Courts'. In contrast, in public law relationships[21] there are examples of supranational courts that one could view as global. Those create and apply public international law that could be seen as 'global'.[22] Absent such truly 'Global Courts' in private relationships the private participants are often applying domestic rules to what are essentially global problems. In some instances the domestic judicial infrastructure is not fit for purpose. And whilst it is clear that domestic courts play a key role in global dispute resolution, any discussion about (anti)specialisation trends in judicial law making needs to take into account the complex web of relevant players involved into account, including the various private participants together with a proper understanding of their incentives and motives.

15.1.3 This Contribution

The metaphor of the Global Village is a useful one to capture today's economic reality as to how global business is conducted. The Global Village should be seen not just in economic terms, but also in legal terms. Whilst the adjective 'global' indicates what the scale and scope of the activities are, the word 'village' suggests that the number of key players is relatively limited and that they are dependent on each other.

This chapter is a first exploratory attempt to explain the phenomenon of global dispute resolution by using a new concept in private adjudication: the notion of the Global Village. Having the Global Village as a starting point of our analysis inevitably leads to an alternative view on specialisation trends in dispute resolution. While specialisation is very much connected to the functioning of national court systems (designed primarily to deal with domestic or national disputes), it fails to capture the realities of the Global Village. It falls short of explaining what is actually going on in global dispute resolution-land and why, while national courts are still

---

[18]Hensler (2011, 2017).

[19]Michaels (2011).

[20]Lehman and Phelps (2008).

[21]Public law focuses on the organization of the government, the relations between the state and its citizens, the responsibilities of government officials, and the relations between states.

[22]Primary forum for the creation of public international law is inter-governmental organizations like United Nations through the codification of customary law by way of international treaties.

very much involved, they are just one category of participants whose traditional role has changed over time and is still changing. Moreover, a different typology for the disputes that arise in this space is necessary to depict this new reality and a matching classification of the dispute resolution mechanisms with respect to these disputes. One cannot even start identifying (anti-)specialisation trends in dispute resolution before one understands which factors and influencers drive these processes.

Section 15.2 identifies the key players inhabiting the Global Village, whilst Sect. 15.3 describes the types of dispute that occur there. Section 15.4 outlines the different dispute resolution methods that are deployed in different types of dispute. Section 15.5 ends with a summary and reflects on the above.

15.2 The Key Players in the Global Village

There are seven categories of key players in the Global Village. These will be discussed below in the chronological order of their appearance in the Global Village.

15.2.1 The Multinationals

The first inhabitants of our Global Village are the multinationals. The world is their market, in which they distribute products and services on a global scale. They prefer to do so with as little governmental interference as possible: the free market is the ideal. Before the existance of the Global Village, economic markets were primarily confined within geographical borders. Motivated by profit maximisation, multinationals look beyond national borders to increase their profits and expand their markets. They are players in a 'global monopoly game' of economic expansion, where markets are identified and conquered on a much grander scale than ever before: European, Asian, North- or South-American, rather than single domestic. To the extent that the latter matter, they are often perceived as a strategic gateway to other wider markets. On this market expansion journey they are accompanied by their trusted advisers, their corporate lawyers who draft trade contracts and prepare joint ventures with the local business partners. The corporate lawyers are the second category of key players in our Global Village.

15.2.2 Global Law Firms: Big Law

The so-called 'Global Law Firms' have been the subject of academic studies on 'Big Law'[23] as have the globalisation of corporate legal services and related

---

[23]Caserta (2020), Henderson (2014) and Ribstein (2010).

developments in the legal profession.[24] These global law firms, predominantly with origins in the US or the UK,[25] but with offices throughout the world, serve corporate clients and proactively develop new services and solutions to support their expanding corporate interests[26] related to economic growth and profit maximisation. The primarily focus of these global lawyers is regulatory and transactional work related to the establishment of new contractual partnerships and joint ventures as well as the litigation or arbitration that flows from the former. However, the future of Big Law is uncertain as a result of globalisation and the increased use of technologies in relation to the provision of legal services.[27] What is certain, is that legal professionals will need to adjust in order to survive and remain successful and profitable. It is also certain that the recent developments in this area will also have implications as to how Big Law assists its multinational clients and the specialisations that they will develop in that regard.

15.2.3 State Regulators and Legislators

Another category of key players in the Global Village are States Regulators and Legislators. The globally expanding multinationals have to deal with them all the time in their market expansion activity. That creates a 'love-hate' relationship that is politically driven. On the one hand, states and their market regulators have a certain self-interest in attracting foreign investors and facilitating their engagement in economic activities in the host state. On the other hand, over time, public interest may require legislative measures that deviate from the initial cooperation projections and lead the foreign investors to believe that they should be compensated for financial losses that they suffer as a result of legislation that is detrimental to their economic interests. The controversy over the attempts of Philip Morris (in the example above) and other multi-national corporations to use investment arbitration to challenge general health, safety and environmental protection regulations derailed international trade negotiations and led to efforts to establish an international court for investment disputes, where transparency and (at least alleged) impartiality would prevail.[28] This brings us to the next category of key players in the Global Village: the NGOs, Consumer Interest Associations and Civil Society.

---

[24]For examples of those, see Galanter and Palay (1991), Spar (1997) and Flood (2007).

[25]Faulconbridge et al. (2008).

[26]Flood (2007).

[27]This is a general trend with respect to the legal profession: Susskind and Susskind (2017).

[28]Howard (2017), pp. 1–52.

15.3 NGOs, Consumer Interest Associations and Civil Society

Globalisation, industrialisation and the expanding power of multinationals in the Global Village have not been met without criticism by NGOs, Consumer Interest Associations and Civil Society. Their concern is increased 'economic protectionism' by home or host states and regulators, at the expense of consumers and environmental interests. In the context of dispute resolution in the Global Village they play three potential roles. First, they act as an originator or activist funder in relation to certain type of global disputes.[29] Secondly, in some (predominantly civil law) jurisdictions they are the only parties that have the right to file collective actions on behalf of or for the benefit of consumers.[30] Finally, NGOs, Consumer Interest Associations and Civil Society are drivers for reform in relation to Global Dispute Resolution. In the EU, BEUC and its sister associations in the EU member states are the main driver for EU legislation in the field of EU collective redress,[31] whilst Civil Society groups were among the main activists opposed to the dispute settlement regime proposed in TTIP and CETA.[32] This invoked discussions in relation to the establishment of an Investment Court System and even a Multiliteral Investment Court.[33] Whilst the incentives of this category of key players seem evident or self-explanatory at first glance, over time, and as the financial stakes increase, they (may) develop their own institutional agenda.[34] That inevitably has or will have an effect on how they deal with global disputes and the dispute resolution mechanisms they invoke in that regard. Moreover, they are often assisted by different types of legal services providers other than corporate law firms. This brings us to the next category of key players in the Global Village.

15.4 Global Claimant Bar?

As multinationals become successful in the establishment of new joint ventures and are growing their global market share, their products and services are distributed on a worldwide scale. Inevitably, when something goes wrong with these products or services that affects a large number of consumers or entities. Their interests are represented by a second group of global lawyers: the ones who construct 'the private

---

[29]E.g. Human rights or climate claims: Greenpeace, Human Rights Watch etc. The Dutch Urgenda case is an example of such an activist litigation.

[30]Belgium, France and Germany are examples.

[31]Siles-Brügge (2017).

[32]Nienaber (2016).

[33]Friends of the Earth Europe (2017).

[34]For further analysis of this phenomenon in relation to their role in collective actions and collective redress see Tzankova (2020).

legal order for mass claims'.[35] This second group of lawyers, are similar to their counterparties in Big Law, predominantly based in common law jurisdictions (US, UK and Australia). They seldom have offices abroad and build instead loose ad hoc networks and relationships with locally-based firms when and where they find that appropriate.

They specialise in litigation on behalf of claimants and work, if not exclusively, at least predominantly, on a contingency fee basis which allows them to share with their clients the fruits of success. This group of global lawyers is continuously exploring the furthest corners of the Global Village in search of the perfect forum that provides them and their clients with the best combination of substance (substantive law), procedure (procedural law) and remuneration (legal costs structure and fee regimes). Similar to the NGOs, Consumer Interest Associations and Civil Society, they also fulfil a number of roles: in addition to their traditional role of legal professionals representing clients in court, they are also claim originators and litigation funders. This category of key players has a substantial financial stake in global disputes and hence a significant impact on how global dispute resolution evolves, on how and where disputes proceed in the Global Village.

15.5   Domestic Courts and Arbitral Institutions

In the meantime, absent global corporate courts, the domestic courts and arbitral tribunals are the two categories of adjudicators with jurisdiction in global disputes. In the early days of the existence of the Global Village they were seen as complimentary to each other, the scope of their competences seemed clear cut and there was 'peaceful co-existance'. With the passage of time and as multinationals expanded their activities the situation has changed or is continuing to change. Due process concerns have made arbitral tribunals increasingly resemble private courts.[36] At the same time domestic courts are keen to attract the clientele of arbitral tribunals and are adjusting their national rules and procedures accordingly. A good example of that development is the introduction of English-speaking commercial courts in non-English speaking jurisdictions (trying to resemble the advantages of arbitration, while preserving its due process features).

The competition in the global dispute resolution arena takes place on different levels. There is not only competition between domestic courts and arbitral tribunals,[37] but also amongst the different English-speaking domestic courts in the non-English speaking jurisdictions.[38] Ultimately, one would expect this to also

---

[35]Hensler (2011).

[36]Verkuil (2005), pp. 963–994; Merrills (2007), pp. 374–377.

[37]Ruckteschler and Stooss (2019), pp. 431–449.

[38]As discussed elsewhere in this book.

influence court specialisation.[39] Moreover, such competition is illustrative of the fundamental changes that are taking place within national court systems in different corners of the Global Village and for the development of an intriguing new phenomenon: the self-positioning of the judiciary as an economic player, a profit centre and yet another legal services provider. That is a step further than the 'managerial judging' signaled by Judith Resnik in 1982.[40] The resolution of global disputes has become a lucrative business, a market where supply and demand follow different market rules. This brings us to the last category of key players in our Global Village.

15.6   Third Party Litigation Finance Providers

The last category of key players in the Global Village is the third party litigation finance providers (TPF). Initially, they emerged in the Global Dispute Resolution space as a response to the ever increasing cost of adjudication. Typically they are described as third parties, unrelated to the dispute at hand, who provide a funding facility on a so-called 'non-recourse basis', to cover all or part of the costs of adjudication, in exchange for a success fee related to the outcome of the litigation.

Largely unregulated, the nature of the third party finance providers varies: they can be publicly listed entities, whose shareholders, e.g. pension funds and the like, appreciate the fact that the performance of this asset class is unrelated to market developments. This adds a welcome diversification to their investment portfolios. Others are spin-offs of insurers or reinsurers or hedge funds and private equity and family offices of high net worth individuals. While in the early days third party litigation financiers would provide funding for single, one off cases or would buy or take over claims at any stage in the proceedings, nowadays their services span a much more diverse menu of options. For example: third party funders finance the enforcement of arbitral awards and related asset tracing or asset recovery activities. They can take over a latent litigation risk in the case of a merger or acquisition, finance a corporate client's dispute resolution portfolio, including costs of defending claims. Similarly: they may also finance the claims portfolio of a law firm working on a contingent basis. If required, TPF can provide insurance for adverse costs orders. In relation to multi-party actions or collective redress, they will also finance book-building activities[41] and will even assist in case origination or litigation project management. Last but not least: they finance companies active in the dispute resolution space such as legal tech platforms and startups in online dispute resolution. Litigation financing has increasingly become a form of corporate finance. The

---

[39]For example the German English speaking commercial court puts an emphasis on its financial expertise, while the Netherlands Commercial Court is emphasizing its utility to handle also complex international multi-party or collective actions.

[40]Resnik (1982).

[41]That means that they will finance the marketing and other related costs of signing up claimants.

next step in that development which marks the growth of the industry is the creation of a new form of reinsurance: the funders share risk among each other with respect to certain claim portfolios. By doing all of these things, TPF also increasingly develop specialisations in the type of disputes or activities that they finance. These examples demonstrate that third party funders are becoming in essence the 'investment bankers' of our Global Village: they interact with and finance the activities of other key players. Because of their central role, the TPF are probably the first ones to spot any emerging trends, including ones in court specialisation.

15.7 Types of Disputes in the Global Village

There are different ways to classify the various types of disputes that can arise in our Global Village. They can be classified according to the nature of the issue at hand, the type of interaction with other disputes or the nature of the parties involved.

15.7.1 Nature of the Issue

One way to classify the disputes is to look at the nature of the problems that they aim to address. Following that line of thinking Michaels[42] distinguishes three categories of global problems, hence global disputes. First, problems that are global by nature e.g. the problems created by global markets, such as fraud on financial markets or cartels. Secondly, there are the problems that are global by design: the global character of the problem is a consequence of its design, as is the case with legal issues arising from the internet, privacy-related infringements and data breaches. Thirdly, there are problems that are global by definition ie. because that is how we choose to frame them, for example human rights abuses, including environmental damage, climate change and pandemics. Michael's conclusion is that whilst these global problems lead to global disputes, there are no 'Global World Courts' to deal with them. It is national judges and court systems that have to act as 'global courts' in private dispute resolution.

15.7.2 Interaction with Other Disputes[43]

Another way to classify global disputes is to look at their interaction and functional connection with other disputes. This approach goes beyond the conventional

---

[42]Michaels (2011), pp. 167–176.
[43]This typology is attributed to Prof. Deborah Hensler (Stanford Law School).

thinking about transnational or cross-border litigation that typically is seen as a single law suit that happened to involve parties, domiciled in different jurisdictions. The classic challenges presented by this type of problems include: where to file a claim; how to achieve service of documents; how to gather evidence; what law prevails and how to ensure enforcement of an award.[44] Nowadays the term transnational or global litigation and dispute resolution increasingly conjures up images of a 'family' of related lawsuits pending in parallel in multiple jurisdictions and before various tribunals. Applying a line of thinking that goes beyond the conventional approach, one that is more in line with contemporary thinking about global dispute resolution, a different typology of global disputes can be distinguished. This is dependent on the nature of the interaction between 'the family of related disputes' and such a distinction leads to two additional types of global dispute.

First, there are the 'families of related disputes', where multinationals use the available dispute resolution mechanisms and the differences between national civil procedures pro-actively and strategically in order to advance their interests or optimise their market position. Some of the examples given above illustrate this: for example the Apple/Samsung 'intellectual property rights'—wars where these companies have been trying to enhance, secure and or protect their global market share. Another example is the British American Tobacco Clean Packaging Act litigation and arbitration disputes against Australia, Uruguay and other countries. As stated above, dispute resolution has become a strategic tool in a commercial effort aimed at economic expansion and profit maximisation. It demonstrates the strategic use of dispute resolution mechanisms available in different parts of the world to promote or obstruct certain business policies viewed by the parties as desirable. Whereas litigation is in nature reactive and traditionally seen as a procedure of last resort (at least in many parts of the world), nowadays it is also used proactively as a tool for global expansion by corporations to advance or promote their corporate goals.[45] This type of dispute generally involves parties that are all more or less repeat players and it assumes that there is more or less a level playing field between them.

The second category of 'families of related disputes' consists of multi-party actions resulting from globally marketed products or services (for example financial services, medical devices or global cartels). The VW emissions scandal and the Trafigura case mentioned above are example of these. Such cases involve a large number of claimants, often dispersed in different jurisdictions, suffering losses attributed to the same corporate or state entity or individuals typically based or domiciled in another jurisdiction. Typically, the claimants and defendants in this

---

[44]Baumgartner (2007), p. 793 reviewing Born and Rutledge (2007).

[45]Indeed, that is an emerging trend identified by Peter Rees, former legal director of Royal Dutch Shell at the IADC Annual Meeting in Vienna, on 9 July 2014. See further Jursys (2012), p. 175: "In order to gain, protect or enlarge their market shares, firms employ various strategies (e.g. technology protection measures or patent thickets). One of the elements of this competition in the innovative industries is litigation: IP right holders sue alleged infringers seeking injunctions and compensation for damages and, on their behalf, alleged infringers may seek declarations for non-liability."

type of case are not equal in terms of financial predisposition and there is also information asymmetry. When it comes to multi-party actions in the transnational or global context, one should note that these might invoke the use of new types of domestic procedure. Until recently modern legal systems have been characterised by cases initiated by a single claimant or a limited number of claimants, pursuing a legal action against one or a few defendants. The key differences amongst legal systems centred on the questions of who had standing to bring which sorts of claim, and which sort of remedies were available. Until the 1990s, class actions and representative litigation brought by one or a few parties on behalf of a larger number of similarly situated persons or entities, were only found in the US and in one province in Canada. Today, an increasing number of countries have adopted some form of representative class action and several others have adopted a non-representative (ie. aggregated) form of group proceeding. The countries that have adopted class actions are diverse.[46] As more jurisdictions have introduced some kind of a collective action, the global exposure of multinationals has increased over time and parties on both sides of the dispute use the differences in national legal regimes to optimise their position.

15.7.3   Nature of Parties Involved

A third way to distinguish global disputes is to do so based on the capacity of the parties involved. On that basis, once again three types of global disputes can be identified. First, there are the so-called business to state or B2S disputes: investors operating on the global market are in search of new markets and new opportunities situated outside their home jurisdictions to increase their market share and to diversify their project portfolio's and related risks. Such opportunities are, not always, but often, to be found in developing jurisdictions or in jurisdictions where the rule of law is 'under construction' or developing as well. Such jurisdictions may welcome and even actively pursue foreign financial investment and matching expertise in various types of long and short term infrastructure projects. A commercially attractive proposition between the developing state and the foreign investor is easy to contemplate. However, over time and also dependent on how the project or the political system in the host country develops, the host company might find itself in—more or less justified—breach of the original investment agreement. This can obviously lead to a state-investor dispute. The British American tobacco disputes are an example of a(n attempt to structure the dispute as a) state-investor one trying to optimise the multinational's legal position.

Secondly, there are the business to business or the so-called B2B-disputes of which the Apple-Samsung litigation is an example. Finally, there are the consumer to

---

[46]Hensler (2016) in: Hensler et al (eds) (2016).

business disputes ('C2B'-disputes), illustrated by the Trafigura and the VW collective actions in the examples above.

15.8 Dispute Resolution in the Global Village

Now that we know who the inhabitants of the Global Village are and the type of disputes that they deal with, let us have a look at the dispute resolution mechanisms that they have at their disposal.

15.8.1 Introduction

Although popular culture[47] and some business lobby organisations[48] might make us think that we are living in an increasingly litigious society, the reality is that most (ordinary) people do not take legal action when something bad happens to them and to the extent that they do, most cases settle and are resolved out of court.[49] Negotiation, mediation and adjudication are conceptually speaking the three main methods to handle disputes. The main difference between negotiation and mediation on the one hand and adjudication on the other is that adjudication is a method of dispute resolution where a neutral third party, a decision maker, determines the outcome of a dispute. Mediation is in essence a form of negotiation that is facilitated by a neutral third party.

Court adjudication and arbitration are the two best known forms of adjudication in the different types of Global Disputes. The main differences between the two are that in arbitration, as opposed to court adjudication, parties are allowed to choose their arbitrator(s), the whole procedure is confidential and the enforcement of arbitral awards is, on a global scale, easier or at least less problematic than the enforcement of domestic court awards.[50] Another advantage that is traditionally attributed to arbitration is that it leads to finality more quickly: an arbitral award is in principle final and often there are no or very limited remedies available to challenge it.[51] In addition to these advantages of arbitration over court adjudication, traditionally arbitration was also considered to be a cheaper and faster dispute resolution method than court adjudication, especially when specific expertise is required. When selecting the arbiters, parties can choose the most appropriate expert in view of the dispute at hand, which speeds up the process and an expert appointment may not be

---

[47]Think of John Grisham's books like Rainmaker, and Netflix series like Suits.

[48]The most prominent example is the American Chamber of Commerce: Rathod, Vaheesan.

[49]Engel (2016).

[50]Green (1997), pp. 175–178.

[51]Mentschikoff (1952), p. 699.

necessary. However, over the years, arbitration has been criticised for becoming expensive, slow and not diverse or inclusive enough.[52]

Different types of global disputes seem to follow a different dispute resolution pattern. Below follows an illustrative overview of the main types of dispute resolution mechanisms used in the B2S, B2B and C2B types of Global Disputes.

15.8.2   B2S Disputes

Typically, state-investor disputes (business to state) are governed by dispute resolution mechanisms that are agreed in special agreements, so-called Biliteral Investment Treaties (BITs). Absent such special agreements, an investment dispute between the host state and an investor would need to be filed before the national courts of the host state. That is seen as a disadvantage for and by the foreign investor, even if it concerns host states with a developed Rule of Law. The more or less explicit assumption is that the national courts of the host state will have the tendency to rule in the interest of the host state. Many states have therefore an agreement with other states that set out the conditions that apply for foreign investments in each other's countries. In other words: when a multinational of country A wants to invest in country B and vice versa, countries A and B negotiate a 'special deal' with each other, that they formalise in a treaty to facilitate investments in each others' economies. The host state of the multinational wants to insure that the company is well protected against expropriations and other events that are detrimental to its assets, when doing business and investing abroad, while the host state of the investment wants to attract foreign investors and offering special arrangements, including a special dispute resolution provision in case of disputes, is often part of the deal. Typically, a BIT contains a dispute settlement clause that stipulates extra dispute resolution options via arbitration for the foreign investors.

15.8.3   B2B Disputes

Business to business disputes in the global context are also often resolved via arbitration, but parties have to have agreed that beforehand, unless they reach such an agreement after the dispute has arisen.[53] There are specialised arbitration institutes for different industries, for example for financial instruments,[54] maritime

---

[52]Slate (2010), pp. 182–198.

[53]Strictly speaking they can also agree on arbitration after the dispute have arisen, but once parties are in disagreement it turns out very difficult for them to agree on anything.

[54]P.R.I.M.E. Finance. https://primefinancedisputes.org.

disputes[55] and energy.[56] The considerations that apply when businesses choose arbitration over court adjudication are, in addition to the advantages that are traditionally being attributed to arbitration, the same as the ones mentioned above with respect to B2S-disputes: an inherent mistrust of the ability of the national courts of the country where the business partner is domiciled to rule impartially on a 'foreign' party's claim, especially when the (financial) stakes are high. One should keep in mind that the B2B-disputes in the Global Village are between businesses situated in different countries.

When businesses make use of national court systems, as the Apple-Samsung example of their 'IP-war' illustrates, that is a strategic choice, part of a pro-active business risk management strategy. The choice as to where to focus to enforce IP-rights is a carefully made one. Some national jurisdictions are more important or relevant for the protection and enforcement of IP rights of multinationals than others.[57] And the 'lucky ones', the national courts selected to deal with these disputes, will also need to find a way to deal with the implications and challenges that go with these strategic choices.[58]

Also, when the disputes involve more than one party, as is often the case in relation to follow on damages claims filed by direct purchasers against members of Global cartels, the use of national court systems, as opposed to arbitration, is a necessity. In cases like this, involving not only multiple claimants, but also multiple defendants, arbitration is simply not a viable option, unless all parties consent to it.[59]

15.8.4   C2B Disputes

Finally, the C2B and disputes. They seem to be the least homogeneous type of disputes in the Global Village when it comes to dispute resolution mechanisms. There are varying attitudes with respect to consumer protection generally in the different corners of the Global Village, which affects also the type of dispute resolution mechanisms applied. For example, within the EU as a general rule, the availability of ADR-mechanisms cannot prevent consumers of having access to the public judicial court system.[60] Also, when consumers who are domiciled in the EU decide to file their claim with a court against a business domiciled in another EU

---

[55]Maritime Arbitration Associations https://icmaweb.com/maritime-arbitration-associations.

[56]E.g. The International Center for Energy Arbitration. http://energyarbitration.org.

[57]For a related discussion of this topic see: Jursys (2012).

[58]Bennett and Granata (2019).

[59]Case C-352/13 *Cartel Damage Claims (CDC) Hydrogen Peroxide SA v Akzo Nobel NV (2015)* EU:C:2015:335. For a more extended discussion of the topic see: Segan (2018), pp. 423–430 and Smith (2019).

[60]See article 46 Directive 2013/11/EU of the European Parliament and of the Council of 21 May 2013 on alternative dispute resolution for consumer disputes and amending regulation.

Member State, they can choose to do so, deviating from the regular rules on jurisdiction, before their home court and not before the court of the defendant.[61] Consumers domiciled outside the EU are still welcome to file their claim before the home court of the EU multinational.

The approach in the US to consumer protection for example is different. While the US class actions regime is traditionally viewed as the most consumer-friendly one in the Global Village, consumers domiciled outside the US will typically find it much more difficult to file a claim against a US multinational before a US court, because of stricter rules on jurisdiction, including the concept of 'forum non-convenience'.[62] In addition, in the US case law with respect to class arbitration has developed that diverts consumer class actions from US courts to US arbitration institutes,[63] a development that would not have been possible in the EU for the reasons pointed out above. However, although consumer arbitration is underdeveloped in the EU, there is emphasis on other forms of ADR, including Online Dispute Resolution, (ODR),[64] resulting from the introduction of the ODR Regulation in 2013.[65] Finally and most recently, the EU has introduced a Directive that aims to cover cross-border collective redress and facilitate the use of TPF, but it is unclear what the impact of these measures will be.[66]

15.9   A Summary and a Reflection

This contribution is a very first exploratory attempt to explain the phenomenon of global dispute resolution via the introduction of the notion of the Global Village and its inhabitants: the multinationals, their global lawyers, states regulators and legislators, NGOs, Consumer Interest Associations and Civil Society, claimant lawyers, domestic courts and arbitral tribunals acting as Global Courts and third party financiers. Whilst the adjective 'global' stipulates the scale and scope of the activities of the relevant players, the word 'village' indicates that the number of key players is relatively limited and that they know, or are at the very least aware of and are dependent on each other.

The main aim of this chapter is to illustrate that whilst domestic courts play a key role in global dispute resolution, there are more relevant participants and any discussion on specialisation or anti-specialisation trends in judicial law-making, needs to take into account the whole web of relevant parties.

---

[61] Art. 18 Brussels I recast.

[62] Duval (1992), p. 650.

[63] Smith and More (2012), pp. 281–302.

[64] For a development of ODR: Mania (2015), pp. 76–86.

[65] Directive 2013/524/EC of the European Parliament and of the Council of 21 May 2013 on online dispute resolution for consumer disputes and amending Regulation.

[66] European Commission (2020).

This chapter takes as a starting point a number of actual pending or recently concluded cases that are examples of different types of disputes in the Global Village. It also attempts to classify these. It demonstrates that different classifications are possible, dependent on the nature of the issue at hand, the type of interaction with other disputes or the nature of the parties involved. The chapter then explores how dispute resolution in the Global Village takes place in relation to one category of global disputes: the one that can be distinguished based on the nature of the parties involved. This initial analysis reveals that there are definitely ongoing (specialisation) trends in dispute resolution, but before one can qualify these properly, additional research is required with respect to each one of the key players identified and their influence on each other and on the resolution of disputes in the Global Village. A few illustrative examples are mentioned below, but the list could certainly be expanded:

How will Big Law evolve under pressure of legal tech and how will that influence its role and performance in Global Disputes?

Will a Global Claimant Bar emerge with Global Claimant Law firms similar to the ones in Big Law and how will TPF affect that development?

Will TPF engage in human rights -litigation and how will that impact that category of global disputes?

Will there be an international court system in B2S (investor-state) disputes?

Will domestic courts overtake the role of arbitral tribunals in B2B disputes?

Will C2B disputes have access to the judicial court system or will they be primarily reverted to ADR, ODR and arbitration? And if so, is that a good or a bad thing?

Will domestic courts develop an expertise in certain types of Global Disputes?

How will the traditional image of the courts as public interest institutions be impacted by an evolving role as economic actors and even 'profit centers'?

Are there other, more adequate or relevant, typologies of Global Disputes?

To what extent does the general rule that most disputes settle or are resolved out of court apply also to Global Disputes and the opportunistic or strategic behavior of the key players? How does the availability of TPF for both multinationals and their customers, the consumers, and shareholders impact the notion of access to justice for all these groups and will that neutralise or enhance investment asymmetries?

While many questions remain unanswered, one thing is clear: the paths to justice in the Global Village remain an unchartered territory.

References

Baumgartner S (2007) Transnational litigation in the United States: the emergence of a new field of law. Am J Comp Law 55(4):793

Bennett A, Granata S (2019) When private international law meets intellectual property law: a guide for judges. World Intellectual Property Organization, Geneva

Born G, Rutledge P (2007) International civil litigation in the United States, 4th edn. Wolters Kluwer, Philadelphia

Bosters T (2015) Collective redress and private international law in the European Union. Wolf Legal Publishers, Oisterwijk, p 71

Business and Human Rights Resource Centre Business and Human Rights Resource Centre Trafigura lawsuits (re Côte d'Ivoire). https://www.business-humanrights.org/en/latest-news/trafigura-lawsuits-re-c%C3%B4te-divoire/

Caserta S (2020) Digitalization of the legal field and the future of large law firms. Laws 9(2):14

Cremer A et al (2015) VW made several defeat devices to cheat emissions tests: sources. https://www.reuters.com/article/us-volkswagen-emissions-software-idUSKCN0SB0PU20151017

Cronin Fisk M et al (2016) Volkswagen agrees to $15 billion diesel-cheating settlement. https://www.bloomberg.com/news/articles/2016-06-28/volkswagen-to-pay-14-7-billion-to-settle-u-s-emissions-claims

Duran P (2019) Volkswagen agrees to Australian settlement over diesel cheating. www.reuters.com/article/us-volkswagen-emissions-suit-australia/volkswagen-agrees-to-australian-settlement-over-diesel-cheating-idUSKBN1W106G?feedType=RSS&feedName=businessNews

Duval J (1992) One-way ticket home: the federal doctrine of forum non conveniens and the international plaintiff. Cornell Law Rev 77(3):650

Engel D (2016) The myth of the litigious society: why we don't sue. University of Chicago Press, Chicago

European Commission (2020) Commission welcomes confirmation of provisional agree-ment to strengthen collective redress in the EU. https://ec.europa.eu/commission/presscorner/detail/en/statement_20_1227

Faulconbridge J, Beaverstock J, Muzio D et al (2008) Global law firms: globalization and organizational spaces of cross-border legal work. Northwest J Int Law Bus 28(3):458

Fenner R, Schneider J (2011) Philip Morris says Australia Plain-Pack law violates treaty. https://www.bloomberg.com/news/articles/2011-06-26/philip-morris-starts-legal-action-on-australian-tobacco-package-law-plans

Flood J (2007) Lawyers as sanctifiers: the role of elite law firms in international busi-ness transactions. Indiana J Global Legal Stud 14(1):35

Friends of the Earth Europe (2017) A new global corporate court system isn't the nswer. Time for Europe to find alternatives. https://www.foeeurope.org/global-corporate-court-multinational-treaty-021017

Galanter M, Palay T (1991) Tournament of lawyers: the transformation of the big law firm. The University of Chicago Press, Chicago

Green ED (1997) International commercial dispute resolution: courts, arbitration, and mediation--introduction. Boston Univ Int Law J 15(1):175–178

Haas P, Kleywegt J (2019) Amsterdam district court recognises Volkswagen Car Claim foundation as claimants in class action against Volkswagen. https://www.akd.eu/insights/amsterdam-district-court-recognises-volkswagen-car-claim-foundation-as-claimants-in-class-action-against-volkswagen-et-al

Henderson W (2014) From big law to lean law. Int Rev Law Econ 38:5

Hensler D (2011) How economic globalisation is helping to construct a private transnational legal order. In: Muller S et al (eds) The law of the future and the future of law. Torkel Opsahl Academic EPublisher, Oslo. http://www.fichl.org/fileadmin/fichl/documents/FICHL_11_Web.pdf

Hensler D (2016) The global landscape of collective litigation. In: Hensler D et al (eds) Class actions in context. E. Elgar, Cheltenham, pp 3–19

Hensler D (2017) From sea to shining sea: how and why class actions are spreading globally. Kansas Law Rev 65(5):965

Howard D (2017) Creating consistency through world investment court. Fordham Int Law J 41(1):1–52

Jursys P (2012) International jurisdiction in intellectual property disputes: CLIP, ALI principles and other legislative proposals in a comparitive perspective. JIPITEC 3(3):175

Kim M (2011) Samsung countersues Apple over iPhone, iPad. https://in.reuters.com/article/us-samsung-apple/samsung-countersues-apple-over-iphone-ipad-idUSTRE73L0DG20110422

Lehman J, Phelps S (2008) Private law defines, regulates, enforces, and administers relationships among individuals, associations, and corporations. In: West's Encyclopedia of American Law, 2nd edn. Gale, Detroit

Mander B (2016) Uruguay defeats Philip Morris test case lawsuit. https://www.ft.com/content/1ae33bc8-454e-11e6-9b66-0712b3873ae1

Mania K (2015) Online dispute resolution: the future of justice. Int Comp Jurisprud 1(1):76–86

Maritime Arbitration Associations. https://icmaweb.com/maritime-arbitration-associations

Matussek K (2020) VW chairman settles another market manipulation case. https://www.bloomberg.com/news/articles/2020-08-20/vw-chairman-poetsch-settles-another-market-manipulation-case

McDonald W (ed) (1997) Crime and law enforcement in the global village. Anderson Publishing Co, Cincinnati

Menn J (2011) Apple sues Samsung over patents for iPad. https://www.ft.com/content/8128db78-6a10-11e0-86e4-00144feab49a

Mentschikoff S (1952) The significance of arbitration – a preliminary inquiry. Law Contemp Prob 17(4):699

Merrills J (2007) The mosaic of international dispute settlement procedures: complementary or contradictory? Netherlands Int Law Rev 54:374–377

Michaels R (2011) Global problems in domestic courts. In: Muller S, Zouridis S, Frishman M et al (eds) The law of the future and the future of law. Torkel Opsahl Academic EPublisher, Oslo, pp 167–176

Nienaber M (2016) Tens of thousands protest in Europe against Atlantic free trade deals. https://www.reuters.com/article/us-eu-usa-ttip-idUSKCN11N0H6

P.R.I.M.E. Finance. https://primefinancedisputes.org

Primary forum for the creation of public international law is inter-governmental organizations like United Nations through the codification of customary law by way of international treaties: http://definitions.uslegal.com/p/public-international-law/

Resnik J (1982) Managerial judges. The Rand Corporation, Santa Monica

Reuters Staff (2016) VW institutional investors file $3.61 billion suit in Germany. https://www.reuters.com/article/us-volkswagen-emissions-lawsuit/vw-institutional-investors-file-3-61-billion-suit-in-germany-idUSKCN0WG2B1

Reuters Staff (2020) Volkswagen offers 830 million euros to compensate German buyers. https://www.reuters.com/article/us-volkswagen-emissions/volkswagen-offers-830-million-euros-to-compensate-german-buyers-idUSKBN2081E4?feedType=RSS&feedName=businessNews

Ribstein L (2010) The death of big law. Wisconsin Law Rev 2010:749

Ruckteschler D, Stooss T (2019) International commercial courts: a superior alternative to arbitration? J Int Arbitr 36(4):431–449

Segan J (2018) Arbitration clauses and competition law. J Eur Compet Law Practice 9(7):423–430. https://doi.org/10.1093/jeclap/lpy039

Shepardson D (2018) Volkswagen agrees to $232 million 3.0-liter Canadian emissions settlement. https://www.reuters.com/article/idUSKBN1F12LC

Siles-Brügge G (2017) Transatlantic investor protection as a threat to democracy: the potency and limits of an emotive frame. Camb Rev Int Aff 30(5):489–506

Slate W (2010) Cost and time effectiveness of arbitration. Contemp Asia Arbitr J 3(2):182–198

Smith V (2019) Collective competition arbitration in the EU: towards an arbitrated European class. King's College London, London

Smith C, More EV (2012) Outsourcing American civil justice: mandatory arbitration clauses in consumer and employment contracts. Texas Tech Law Rev 44(2):281–302

Spar D (1997) Lawyers abroad: the internationalization of legal practice. Calif Manag Rev 37(3):8

Sterling T (2017) Dutch group to launch lawsuit against VW over emissions cheating. https://fr.reuters.com/article/idUSL1N1JA0E6

Susskind R, Susskind D (2017) The future of the professions: how technology will trans-form the work of human experts. Oxford University Press, Oxford

The International Center for Energy Arbitration. http://energyarbitration.org

The Times staff (2008) Ivory Coast turns to UK in class action over toxic waste. In: Thetimes.co.uk. https://www.thetimes.co.uk/article/ivory-coast-turns-to-uk-in-class-action-over-toxic-waste-pfk9w0l0tqq

Tobacco plain packaging — investor-state arbitration. https://www.ag.gov.au/international-relations/international-law/tobacco-plain-packaging-investor-state-arbitration#decision-on-australias-preliminary-jurisdictional-objections

Tzankova IN (2020) Legal standing in collective redress. In: Stadler A et al (eds) Collective and mass litigation in Europe. Model rules for effective dispute resolution. E.Elgar, Cheltenham, pp 127–152

Verkuil PR (2005) Privatizing due process. Admin Law Rev 57(4):963–994

Part V
Concluding Remarks

Chapter 16
Constituting a Civil Legal System Called "Just": Law, Money, Power, and Publicity

Judith Resnik

Abstract From the vantage point of a world reorganized by the COVID-19 pandemic and riven with political and social conflicts, this book is a powerful testament to how embedded dispute resolution systems are as normal facets of ordinary good governance. The shared commitments are to measured, consistent, and accessible means of obtaining relief for allegedly unlawful behavior. What the authors debate are not the goals of supporting dispute resolution services but the modalities for doing so. The questions are how and who responds to calls for legal help.

This volume thus represents the success of political and social movements that have shaped the expectations, practices, culture, and laws of dispute resolution systems in the last centuries and, more recently, have brought to the fore concerns about a "justice gap." Several chapters hone in on the distance between what systems purport to provide and what they deliver, as demand exceeds the supply of responders.

But demand for what? The core questions include what kinds of harms merit legal recognition as well as whether, were all claimants able to obtain responses, the resulting procedures would be part of a civil legal system worth calling "just." Analysis of these justice questions entails considering the metrics to choose when assessing the substantive rights and entitlements recognized, the processes provided, and the quality of results. How does one measure whether the quantum of legal protection and the invocation of those rights and entitlements are optimal or reflect under-protection, over-protection, under-claiming or over-claiming? What factors are the bases for assessing the various processes espoused or criticized by the chapter authors? What are the baselines for assessments of outcomes? These queries bring

---

Thanks are due to this volume's editors, Xandra Kramer, Alexandre Biard, Jos Hoevenaars & Erlis Themeli, who invited me to participate and from whom I learned a great deal when speaking at the conference that is the genesis of this book. This chapter builds on related work, including the co-authored Representing Justice (2011) and *The Functions of Publicity and Privatization* (2019b).

J. Resnik (✉)
Yale University, New Haven, CT, USA
e-mail: judith.resnik@yale.edu

X. Kramer et al. (eds.), *New Pathways to Civil Justice in Europe*,
https://doi.org/10.1007/978-3-030-66637-8_16

into focus another critical issue, that of perspective. What are the vantage points from which to understand the civil legal system so as to make judgments about whether a system is just or unjust? These are the issues I address in the chapter that follows.

16.1   The Interaction of Norms, Practices, and Doctrine

Discussions of implementation are at the heart of this volume. In this brief commentary, I step back to ask prior questions about the normative aspirations, the doctrinal mandates, and the pragmatics of contemporary civil justice systems. I explore some of the law and the political economy of the choices pursued under the rubric of "paths to a civil justice system," and I underscore three interrelated facets to be taken into account when assessing the justice of a legal system.

The first is about the substantive entitlements a civil justice system protects. The discussion of consumers, household members, and employees reflects the range of rights that political movements have recently brought into being. But the status quo neither should be taken for granted nor be seen as intrinsically optimal. Courts have been one venue for debate about who merits recognition as entitled to law's protection, about the forms procedures take, and the kinds of remedies to be made available. Hence, new modes and technologies need to address whether and how they will contribute to norm development. If they do not, they are at risk of being vehicles for stagnation or retrenchment.

My second concern focuses on the extent of government support for courts, for other forms of dispute resolution, and for those who seek to participate. Subsidies of various kinds are necessary to ensure that all members of the body politic are empowered to use the mechanisms created. Litigant asymmetries raise significant problems of fairness for dispute resolution. The diversity of kinds of legal rights raises a host of complex questions about line-drawing. Decisions need to be made about what kinds of claimants to encourage and what forms of economic transfers— from the government to individuals or among disputants—to provide or require and about how aggregate procedures can help.

Third is the issue of the public face (or not) of dispute resolution systems. The obligation of courts to function in public is longstanding, but the shift to other forms of government-sponsored or government-obliged processes does not always entail access for third parties, who are neither disputants nor decision-makers. The activities as well as the results of new modes need to be available to the public (more accurately, as detailed below, the many public(s)) so that questions of the underlying legal rights, the range of remedies, and the procedures can be the subject of informed discussions about the justice of the practices.

Knowledge is required about whether pathways (using various technologies) enable people to get into courts or their alternatives. Obtaining that information requires both learning about the range of users and observing the processes real-time.

Only then can one know whether justice is a goal embedded in the new routes and that justice is a result of the civil remedial structures provided.

16.2   From Exclusionary Judicial Systems to Mandates for Egalitarian Redistribution of Authority: Participatory Parity in Courts

What the 15 chapters in this volume make plain is that the human rights movements of the last century have ensconced new metrics of what makes a civil legal system just. To appreciate the shift requires a glance back in time, as adjudication is an ancient rite. Indeed, historians of Europe identify the need for dispute resolution as one of the reasons for the rise of city-states in the late Medieval period. The physical embodiment of those practices can be seen in the extant town halls of Renaissance Europe and in the thousands of segregated, purpose-built courthouses that have since become icons of government.[1]

The old and the newer structures bear testament to the intertwining of political, legal, and judicial power. Governments need their members and residents to participate in adjudicatory processes as one means of promoting peaceful resolutions, of supporting economic growth, and of generating and reinforcing states' own authority to function. Adjudication (whether in civil, criminal, or administrative tribunals) confirms and produces power.

Court proceedings were once deeply exclusionary: a narrow band of the population was legally entitled to redress. Around the world, civil justice systems historically excluded people by gender, marital status, race, nationality, class, and much else. In contrast, today, constitutional democracies oblige their legal systems to welcome as full participants all persons, including those with limited economic resources. Women and men of all colors have gained juridical capacity to serve in the full range of roles, from litigant and witness to lawyer, staff, and judge.

The changing face of judiciaries and the growth in demand for adjudicatory services and for other "paths" to civil justice[2] is an artifact of a host of new legal rights for family members, employees, tenants, consumers, and detainees, and of aspirations that all individuals should be able to live in safe environments and be treated with dignity and respect. The numbers of people seeking courts' help is one marker of the success of the link between these commitments and civil justice systems. The recent expansion of rights not only have brought new claimants *to* courts but also have changed the law and practices *of* courts, which are now understood as obliged to welcome diverse users.

Given the history of courts as exclusionary institutions that implemented racialized hierarchies and regimes of colonialism and subordination, we have much to

---

[1]Resnik and Curtis (2011).
[2]See Genn (2009, 2018).

celebrate in these developments. Courts have come to represent—and to present themselves as—venues of equality in which power redistribution is requisite to justice and hence to courts' own legitimacy. The result is that governments have to devise means of implementing the concept of *participatory parity* in the entry to and use of their dispute resolution systems.

Making good on that promise is, however, complex. Democracy not only has changed adjudication, but also has challenged it profoundly. As authors in this volume discuss, some of the new technologies and modes of dispute resolution aim to respond to the numbers of people seeking assistance and to the problems of unequal access. But unlike court-based adjudication, for which open and public access is one of the signature features,[3] few of these new processes build in mechanisms to include third parties. Moreover, one ought not take for granted the stability of the principle of participatory parity because not all of the alternatives to courts make provisions to subsidize or otherwise assist users.

16.3   New Obligations to Lower Entrance Barriers

Because the idea of government subsidies for needy litigants is relatively novel, unfolding, and potentially unstable, more needs to be said about its doctrinal roots and scope. I explore these issues by discussing a few decisions from the United States and the United Kingdom Supreme Courts, as they called on governments to reduce barriers to access by waiving or lowering court fees.

A half-century ago, in the early 1970s, a group who described themselves as "welfare recipients residing in Connecticut," filed a class action lawsuit and argued that state-imposed fees of sixty dollars for filing and service, coupled with no mechanism to waive that requirement, violated the U.S. Constitution by precluding them from getting divorced. In 1971, in *Boddie v. Connecticut*, the U.S. Supreme Court agreed.

In John Marshall Harlan's opinion for the Court, he explained that the combination of "the basic position of the marriage relationship in this society's hierarchy of values and the . . . state monopolization" of lawful dissolution resulted in a due process obligation by the state to provide access.[4] This decision was the first in U.S. history that identified the constitutional obligation to waive fees in civil litigation for people unable to afford the filing costs to obtain a divorce.

To think of the issue only in terms of the parties is to miss the perspective of the government, whose needs courts routinely serve. As Justice Harlan wrote:

> Perhaps no characteristic of an organized and cohesive society is more fundamental than its erection and enforcement of a system of rules defining the various rights and duties of its

---

[3]Resnik (2019b).

[4]*Boddie v. Connecticut*, 401 U.S. 371, 374 (1971).

members, enabling them to govern their affairs and definitely settle their differences in an orderly, predictable manner.[5]

As this brief excerpt reflects, the potential scope of the obligation to ease access could well include all kinds of civil disputes. Moreover, such assistance could range from fee waivers to subsidies for transcripts, experts, and attorneys.

Within short order, the U.S. Supreme Court retreated from this formulation by limiting the reach of its own understanding of when and why governments ought to subsidize courts and their users. The Court declined to recognize poverty as a suspect classification that would have triggered equal protection obligations across a range of legal domains.[6] Instead, the Court relied on an alchemy of constitutional commitments to due process and equal protection to recognize a narrow obligation to protect low-income, low-resource litigants when in certain forms of conflict with the state.[7] A related line of cases used this constitutional approach to conclude that governments could not use incarceration as the penalty when people lacked resources to pay fines and fees without first inquiring into their ability to pay.[8]

The constitutional law decisions interacted with legislative action. In 1974, the U.S. Congress chartered the Legal Services Corporation (LSC) to provide federally subsidized lawyers authorized to represent a segment of people too poor to seek civil legal advice.[9] Yet the LSC has never been funded sufficiently to meet the needs of those eligible for its services.[10] In 1976, Congress also provided for fee-shifting from losing defendants to successful civil rights plaintiffs to encourage the pursuit of such claims.[11]

Furthermore, revisions of federal procedural rules in the 1960s permitted class actions and other forms of aggregation that enable cost-sharing among litigants and provide incentives for lawyers to represent groups.[12] These group-based lawsuits are usually understood as enabling new plaintiffs to enter courts, yet these aggregations also work at times to the benefit of defendants, when they seek binding resolutions to preclude additional lawsuits.[13]

---

[5] *Boddie*, 401 U.S. at 374.

[6] See *San Antonio Indep. Sch. Dist. v. Rodriguez*, 411 U.S. 1, 16–18 (1973).

[7] The examples in addition to *Boddie v. Connecticut* include *Gideon v. Wainright*, 372 U.S. 335, 342–44 (1963); and *M.L.B. v. S.L.J.*, 519 U.S. 102, 106–07 (1996). The limited approach to requirements for lawyers, even when an individual faces months in jail, can be seen from *Turner v. Rogers*, 564 U.S. 431 (2011). See generally Resnik (2011a), Resnik (2000), pp. 2132–2137.

[8] See *Bearden v. Georgia*, 461 U.S. 660, 672–73 (1983); *Tate v. Short*, 401 U.S. 395, 397–99 (1971); *Williams v. Illinois*, 399 U.S. 235, 240–41 (1970).

[9] See, e.g., Houseman and Perle (2007).

[10] See, e.g., Legal Services Corporation, 2018 Annual Report; Legal Services Corporation, 2019 Annual Report.

[11] The Civil Rights Attorney's Fees Award Act of 1976, 42 U.S.C. § 1988(b); Farhang (2010).

[12] The history and current issues are explored in two symposia on the fiftieth anniversary of the class action rule. See Resnik (2017a, b).

[13] See, e.g., *Mullane v. Central Hanover Bank*, 339 U.S. 306 (1950).

As discussed below, retrenchments came thereafter. The Supreme Court has narrowed the reach of the principles it announced in *Boddie*. The legislature has not sufficiently funded services for civil legal aid. Attacks are underway to limit the use of class actions and other aggregate procedures, and during the last two decades, the U.S. Supreme Court has read the 1925 Federal Arbitration Act to permit providers of goods and services and employers to require claimants to forego the use of courts and to proceed, if at all, through single-file private arbitration.

Boddie centered on the role that courts play in family life. Counterpart in Europe are cases such as the 1979 *Airey* decision of the European Court of Human Rights, which recognized rights of access to civil remedial processes; effectuation sometimes involves legal services, such as when family dissolution is sought and the process is complex.[14]

In addition to households, courts have been foundational to markets, as adjudication provides one mechanism to enforce horizontal obligations among individuals and entities in contemporary societies. The need for governments to lower barriers to such litigation was the basis for *R. (in the Application of UNISON) v. Lord Chancellor*, rendered in 2017. Evidencing an understanding broader than that of the U.S. Supreme Court, the U.K. Supreme Court found unlawful the high fees the government had imposed for use of its employment tribunals.

Writing the central opinion for the Supreme Court, Lord Reed provided an aspirational account of the role for courts:

> Every day in the courts and tribunals of this country, the names of people who brought cases in the past live on as shorthand for the legal rules and principles which their cases established. Their cases form the basis of the advice given to those . . . now before the courts, or who need to be advised . . . [that] their claim might fairly be settled, or . . . that their case is hopeless. . . . But the value to society of the right of access to the courts is not confined to cases in which the courts decide questions of general importance. People and businesses need to know, on the one hand, that they will be able to enforce their rights if they have to do so, and, on the other hand, that if they fail to meet their obligations, there is likely to be a remedy against them.[15]

Lord Reed also noted in his opinion that resolutions often come through negotiation or mediation; yet:

> those procedures can only work fairly and properly if they are backed up by the knowledge on both sides that a fair and just system of adjudication will be available if they fail. Otherwise, the party in the stronger bargaining position will always prevail.[16]

Even though "judicial enforcement of the law is not usually necessary, and . . . that the resolution of disputes by other methods is often desirable," the Court required tribunals to be open to people of limited means, asserting legal rights.

---

[14] *Case of Airey v. Ireland*, 32 Eur Ct HR Ser A (1979).

[15] *R (on the application of UNISON) v. Lord Chancellor*, UKSC 51 para. 70, 71.

[16] *R (on the application of UNISON) v. Lord Chancellor*, UKSC 51 para. 72.

16.4 Affirmative Obligations to Provide Dispute Resolution Services

This brief account of a few legal rulings exemplifies the development of affirmative obligations to open courthouse doors. A large literature debates the roles courts play in enforcement of economic and social rights,[17] but less attention has been paid to courts as themselves *services* that governments must provide to individuals. Part of the reason courts go unrecognized as a genre of government provisioning akin to health, education, and housing is that courts are a longstanding feature of political orders, democratic or not.

Along with the related services of policing and prisons, courts are one of a network of government institutions that could be part of sustaining wellbeing and, given the new egalitarianism of courts, could (if living up to democratic aspirations) be mechanisms for resource redistribution. Bringing courts into the fold of social and economic rights underscores that they share the problems that haunt discussion of those rights. The questions include: what branches of government decide levels of funding; what taxes (called fees, fines, assessments, surcharges, and the like in this context) can be imposed on users; what subsidies are required, and what forms of rationing are licit? The *Boddie* and *UNISON* decisions answered aspects of these questions, as they insisted on lowering barriers to entrance for subsets of litigants— certain private parties in conflict about particular kinds of claims and dependent on the state to provide the structure for resolution.

But how broad are the mandates? The aim to lower transaction costs is part of what drives discussions in this volume that call for alternative dispute resolution (ADR) and online dispute resolution (ODR) or their mix. Another segment of this volume focuses on the role played by attorneys. While some individuals choose to represent themselves, many lack the means to have lawyers and instead navigate procedures with little or no expert guidance. Their needs prompt interest in rethinking how to remake procedures to lower the reliance on lawyers.

A question less explored in this book is whether, in addition to circumstances when access fees must be waived, governments have to do more to equip civil litigants through an array of services, of which lawyers are but one. Attention needs to be paid to the drivers of political and legal movements that could widen or limit the obligations of governments to facilitate use of civil justice, whether through courts, lawyers, or other routes.

Experiences in the United States provide grounds for concern. In the last decade and especially after the recession of 2008, localities looked to courts as "revenue centers" and increased the fees imposed on participants.[18] A host of what have come to be called "legal financial obligations" (LFOs) are assessed for a wide array of court-related activities.

---

[17]Resnik (2019a).

[18]See generally Resnik et al. (2018, 2019).

The expanding reliance on fees and assessments has affected understandings of what courts represent—seen less as venues for rights pronouncement and more as discriminatory extractors of money from people seeking help from or hailed into court. "Court debt" comes from financial obligations that individuals incur in civil, administrative, and criminal litigation, as legal systems charge fees at entrance, for subsequent filings. In some jurisdictions, when civil defendants respond, they too must pay fees unless those individuals seek court recognition that they are too poor to do so.[19] Courts impose charges on litigants for transcripts of proceedings, to register to obtain "free" public defenders, and to use civil and criminal diversion programs, including court-based arbitration.[20] And, as the U.S. Supreme Court detailed in 2017 in *Nelson v. Colorado,*[21] not all jurisdictions return the assessments associated with criminal proceedings when individuals are acquitted.

The harms of court debt are not experienced equally. The impact of such practices is felt most acutely by people with limited resources and by communities of color, either because they seek assistance from the legal system or because they are subjected to over-policing, prosecution, and punishment.[22] A growing body of empirical evidence documents the racial inequalities when fees are assessed and surcharges imposed. The debt associated with the legal system undermines individuals, families, and communities.[23] Nonpayment in some jurisdictions can be met with driver's license suspensions (and then more fines for driving without a license),[24] and the loss of voting rights.[25]

The grim picture of courts that I have just sketched needs to stand alongside the model put forth by Lord Reed, who discussed the utility of courts' availability for the social order and framed legal principles to open doors to the state's dispute resolution system. Some of the methods discussed by authors of chapters in this book hone in on access issues, while others assume that ADR, ODR, and other new technologies will be intrinsically more hospitable to users. That empirical question cannot be answered without data collection to understand the demographics of actual and potential users.[26] In addition to the need for such research, few of the chapters directly address either the question of norm generation and development or the issue

---

[19] A chart detailing examples of fees is at Resnik (2018a), p. 664.

[20] See, e.g., generally Statutory Court Fee Task Force, Illinois Court Assessments (2016) [hereinafter Illinois Court Assessments 2016].

[21] *Nelson v. Colorado,* 137 S. Ct. 1249 (2017).

[22] The U.S. Department of Justice's report on Ferguson and the subsequent litigation and settlement provide one of many examples. See Civil Rights Div., U.S. Department of Justice, Investigation of the Ferguson Police Department (2015) [hereinafter Ferguson Report]. See also Bell (2018), Smith (2018), pp. 2317–2319.

[23] See generally Harris (2016).

[24] See, e.g., *Robinson v. Purkey,* 326 F.R.D. 105 (M.D. Tenn 2018), reversed, 814 Fed. Appx 991 (6th Cir. 2020). See also Fowler v. Benson, (24 F.3d 247 (6th Cir. 2019).

[25] *Jones v. Governor of Florida,* 975 F. 3d 1016 (11th Cir. 2020).

[26] See Byrom (2019a, b).

of third-party access in the use of ADR, ODR, and AI, and these are the questions to which I turn.

16.5 Open to Whom? Participatory Observers as Well as Disputants

On both sides of the Atlantic Ocean, "open justice" has been a rallying cry and, in some instances, a description. The concept is an artifact of political agendas of the Enlightenment. Governments committed to expanding nation-state power had the economic resources on public buildings and apportioned funds dedicated to constructing courthouses to serve as icons of law, justice, and their own authority. Persons walking into courtrooms not only had rights to observe what transpired therein, but also governments hoped that what they saw would prompt or renew commitments to the rule of their law. The professionalization of judges, lawyers, and architects, interacting with political commitments, forged a system in which court-houses became a signature of governments. The commitments in law to judicial processes being open (what I have called *doctrinal openness*) intersected in some eras with functional openness, and both were in service of the need to build state power.

The "right to a public hearing" for criminal and civil proceedings is a familiar refrain in European law. The U.S. Supreme Court has many times insisted that criminal trials and related proceedings be open to the media and the public in general. Lower courts recognize a right to civil trials and the hearings related to those processes.[27] Thus, access to courts has come to reference both the right of individuals to bring cases to courts and the right of third parties to watch. While litigation is often styled as a triangle, with the judge at the apex dealing with opposing plaintiffs and defendants, the depiction of adjudication ought to be a square, with a fourth line to denote the audience.

That fourth line has political implications, as openness is also a route to challenge state power. As Jeremy Bentham said long ago: "Publicity is the very soul of justice. . . . It keeps the judge himself, while trying, under trial."[28] Bentham imagined that what he called a "Tribunal of Public Opinion" would, through observation, be able to see whether judges were self-interested (which he thought they were) and hence could form critiques to press for changes. Given Bentham's critique of "Judge & Co. (to wit, lawyers), ADR advocates could well invoke him, as Bentham pressed for

---

[27]See *Press-Enter. Co. v. Superior Court* (Press Enterprise I), 464 U.S. 501, 503–05 (1984); *Richmond Newspapers, Inc. v. Virginia*, 448 U.S. 555, 559–63, 580 (1980) (plurality opinion); see also Resnik (2018b). The Sixth Amendment right of the defendant is sometimes either itself the basis of access by third parties or related to a First Amendment right or "freedom" of the public to "listen." See *Richmond Newspapers*, 448 U.S. at 576.

[28]Bentham (1843a), pp. 573, 582.

procedural revision as well as for lower court costs. Bentham famously termed filing fees a "tax on distress."[29]

My analysis of the new metrics of legitimacy for courts reflects that they have become venues in which norms of democracy can take material shape. Bentham saw courts as "schools for justice" because he thought judges would naturally want to explain their decisions to their audience. For me, the state is not only a teacher but also a *student*, reminded that all of us have entitlements in democracies to watch power operate and to receive explanations for the decisions entailed. The observers are, in this account, a necessary *part* of the practice of adjudication, anchored in democratic political norms that the state cannot impose its authority through unseen and unaccountable acts. Therefore courts are, like legislatures, a place in which *democratic practices* occur in real-time.

My analysis also assumes that law and norms—substantive and procedural—are not fixed but are constantly dynamic and debated and that court-based processes are one venue for those exchanges. This proposition prompts my concerns about the functional privatization of dispute resolution and the use of online forms. Underlying the use of some fast-track techniques is the assumption that the job of law is to take the law "as is" and apply it to individual problems. But how do we know what the law is? Or how can we push for changes?

Moreover, we cannot have the kind of unvarnished faith in public processes that Bentham espoused. He presumed the plausibility of constituting a singular public, understanding its own self-interests, aggregating preferences, and therefore enhancing the general welfare. In contrast, in the twenty-first century, we know of the many competing and deeply divided public(s), with different understandings of their own self-interests than what others ascribe to them.[30] Today, political and critical theorists insist on the construction of preferences and the multiplicity of points of views,[31] just as art historians remind us that cubism broke the linear plane and refuted the singular perspective valorized in Renaissance art.[32]

Further, we know well about another kind of public—what I term a "predatory public," trolling on the internet in a manner that can entail personal aggression against individuals and impose significant harms.[33] The injuries come from a too-easy dissemination of information (true and false) about individuals. Thus, Jeremy Bentham is invoked not only as the central theorist for the much-admired publicity of justice's "soul," Bentham is also the touchstone for modern public relations, advertising, and propaganda. The methods of manipulation have expanded through technologies, which are exemplified by conflicts over the impact and use of sites like Facebook.

---

[29]Bentham (1843b). See also Resnik (2011b).

[30]Fraser (1992).

[31]See, e.g., Mansbridge (2001).

[32]See, e.g., Crary (1992).

[33]Examples are provided by many. See, e.g., Eltis (2011).

16.6 Repeat Players, Privatization, and Public Involvement

The entrenchment of new rules of privatization reflect what Marc Galanter described as the ability of "repeat players" (the "haves" in his classic article) to come out "ahead" by using their resources and knowledge to structure procedures that benefit their interests rather than those of "one-shot" players.[34] Galanter explained that reiterative involvement in legal processes provides insights into (and the potential for authority over) the procedures that have substantive impacts on rights and remedies. Understanding the incentives of governments, other entities such as corporations, judges, and lawyers—all of whom are the repeat players—is central to appraising the new rules proffered and some of which are installed.

Many of the contemporary procedural innovations are justified as requisite to "open justice." Exemplary is the 2016 Report entitled *"ODR and the Courts: The Promise of 100% Access to Justice?"*[35] Through a series of images and commentary, the monograph volume outlines steps for responding to conflicts. Depicted are individuals behind computers working through whether they can reach a resolution. In another frame, a person is labeled as a mediator, and another a judge.

But the public is not in sight. The text of the monograph reflects its title, insistent that ODR will promote users' "fairness experience;"[36] the "users" referenced are disputants. Unlike the 2017 *UNISON* decision of the U.K. Supreme Court, requiring that filing fees be limited in employment tribunals because of the general need to know about the enforceability of rights, "which underpins everyday economic and social relations,"[37] this monograph neither addresses the public nor describes how users and consumers should be understood as citizen-agents empowered to participate in shaping dispute resolution processes.

The exclusion of the public is not inevitable. Some ODR processes, such as those underway in the courts of British Columbia, include efforts to preserve the principle of openness[38] even as ODR is becoming "the court." Policymakers describe their provisions as responding to concerns about individual privacy and the appropriation of web-based information while maintaining commitments to institutional

---

[34]Galanter (1974).

[35]HiiL (2016) p. 38.

[36]HiiL (2016), p. 41. The discussion of informational justice, distributive justice, restorative justice, procedural justice, and interpersonal justice, *id.* p. 42, does not address a role for an observing public. "Transparency of outcomes" is in view, but not of process. The monograph spoke of concerns about how to scale up ODR to lower marginal costs (*id.* p. 54) and to enable a "respectful dialogue" (*id.* p. 44). The monograph did not provide the metrics of respect.

[37]*R (on the application of UNISON) v. Lord Chancellor*, UKSC 51 para. 71.

[38]British Columbia Civil Resolution Tribunal Rules, pp. 1–39 (May 1, 2021)   https://civilresolutionbc.ca/wp-content/uploads/2021/04/CRT-Rules-in-force-May-1-2021.pdf [hereinafter British Columbia CRT Rules].

openness.[39] An online dispute resolution process in British Columbia's Civil Resolution Tribunal ("CRT") aims to shift a variety of claims away from what was an in-person, open court-based system that had generally been open to the public and move those exchanges on line.[40]

In short, while celebrating ADR and ODR as answers to the "global crisis" in access to justice, these new technologies focus on one sense of openness—*accessibility* for disputants—in part through lowering the cost of the process. Often ignored is the other sense of openness, the role of third parties welcomed to observe. And, relatedly, also ignored is a role for collective action. The models are focused on single-file decision-making rather than on group-based information and resource sharing. This approach exemplifies a form of complacency about the status quo. The implicit assumption is that the law as we have it is good but what we are lacking is access to it. And for some proponents of ADR/ODR, the exclusion of the public is a method of claim suppression by limiting information about potential injuries and routes to redress.

But what about how the law could/would/should change—in all directions? When it rejected high filing fees in the Employment Tribunal in the U.K., the Supreme Court insisted that access to courts was not "of value only to the particular individuals involved;" the Court invoked a 1932 ruling, which was an ordinary dispute that resulted in a new rule; producers of consumer goods were under a duty to take care of the health and safety of the consumers of those goods, which Lord Reed described as "one of the most important developments" in twentieth-century U.K. law.[41] Theorists from Habermas to Pierre Bourdieu have analyzed the interplay between fact and law and the reflexivity that constructs our professional habitus.

Procedures always allocate authority and, as Jeremy Bentham instructed long ago, access by the public is requisite to the capacity to scrutinize, let alone to discipline, the decision-making and the norms that undergird it. Without third-party access to the processes and outcomes of ADR/ODR, and to the formulas and algorithms that underlie AI, we cannot know what judgments, predicated on what understandings of people, practices, facts, and obligations, are being promoted. Without some forms of public access, we cannot know whether fair treatment is accorded regardless of litigants' status, and the relationship of remedies to harms. Without oversight, we cannot ensure that decision-makers are independent of parties. And without public accountings of how norms are being applied, we cannot consider the need for revisions of underlying rules, remedies, and procedures by which to decide claims of right. We lose the very capacity to debate what our forms and norms of fairness are. Whether called "court," or "ADR," or "ODR," we cannot, without both forms of openness, decide whether the paths, processes, or resolutions are just.

---

[39]*British Columbia CRT* p. 3. *See* Thompson (2017). British Columbia Civil Resolutions Tribunal, Access to Information and Privacy Policies, July 2020, pp. 1–14, https://civilresolutionbc.ca/wp-content/uploads/2019/02/Access-to-Info.

[40]British Columbia CRT Rules.

[41]*R (on the application of UNISON) v. Lord Chancellor*, UKSC 51 para. 69.

References

Bell MC (2018) Hidden laws of the time of Ferguson. Harv Law Rev Forum 1:132

Bentham J (1843a) Rationale of judicial evidence: "of publicity and privacy, as applied to judicature in general, and to the evidence in particular". In: Bowring J (ed) The works of Jeremy Bentham, vol 6. William Tate, Edinburgh

Bentham J (1843b) A protest against law-taxes: showing the peculiar mischievousness of all such impositions as add to the expense of appeal to justice. In: Bowring J (ed) The works of Jeremy Bentham, vol 4. William Tate, Edinburgh

British Columbia Civil Resolution Tribunal Access to Information and Privacy Policies, https://civilresolutionbc.ca/wp-content/uploads/2019/02/Access-to-Info-in-CRT-Case-Records-20190220.pdf); British Columbia Civil Resolution Tribunal Rules, effective May 1, 2021, https://civilresolutionbc.ca/wp-content/uploads/2021/04/CRT-Rules-in-force-May-1-2021.pdf

Byrom N (2019a) Developing the detail: evaluating the impact of court reform in England and Wales on Access to Justice, Report and recommendations (The Legal Education Foundation, October 2019)

Byrom N (2019b) Digital Justice: HMCTS data strategy and delivering access to justice, Report and recommendations (The Legal Education Foundation, October 2019)

Crary J (1992) Techniques of the observer: on vision and modernity in the nineteenth century. MIT Press, Boston

Eltis K (2011) The judicial system in the digital age: revisiting the relationship between privacy and accessibility in the cyber context. McGill Law J 56:289

Farhang S (2010) The litigation state: public regulation and private lawsuits in the U.S. Princeton University Press, Princeton

Fraser N (1992) Rethinking the public sphere: a contribution to the critique of actually existing democracy. In: Calhoun C (ed) Habermas and the public sphere. MIT Press, Boston

Galanter M (1974) Why the "Haves" come out ahead: speculations on the limits of legal change. Law Soc Rev 9:95

Genn H (2009) Judging civil justice. Cambridge University Press, Cambridge

Genn H (2018) Annual Birkenhead lecture online courts and the future of justice. Graya

Harris A (2016) A pound of flesh: monetary sanctions as punishment for the poor. Russell Sage Foundation, New York

HiiL (2016) ODR and the Courts: The Promise of 100% Access to Justice?, http://www.onlineresolution.com/hiil.pdf

Houseman AW, Perle LE (2007) Centre for law & society policy, securing equal justice for all: a brief history of civil legal assistance in the United States 19–22. https://www.clasp.org/sites/default/files/public/resources-and-publications/files/0158.pdf [https://perma.cc/8JRV-GC8U]

Legal Services Corporation (2018) Annual Report; Legal Services Corporation (2019 Annual Report)

Mansbridge J (2001) The descriptive political representation of gender: an anti-essentialist argument. In: Klausen J, Maier CS (eds) Has liberalism failed women?: Assuring equal representation in Europe and the United States. Springer, New York

Resnik J (2000) Money matters: judicial market interventions creating subsidies and awarding fees and costs in individual and aggregate litigation. Univ Pa Law Rev 148:2119

Resnik J (2011a) Fairness in numbers: a comment on AT&T v. Concepcion, Wal-Mart v. Dukes, and Turner v. Rogers. Harv Law Rev 125:78

Resnik J (2011b) Bring back Bentham: "Open Courts," "Terror Trials," and Public Sphere(s). Law Ethics Human Rights 5:226

Resnik J (2017a) Reorienting the process due: using jurisdiction to forge post-settlement relationships among litigants, courts, and the public in class and other aggregate litigation. N Y Univ Law Rev 1017(92)

Resnik J (2017b) "Vital" state interests: from representative actions for fair labor standards to pooled trusts, class actions, and MDLs in the Federal Courts. Univ Pa Law Rev 165:1765

Resnik J (2018a) A2J/A2K: access to justice, access to knowledge, economic inequalities, and open courts and arbitrations. North Carolina Law Rev 96:605

Resnik J (2018b) The contingency of openness in courts: changing the experiences and logics of the public's role in court-based ADR. Nevada Law Rev 15(3):1631

Resnik J (2019a) Courts *and* economic and social rights/courts *as* economic and social rights. In: Young KG (ed) The future of economic and social rights. Cambridge University Press, Cambridge

Resnik J (2019b) The functions of publicity and of privatization in courts and their replacements (from Jeremy Bentham to #MeToo and *Google* Spain). In: Hess B, Koprivica A (eds) Open justice: the role of courts in a democratic society. Nomos, Baden-Baden

Resnik J, Curtis D (2011) Representing justice: invention, controversy, and rights in city-states and democratic courtrooms. Yale University Press, Yale

Resnik J et al (2018) The Arthur Liman Center for Public Interest Law at Yale Law School, Who Pays? Fines, Fees, Bail, and the Cost of Courts (2018) https://law.yale.edu/sites/default/files/area/center/liman/document/liman_colloquium_book_04.20.18.pdf

Resnik J et al (2019) The Arthur Liman Center for Public Interest Law at Yale Law School, Ability to Pay https://law.yale.edu/sites/default/files/area/center/liman/document/liman_colloquium_book_combined_cover_march_21_2019.pdf

Smith FO (2018) Abstention in the age of Ferguson. Harv Law Rev 131:2283

Statutory Court Fee Task Force, Illinois Court Assessments (2016) Findings and Recommendations for Addressing Barriers to Access to Justice and Additional Issues Associated with Fees and Other Court Costs in Civil, Criminal, and Traffic Proceedings. http://www.ilga.gov/reports/special/Statutory%20Court%20Fee%20Task%20Force%20Report.pdf

Thompson D (2017) Rationalizing Openness: Access to British Columbia Court and Tribunal Records in a New Era of Technology and Privacy (manuscript)

U.S. Department of Justice, Civil Rights Division (2015) Investigation of the Ferguson Police Department, https://www.justice.gov/sites/default/files/opa/pressreleases/attachments/2015/03/04/ferguson_police_department_report.pdf

Case Law

Mullane v. Central Hanover Bank, 339 U.S. 306 (1950)

Gideon v. Wainwright, 372 U.S. 335, 342–44 (1963)

Williams v. Illinois, 399 U.S. 235, 240–41 (1970)

Tate v. Short, 401 U.S. 395, 397–99 (1971)

Boddie v. Connecticut, 401 U.S. 371, 374 (1971)

San Antonio Indep. Sch. Dist. v. Rodriguez, 411 U.S. 1, 16–18 (1973)

Case of Airey v. Ireland, 32 Eur Ct HR Ser A (1979)

Richmond Newspapers, Inc. v. Virginia, 448 U.S. 555, 559–63, 580 (1980)

Bearden v. Georgia, 461 U.S. 660, 672–73 (1983)

Press-Enter. Co. v. Superior Court (Press Enterprise I), 464 U.S. 501, 503–05 (1984)

M.L.B. v. S.L.J., 519 U.S. 102, 106–07 (1996)

Turner v. Rogers, 564 U.S. 431 (2011)

Nelson v. Colorado, 137 S. Ct. 1249 (2017)

R (on the application of UNISON) v. Lord Chancellor, [2017] UKSC 51

Fowler v. Benson, (24 F.3d 247 (6th Cir. 2019)

Jones v. Governor of Florida, 975 F.3d 1016 (11th Cir. 2020)

Robinson v. Purkey, 326 F.R.D. 105 (M.D. Tenn 2018), reversed, 814 Fed. Appx 991 (6th Cir. 2020)

Lightning Source UK Ltd.
Milton Keynes UK
UKHW020931081022
410083UK00003B/5